M000249246

Silent Players

Silent Players

A Biographical
and Autobiographical Study
of 100 Silent Film Actors and Actresses

Anthony Slide

THE UNIVERSITY PRESS OF KENTUCKY

Publication of this volume was made possible in part by a grant
from the National Endowment for the Humanities.

Copyright © 2002 by The University Press of Kentucky

Scholarly publisher for the Commonwealth,
serving Bellarmine University, Berea College, Centre
College of Kentucky, Eastern Kentucky University,
The Filson Historical Society, Georgetown College,
Kentucky Historical Society, Kentucky State University,
Morehead State University, Murray State University,
Northern Kentucky University, Transylvania University,
University of Kentucky, University of Louisville,
and Western Kentucky University.
All rights reserved.

Editorial and Sales Offices: The University Press of Kentucky
663 South Limestone Street, Lexington, Kentucky 40508-4008

06 05 04 03 02   5 4 3 2 1

Frontispiece: Douglas Fairbanks holding Charlie Chaplin and Mary Pickford.

Library of Congress Cataloging-in-Publication Data

Slide, Anthony.
    A biographical and autobiographical study of 100 silent film actors and actresses /
Anthony Slide.
        p. cm.
    Includes bibliographical references and index.
    ISBN 0-8131-2249-X (alk. paper)
1. Motion picture actors and actresses—United States—Biography—Dictionaries.
2. Silent films—UnitedStates—History and criticism. I. Title.
PN1998.2 .S547 2002
791.43'028'0922—dc21   2001007529

This book is printed on acid-free paper meeting
the requirements of the American National Standard
for Permanence in Paper for Printed Library Materials.

Manufactured in the United States of America.

This book is dedicated to
Edward Wagenknecht,
my mentor, friend,
and whilom co-author.

Contents

Preface

As the title indicates, this volume is devoted to a wide spectrum of silent film performers, from the legendary stars to those who were little more than extras. In the silent era, to be a star meant to have one's name above the title—there was no other definition—and so, it might be noted, the majority of players herein do not fall into that category but were rather leading ladies and leading men. I knew many of the players personally, some very well, hence the subtitle "A Biographical and Autobiographical Study." Wherever appropriate, I have discussed my relationship with and my personal observations of the performer. The hundred actors and actresses represented herein are my personal choices of some of the best, brightest, or most unusual of silent players. (The unlikely plot twists in many silent films are nothing compared to the extraordinarily strange and often sad lives led by many of the players from the silent era.)

I make no apologies for absences that may cause personal distress to overly enthusiastic fans. You have your opinions and I have mine. At the same time, I would point out that within the main entries I have discussed many players whom I did not choose to feature. The index will help to locate commentary on these individuals.

Unless otherwise indicated, all quotes are from interviews or conversations with me. Comments have been edited, but no words have been added nor changes made to the context. Occasionally, I have merged interviews or conversations that took place at different times.

Aside from those of whom I write, I have met many other silent players through the years, including Gertrude Astor, Yakima Canutt, Janet Gaynor, May McAvoy, Patsy Ruth Miller, and Carmel Myers. My dismissal of these in favor of others is as hard for me to justify as it may be for some readers to accept. I did not necessarily dislike the rejected ones, although I have to admit that Patsy Ruth Miller's right-wing opinions and racist views on "niggers" were as difficult to tolerate as Carmel Myers's snobbery. Both Priscilla Bonner and Mrs. Wallace Reid shared my opinion of Patsy Ruth Miller; "No one cared for Patsy Ruth Miller," they assured me in unison. For her comedic performance opposite Harry Langdon in *The Strong Man* alone, Gertrude Astor deserves some sort of recognition, and perhaps some day she will get it. Yakima Canutt was a true gentleman, kind and generous, and, despite his many silent film appearances, I do feel he belongs more in a study of stuntwork in later decades.

I might well have discussed Baby Peggy (Diana Serra Cary), but she has done a pretty good job of writing of her career herself. Aileen Pringle was unwilling to meet with me, but then spent a good hour on the telephone talking of nothing with great enthusiasm. I knew two of Roscoe "Fatty" Arbuckle's wives, his first Minta Durfee and his last Addie McPhail. I didn't know Minta well enough to have an opinion of her, and Addie's career belongs to the sound era. Addie worked as a volunteer at the Motion Picture Country Hospital and would sit with Minta while she was a resident there at the end of her life. Fans would visit, respectfully addressing Minta Durfee as "Mrs. Arbuckle," while the real and last "Mrs. Arbuckle" sat by and said nothing.

I met Beverly Bayne on a couple of occasions, but all she wanted to do was complain of her former costar and husband Francis X. Bushman. Riza Royce, the first Mrs. Josef von Sternberg, told me how she would play hookey from school to work for D.W. Griffith. At the age of 92, Ann Little told me how she never liked acting and that all she wanted was to own her own ranch.

Silent Players is intended to serve not only as a lively and entertaining study of a hundred actors and actresses from the American silent cinema but also as a reference work. The entries provide facts of the life and career of each individual, and they offer glimpses into many aspects of silent film performance, from makeup to the art of pantomime. Even modern themes, such as homosexuality and sexual harassment, are explored. The silent players I have known were anything but silent, as this book reveals.

Biographical citations are provided for each of the players, primarily from sources contemporary with their careers. I have made every effort to read these articles and have deliberately omitted those that contain no useful content or commentary. I see no point in referencing pieces on clothing or hats worn by the ladies under discussion, nor do I care about patently false stories, minor acts of bravery, or stunts that were obviously executed by others. The fan magazines and their writers deserve immense praise for the intelligence and style that they displayed, but it should be noted that many fan magazine writers of the teens and 1920s were also paid publicists for the stars of whom they wrote, and their opinions are seldom without bias. (Herbert Howe, who was one of the best fan magazine writers of the period, went even further in his personal relationship to one of his subjects and was for several years in the 1920s the lover of Ramon Novarro.)

Catalogs of film titles hold little appeal, and I have avoided the temptation to make long lists of meaningless titles. If for no other reason than space considerations, I have chosen not to include filmographies. With the publication of the *American Film Institute Catalog*, on the editorial board of which I am honored to serve, a complete record of appearances in feature-length productions by actors and actress from the teens through the 1940s and beyond is readily available.

The Silent Players is not intended as a catalog of tired, old facts, a rehash of half-true anecdotes. Rather, I would like to believe it is a revisionist, almost revolutionary, text, a story of vibrant and appealing personalities, talented individuals, whose works and lives make compelling reading.

Acknowledgments

In many ways, this book has been more than thirty years in creation, during which time I have utilized the facilities of many major archives and libraries, including the British Film Institute, the Frances Howard Goldwyn/Hollywood Regional Library, the International Museum of Photography at George Eastman House, the Library of Congress, the Los Angeles Central Library, the Los Angeles County Museum of Natural History, the Museum of Modern Art, the University of California at Los Angeles, the University of Southern California, the Wisconsin Center for Film and Theater Research, and, most important, the Margaret Herrick Library of the Academy of Motion Picture Arts and Sciences. I thank the countless staff members who have helped me at all those institutions and would like to make special reference to Stacy Behlmer, Elaine Burrows, Ned Comstock, Mary Corliss, Patricia Coward, Carol Cullen, Sally Dumaux, Barbara Hall, Steven L. Hanson, Rita Horwitz, Robert Knutson, Audree Malkin, Linda Mehr, Alice Mitchell, Helene Mochedlover, David Parker, George Pratt, Howard Prouty, Patrick Sheehan, Charles Silver, Mildred Simpson, Dace Taub, and Jean Tucker.

I am lucky to have known through the years some of the personalities who dominated these institutions. As a young man, I fought with Ernest Lindgren at the National Film Archive in London, arguing against his policy of non-access to most of the collection. Somewhat more mature today, I now realize that his intentions were honorable and that his primary concern was preservation and conservation. I met Henri Langlois and Mary Meerson of the Cinémathèque Francaise, who promised everything that Ernest Lindgren denied, but, in the end, could deliver nothing. When I first visited George Eastman House as the guest of George Pratt, I timorously asked if I might be allowed to view a few films. George was too scared of his boss to make the request on my behalf, but when I plucked up the courage to face the infamous James Card, he looked at the screening schedule and summarily canceled all promised screenings for that week and allowed me free access to any silent films I might wish to see. That is the way it used to be with many archives. If the curator liked you, there was nothing he or she would not do. If your personality was unappealing, you might just as well look for a new calling in life.

Today, so much is accessible on videotape that younger film enthusiasts find it difficult to believe that once one had to rely on archivists and 8mm and 16mm film distributors for screening prints. Through Blackhawk Films and its founder Kent Eastin, we were able to acquire 8mm prints of many classic silent films (and quite a few obscurities). Edward Wagenknecht captured the sense of excitement that ownership of those films meant when he wrote in his autobiography, *As Far as Yesterday*, "If in the days of my youth, anybody had told me that I might someday own my own copies of the great D.W. Griffith films, I should probably, had I believed him, died of joy."

In the late 1970s and early 1980s, for five years I wrote a monthly column on film collecting in *Films in Review*. I remember Tom Dunnahoo's Thunderbird Films and Bob Lee's Essex Film Club as the primary sources for rare prints. Bob Lee is no longer with us, but Tom Dunnahoo is still alive, and I wish that we might all acknowledge just how much he did for the collector and the film enthusiast by standing up to the F.B.I. and others who tried to close him down. Eventually, Tom was sent to jail on a trumped up charge, badly beaten in prison, suffered a stroke, and now clings to life. Tom Dunnahoo paved the way for the video entrepreneurs who followed him. He is a true pioneer to collectors of both silent and sound films.

The majority of private individuals, celebrities, and others whom I would like to thank are mentioned in the text, but among those who are not and deserve thanks are Rudy Behlmer, DeWitt Bodeen, Charles G. Clarke, Jim Curtis, Bob Dickson, Geoffrey Donaldson, Billy H. Doyle, William K. Everson, George Geltzer, Alan Gevinson, Denis Gifford, Sam Gill, Robert Giroux, Herb Graff, Buckey Grimm, Jere Guldin, Randy Haberkamp, Patricia King Hanson, Mike Hawks, Lawrence F. Karr, Marty Kearns, Richard Lamparski, Arthur Lennig, Leonard Maltin, George J. Mitchell, Cody Morgan, Lisa Mosher, Liam O'Leary, David Pierce, Andre Soares, George Stevens Jr., Charles Takacs, Ralph Wolfe, and Hans Wollstein.

The bulk of the illustrations are from my own collection; additional photographs were provided by the Margaret Herrick Library of the Academy of Motion Picture Arts and Sciences and the Museum of Modern Art.

A Personal Odyssey

Silent film, the truth at sixteen frames per second, has dominated much of my adult life. It has brought me happiness through the individuals I have met as a result of my interest, and it has also resulted in endless frustration in regard to both the lack of interest in the genre and the combined efforts of many who debase it through distribution of misinformation, arrogant and often worthless opinions, and shoddy presentation. The silent film we see on screen today is not what was viewed by an audience contemporary to the film. No matter how fine, dedicated, or caring the preservation or restoration, an acetate 35mm print of a silent film can never look as good as an original 35mm nitrate print. An archivist can make every effort to reproduce the tints and/or tones of the original, but the end product will never be the same.

Technicians may argue over silver content in the nitrate film against that in an acetate or safety print, assure us that their best efforts have replicated the original, but I know differently. I fell in love with silent films because, week after week as a young man, I saw original 35mm nitrate prints of silent films.

I was born and educated in Birmingham, England, and had my first work experience at the age of sixteen in the Northern city of Hull. I subsequently escaped from there and from my family to London, where I worked in local government by day and tried desperately to find a niche in the film field. My first involvement in film in the mid-1960s was as honorary secretary of the Society for Film History Research, a group of dedicated scholars and non-scholars concerned with the more esoteric aspects of motion picture history. My first published essay, "William Morton and His Cinemas," dealing with an early film exhibitor in Hull, appeared in the December 1963 issue of the Society's journal, *Cinema Studies*. During that same period, I was involved in the formation of the Cinema Theatre Association, which was concerned with the movie theatre as a building, and whose newsletter I edited.

In London, I was lucky enough to meet a middle-aged silent film collector named Bert Langdon. Each Saturday night, Bert would screen original 35mm nitrate prints of silent films in his apartment in the Camden Town area of London. He utilized a hand-cranked, vintage 35mm projector and would accompany the films with contemporary music selected from a wide range of 78-rpm recordings. Because he had only one projector, there would be a break between reels, but because he had two turntables, he was able to keep the music playing constantly throughout the screening, fading in and out from one recording to the next. Incredibly, he operated both the projector and the turntables single-handedly. Only after Bert suffered a stroke and I took over the cranking of the projector did I realize just how remarkable was Bert's presentation. It was hard enough to keep the projector turning at a constant speed, trying to ignore the muscle ache, let alone to operate two turntables!

Bert Langdon was no wealthy collector. He lived with his wife and son in a council flat—what in America would be termed subsidized housing—and purchased his films for a few dollars a reel at flea markets and the like. What wonderful films they were. There, for the first time, I saw a Mary Pickford feature, *The Hoodlum* (1919), and could comprehend the vibrancy of her personality. Bert owned the only extant print of a 1924 British feature film, *Reveille*, starring Betty Balfour and directed by George Pearson. I fell in love with both the production and Betty's performance and had the good fortune to meet and become friendly with both her and her director. Another wonderful British film was *The Rat* (1925), starring Ivor Novello and Mae Marsh, and Bert's print featured a hand-colored sequence of French nightlife. Through Bert, I discovered just how many ways there were to color silent films. I even saw Kinemacolor projected—and it was extremely difficult to crank the projector at twice the normal speed in order to obtain a satisfactory merging of the two primary colors.

The regular Saturday night group at Bert's did not comprise what would today be termed film buffs. There was another 35mm film collector, Frank Shelton (who specialized in early talkies), Harold Dunham (who wrote pioneering articles in *Films in Review* on Robert Harron and Mae Marsh), two sisters, Cis and Roz, whose interest in film began in the 1920s, and occasional visitors, including conductor John Lanchbery, Kevin Brownlow, and a young director named Ken Russell. Two of my favorite films from Bert's collection were Marshall Neilan's *The River's End* from 1920 and a James Fitzpatrick "Music Masters" short from the mid-1920s on the life of Ethelbert Nevin. (I recall that when I saw Ken Russell's *The Boy Friend* [1971] for the first time I was surprised to recognize that one of the musical numbers was very obviously based on a sequence from the Fitzpatrick production.)

Through Bert Langdon, I was introduced to a unique community of film collectors and enthusiasts. John Cunningham, who had an amazing collection of original 35mm prints of silent and sound films, was a chemist. He could handle his own duplication of prints, even mixing dyes to approximate the original tints. Later, John began to sell 8mm and 16mm prints of some of his titles through his own company, Breakspear Films. John stored his films in a World War Two air raid shelter in the back garden. More typical of 35mm film collectors was David Gillespie, whose hundreds of nitrate reels were kept in every available space in his South London home. His mother would sit watching television surrounded by film cans. A collector who was just starting out at this time was Ron Grant, who went on to create his own film archive, the Cinema Museum in East London.

In London at that time, there were still two fan clubs honoring silent screen personalities. Audrey Homan had the Ramon Novarro Fan Club, and Leslie Flint headed the Rudolph Valentino Memorial Guild. I was a member of both. The Rudolph Valentino Memorial Guild met in Leslie Flint's sumptuous basement apartment at 140 Westborne Terrace, close to Paddington Station, a house formerly occupied in its entirety by George Arliss. Leslie had a little theatre that sat between twelve and twenty, and there he would screen 16mm prints of *Blood and Sand* (1922), *The Eagle* (1925), *Son of the Sheik* (1926), and other Valentino titles. The Ramon Novarro Fan Club was a more homey group. The ladies knitted assorted garments for Ramon, and on his birthday, we all sang to him over the telephone.

Leslie Flint was a well-known voice medium, and at seances, he would have lengthy conversations with Valentino. I was never invited to attend, being a nonbeliever, but once in his living room, I did point out a strange cloud that seemed to be hanging down from the ceiling. Flint explained that I was seeing Valentino's ectoplasm, which had yet to dematerialize after his latest contact. Leslie Flint was very kind to me and arranged with the elderly lady who owned 140 Westbourne Terrace for me to rent a second-story apartment there. Once I invited the Ramon Novarro Fan Club over to see a short film, and when the projector failed to work, Leslie very generously suggested that the Ramon Novarro fans might meet in Valentino's theatre—and also served us afternoon tea. It was all very English and all very civilized.

In 1968, I meet a young film editor named Paul O'Dell, and together we founded *The Silent Picture*, which we proudly promoted as the only serious quarterly devoted to the art and history of the silent film. *The Silent Picture* ran through 19 issues and eventually ceased publication in 1974. Initially, Paul took care of the layout and design. When he decided to move on to other projects, I was assisted in that area by the staff of the cataloging department at the National Film Archive, who billed themselves as Catra. Finally, I was lucky to find an enthusiastic and professional designer in Stefan Dreja, who created a new logo for the magazine and became a good friend. Business affairs for *The Silent Picture* were handled in later years by Garth Pedler.

The Silent Picture is generally forgotten today, but among its contributors were DeWitt Bodeen, Kevin Brownlow, Thorold Dickinson, Lotte Eisner,

Stuart Kaminsky, Anna Neagle, Liam O'Leary, Dilys Powell, and Lotte Reiniger. Jeffrey Richards, with whom I had attended King Edward VI Grammar School in Birmingham, England, and with whom I first explored the magical film-related holdings of the Birmingham Public Library, wrote a major piece on Leni Riefenstahl's visual style. We published interviews with many from the silent era, and Blanche Sweet contributed an essay on *Judith of Bethulia.*

The demise of *The Silent Picture* was due in part to production costs that were never met by the income from sales, which ranged from 500 to 1,500 copies per issue. The British Film Institute made a small financial contribution, then withdrew its support after a prominent film critic spoke against us at a grants committee meeting.

Also in 1968, I began my first professional involvement in film with the Tantivy Press, which had been founded by Donald Cowie to publish books on antique collecting. Cowie's son, Peter, took over the press and began publication of *International Film Guide,* at first on his own and then with a staff of one, Allen Eyles. I joined Peter and Allen in 1968, and Peter embarked on a program of publishing paperback film books as well as the journal *Focus on Film,* edited by Allen. Thanks to Peter, in 1970, I was able to publish my first book, *Early American Cinema.*

As a result of that book, and thanks to support from Kevin Brownlow, film collector David Bradley, and others, I was awarded a one-year scholarship in 1971–1972 by the American Film Institute. I had already spoken with quite a few silent film figures in the United Kingdom, but when I came to Los Angeles to research early American cinema, my contact with the last remnants of a forgotten era expanded. I remained with the American Film Institute and moved to its Washington, D.C., headquarters, where I set up the 1911–1920 volume of the *American Film Institute Catalog* and served as the Institute's associate archivist.

In 1975, I returned to Los Angeles as resident film historian of the Academy of Motion Picture Arts and Sciences, a position I held until 1980. Since then, I have had no professional association with any institution but have tried to remain gainfully employed as an independent film scholar.

With me when I returned to Los Angeles was Robert Gitt, currently preservation officer of the UCLA Film and Television Archive, who has an international reputation for his work in film preservation and restoration. Bob and I first met in 1971 just as I was about to leave Los Angeles, and since 1977 we have lived together in Studio City, California. (The first housewarming gift we received came from Madame Olga Petrova; it arrived two days after her death.)

Bob and I have hosted countless dinner parties, Fourth of July parties,

New Year's parties, and other festivities, at which our guests (and our good friends) have included Billy Bakewell, Priscilla Bonner, Mary Brian, Ruth Clifford, Viola Dana, Ethel Grandin, Esther Ralston, cinematographer Karl Struss, Margery Wilson, and many others. (From a more modern era, we have entertained Beulah Bondi, Phil and Ginnie Brown, Ann and Andre De Toth, Norman and Peggy Lloyd, Curtis Harrington, Rose Hobart, Marsha Hunt, Jack Larsen, Doris Nolan, Dido [Madame Jean] Renoir, and Pippa Scott.) We have enjoyed such good times together that to recall any specific moment is impossible and would only serve to emphasize that our numbers have dwindled to a precious few. (I must mention, however, the annual February 17 birthday party. On this day—different years—Priscilla Bonner, Mary Brian, Ruth Clifford, and our dog, J. Stuart Blackton, celebrated their collective birthdays. Year after year, it was always such a happy day.)

One special guest and special friend was Herb Sterne (1906–1995), former publicist and journalist, who had enjoyed close personal friendships with D.W. Griffith, Lillian Gish, Mary Pickford, and others. Herb's sister Meta had been John Ford's script girl from 1936 and had earlier worked at Universal, where her films included *The Phantom of the Opera* (1925). Her younger brother was always a film enthusiast, and she helped him find work as an extra in the late 1920s. Herb's first professional engagement was as film critic for *Rob Wagner's Script*, the West Coast equivalent of *The New Yorker*, for which Herb wrote in the 1930s and 1940s and also contributed a society column under the name of Dan Rich.

Herb organized the first D.W. Griffith retrospective, at the University of Southern California, in the early 1940s. The director attended screenings, accompanied by Lillian Gish, Jean Renoir, Preston Sturges, and Dudley Nichols. In 1942, Herb became a critic with *The Hollywood Reporter* and a couple of years later began work as publicist at Columbia. After his death, I inherited Herb's cherished memorabilia, including one of Pickford's curls. According to Herb, one evening at dinner he had chastised the actress for giving a curl to the Los Angeles County Museum of Natural History but not to him. Pickford ordered the butler to bring a pair of scissors, and then and there she cut off a curl for Herb. The hair was subsequently carefully boxed and "laquered" by the hairdressing department at Columbia. Herb was for many years a resident of the Motion Picture Country House, and we enjoyed frequent lunches and dinners there with him and other residents. And we enjoyed the company of Herb and his fellow guests at our house.

(The Motion Picture Country House facility consists of individual cottages, the lodge, and the hospital and is located in Woodland Hills, a Los Angeles suburb in the West San Fernando Valley. Because so many residents and non-residents of the Country House facility end their days in the Motion Picture Country Hospital, Woodland Hills is probably the place of death for more members of the American film industry than any other community.)

I have written much on the history of the motion picture, both silent and sound, as well as many other areas of popular entertainment. To date, I have avoided any personal intrusion into those histories. This book is the exception in that it is very personal in terms of its content. As I complete the manuscript, I am painfully aware that all my friends from the silent era, excepting Mary Brian, are gone. To a large extent, that fact makes it easier rather than harder for me to put thoughts down on paper. I can tell the truth without any unnecessary wounding of feelings, and I can also display some (but not very much) personal emotion. With *Silent Players*, I say goodbye to my friends and to a part of my life that has meant so much to me and that can never be repeated. As Olga Petrova wrote of something I had written about her, it is both an *ave* and a *vale*.

Silent Players

MIGNON ANDERSON

She was a sad little creature, one might almost say pathetic, as unworldly as many of the ingénues she had played at the Thanhouser Company in the early teens. She lived in a small apartment, almost across the street from Warner Bros., a studio that had not existed when she was a leading lady. The world scared and confused her, and she was genuinely shocked that she was living next door to a young man and a woman who were not married to each other.

One of her leading men at Thanhouser had been James Cruze, who went on to direct *The Covered Wagon* (1923) and *Old Ironsides* (1926). While at Thanhouser, he gave Anderson the nickname of "fillet mignon." Cruze was engaged to marry actress Betty Compson, and the two would give riotous and drunken parties that continued until all involved had collapsed. Mignon Anderson was a guest at one such party, arrived early, and was invited up to Compson's room while she readied herself for the evening. To poor little Mignon's anguish and discomfort, Compson entertained her with bawdy stories while sitting, nude, at her dressing table.

Surprisingly, Mignon Anderson, for all her innocence, was born into a theatrical family—in Baltimore, Maryland, on March 31, 1892. Her father, Frank Anderson, was reasonably prominent on stage until his death in 1914, and he found roles for his daughter with a number of legendary theatre personalities, including Richard Mansfield, Julia Marlowe, and Joseph Jefferson. As Mignon recalled for me, "I started posing for clothes, and I met people who were working in the picture business, who were also posing for clothes. I was invited to go to the Thanhouser Company and meet Mr. Thanhouser, because in those days, I was supposed to look like Mary Pickford—I really didn't. That's what the Thanhouser advertised me as, 'The Second Mary Pickford.' I started right in, and I was put under contract, and stayed with them for six years."

Founded in 1910 by theatrical entrepreneur Edwin Thanhouser—"He was German, you know, and very tight about money," commented Mignon—the Thanhouser Film Corporation (the "Th" was pronounced "F") was located in New Rochelle, New York, and remained in existence through 1918. None of its films are particularly memorable. Some are very bad. A couple from 1916, *The World and the Woman* and *Fires of Youth*, starred Jeanne Eagles in her first screen role. Mignon Anderson's most spectacular film for the company was *The Mill on the Floss*, released in December 1915, in which the flood sequences easily steal the production away from Mignon and her fellow players.

Anderson had been engaged to actor Irving Cummings, but when her family discovered he was Jewish, and his family discovered she was a gentile, there was mutual outrage, and the engagement was called off. In 1916, Mignon married a fellow Thanhouser player, Morris Foster, and the couple left the studio to join Ivan Productions, created by Ivan Abramson. Abramson specialized in exploitation films, and Mignon Anderson starred for him in *The City of Illusion* (1916), playing a Southern aristocrat who almost ruins the lives of both her husband and her lover.

In January 1917, Anderson moved on to Universal, where she worked with various directors, including two of its most prominent female filmmakers, Lois Weber and Ida May Park. By 1918, the actress had left Universal, and for the remainder of her relatively short career she worked as a freelance player. She made her last screen appearance, *Kisses*, for Metro in 1922. At the end of her career, she was not paid too badly, earning $250 a week, compared to the weekly stipend of $50 that another pioneering actress, Ethel Grandin, was earning at the studio at that time.

Mignon retired, and Morris Foster gave up acting and spent 17 years in the wardrobe department at Paramount. He died on April 24, 1966, and Mignon died, in Burbank, California, on February 25, 1983.

Bibliography

Holmes, Harriet. "Winsome Mignon Anderson, the Little Dresden China Girl." *Photoplay*, November 1913, pp. 59–60.
"Mignon Anderson's Career." *Moving Picture Stories*, June 29, 1917, p. 24.

MARY ASTOR

It would be foolish to claim that Mary Astor was a great silent star. She was certainly a pretty ingénue, but there was little substance to her performances. Only with the coming of sound and her own maturation as a woman did she develop a dignity and strength to her characterizations. After 1930, whether she played heroine or villainess, Astor asserted her presence and commanded attention.

In her silent films, Astor has much the same innocuous quality as Mary Philbin, and, curiously, both women were dominated by their fathers. Mary was a member of the informal social club that called itself the Regulars, and, according to Priscilla Bonner, at her father's insistence she wore long underwear to the meetings. Eventually, because her father took his daughter's studio income, the actress could not even afford to pay the club's weekly dues. As she matured and gained in sexual knowledge, in large part thanks to an affair with John Barrymore, Mary Astor gradually developed as an actress. There is little difference between her performance opposite Barrymore in *Beau Brummel* (1924) and *Don Juan* (1926), but by 1930, she was obviously an actress worthy of attention.

Mary Astor (Quincey, Illinois, May 3, 1906–Woodland Hills, California, September 25, 1987) was one of the contestants in the "Fame and Fortune" contest organized by *Motion Picture Classic*, and in the April 1919 issue, she appears, under her real name, Lucile V. Langhanke. The magazine even provides would-be fans with her address at 1120 East 47th Street, Chicago. In 1920, Lillian Gish directed a screen test of Astor for D.W. Griffith; Gish believed that Astor was another Clarine Seymour, but Griffith did not care for the actress and took an instant dislike to her father. Astor once told me that she had often thought her life might have been different had she become a member of the director's company.

One of Astor's earliest starring roles is in the 1922 Triart short, *The Young Painter*, competently if not impressively directed by Herbert Blaché. Mary recalled that the exteriors were filmed at Charles Tiffany's estate at Oyster Bay, Long Island, and the interiors at a small studio on New York's West 56th Street. In *Second Fiddle*, released in January 1923, she is the heroine to Glenn Hunter's bucolic hero, who has problems asserting his masculinity. The film, directed by Frank Tuttle, makes good use of rural locations on the Eastern seaboard, but the leading man is as effeminate and ineffectual as the leading lady. It soon became clear to producers that with her good looks but weak personality, Mary Astor was best opposite a strong leading man such as John Barrymore or Douglas Fairbanks Sr.

Thanks to her relationship with Barrymore and a marriage to director Kenneth Hawks, who died in 1930, Mary Astor came of age. Voice coach Margaret Carrington, to whom Astor was directed by John Barrymore, also had a role in the actress's development. Astor made more than thirty sound films between 1930 and 1936, among which *Red Dust* (1932) and *The Kennel Murder Case* (1933) stand out, but the first classic Mary Astor performance comes with *Dodsworth* in 1936. Her introduction to the audience, with its reference to alcohol, is on a par with Garbo's first words in *Anna Christie*. Walter Huston, the title character, asks the ship's steward for something "quieting to the nerves." From the depths of a ship's deck chair comes the voice of Mary Astor as Mrs. Cortright: "Why don't you try stout, Mr. Dodsworth?"

A scandal that same year involving a custody suit over her daughter and the public revelation that Astor had kept a diary in which she wrote of her love affair with playwright George S. Kaufman came close to ending her career. Ultimately, the actress triumphed over adversity and continued on in a career that included *The Maltese Falcon* (1941), *The Palm Beach Story* (1942), *Meet Me in St. Louis* (1944), *Little Women* (1947), and even *Return to Peyton Place* (1961) and *Hush Hush...Sweet Charlotte* (1965).

In ill health and seeking security, Mary Astor moved into a cottage at the Motion Picture Country House in 1974, along with her canary, Prince Carol (of Romania). She acquired a tricycle and would pedal around the grounds and to and from her cottage and the dining room, where residents were expected to sit two or four to a table. Mary had no desire to socialize with her fellow guests, none of whom had attained her stature within the industry. She was given a table to herself close to the dining room entrance, and there she would sit, seldom acknowledging anyone and certainly not inviting daily greetings or enquiries as to her well-being.

After an introduction to Mary Astor, one might speak to her, but only if she spoke first. People just did not intrude upon her world uninvited, although she welcomed some assaults on her privacy, including a cover story in the February 1980 issue of *Life*. If Mary chose to have a conversation, the language would often be salty and spiked with four letter words.

One day at breakfast, Mary Astor came over to Herb Sterne and asked him what he was reading. Herb always had a rather eccentric taste in reading matter, and the book happened to be a novel by Elinor Glyn. Astor remembered that when she was being considered as Douglas Fairbanks's leading lady in *Don Q, Son of Zorro* (1925), she had been invited to dinner at Pickfair. Also present was Elinor Glyn, who pointed out that Astor's curly hair was not right for a Spanish role. To illustrate how the hair might be straightened, the author picked up a pat of butter and smeared it into the actress's hair. To quote Mary Astor, "I was goddamn fucking mad." (Mary Brian once described Elinor Glyn to me as "the Theda Bara of literature.")

Mary Astor and Ann Harding appeared together in the 1930 version of *Holiday*, with Harding in the role later played by Katharine Hepburn and Astor in the part taken in the 1938 film by Doris Nolan. Astor and Harding had no great respect for each other on or off the set, and Mary succinctly described Harding as "a piece of shit." Certainly, neither actress does anything in the film of which to be ashamed, and Ann Harding's delivery of her lines is so close to that of Hepburn's in the later production that one has to believe that Hepburn saw the earlier film before appearing in the remake.

I was able to persuade the Library of Congress to loan a 35mm print of *Holiday* for a screening at the Motion Picture Country House on January 7, 1979. Astor was delighted to have an opportunity to view the film and was remarkably pleasant, given her usual volatility. She stayed after the screening to talk with her fellow residents and staff members and signed autographs for all. (Earlier, in August 1976, she had agreed to my screening *Don Juan* at the facility, and while she refused to speak about its making, she did enjoy the program and respond to the applause.)

Just before her death, Mary asked Robert Gitt and me to screen *Dodsworth* for her. It was her favorite film, and at its close the actress was in tears. For the first time, she spoke to us of the infamous diary, recalling that when she went to see *Dodsworth* at Grauman's Chinese Theatre she disguised herself with a headscarf and glasses. At her first appearance on screen, the audience applauded, and Astor knew that her public remained faithful to her despite the revelations about her sex life.

Bibliography

Anderson, Lindsay. "Mary Astor." *Sight and Sound*, autumn 1990, pp. 230–239.
Astor, Mary. "Great Lovers of the Screen: John Barrymore." *Photoplay*, June 1924, p. 90.
———. *My Story: An Autobiography*. Garden City, N.Y.: Doubleday, 1959.
———. *A Life on Film*. New York: Delacorte Press, 1971.
Calhoun, Dorothy. "The Tragic Story Behind Mary Astor's Diary." *Motion Picture*, November 1936, pp. 38, 69, 71, 83.
Hall, Harold R. "The Tale of an Old-Fashioned Girl." *Picture-Play*, December 1929, pp. 43, 109.
Levenson, Lewis F. "Traveling the Road to Success with Mary Astor." *Movie Weekly*, September 9, 1923, pp. 11, 29.
"Mary Comes On." *Photoplay*, May 1930, p. 44.
"People We Like: Mary Astor." *Sequence*, Summer 1948, p. 13.
Talmey, Alma. "I Don't Want to Play a Luring Lady." *Movie Weekly*, July 4, 1925, pp. 25–26.

WILLIAM BAKEWELL

Billy Bakewell, as everyone called him, was one of the few actors and actresses from the silent era to have been born in Hollywood—on May 2, 1908. He was a star-struck teenager who frequented the studios, watching production and seeking work as an extra. In January 1928, Central Casting listed him as one of the 29 extras who had graduated to featured roles on screen, and he was making $75 a week. (Sue Carol, Sally Eilers, James Murray, and David Rollins were also mentioned.)

Billy never lost his fascination with the film industry, and even after retiring from films and embarking on a new career as a Beverly Hills realtor, he would still assure us that he was available for any role, directing all enquiries to his agent who now resided at Forest Lawn. Billy was a dear, gentle-spoken man, with a great sense of humor, who always had time for a friendly conversation. He walked down the street as if he was leading a band; he would start a story with "Don't stop me if you've heard this—I'm going to enjoy hearing this one myself." He and his wife, Diane, lived in an elegant townhouse adjacent to the Mormon Temple in West Los Angeles.

Pride of place was given to the "iron mask" from Billy's last silent film, *The Iron Mask* (1929), in which he had played the crucial role of Louis XIV and his twin, and was privileged to work with his hero, Douglas Fairbanks Sr. "As a kid growing up in Hollywood, Douglas Fairbanks was my idol. He was the idol of every boy in America. They used to work on Saturdays in those days, and on days off of school, I'd go down to Formosa [the site of the Pickford-Fairbanks studios] and look through the wire fence and watch Doug Fairbanks shooting *Robin Hood* [1922] and *The Thief of Bagdad* [1924]. Then years later, one day my agent called me: you've got a great part in *The Iron Mask*. It was the greatest thrill of my life. I had fencing lessons. I had horseback riding lessons. It was a great experience. It was the heyday of Pickfair, the Buckingham Palace of the picture business, and I was always invited. It was a great thrill."

Billy's first film appearance, as a trainbearer, was in the Raymond Griffith comedy, *He's a Prince*, a parody on the life of the Prince of Wales, released in October 1925. In a role somewhat more prominent but still uncredited, he played the historical naval figure, James McDonnaugh, in *Old Ironsides* (1926). Bakewell played Norma Shearer's younger brother in two MGM romantic comedies, *The Waning Sex*, released in September 1926, and *The Latest from Paris*, released in February 1928.

In 1927, Billy went on location for the first time, to play the roommate of William Haines in *West Point*. Because Haines was homosexual, MGM nervously arranged for Billy's mother to accompany him to the military academy.

She had no understanding of what the problem might be. From West Point, Bakewell moved on to the U.S. Naval Academy for *Annapolis* (1928). He was a typical college kid in *Harold Teen* (1928) and was featured as a juvenile in two of D.W. Griffith's last silent films, *The Battle of the Sexes* (1928) and *Lady of the Pavements* (1929). In all, Billy can be seen in nineteen silent feature films and three short subjects for Fox: "In the silent days you did learn the lines that you were supposed to speak, but technique-wise, before you spoke an important line, it was important that you register the expression, the thought, in advance, because the cutter then could have a clean cut in which to inject the subtitle. In other words, you had to time it, to register enough ahead before you spoke so that it would fit in. They would see the expression, which is good, because you're supposed to think before you speak anyway.

"It was not uncommon for two companies to be working on opposite ends of the same stage. Silence wasn't necessary, and a sort of fraternal camaraderie developed very often. They used to have Cooper-Hewitt lights overhead that cast a kind of pea-green, thickly green glow between shots. If you weren't working at the moment and you had a little time, you'd wander over, maybe visit with another company. At Fox–Western Avenue, I can remember I was doing a picture with Madge Bellamy called *Bertha, the Sewing Machine Girl* [1926]. I was supposed to be the delivery boy of this modiste shop. And Walter Pidgeon was working in a picture with Alma Rubens at the opposite end. He was a very nice guy and we got to be friends, and it's funny, you know, when you're a kid, I looked at him and thought he must be over fifty years old. He was about 29, I suppose. When we broke for lunch, we would go to the Assistance League Tea Room behind the Fox studio."

After six sound films, Billy Bakewell appeared as the fresh-faced young German recruit, Albert Kropp, in *All Quiet on the Western Front* (1930). This role remains his finest, and it led to a deep and lasting friendship with the film's star, Lew Ayres. Billy writes of the film and 86 additional sound features in his autobiography, *Hollywood Be Thy Name*, which I had the pleasure to edit, proof, and index. "You are my mentor and it could not have happened without you," reads Billy's inscription in my copy of the book.

Billy had contracted leukemia, and so his death in Los Angeles on April 15, 1993, was not a complete surprise. Mary Brian, who had been Billy's leading lady in *Harold Teen* and was a close friend of both him and Diane, overcame her grief by spending a day whacking at weeds in the garden.

One of the speakers at Billy's memorial service, held at the Motion Picture Country House (where he had been a longtime member of the board), was Ginger Rogers, who was very obviously grief-stricken. Some time later, I was asked to interview her in regard to the founding of the Screen Actors

Guild. She was not a pleasant interview subject. "I'm telling you now I remember nothing," she insisted at the start of the conversation. She kept calling me "dear" in a far from friendly manner but with not quite the same amount of venom she directed toward "Mr. Astaire." Then I mentioned my friendship with Billy Bakewell. What a change in manner! "Bless your heart, I'm sorry I can't give you a more colorful description of things," apologized Ginger. Anyone who was a friend of Billy—"a real friend, a wonderful man, they don't come any better, he was loved by everybody"—was a friend of Ginger. Billy Bakewell was the type of guy who could create a warm circle of friendship from a very disparate group.

Bibliography

Bakewell, William. *Hollywood Be Thy Name: Random Recollections of a Movie Veteran from Silents to Talkies to TV.* Metuchen, N.J.: Scarecrow Press, 1991.

Manners, Dorothy. "The Native Son Also Rises." *Motion Picture Classic,* January 1929, pp. 55, 84.

Shelps, Margarita Lorenz. "William Bakewell." *Films in Review,* December 1990, pp. 514–523.

York, Cal. "William Bakewell." *Photoplay,* December 1929, p. 40.

THEDA BARA. *See* **THE VAMPS**

Lina Basquette (left), with Marie Provost, in *The Godless Girl* (1929)

LINA BASQUETTE

There can be few autobiographies as outrageous as Lina Basquette's *Lina: DeMille's Godless Girl*, almost every page of which consists of remembered conversations dealing in large and intimate part with her sex life, the early death of her first husband, and, most entertaining of all, her attempted rape by Adolf Hitler. Norma Desmond did not have such a life! The book contains exaggeration and curious inconsistencies, if not downright lies, but it is all so entertaining that nobody should care. In a way, the autobiography's title reveals all—Basquette made only one film for which she is vaguely remembered, and that is as much for the director as for her performance.

When talking with Basquette, one was aware first of the twinkle in her eye and the measured appraisal of any good-looking man who walked by (straight or gay). Her behavior was difficult to resolve with her appearance; she wore her silver hair cropped short and she was well dressed but nonetheless grandmotherly.

Lina Basquette was never really what she claimed to be. Born in San Mateo, California, on April 19, 1907, she did indeed enter films, as a dancer, in 1916 with Universal, but while these productions were billed as "Lina Basquette Featurettes," they were no more than one half-reel (or five minutes) in length and certainly had no impact on audiences at the time. As a result of her work on the New York stage in the 1920s, again as a dancer, she was able to revive her film career (if she ever really had one), but the six features she made in 1926 and 1927 were as unimportant as her performances in them. She worked on stage, in the Ziegfeld *Follies*, with Louise Brooks, and Basquette is lucky that she was the subject of a *New Yorker* profile by the author who also wrote the only biography of Brooks. It leads to a comparison that is flattering to Basquette, but totally preposterous.

As a result of her performance in the 1928 crime melodrama, *The Noose*, Cecil B. DeMille offered her the leading role in *The Godless Girl*. As its militant title character, Lina Basquette proselytizes atheism at her high school, and when a riot leads to the death of one of the other students, she is sent to the state reformatory. Like many of DeMille's films, *The Godless Girl* has a rightwing message—this time the need for discipline in the classroom—although it does lay bare the brutality of juvenile crime facilities. The film is so bad that it is fun, and Lina Basquette looks most attractive, even after her hair has been shorn in the reformatory. She is less pleasing in the closing scene, which, unlike the rest of the film, has spoken dialogue, was directed not by DeMille but by Fritz Feld, and makes one wish that the silent film era might never have ended.

Lina Basquette's private life at this time was every bit as exciting as the plotline for *The Godless Girl*, but with far more serious overtones. In 1925, she had married Sam Warner, arguably the most intelligent of the Warner Brothers, who had shepherded the company into the sound era with the acquisition of the Vitaphone system. Lina gave birth to a daughter in 1926, but within a year she was a widow when Sam died unexpectedly. His family did not care for his gentile bride and were able to force Basquette to permit Harry Warner and his wife to become the child's guardians in return for a cash settlement. In August 1930 she made the obligatory suicide attempt—very obviously little more than a publicity ploy—and it was not the only such attempt. When Basquette married her cameraman from *The Godless Girl*, J. Peverell Marley, he became the second of her seven husbands

Curiously, *The Godless Girl* found an audience in both the Soviet Union and in Germany. There can be few films that appeal both to communists and fascists, but, when the film was suitably edited, the former applauded its message and the latter took their cue from Hitler, who despised all religion. Despite appearing only in American B pictures of the 1930s, and not too many of those, Lina Basquette claimed to have become Hitler's favorite film star. With her jet-black hair and Semitic features, she seems an odd choice for the Fuhrer's affection, and Hitler must have used considerable ingenuity to seek out her work at a time when most Americans would have been hard-pressed to know Basquette's name, let alone to have seen her films. Nevertheless, according to Lina Basquette, she came to Germany for a visit in January 1937, was introduced to Hitler at Berchtesgaden, and was invited to become Germany's biggest star. She also became the subject of attempted rape, but she escaped the Fuhrer's assault by pointing out that her grandfather was Jewish. The next day, Lina Basquette left Germany, and the next year, her film career ended for the remainder of the decade, presumably through the closure of the German market.

Lina Basquette had much more to recount in similar outrageous tone. She claimed she was involved during the Second World War in some form or other of espionage in South America, and it is difficult to figure out which side she was working for, if any. She made one last, very minor screen appearance, as a movie star in *A Night of Crime* (1943), before embarking on a new career in the late 1940s as a breeder of Great Danes. "Stay as close to dogs as possible," Lina told me. "They, on the whole, seem to have more common sense than the human race." She died in Wheeling, West Virginia, where she had lived since 1975, on September 30, 1994.

Bibliography

Paris, Barry. "The Godless Girl." *The New Yorker*, February 13, 1989, pp. 54–73.

Sewald, Jeff. "Return of the Godless Girl." *American Film*, January/February 1992, p. 14.

MADGE BELLAMY

Louise Dresser is *The Goose Woman*, a sort of rural bag lady, in the 1925 Universal film. Her real life equivalent was Madge Bellamy (Hillsboro, Texas, June 30, 1899–Upland, California, January 24, 1990), who lived her final years in Ontario, California, in semi-rural squalor, her attire and her surroundings equally distressed. Everything about Madge Bellamy was a mess. With her below-the-shoulder wig of golden curls, she looked as if she was understudying Bette Davis in *What Ever Happened to Baby Jane?* Even her autobiography, *A Darling of the Twenties: Madge Bellamy,* is rather a hodgepodge, with an appendix of correspondence, much of which makes no sense whatsoever.

From the stage, where she had made her debut at the age of five and on which her biggest success came in 1919 playing opposite William Gillette in *Dear Brutus,* Bellamy moved on to films in the 1920s as producer Thomas H. Ince's top female star. Her screen debut, prior to the Ince contract, was as Geraldine Farrar's daughter in *The Riddle: Woman* (1920). The next year, she made her Ince debut in *The Cup of Life* as the adopted white daughter of a Chinese merchant. The film was a silly melodrama, as were too many of Madge's Ince films. In Bellamy there was more than a hint of Mabel Normand to her face and her demeanor, and yet she was stuck in improbable dramas such as *Soul of the Beast* (1923), in which her costar is Anna May the elephant. Director John Griffith Wray "would sit under the camera tripod, with his megaphone, and scream all the way through the picture," recalled Madge. (Wray directed Blanche Sweet the same way in *Anna Christie*.) Bellamy needed fewer directors like John Griffith Wray, more farces such as *The Hottentot* (1922), in which she played opposite light comedian Douglas MacLean, and fewer romances opposite the likes of Lloyd Hughes.

The dreary adaptation of *Lorna Doone,* released in October 1922, made Bellamy a star and led Ince to feature her in a series of specials produced by Regal Pictures, Incorporated. She was now "the exquisite Madge," but the title was worthless without matching productions, and the vehicles Ince was able to provide were inferior.

In 1924, the actress became an independent player. She had the good fortune to star opposite George O'Brien in John Ford's *The Iron Horse,* released in October 1924, but, as ill fortune would have it, the film is one of the director's least inspiring, nothing more than a dull historical epic in which the performers are secondary to the building of a railroad. Madge stayed at Fox throughout the remainder of the silent era, playing again for Ford in *Lightnin'* (1925) and also working for such prominent directors as Frank Borzage and Victor Schertzinger. She told me—and I don't know if I believe her—that she was to have played Diane in *7th Heaven* (1927), but that while Bellamy was shooting location footage in France, the role was assigned to Janet Gaynor.

With the coming of sound, Madge Bellamy's career wound quickly down, and she made only nine films between 1929 and 1945. *White Zombie* (1932), in which she has second billing after Bela Lugosi, is the best known and also the worst received. Writing in *Liberty* (September 10, 1932), Frederick James Smith commented, "If you do not get a shock out of the thriller, you will get one out of the acting. It should worry even a zombie." Bellamy expected to star in the next film from the producers, the Halperin Brothers, but, perhaps wisely, they selected Carole Lombard for *Supernatural* (1933). Following her final screen role in *Northwest Trail*, a Bob Steele Western released in November 1945, Madge returned briefly to the stage in an undistinguished Los Angeles production of *Holiday Lady*.

Beautiful but dumb is how Madge Bellamy was described in the 1920s. Whether she was simply stupid or manipulative remains unclear. Her private life suggests both. Her 1928 marriage to broker Logan Metcalf lasted a mere four days. In 1943, she was convicted and received a suspended sentence for shooting at her boyfriend, millionaire lumberman Albert Murphy. She confounded Murphy and just about everyone else by suing him for divorce, despite the fact that the two were not married. Bellamy claimed a 1941 "mutual consent" marriage in Nevada was valid, although the court found otherwise.

Throughout her life, Madge Bellamy was exploited by her parents and by Hollywood. In pathetic old age, she at least enjoyed the interest of young film buffs, who saw in her eccentric attire and faded hairpiece a link to the exotic era of silent films.

Bibliography

Beach, Barbara. "A Lighted Torch." *Motion Picture Classic*, January 1921, pp. 46–47, 88.

Bellamy, Madge. *A Darling of the Twenties: Madge Bellamy*. Vestal, N.Y.: Vestal Press, 1989.

Drew, William M. "Madge Bellamy." In *Speaking of Silents: First Ladies of the Screen*. Vestal, N.Y.: Vestal Press, 1989, pp. 6–35.

Gebhart, Myrtle. "The Gold Girl." *Motion Picture*, April 1922, pp. 54–55, 101.

———. "Another Blue Bonnet." *Picture-Play*, August 1922, pp. 57–58, 96.

Jordan, Joan. "Madge Make-Believe." *Photoplay*, March 1921, p. 54.

Larkin, Mark. "Giving the Men a Break." *Photoplay*, March 1929, pp. 28, 97.

Manners, Dorothy. "A Salvaged Ingenue." *Picture-Play*, December 1924, pp. 34, 115.

Smith, Agnes. "Peroxide Pep." *Photoplay*, October 1926, pp. 31, 128.

CONSTANCE BINNEY

Back in the 1970s, there was an aging film buff in Washington, D.C., by the name of Tom Fullbright. For somewhat obvious reasons, including a penchant for aging actresses (very much a gay trait), he had the nickname of "Fruity" Fullbright. Tom came up with the notion of presenting "Rosemary Awards" to individuals from the silent era who were largely forgotten at the time—and back then film buffs were less determined in their desire to honor any actress of the past, no matter how trivial the career or how minimal the performance. I had something of a reputation as a film historian, or at least as the author of a handful of books on silent film, so Tom Fullbright asked me to make the presentations to his selected actresses. This was no Oscar event; to most of the audience, the presenter was as obscure as the presentees.

Thus it was that on April 30, 1974, I found myself in a church hall in Brooklyn, New York, presenting a Rosemary Award to Constance Binney before an audience of aging parishioners, including a bemused if not downright confused Butterfly McQueen. Miss Binney, who had once been a major Broadway leading lady and one of Paramount's top stars of the late teens no longer had the look of a piquant beauty for which she had been renowned, but resembled more an affluent aging housewife.

Binney had come to fame on stage as Penelope Penn in Rachel Crothers's *39 East*, which ran for 160 performances on Broadway, beginning March 31, 1919, and subsequently toured the U.S. At the time, Edward Wagenknecht described it as "a homey sort of play—real comedy not farce—about the daughter of a minister—'who is not a very good preacher but a perfectly darling man.'"

On screen, Constance Binney, along with her younger sister Faire (1900–1957), had made her debut the previous year in director Maurice Tourneur's first independent production, *Sporting Life*. The film led to a starring role opposite John Barrymore in *The Test of Honor* (1919) and a contract with Paramount's subsidiary, Realart. She was hailed as one of the screen's prettiest ingénues, with a natural film personality. *Photoplay*'s Julian Johnson waxed lyrical, "Her mouth was very serious, but her eyes were dancing. Her face was the face of the child of a Salem elder, the contained but tremendously potential loveliness that so intrigued Hawthorne and bedeviled John Alden."

Unfortunately, history has not been kind to Constance Binney. Most of her films have not survived; only two are available for reassessment. *Erstwhile Susan* (1919), directed by John Robertson, is the Cinderella tale in reverse; the fairy godmother in the form of the stepmother changes Constance Binney's drab existence, successfully subduing a father and two brothers, who have heretofore treated Binney's character as a drudge. Character woman

Mary Alden is delightful as the stepmother, at first seemingly coy and spinsterish, but for the first two reels Binney adopts make-up remarkably similar to that utilized later by Lois Wilson for *Miss Lulu Bett*—and equally unflattering. With her upturned nose and slightly plump features, Constance Binney is very much an actress in the Mae Marsh rather than the Lillian Gish tradition, more earthy than ethereal.

Constance Binney is also represented in the archives by the first reel of her 1921 feature, *First Love,* in which she goes out on her first date, receives her first kiss, has her first argument with her parents, and—because, as a title tells us, "First Love—blind and impetuous—knows no middle"—leaves home. A promising start for a film whose director, Maurice Campbell, has no reputation.

In all, Constance Binney starred in fourteen feature films between 1918 and 1923; sister Faire continued on screen for few years longer. In 1924, Binney made one last New York stage appearance, a starring role in the George Gershwin musical *Sweet Little Devil,* before retiring completely from stage and screen. Binney married three times, to wealthy businessmen, but all of them ended in divorce. Constance Binney (born June 28, 1896, New York) died in Whitestone, New York, on November 15, 1989.

Bibliography

Binney, Faire. "My Sister Constance." *Filmplay,* June 1922, pp. 6–7, 52.
Boone, Arabella. "The Day of the Deb." *Photoplay,* September 1920, pp. 28–29, 116.
Bruce, Betsy. "Constance Seeking." *Motion Picture,* November 1920, pp. 33, 99–100.
Cole, Phoebe. "Dancing into Focus." *Filmplay,* September 1921, pp. 20–21, 56.
Curley, Kenneth. "Constance: The Brute Breaker." *Motion Picture,* May 1922, pp. 44–45, 95.
Johnson, Julian. "Plymouth Rock Chicken." *Photoplay,* September 1919, pp. 33–34, 130.
Boone, Martin. "Cinderella Lives Again." *Picture-Play,* April 1922, pp. 49, 100.
Smith, Frederick James. "Youth and Constance Binney." *Motion Picture Classic,* January 1921, pp. 16–17.
Williams, Louise. "Back-Stage with Constance Binney." *Picture-Play,* September 1920, pp. 68–69, 85.

Priscilla Bonner (right) with sister Margerie.

PRISCILLA BONNER

Priscilla Bonner's forté was playing the innocent, virginal heroine. "I was in rags a lot of the time and it was always raining. I was dragged through rainstorms and it was snowing and people were abusing me. That was my screen life," she once commented. In real life, she was a shrewd businesswoman with a keen interest in money. On a road trip to San Francisco, she pointed out the oilrigs off the coast of Santa Barbara, ugly and offensive to most passersby, but to her, an investor, a potential source of revenue. She was very good at entertaining friends with stories that showed her in a humorous light, and always with an innocence that one strongly suspected was false. "I know I had talent," she once told me, "but I also knew it wasn't enough to make an impression."

Born in Washington, D.C., on February 17, 1899, Priscilla Bonner enjoyed dancing at school, and there she was approached by a young vaudevillian, asking if she would like to join his act on the Orpheum Circuit. Priscilla was thrilled, her parents outraged. Mother put a stop to the proposed teaming, but she did allow Priscilla to come out to Los Angeles, properly chaperoned: "I went out to Metro, and there was a casting director there. I was very nicely dressed, as a very young girl would be, with my hair hanging down my back. He said, 'What experience do you have?' I said, 'Oh, I haven't any experience, but I expect you to give me some.' He leaned back in his chair and said, 'Jesus Christ!' Of course I wasn't used to such language, and I was shocked, but the end of the thing was he gave me some extra work. I didn't know I was an extra and I didn't know I was to be paid. So I worked four or five days and I never collected any money. I was the original freshman. I knew nothing.

"Then I decided I would like to have something a little better and I went down to the Ince studio where Charles Ray was working. They saw me as the type of girl they wanted, so I ended up playing the lead with Charles Ray [in *Homer Comes Home* (1920)]. I bought all my clothes, which the studio would have paid for, but nobody told me. When they found out how stupid I was, they just let me.

"When I got through with that picture, I went out to Metro, and the casting director said, 'Hello, how are you? What have you been doing?' I said, 'I just finished playing a lead with Mr. Charles Ray.' He leaned back in his chair and again said, 'Jesus Christ!' So I ended up playing leads with Jack Pickford, Tom Moore, Will Rogers. It just went on. I had no fear because I was raised in a home of protection. I wasn't afraid of anything or anybody. I had no fear of not getting work because I had come all this way to get it. Also, my innocence protected me, as it always does you know."

In 1920 Bonner made *Honest Hutch* (1920) with Will Rogers and *Of-*

ficer 666 with Tom Moore. The titles are irrelevant, but the leading men are impressive. The same year, Priscilla was cast opposite notorious womanizer Jack Pickford in *The Man Who Had Everything*: "Jack Pickford was marvelous to me. He treated me like a little sister and protected and watched over me. I think I was much too innocent, much too young for him. He was probably the most charming man I have ever met. He took me out to dinner at the Alexandria Hotel and we held hands under the table. He asked me, 'Are you a virgin?' I was so embarrassed because there are certain subjects one does not talk about. I said, 'Yes, why?' He replied, 'It's a pity because virgins are too much trouble. I'll leave you for someone else to have fun with, and then we'll get back together.' I think eventually we would have married had he not died so young."

Another man with a bad reputation as a lecher was director Marshall Neilan, for whom Priscilla appeared as a schoolteacher in his 1921 production of *Bob Hampton of Placer*: "I was on the set and somebody came from another studio, and Mr. Neilan in a loud voice called out, 'Where's Priscilla? Bring her over here.' Then he turned to this man and said, 'We've got a virgin. You are a virgin, aren't you dear?' I was a joke, a company joke. The more I blushed, the more they enjoyed it."

While she might talk about her innocence and her virginity with candor, she was anything but candid when it came to her personal life. Priscilla spoke only of one, lasting marriage—a second one. She made no reference to an earlier wedding to Alan Wyness, which took place in Riverside, California, on May 28, 1921, after which she retired from the screen. A final divorce decree was issued in December 1925, Priscilla claiming that her husband had deserted her the previous year, when in all probability, the couple split much earlier. Priscilla was forced to try to rekindle her career with small, insignificant roles in *Shadows* (1922), *Hold Your Breath* (1924), *Charlie's Aunt* (1925), and others.

In July 1925, Priscilla was thrilled to be invited to John Barrymore's suite at the Ambassador Hotel, where she was told she would be his leading lady in *The Sea Beast*. "He said, 'Are you afraid of me?' I said, 'Yes, Mr. Barrymore.' He said, 'My friends call me Jakie,' and I said, 'Yes, Mr. Barrymore.' He looked at me rather quizzically and I could see he didn't like it. I said, 'Don't worry, it'll be all right on the set; as I'm playing the character, I'll be the character, and I won't be afraid of you then. I'm only afraid of you personally.' That didn't make much of a hit with him." Priscilla recalled that Barrymore looked dirty and smelled dreadful. Barrymore's body odor was a major problem. (Jetta Goudal, who also lived at the Ambassador Hotel, similarly described him as "smelly and greasy.")

Neither body odor nor Priscilla's acting ability caused her to lose to role, but rather Barrymore's meeting and infatuation with Dolores Costello. Again, Priscilla was summoned to the Ambassador Hotel. Barrymore was horrified when she burst into tears and fled the room. He wrote her a six-page handwritten note, containing $500 in cash, as an apology and an assurance that her acting was fine. (Later, Priscilla met Costello's father, Maurice, at Columbia; he was extremely upset that his daughter was under Barrymore's spell and told Priscilla, "He is depraved.") Priscilla kept the note and when in the early 1980s, she gave it to me she wondered why she had kept it in lieu of all the other memorabilia relating to her career that she might have retained.

As early as 1921, Priscilla appeared as a second lead to Viola Dana in *Home Stuff*. Neither she nor Vi could recall working together. Priscilla was bothered that she was cast in support of a female star. She appears in Clara Bow's most famous film, *It* (1927), as a single mother whose baby is to be seized by the authorities: "I didn't want to support a feminine star, but I had to, so I did it with the best grace possible. She was all dressed up and looked beautiful and I was in rags. She [Bow] was very pleasant to me and I was very pleasant to her. But, you see, when you support a star of the size and magnitude of Clara Bow, you play always with your left ear to the camera."

Priscilla faced a similar problem in John Ford's *Three Bad Men* (1926): "Olive Borden played the lead and Olive Borden was just so beautiful. I played the character ingénue. Lou Tellegen was in the picture and he beat me with a whip. That was very dramatic. But I was all cut out. Olive Borden was so adorable, they used three reels of her and cut out everything that was dramatic in the picture. By the time they got through, it was mostly Olive taking a bath in a barrel."

Mrs. Wallace Reid (she was so billed) had entered film production following the drug-related death of her husband. Her first two films were produced in association with Thomas H. Ince, but for her third effort, *The Red Kimona* (1925)—a strange main title misspelling for *Kimono*, which was corrected in the publicity for the film—she formed her own company. Priscilla was hired to play the central character, Gabrielle Darley, who is forced into prostitution but regenerates herself through hard work. The role was perfect for Priscilla, but her mother disagreed. "If your father had known what this film was about, he would not have permitted you to appear in it," Priscilla's mother told her at the first Los Angeles screening. When Priscilla excused herself to meet with reporters, her mother responded, "The press! You mean this will be in the newspapers!"

Someone else unhappy with the film, and far more important, was Gabrielle Darley, on whose life story the film was based and who had since married a prominent St. Louis businessman. She sued, claiming the film denied her the right "to pursue and obtain happiness," as guaranteed by the California constitution. Eventually, in 1931, she won, and Mrs. Reid began the decade penniless.

Priscilla and Mrs. Reid remained close friends, but when I took the former to visit Mrs. Reid in the Motion Picture Country Hospital in January 1977, she did not know Priscilla.

If modern audiences know Priscilla Bonner at all, it is because of her role as Harry Langdon's leading lady in *The Strong Man* (1926) and *Long Pants* (1927) at the time the comedian was rejecting the advice of his director Frank Capra. In the latter, she has the quintessential Priscilla Bonner role of an innocent blind girl, Mary Brown, unable to see the basic foolishness in Harry Langdon: "That was a very poignant scene where the little, funny-looking man stands in front of the girl to whom he is a dream man and she can't see him, so he always will be. It's a beautiful situation, and they didn't want a girl who was a comedienne to play it. The second picture, there was much trouble and dissension. I never saw the picture because the reviews weren't too awfully good. Frank Capra was the great director, later proven. He was a quiet director, not flamboyant. He embraced you with his smile. Harry Langdon was in his time compared to Chaplin, and he might have gone on because there was something so tragic about his comedy. His timing was magnificent. But fate intervened. He should have stayed with Capra. Capra would have soared with him. There were other people in there, of course. There was this woman he married, who was not a very smart woman. It was a sad situation, a tragedy. Like so many highly gifted men, he was perhaps not too stable."

Priscilla had a younger sister, Margerie (1905–1988), who was also a close friend and a frequent dinner guest at our house. Just as Priscilla would usually hold out her wine glass for more, Margerie loved her vodka. She followed Priscilla into films in 1920 but never achieved any major success. What she did do was marry Malcolm Lowry, whose novel, *Under the Volcano*, is a cult classic if not a work of popular fiction. Priscilla did not approve of Malcolm, whose drinking was legendary. On one visit to Priscilla's home, he managed to leave the bath water running and to soak not only the bathroom floor but also the carpeting on the stairs, after which Priscilla ejected the pair. (When Priscilla told Preston Sturges that she did not like Lowry "because he is not polite and he is not a gentleman," the director smiled and nodded in agreement.)

In old age, Margerie was such a Beverly Hills matron that it was difficult to imagine her and Lowry living together in semi-poverty and squalor. It must have been an odd relationship. Margerie came with Robert Gitt and me to view the National Film Board of Canada documentary, *Volcano: An Inquiry into the Life and Death of Malcolm Lowry* (1977). I felt more and more uncomfortable sitting next to Margerie as the film discussed Lowry's penis size and his latent homosexuality. Margerie seemed disinterested—perhaps she already knew what the film had to relate—and after the screening, she happily invited everyone back for cocktails.

Margerie and Priscilla appeared together as sisters in one film, *Paying the Price*, released by Columbia in April 1927. Priscilla dismissed the film as "that awful picture," which it probably was, and complained that Harry Cohn had told her that she had no sex appeal.

Two years later, Priscilla retired from the screen and married a prominent Beverly Hills physician, Bertram "Bertie" Woolfan. "He said let's get married and no more work. He was a pretty forceful man and a very strong man. I knew I couldn't have a career and him. I had to make a decision right there," said Priscilla. In reality, it seems likely that Priscilla's voice was not ideally suited to talkies and that the end of the silent era was a good time to marry and retire.

Bertie Woolfan was well known in the film community; for many years he was the studio doctor at 20th Century-Fox, and he even has a credit as a consultant on a 1925 silent film, *The People vs. Nancy Preston*. Beginning in 1932, he also enjoyed a close personal relationship with director Preston Sturges. When Sturges was asked to entertain an important but taciturn Paramount executive, he decided that Priscilla should sit next to him because "she can talk to a telephone pole." In old age, Priscilla was interviewed frequently about Sturges and never really admitted that her friendship with the director was the direct result of her husband's relationship with him. She was very much a secondary character in the threesome. In fact, if it was not so obvious that Sturges was heterosexual, one might even be inclined to ponder a gay relationship between him and Bertie. Priscilla once commented that she was sure that the relationship between the two men was far from natural and that if Bertie had had to choose between her and Preston, he would have chosen Preston.

Bertie Woolfan killed himself in December 1962. He chose a horrendous method of suicide for a doctor, who could so easily have selected a painless and quiet means of death. Soon after waking one morning, Bertie took a gun and shot himself. Priscilla came running to his side. The foolish man had not aimed the weapon accurately, but he lay in his wife's arms and bled to death, while telling the paramedics who had been summoned that he, as a doctor, forbade them to treat him.

As she grew older, Priscilla became very parsimonious. Despite a stock portfolio worth in excess of two million dollars, Priscilla pleaded poverty. Sister Margerie had been living for some time in a small Beverly Hills apartment with Marian Blackton Trimble, the widow of director Larry Trimble and daughter of Vitagraph co-founder J. Stuart Blackton, whom she had known since the 1920s. In retrospect, I realize it was a lesbian relationship. Priscilla may have realized this far sooner; she broke up the couple by insisting that a decline in the value of her stocks made it imperative that Margerie share an apartment and expenses with her.

In time, Margerie suffered a stroke and was eventually shuffled off to a retirement facility. The stroke was blamed on the Lowry marriage. "Malcolm was a genius, but he was also a maniac, and you can't live with a maniac for eighteen years and not pay the price," Priscilla commented. She claimed Margerie was no longer aware of her surroundings and ceased visiting her, but when college professor Betty Moss, who had been a good friend to Margerie, brought her to the screening of John Huston's 1984 adaptation of *Under the Volcano*, it was obvious that despite her loss of speech Margerie was still mentally alert. Avidly she studied what was taking place on screen, watching a film in which the central female character is based on her, often with tears in her eyes.

With Margerie's death, Priscilla gave up her apartment and moved into a retirement facility in Beverly Hills. Eventually, Robert Gitt and I persuaded her to move to a location closer to us, and we would visit her each weekend. She was highly amusing. On one occasion, she announced that she had been reading the Bible, "and it's a crashing bore! I've read Genesis and now I'm reading Exodus. And it's getting no better!"

Priscilla would eat ravenously when invited for dinner, but when she had to pay for the food, she was not hungry. Every penny was put aside for the cause of reincarnation, with which she became obsessed. At her death on February 21, 1996, she left her estate to the University of Virginia, for the purpose of creating a research fellowship in her and Margerie's name. Poor Bertie was forgotten. For months before her death, Priscilla had been announcing that she would take everyone out for a formal dinner on March 30. On her deathbed, she told Betty Moss, "Tell the boys I won't be able to have the dinner." We joked that she would do anything to get out of paying for a meal.

Bibliography

Carlisle, Helen. "The Girl Who Lost and the Girl Who Won." *Movie Weekly*, September 19, 1925, pp. 30–31.
Moore, Molly. "Talent Plus." *Motion Picture Classic*, January 1921, pp. 18, 80, 82.
Slide, Anthony. *The Silent Feminists: America's First Women Directors*. Lanham,

Maryland: Scarecrow Press, 1996. See pages 89-92 for a discussion of the making of *The Red Kimona*.

———. "The Film Career of Margerie Bonner Lowry." *The Malcolm Lowry Review* 29 and 30, fall 1991 and Spring 1992, pp. 20-26.For a discussion of Margerie Bonner's career.

Stuart, Clyde. "Priscilla Finds Romance." *Motion Picture*, October 1921, pp. 68–69, 85.

HOBART BOSWORTH

Hobart Bosworth brought a sense of strength and nobility to the screen. He was a pioneering actor who seemed to continue on forever, as virile and capable in roles of the 1930s as he appeared two decades previous. Bosworth was the Dean of the Screen, and as such he symbolized old Hollywood. "I remember him so well as a young boy," said Charles "Buddy" Rogers, who played his son in *My Best Girl* (1927), "We had a bridle path in Beverly Hills, and he had this big white stallion. My first memory of glamour Hollywood was to see him and Valentino—to see those two men riding." Bosworth's pure white Palomino Arab, Cameo, was as much a part of the Hollywood scene as its owner; he appeared on screen in *The Man Alone* (1923), participated in the 1926 and later editions of the Rose Parade, and was even the subject of a feature-length article in the April 1, 1926, edition of *Farmers Home Journal*. "With your white hair and your blue eyes, Hobe, you look jes' like your hoss," wrote Will Rogers, who died the same year as Cameo, 1935.

Born in Marietta, Ohio, on August 11, 1867, the son of a Civil War sea captain, Hobart Bosworth ran away to sea at the age of twelve. While on shore leave in San Francisco in June 1885, he was persuaded to join McKee Rankin's stage company, and he embarked on a major theatrical career. (In 1909, he and Selig would film Rankin's play *'49*.) He was with Augustin Daly from 1888 to 1898, with Henrietta Crosman in 1903, with Mrs. Minnie Maddern Fiske in 1903, and with Florence Roberts in 1904. While with Amelia Bingham in St. Louis in 1902, his female fans gave Bosworth the nickname "Violets" because of the blueness of his eyes. In 1906, Bosworth became leading man, director, and stage manager with the Belasco Theatre stock company in Los Angeles, where the players included Lewis Stone, Charlie Ruggles, Elmer Clifton, Alfred Paget, and director-to-be Joseph DeGrasse. Two years later, in association with the Belasco Theatre, the actor founded the Hobart Bosworth Institute of Dramatic Arts.

Hobart Bosworth was first diagnosed with tuberculosis in 1899, and by 1905 his weight had dropped from 204 to 139 pounds. The disease was still present in 1909, when he left the Belasco Theatre and considered retirement. He was persuaded by director Francis Boggs of the Selig Polyscope Company, the first major production entity to establish a studio in Los Angeles, to star in a one-reel drama dealing with the political situation in Turkey and entititled *In the Sultan's Power*, which was released on June 17, 1909. After completion of the production, Bosworth went to San Diego in an effort to regain his health in a warmer clime but was offered, and accepted, a contract with Selig at its new studio in Edendale, near downtown Los Angeles. From

Selig, the actor formed an alliance in August 1913 with H.T. Rudisill and Frank A. Garbutt and formed a new company, Bosworth, Inc., to produce feature films based on the works of Jack London. The first was *The Sea Wolf*, filmed in 1913, with Bosworth in the title role of Wolf Larsen, followed by seven more Jack London adaptations in 1914. The company, which also boasted the presence of director Lois Weber and her husband Phillips Smalley, was absorbed by Paramount in 1916, but a year earlier its founder had moved on and become a Universal star. The actor returned briefly to production in 1921 with two films, *Blind Hearts* and *The Sea Lion*, directed by Rowland V. Lee.

As evidenced by his 1921 productions and the earlier adaptations, Bosworth had a great love of the outdoors and of the works of Jack London. In 1917, he embarked on a major vaudeville tour, playing opposite Ethel Grey Terry in a 26-minute version of *The Sea Wolf*. His most memorable screen appearance in the teens is in *Behind the Door* (1919), in which he plays Oscar Krug, who skins alive the German submarine lieutenant (Wallace Beery) responsible for the rape and murder of his young wife. This role reveals an incredible bitterness to Bosworth's characterization that is lacking from most of his screen work. In an unusual concept, Bosworth appeared on stage in January 1920 at Grauman's Theatre in Los Angeles, with James Gordon and Richard Wayne; the film was stopped immediately after the German captive has been taken behind the door, and the next expository scene was performed live.

Bosworth was as adept at historical characterizations as he was at modern roles. He could play Bill Sikes in *Oliver Twist* (1916) or Cortez in *The Woman God Forgot* (1917). Other men of his age might become character actors, but he remained a featured player, appearing in more than 60 films in the 1920s and more than 20 in the 1930s. He made his last screen appearance in Ray Enright's 1942 production of *Sin Town* and died in Glendale, California, on December 30, 1943.

The actor had the misfortune to be married to a young, over-caring wife, who was obsessed with the preservation of his career and his image. I was one of many who received scathing telephone calls from the widow; she denounced me for what I considered a laudatory piece on Bosworth but one that failed to do him justice. In order to "preserve" his work, the widow moved his personal 35mm nitrate film prints out to the desert community where she lived and where they decomposed in the high heat and high humidity. A handful of reels were eventually salvaged for preservation by the Library of Congress, and, after her death, Bosworth's papers, which strangely lack important primary documentation on much of his silent career, came to the Margaret Herrick Library of the Academy of Motion Picture Arts and Sciences.

Bibliography

Beach, Barbara. "The Pioneer of the Shadowed Drama." *Motion Picture*, February 1922, pp. 42, 88.

Belfrage, Cedric. "Mark My Words." *Motion Picture*, April 1928, pp. 34, 100, 107, 109.

Bosworth, Hobart. "The Picture Forty-Niners." *Photoplay*, December 1915, pp. 75–81.

"Bosworth's Art Analyzed by Critic." *Moving Picture Weekly*, September 18, 1915, p. 19.

Cheatham, Maude S. "Sea Dog Bosworth." *Motion Picture Classic*, December 1919, pp. 18–19, 76, 81.

Oettinger, Malcolm H. "A Man Who Refused to Die." *Picture-Play*, March 1921, pp. 50, 92.

"People You Pay to Know." *National Magazine*, May 1918, pp. 277, 279.

Squier, Emma-Lindsay. "A Prophet of the Cinema." *Picture-Play*, November 1925, pp. 90, 107.

Williams, Tony. "The War of the Wolves: Filming Jack London's *The Sea Wolf*." *Film History*, vol. IV, no. 3, 1990, pp. 199–217.

EVELYN BRENT

The majority of silent film players never took themselves too seriously, but few were willing to spare the time to view what they considered to be their worst screen appearance. An exception was Evelyn Brent, who sat down and watched with obvious amusement (and a few quite salty comments) her 1922 British feature *Trapped by the Mormons*. Between 1920 and 1923, Brent made thirteen films in Europe, ten in England, two in the Netherlands, and one in Spain. The last, *The Spanish Jade*, co-starring Marc MacDermott, was directed by John Robertson and Tom Geraghty for Famous Players-Lasky and is the best of the bunch. *Trapped by the Mormons*—along with its sequel, *Married to a Mormon*, both released in 1922—is the worst, an incredibly lurid production dealing with the Mormon "menace." Director H.B. Parkinson took advantage of the public agitation surrounding the missionary work of the Mormon Church in Britain and the suggestion that virginal English girls were being lured back to Utah and a life of sin. (Apart from being an extremely bad director, H.B. Parkinson was also an exploitative one and in 1926 produced *The Life Story of Charles Chaplin*, starring Chick Wango, which was suppressed by the comedian.)

A solemn-faced actress with a smoldering intensity, Evelyn Brent's features carried a vague hint of the mysterious. Cool and beautiful, she seldom smiled, perhaps because she had little to smile about. The actress was the archetypal gangster's moll in her best films, *Underworld* (1927) and *The Dragnet* (1928), both directed by Josef von Sternberg. Brent was a favorite of the director, and he also cast her as the Russian spy in *The Last Command* (1928). One of her minor films very much deserving of rediscovery is *Women's Wares*, a 1927 Tiffany production directed by Arthur Gregor. Brent's character uses men to her advantage, and the scene in which she agrees to spend the night with Larry Kent is told entirely in close-up, without a subtitle. Only at the conclusion of a sequence illustrative of not only Brent's talent but also that of the generally under-regarded Larry Kent do we need a title to explain the character's behavior: "From now on, I'll promise them everything and give them nothing." The sophistication and innuendo of the storyline is best exemplified when Brent's roommate Gertrude Short looks through the overnight bag of Richard Tucker, who is paying the apartment rent for both women. She discovers bath salts, "a purifying deodorant for mouth and stomach," and an unidentified item that causes Short to hide her eyes in horror and to crawl away.

Born Mary Elizabeth Riggs in Tampa, Florida, on October 20, 1899, to a fourteen-year-old Italian mother and a seventeen-year-old Irish-American father, the actress had a miserable childhood. Her father died when she was three years old, and her mother died and left her penniless at the age of fourteen. She visited the studios at Fort Lee and began appearing as an extra, with her first credited role, as Betty Riggs, in Maurice Tourneur's 1914 production of *The Pit*. She met Olga Petrova while appearing in the Metro production of *The Soul Market* (1916), and the former encouraged her career. "She was a lovely child, loveliest of the group and talented," Petrova told me. The actress changed her name to Evelyn Brent with *The Lure of Heart's Desire* in 1916 and the size of her roles gradually increased.

By 1920, she had saved $500, and with a girl friend, decided to visit Europe. Brent made her first British film, *The Shuttle of Life*, opposite C. Aubrey Smith that same year. "In London I had the happiest time I ever had in all my life," she recalled. She alternated between film and stage work, and as a result of her British career, Brent returned to the United States as a "British Beauty" and a star. She came to California for the first time and revived her American career with Metro's *Held to Answer* (1923) in which she was directed by Harold Shaw, who had himself spent many years in the British film industry.

From 1926 to 1930, Evelyn Brent was under contract to Paramount and was one of the stars of the studio's first talkie, *Interference* (1929). She made 56 more sound films, with the roles gradually getting smaller and the productions quickly diminishing in importance and quality. Her last film, in 1950, was *Again Pioneers* for Religious Film Associates. Despite, or perhaps because of, three marriages, she ended her life as a lesbian, living with actress Dorothy Conrad in a small Westwood apartment, where she died on June 4, 1975.

Bibliography

Albert, Katherine. "She Eats and Tells." *Photoplay*, January 1931, pp. 40, 120.
Biery, Ruth. "Suicide Never Pays." *Photoplay*, May 1928, pp. 33, 120–122.
Bodeen, DeWitt. "Evelyn Brent." *Films in Review*, June 1976, pp. 339–360.
Hall, Gladys. "Confessions of the Stars: Evelyn Brent Tells Her Untold Story." *Motion Picture Classic*, July 1929, pp. 28–29, 66, 90.

MARY BRIAN

Mary Brian is the greatest of the screen ingénues from the silent and early sound era. She is a competent, intelligent, and compliant actress who exudes a natural charm and personality. There is never anything forced or artificial about her performances, no matter if the storylines are not always believable. Because she appears to have faith in what is transpiring on screen, so do we, the audience, believe. It is rather like the line in *Peter Pan*, in which Mary made her debut, when the audience is asked if they believe in fairies. Of course, we do, and so do we believe in Mary Brian.

I doubt there is any other actress who was so popular among her contemporaries. In 1932, she was away from her studio for her birthday, the first time she had not been there in eight years. Juvenile Russell Gleason made a film, which Mary later gave to me, in which everyone on the lot, and many off it, wishes her a happy birthday. They are all there, from the giants of the cinema, including Douglas Fairbanks and W.C. Fields, to leading players, such as Lew Ayres, Johnny Mack Brown, Louise Fazenda, Ginger Rogers, Ben Lyon, Jack Oakie, and Lois Wilson, and directors, including Herbert Brenon, Eddie Sutherland, and Frank Tuttle.

Brian was described as Hollywood's social arbiter for the younger set. A young actor could not be a popular man-about-town until he had "dated" Mary Brian and received her seal of approval. Once Mary Brian had been out with an actor, it was said that any other actress could be seen with him and not risk losing her reputation. As *Modern Screen* described her in 1934, she was "The Girl of a Thousand-and-One Boy Friends." Among the leading men who were Mary's beaux (as she always referred to them) were Lew Ayres, Billy Bakewell, Gary Cooper, Russell Gleason, Jack Oakie, George Raft, Gene Raymond, Charles "Buddy" Rogers, and Rudy Vallee. In the summer of 1932, it was rumored that Ken Murray (with whom she was appearing in vaudeville) and Mary had married. And her "dates" were not limited to Hollywood types. In 1932, Mary was frequently seen in the company of boxer Jack Dempsey, and in 1935, there were rumors of an engagement to Gerald Lambert, heir to the Lambert Listerine fortune. Of her beaux, Mary named George Sanders the most intelligent. He begged her to marry him, and when Mary refused, he responded, "But I have dismissed my mistress, and who is going to iron my shirts now?"

Mary Brian was engaged to both Dick Powell (she was his leading lady in his first film, *Blessed Event*) and Cary Grant and came very close to marrying the latter. In later years, she remembered visiting Powell and his then-wife June Allyson, along with Glenda Farrell. Powell turned to the latter and commented wryly, "I should have married Mary." The relationship between Mary Brian and her beaux never caused jealousy or animosity. When Dick Powell saw Mary in the company of Jack Oakie at the Cocoanut Grove, he demanded to know, "What's the big idea?" Mary replied, "Oh, Jack's back for retakes."

"I need to explain beaux," says Mary. "This is a whole different time. I'm not saying this is a better time or a worse time. I'm not sitting in judgment. A beau is someone you meet. They're interested in you and you're interested in them. You're taken out to dine and dance. And we used to go dancing all the time. They're beaux, and they're chums and they're friends. If you have a chance to go out with a lot of people, it's not promiscuous. It's just they like you. Now, if they say they're going out with some person, they mean that you're having an affair with them.

"Sometimes, they [the studio] did try to make a romance out of it. One of the friendships of my life was June Collyer Erwin. We were in a picture with Buddy [Rogers], and the studio wanted to make a feud that he was going with her, and the two of us were at swords' points on the picture. Buddy and I had worked together and we were chums. Buddy loves to flirt. It was never really serious. He took out June a few times. It didn't bother me. But June came to me and she said, 'They're trying to make us rivals. I don't want it. I want you for my friend.' I thought, 'How nice.' And we did become great friends."

Born Louise Byrd Dantzler in Corsicana, Texas, on February 17, 1906, Mary Brian did not have an easy childhood. Her father, an oculist, died in an accident when she was a month old, and her mother was forced to return to work in order to pay off debts built up not by her husband but by his partner, who had left town. She moved Mary and her brother, Terry (who was later a bandleader and vocalist) to their grandmother's home in West Texas. Dorothy Scarborough visited there and used the experience as a background for her harrowing novel, *The Wind;* even today, Mary notes that the only thing that frightens her is the wind. When Mary's aunt moved to Long Beach, her mother took her family also, and in 1923, Mary Brian entered a bathing beauty contest in the hope of winning the $25 prize money. She didn't, but one of the judges, Esther Ralston, who was to become Mary's lifelong friend, insisted, "You've got to give that little girl something."

The "something" was the promise of a test at Famous Players–Lasky for a role as one of the children in the about-to-be filmed adaptation of *Peter Pan.* Betty Bronson had already been cast in the title role, and Mary was sent in to be interviewed by director Herbert Brenon: "Herbert Brenon had an eye operation of some kind and his office he had to keep dark. When anybody came in, he turned the light off. He asked me a few questions. Is that your hair? Out of the blue, he said, 'I would like to make a test.' Even to this day I will never know why I was that lucky. They had made tests of every ingénue in the business for Wendy. He had decided he would go with an unknown. It would seem more like a fairy tale. It wouldn't seem right if the roles were to be taken by someone they [the audience] knew or was divorced. I got the part. They put me under contract.

"Herbert Brenon was supposedly a very difficult man. He was very strict—not particularly with the children. He knew I had no experience. I did what he told me. I made several pictures with him, and he was always wonderful to me." Many years later, after both Mary and Brenon had retired, the latter began work on his autobiography. His Wendy had taken up painting as a hobby, and the director asked her to create an oil painting of a scene from *Peter Pan* as a cover illustration for the book. The autobiography was never completed, but the painting still hangs in Mary's Studio City home—in the kitchen.

The studio named the actress Mary Brian: "Byrd was the family name. When I was first starting, it didn't seem important one way or the other." Famous Players-Lasky created a problem for itself and for its new ingénue when it decided to knock two years off her age, because they decided that Wendy could not be more than 16 years old: "They wanted me to be younger. Then, the minute they put me in more leading roles, they wanted me to be older." In later years, when asked as to her real year of birth, Mary would always explain that her age was "negotiable."

From *Peter Pan*, Mary Brian was starred opposite Douglas Fairbanks Jr. in *The Air Mail* (1925): "We were juvenile juveniles." Herbert Brenon directed her in *The Little French Girl* (1925), for which she went on location to Bermuda, *The Street of Forgotten Men* (1925), and *Beau Geste* (1926). Playing opposite Raymond Griffith in *A Regular Fellow* (1925) and opposite Arthur Lake in *Harold Teen* (1928), Mary demonstrated her comedic talents, and with *The Enchanted Hill* (1926), she proved an idyllic Western heroine. For *More Pay—Less Work*, released in July 1926, Mary was loaned out to Fox, and filmed on location in San Francisco with Charles "Buddy" Rogers, another lifelong friend. Earlier, she had been loaned out to MGM for *Brown of Harvard* (1926) opposite William Haines: "They had a whole different system at MGM. They had a lot of people under contract but they didn't use them as often. They were teaching them many things, singing and dancing. Paramount did give me a chance and I did have a wonderful time there. I made friends that I've had all my life. But we just worked—and we were loaned out too. But Paramount was still better than Universal or some of the other studios."

Initially, Mary was not aware that Haines was gay. "I was around that all the time, and it didn't seem that it was that big a deal. I just took it for granted when his friend, Jimmy Shields, used to come on the set quite often to see him. There were art directors, wonderful integral parts of the business, that were taken for granted. You admired them for their talent. It was no big deal."

The only actor of whom Mary has anything negative to say is Wallace Beery, her leading man in *Behind the Front* (1926), *Partners in Crime* (1928), *The Big Killing* (1928), and *River of Romance* (1929): "I never understood Gloria Swanson marrying him, because he was a cruel man. He played jokes, but they were not funny jokes. They were cruel jokes. On this one particular picture, we had been fighting the sun and it was not easy to get this one shot. Wallace Beery got his plane and would fly over the set and ruin every take. This is funny? You'd see him on the screen and he looked like a big, loveable chump. I was not overly fond of him.

"I think in *Behind the Front*, there was a scene where I was supposed to sit in a sidecar. We got out on location and they said, 'Can anyone here drive a motorcyle?' This one man said yes. We were zig-zaging all over the place. They kept yelling to the man, 'Shut it off.' I don't think he'd ever driven a motorcycle before. I had the ride of my life. I wasn't frightened. It was funny. I think that pleased Wallace Beery."

The director of the first Beery-Brian film was Edward "Eddie" Sutherland, whose humor was far more appealing to the actress: "He loved to play jokes on me, but it was all done in a very good humored sort of way. It was never condescending. He would come over and say, 'Listen to Uncle Eddie.' He was always doing things to make me laugh and relax. I was used to working with the guys. I wasn't averse to working and taking suggestions. I got along fine. I don't think they were exceedingly tough on women. The same people worked at the studio on most of the pictures, and they felt like they raised me. They were protective. They always included me in. If they decided to have a cookout or whatever, we all did it together. They had a lot of practical jokes going, but not because I was a woman. It just passed the time."

In 1927, Mary Brian made the first of her films with comedian W.C. Fields, *Running Wild* and *Two Flaming Youths*. With the coming of sound, she was again Fields's daughter in *The Man on the Flying Trapeze* (1935). The two became good friends, and even today, when Fields's grandson Everett comes over, he always addresses Mary Brian as his Aunt Mary: "You always played comedy entirely different than if you're playing straight and natural. Fields always wanted it spontaneous. He would ask me to go and do something that we had never rehearsed. The thing is he knew he could count on me to do certain things and never look as if I don't know what it is. A comedian depends on the straight man. It's an ear for timing that you have to develop.

You have to be on the alert all the time. Their timing depends on what you feed them."

Mary Brian made an easy transition to sound, and she was immediately featured in three films with classic status. She is Molly Wood opposite Gary Cooper in *The Virginian* (1929). George Cukor directed her in his 1931 screen adaptation of the Edna Ferber/George S. Kaufman comedy, *The Royal Family of Broadway*. And she is Pat O'Brien's fiancée, Peggy Grant, in Lewis Milestone's adaptation of Ben Hecht/Charles MacArthur's *The Front Page* (1931), for which she was loaned out to producer Howard Hughes: "It was fun. It was different. At the time, it was something of a sensation because they had never overlapped dialogue before. You spoke, they spoke, then you spoke. We rehearsed for about two weeks. The thing was we got into shooting, and Louis Wolheim, who was playing the managing editor, died. [Replacement] Adolphe Menjou was just the opposite to Wolheim, a very cultured, well educated man. He didn't change the tone of the picture, because this was so worked out. This was a fun picture. Milestone used to call and say, 'Come on in by noon tomorrow.' I'd say, 'I'm not in that scene.' He'd say, 'Come on over. I just thought we'd all have fun.' They had all these reporters who were comedians, and they all hated to get up in the morning. So we started at noon, stopped for a long dinnertime, and they all had good tales. Some of them were great raconteurs. We would go until dawn many times. And we had good food!

"Howard Hughes used to come on part of the set and watch. He was very shy about it. Sometimes he'd come in and talk to Milestone, but never in an authoritative way. I don't mean that he was timid about it. He had definite ideas. It was like he was a visitor. We never felt that we knew him that well."

That Paramount chose not to renew Mary's contract in 1932 came as a major shock to her. "I had been there every day of the week for all that time. Other things did come along, but because you had worked there ever since you started, it was like leaving home for the first time. I shed a few tears." Later, she returned to Paramount in 1934 for *College Rhythm* and *Private Scandal*. "A sort of bitter sweet thing. I enjoyed it one way. It's hard to describe how I did feel."

After that Mary made poverty row productions and major studio productions. She was a big enough star that on May 5, 1935, she was asked to christen the first sky sleeper for American Airlines at the Grand Central Air Terminal in Glendale. The number of her young men was still the subject of much publicity, and around the same time, *The Hollywood Reporter* suggested that an appropriate title for a Mary Brian film would be *No One Man*. Mary starred in three films in the United Kingdom, and while making *Once in a Million* (1936, released in the U.S. as *Weekend Millionaire*) there, she also appeared on stage in the André Charlot revue, *Stop— . . . Go!* Mary's final British film was *The Amazing Quest of Ernest Bliss* (1936), cut from 80 to 56 minutes for U.S. release in 1937 as *Romance and Riches*. Starring opposite Mary was Cary Grant, with whom she began a serious relationship that might well have ended in matrimony: "We had a misunderstanding after about a year-and-a-half or two. We were going to get married. I'm kind of independent. I guess it could have been smoothed over, but I got on a plane and went to New York and signed up for a show. A lot of time went by. He was frugal, but I understand that because I am sort of a child of the depression. He came from a poor background. But I never found him stingy. Could he have been bisexual? I don't think so." As to the supposed relationship with Randolph Scott and the shared beachhouse in Santa Monica: "I don't think that means anything. He'd pick me up at Toluca Lake, take me down to the beachhouse on Sunday. He was working the rest of the time. And there were always people at the beachhouse. People misinterpret a lot of things."

Mary Brian appeared to retire from the screen in 1937, and she ended the decade with two stage productions, neither of which made it to Broadway. Hoagy Carmichael and Johnny Mercer provided the songs for *Three after Three*, which opened at the Shubert Theatre, New Haven, on November 24, 1939, and marked the American stage debut of French actress Simone Simon. Mary was starred along with Bruce Cabot and Betty Furness in *Off the Record* by Parke Levy and Alan Lipscott, which opened at the McCarter Theatre, Princeton, New Jersey, on December 1, 1940.

America's entry into the Second World War gave Mary a new opportunity, not to revive her career but to do something that she considered worthwhile. Through the years, she has spent more time discussing her work entertaining the troops than she has in resurrecting her film career. She is so proud to have been there in the South Pacific and in Europe, on board the Enola Gay immediately after it dropped the atomic bomb on Hiroshima, and at the Battle of the Bulge.

Mary has never discussed her first marriage to illustrator Jon Whitcomb, which took place in Hollywood on May 4, 1941; it ended in a Reno divorce six weeks later. She never tires talking of her marriage to film editor George Tomasini, which took place in Santa Monica on June 26, 1947, and lasted until his death. I have always felt she was more proud of her husband's work on the films of Alfred Hitchcock than she was with her own screen career.

"My life was changed by the war," she explained. "I think you get a perspective when you see people die, when you go to the hospitals. I met some of the finest people, people whom you'd refer to as little people, but I'd never refer to them as little people. Why did I choose George, when there was Cary or Dick? I think that George getting out of the service at the same time [as I did]. We had a common bond. I looked at him as a person, not as somebody who is on this side of the camera or that side of the camera. He was a very honest person. He was kind. He was as handsome and charming as any man I've ever worked with."

Mary Brian appeared in a handful of undistinguished films in the 1940s. She barely has recollection of them. She also worked briefly in television in 1954 and 1955, appearing on *Meet Corliss Archer* and *Strike It Rich*. But the enthusiasm was gone, replaced with a dedication to her painting: "This was as fulfilling as anything else I did in pictures. I don't want to feel I'm not working in pictures, so I'm nothing. That is what I want to do for myself."

She may be retired from the screen, but Mary Brian is still a consummate actress. She has never lost her sense of theater. Whatever she does is a unique performance, permeated with a natural, and honest, charm. She also has an inner beauty that is obvious and genuine, almost more attractive than the exterior good looks. I have known Mary for a long time—we were introduced by mutual friend Priscilla Bonner—and it seems that as far back as I can recall, Mary Brian has been an important part of my life. She was there, hosting my surprise 50th birthday party. She has been with Robert Gitt and me on trips as far away as San Francisco and as close as weekly visits to the supermarket.

Whenever Mary Brian comes over to the house, actor Norman Lloyd greets her, in his own inimitable and theatrical style, as "My Mary." That is what Mary Brian has been to her beaux, to her friends, to her fans, and to the world. My Mary.

Bibliography

Albert, Dora. "O.K.d by Mary Brian." *Silver Screen*, September 1933, pp. 28–29, 59–61.

Brundige, Harry T. "Mary Brian." In *Twinkle, Twinkle, Movie Star!* New York: E.P. Dutton, 1930, pp. 100–109.

Cannon, Regina. "What's the Matter with Mary?" *Modern Screen*, June 1934, pp. 69, 108–109.

"The Girl on the Cover." *Photoplay*, May 1930, p. 14.

Goldbeck, Elisabeth. "The Woman Pays Back." *Motion Picture*, August 1930, pp. 55, 90.

GLADYS BROCKWELL

Both physically and emotionally, Gladys Brockwell (Brooklyn, New York, September 26, 1894–Los Angeles, July 2, 1929) was an outstanding presence on screen. There was a majesty to her leading roles with William Fox from 1916 to 1920, and her performances mask the cheapness of productions ranging in cost from $25,000 to $30,000. Born Gladys Lindeman, the actress had adopted her mother's maiden name when she embarked on a lengthy stage career—a leading lady at age fourteen with her own company at seventeen—prior to her 1913 entry into films with Lubin.

The thirty-three feature films in which Brockwell starred for Fox were all either melodramas or Westerns, but the characterizations, while primarily modern, were considerable in range. Brockwell played both mother and child in *Sins of Her Parents*, released in November 1916, and directed by Frank Lloyd, a distinguished director in strong need of reevaluation. She had the dual role of sisters in *The Moral Law*, released in February 1918, and was both a wealthy heiress and her maid in *Her One Mistake*, released in April of the same year. In *Conscience*, released in October 1917, and initially intended as a starring vehicle for Theda Bara, Gladys Brockwell appeared in eight roles, including personifications of many of the deadly sins.

Immediately prior to her work at Fox, Brockwell had played a prima donna in Universal's 1916 production of *The Crippled Hand*, and it was a role that perhaps she also played in real life. Producer William Fox certainly branded her as such, and his virulent comments, in all probability, limited the star's work in the 1920s.

After leaving Fox, which failed to appreciate just how good an actress she was, Brockwell appeared as Nancy Sikes in the Jackie Coogan version of *Oliver Twist* (1922). It was the role of which she was most proud, although she must have found some satisfaction in the ferocity of her performance as poor Janet Gaynor's evil sister Nana in *7th Heaven* (1927). She made an easy transition to sound in the first all-talkie feature-length production, *Lights of New York* (1928), playing the much maligned, aging mistress of villain Wheeler Oakman, whom she eventually murders. She died early of a punctured appendix as a result of an automobile accident. "I've lived, I've loved, and I've lost," she proclaims in her confession to the killing in *Lights of New York*, but it is audiences who lost a great potential character star of the 1930s with the death of Gladys Brockwell.

Bibliography

G.W.B. "Being a Chat with Gladys Brockwell." *Motion Picture Classic*, October 1917, pp. 22–23.

"Gladys Brockwell with Fox Three Years." *The Moving Picture World*, August 10, 1918, pp. 822–823.

Handy, Truman B. "Iconoclast." *Motion Picture Classic*, September 1922, pp. 36–37, 90.

Kingsley, Grace. "Rich Girl, Poor Girl, Beggar Girl—Thief!" *Photoplay*, April 1917, pp. 127–129.

McKelvie, Martha Groves. "A Glance at Gladys." *Motion Picture*, June 1919, pp. 45–46, 104.

Kate Brue, with Richard Barthelmess, in *Way Down East* (1920).

KATE BRUCE

A number of actresses gained fame for their characterizations as mothers in silent film. Mary Maurice was a pioneer with the Vitagraph Company. In the 1920s, Mary Carr was made up above her years to portray mothers, most notably the central character in *Over the Hill to the Poorhouse* (1920). Vera Gordon was the stereotypical Jewish mother in *Humoresque* (1920) and, later, in the "Cohens and Kellys" series of feature films (1928-1930). Then, of course, Belle Bennett played the tragic *Stella Dallas* (1925), watching her daughter's wedding through a window. But the mother of all mothers is Kate Bruce (1858–New York, April 2, 1946).

With his Victorian sentimentality and morality, D.W. Griffith held mothers in high esteem, and no actress was ever considered suitable for the role in most of his films except Kate Bruce. She is the "fussy little mother" in *Hearts of the World* (1918), the matriarchal figure in *Way Down East* (1920) "whose gentle soul is as sweet as her beloved Bible," and even a little crafty and sly mother nudging her daughter into courtship in *True Heart Susie* (1919). When she wasn't working for Griffith, as she was through most of the 1910s, Kate Bruce in the 1920s was a mother to Thomas Meighan (*City of Silent Men* in 1921), Richard Barthelmess (*Experience* in 1921), Milton Sills (*I Want My Man* in 1925), Gladys Hulette (*A Bowery Cinderella* in 1927), John Bowers (*Ragtime* in 1927), and Olive Borden (*The Secret Studio* in 1927).

Virtually nothing is known of Kate Bruce's early life. Lillian Gish told me she believed that Brucie, as she was known, was born in Ohio and might possibly have worked as a nurse in a lunatic asylum. Why she should have entered films, nobody knows, but she joined the American Biograph Company in 1909 and remained there, working under Griffith's direction, through 1913. She has the minor role of a Babylonian mother in *Intolerance* (1916) and makes her last silent film appearance for Griffith in *The White Rose* (1923) as an aunt. The size of the part does not appear to have bothered the actress in the slightest: she could play a major or a minor role for Griffith, and just as well play a bit part, again as a mother, in Thomas Ince's *Civilization* (1916).

I had always assumed that Kate Bruce ended her career in 1927, and I was amazed while watching Griffith's last film, *The Struggle* (1930) for the first time to see the actress make a fleeting appearance. I nearly fell out of my seat with excitement at the Museum of Modern Art. At what proves to be a catastrophic party, the doorbell rings, and in walks Kate Bruce. She is led to a partly obscured chair, and there she sits, sipping a nonalcoholic beverage. What a curious screen farewell to Kate Bruce.

Blanche Sweet recalled her as "a dear person, very quiet, very calm. Rather shy. She never had much to say. She played a great many of the mothers, of course, always the sweeter, gentler character—she was that." The actress may not have been quite as sweet and innocent as depicted on screen or as remembered by her co-workers. As far as is known, she was never married and was never a mother. More likely, she was a lesbian. Griffith's first wife, Linda Arvidson, wrote a 1926 memoir, *When the Movies Were Young*, which is very much a silent version of Kenneth Anger's *Hollywood Babylon*. Arvidson provides much suggestive material on the sexual behavior of the acting members of the American Biograph Company. Considerable space is devoted to "the saintly 'Brucie,'" who "pillowed in her lap or on her shoulder by turns, all the feminine heads of sufficient importance." Arvidson notes that the actress provided overnight accommodation for those living too far away from the studio to answer an early morning call. "She had a strong maternal complex, had the maidenly Kate Bruce."

Lillian Gish may not have succumbed to Brucie's charms, but she and her sister did take care of the actress in later years. As she told me, she and Dorothy paid Bruce's rent on a small hotel room on Madison Avenue. She lived such an austere life that Lillian always felt that she should have been a nun. She was "so alone, no plant, no cat, no dog, not even a goldfish." Lillian's maid would go down to the hotel once a week to check that everything was satisfactory, and two or three times a week, Brucie would come around for dinner. When Lillian's mother was alive, the two would work on jigsaw puzzles after the meal. Once seated for dinner, the actress would realize she had left her pocket book in the other room and worry that it might be stolen. In fact, all it contained were safety pins.

When Brucie died, Lillian was in Europe, and Dorothy made all the arrangements for the funeral. She could trace no relatives. The sisters went through Bruce's possessions and discovered that she had kept everything they had ever given her. In one trunk, they found the black evening dress they had presented her with for the premiere of *Way Down East*. It had been eaten away by moths and fell apart in their hands.

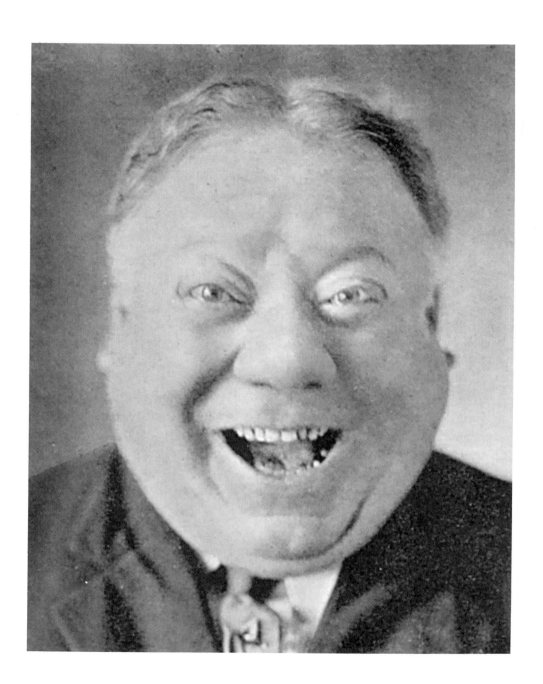

JOHN BUNNY

John Bunny was the first internationally recognized film comedian. He was also the most famous fat comedian of his day, at a time when fat meant cute and cuddly rather than obese and unattractive. There had been earlier fat comedians, most notably John Cumpson at American Biograph, featured in the 1908–1909 Jones family series, and there would be later ones, such as Roscoe "Fatty" Arbuckle, whose fame became infamy and whose obesity only added to the public horror and outrage when he was accused of rape-murder.

John Bunny was as innocuous as his predecessors, but he was no Roscoe "Fatty" Arbuckle. His characterizations contain nothing creative, and he uses no knockabout or slapstick comedy. His comedy is all very middle-class and very polite. Often so dull is the storyline that the comedy is difficult to uncover. Time and again one wonders if audiences ever did laugh at his work, and, if so, why? After John Bunny, what a welcome relief must have been Charlie Chaplin, Buster Keaton, or even, God forbid, Larry Semon (who, like Bunny, came to fame with the Vitagraph Company).

Born in New York on September 21, 1863, Bunny was active on stage for many years without making an impact. He entered films with Vitagraph in October 1910, welcoming the steady employment that the motion picture offered to second-rate theatrical types such as he undoubtedly was. Until his death in Brooklyn (where the Vitagraph studios were located) on April 26, 1915, John Bunny appeared in more than 150 one-reel and half-reel shorts for the company, often teamed with the thin and spinsterish Flora Finch (1869–1940). He was a natural for the leading role in *Pickwick Papers*, filmed in England by Vitagraph and released as a two-reel special on February 28, 1913.

Pickwick Papers, like many of Bunny's films, was directed by Larry Trimble, whose daughter, Jan Zilliacus, described the comedian as "very bad-tempered, very difficult. He upstaged everyone. He was an old egocentric. He always wanted the camera on him. He wasn't as mean as W.C. Fields, but he was verging on it." Marian, Trimble's widow and daughter of Vitagraph co-founder J. Stuart Blackton, complained to me of Bunny's fatuous grins: "Even at a very early age I thought him repulsive and of course he had a foul disposition." "I wasn't awfully fond of Bunny," said Vitagraph leading man James Morrison. "He looked down on anybody who wasn't as great as he was." Bunny was equally unpopular with his leading lady and Vitagraph co-founder Albert E. Smith admitted that Bunny and Flora Finch "cordially hated each other."

The animosity generated by John Bunny is almost apparent in his film performances. You know not to like or to trust him. He is not your kindly uncle but more likely the older relative who sexually abuses his nephew or niece while offering them candy and chocolates. Yet contemporary audiences took delight in John Bunny and his work. When he died, commentators realized for the first time the power of the motion picture and the influence that its players had on the public. Mrs. Albert E. Smith showed me a voluminous scrapbook containing nothing other than published obituaries of the comedian from newspaper and magazines around the world. Even her husband had allowed the early public perception of Bunny to interfere with the integrity of his history of Vitagraph. In *Two Reels and a Crank* (with Phil A. Koury, Doubleday, 1952) Smith has nothing but praise for Bunny, but the original, unpublished manuscript, contains nothing but negative comment.

Bibliography

"The Art of John Bunny." *The Bioscope*, May 6, 1915, pp. 509–510.

Bunny, John. *Bunnyisms*. New York: Kraus Manufacturing Company, 1914.

———. "How It Feels to Be a Comedian." *Photoplay*, October 1914, pp. 111–113.

Dunham, Harold. "John Bunny." *The Silent Picture*, no. 1, winter 1968, unpaged.

Gill, Sam. "John Bunny Checklist." *The Silent Picture*, no. 15, summer 1972, pp. 8–15.

Lanier, Henry Wysham. "Coquelin of the Movies." *World's Work*, March 1915, pp. 566–577.

Slide, Anthony. *The Big V: A History of the Vitagraph Company*. Metuchen, N.J.: Scarecrow Press, 1987.

LON CHANEY. *See* **THE LEGENDS**

CHARLIE CHAPLIN. *See* **THE LEGENDS**

RUTH CLIFFORD

Ruth Clifford enjoyed two very distinct film careers, the first as a silent star and the second, in later years, as a member of John Ford's stock company. Her innocent, slightly worried looks coupled with a pretty, natural beauty made her an ideal silent ingénue. Ruth's primary credentials for membership in the John Ford stock company were an Irish accent and Irish ancestry. The Irish connection was a little weak in that she was born in Pawtucket, Rhode Island, on February 17, 1900, and both her parents were born in England. "Mine is not an Irish accent—I'm accused of being a Bostonian," she once told me, but her accent was sufficiently Irish for her to be a member of the Abbey Theatre Company when it toured the United States in the 1940s and for her to play leads in classic Irish plays.

After she had appeared, as an extra, in two 1914 Edison films, starring Viola Dana, Ruth was introduced to films at Universal in 1916 by an aunt, actress Catherine Wallace; her first credited role is in *Behind the Lines*, directed by Henry McRae, a longtime, unremarkable filmmaker:

"I had stood and watched many, many times Henry McRae shooting the films. I had watched the people put the green shadow and the blue shadow over their eyes. I was fascinated. In fact I was terribly, terribly stage-struck. He asked me, 'Would you like to play a scene?' Needless to say, I was breathless. The scene was a hospital room, and foreground of the camera was a bed with a very lovely, young girl lying in it. She is my oldest sister and she has been very ill. At the foot of her bed was her sweetheart Harry Carey, a very dear man. He had his hand under his left arm, which was his habit, standing looking at the girl. The director would direct you as you worked. He told me to open the door, which was background, enter the scene. My knees were shaking. The director whispered, 'She has been very, very ill. Call her name, Anna.' So I said, 'Anna.' He said, 'Call it again.' 'Anna.' There was silence. There was no motion. The director said, 'She's dead.' It affected me so that I knelt down by the bed and I started to cry and I couldn't stop crying.

"Those tears gave me a contract. I was sixteen, and I had a contract for $75 a week, going up to $150. It was worth the tears."

Ruth Clifford remained under contract to Universal through 1919 and had vivid memories of the company and the original studio tour at Universal City: "They charged for people to come in, and they would sit on tiers, like you do at a football stadium. They would watch, because the stages were open. They would have canvas sheets at the top to kill the direct sunlight, but it was all in daylight with the additional foreground light."

Artificial light was provided by carbon arc lamps, manufactured by the

Kliegl Bros. and known as Klieg lights: "The Klieg lights were wicked. It was a square metal frame. I don't know if you'd call them prongs or not, but there were two that met in the middle, and the minute they hit, it formed an ice blue, ice-cold, but very hot light. That Klieg light could burn your eyes, even if you were not looking directly at it. And in the silent days, they used a lot of those, because the lighting was flat and mostly straight on. Carmel Myers showed me how to use tea bags to put on your eyes, to soothe your eyes when they were burned. It was pretty mean, but a cameraman said to me one time when I told him that they hurt, 'Well the more they hurt Ruth, the better you're going to look.'"

The director with whom Ruth Clifford was most associated at Universal was Rupert Julian, who made twelve of her early films and also co-starred in four of them. The most prominent of these is *The Kaiser, The Beast of Berlin,* an anti-German propaganda film, released in March 1918, which took advantage of Julian's remarkable likeness to the Kaiser. (Julian also played the Kaiser in a number of later films.) Julian's wife, Elsie Jane Wilson, also directed Ruth in two feature films, *The Lure of Luxury* (1918) and *The Game's Up* (1919):

"I was given a director, an Australian actor, a very wonderful man, Rupert Julian. [Julian was actually born in New Zealand.] His wife, Elsie Jane Wilson, co-directed. She had been an actress in Australia. We'd sit down and talk about the scene before we ever got on the stage. He was a very good actor. He liked to act. He'd do the women's scene as good as the women do. We had scripts. We spoke lines. If they said, 'I love you,' you could see a person say, 'I love you.' A lot of motioning and emotion in those days. Would that the youth of today could have the real joy with the innocence that existed. As the old German woman said, 'We get too soon old and too late smiles.' They were honest-to-God innocent days. It was an entirely different world, but a very beautiful world.

"Rupert Julian would talk very gently to you, and he would always come up with surprises, as John Ford used to do, in scenes as he directed you. There are certain things that you can't rehearse. John Ford said, 'The first take, even with fluffs, is always the best.' The minute the word action occurs, something is turned on and the actor goes." Over lunch once, Ruth confessed to me that she had been fascinated by Julian's stiff moustache and had always wanted to touch it.

Aside from Rupert Julian, Ruth Clifford was also associated at Universal with actor Monroe Salisbury, her leading man in six films between 1917 and 1919. What she remembered most about him is the shock, at their first love scene, to discover not only that he was old but also that he was wearing a toupée.

After leaving Universal, Ruth Clifford worked independently, appearing in 25 feature films of the 1920s. Her favorite was the Al and Ray Rockett production of *Abraham Lincoln* (1924), in which she appeared as Ann Rutledge opposite George A. Billings in the title role. Only a portion of the film survives, and it is probably not as fine a production as Ruth chose to recall. A year earlier, she had played opposite John Gilbert in *Truxton King*; the actor, through a written note, asked her to marry him, but, as a good Catholic, she could not consider a relationship with a divorced man. The best of her surviving silent features is Clarence Brown's 1924 production of *Butterfly*, in which she plays Hilary, a woman who sacrifices her own career for that of her younger sister, Laura La Plante: "I had never been in love when I made that film. I had never had a physical experience. And so I think the character is me. I was as introverted as the character I was playing." Ruth contributes a marvelous, understated performance, and it must have been galling when Clarence Brown told her at the film's completion that he had wanted Irene Rich rather than her for the part.

Like so many other actors and actresses, Ruth Clifford made her sound debut in Warner Bros. 1929 production of *The Show of Shows*. It did nothing for her; she was simply another star name in the cast list.

On December 5, 1924, Ruth Clifford married James Cornelius, a prominent real estate developer and the son of a Los Angeles banker—the couple separated in 1934—and while she continued to appear on screen in the 1930s and 1940s, she was more interested in bringing up her son, James Junior, born in 1930, and who was an actor until his early death in 1956: "I had matured. I had experienced the crash. I had had a baby, and the baby's first tooth meant more to me than one whole block of Wilshire Boulevard. When I went back to work, I needed to work. Of course, I was older. I was in my thirties, and I did some pretty good parts. When I got into my forties, I knew that I was suited to the parts of that age. I grew up slowly. I know that. But when I did finally mature sufficiently, my ability increased."

Ruth Clifford had starred for John Ford as early as 1923 in *The Face on the Barroom Floor*. In the 1940s, the director began to use her as a member of his stock company, often in uncredited and sometimes cut roles. (For example, in *The Quiet Man*, Ruth's scene with John Wayne on a train was shot but cut from the released version of the film.) In particular, Ford liked having Ruth with him on location, because she could play bridge. Ford took his bridge games very seriously. Once, when his partner Ruth trumped his ace, he told her, "*You* won't be in my next film." Often during shooting, Ford would turn to the actress and ask, "Are you in a state of grace, Ruth?" He would make her laugh by asking, "I wonder where Rupert Julian is tonight?" (He had died in December 1943.) Ruth's favorite role for Ford was as medicine show performer, Floretty "Florey" Phyffe in *Wagon Master* (1950):

"He would befriend anyone. His bark was louder than his bite. He was without a doubt one of the most wonderful persons I have ever known in my life. His memory was like an elephant's. The cowboys that worked extra in the Universal days grew up and became extras or bit players. In every John Ford film until he died, he would have those old faces sitting on a porch, riding a horse with their back to the camera into the sunset, not heard, but there, because it gave them an income, residuals, unemployment benefits."

Aside from the John Ford productions, Ruth Clifford could be seen on television in the 1950s in episodes of *Highway Patrol* and also in many television commercials. As late as 1968, she pops up as a housekeeper in Barbra Streisand's *Funny Girl*.

I first met Ruth Clifford in 1977, when she invited Herb Sterne, Robert Gitt, and me to dinner at her Sherman Oaks condominium. When she moved to a cottage at the Motion Picture Country House, we would see her often. She would come over for dinner, and she was most generous in inviting us to restaurants. She always wanted to have a good time and insisted that her companions do likewise. Into her nineties, she was taking cruises to Hawaii or Alaska. She did not stand on ceremony. Once when Robert's car broke down, we had only a van to transport Ruth and Herb to dinner. Herb sat up front, and Ruth, a ninety-year-old lady, happily clambered into the back and laid down on the floor. What she did not like was to be interviewed, and she would clam up when a tape recorder was placed in front of her, experiencing a strange memory loss. I did arrange for her to appear in a 1984 Ulster Television production, *A Seat in the Stars: The Cinema and Ireland*, and she also participated in my documentary, *The Silent Feminists: America's First Women Directors*. It was so typical of Ruth that after filming her segment of the Irish documentary, she insisted on taking the entire and excessively large crew of fourteen out to an expensive dinner.

Ruth was an extremely devout Catholic and always seemed to be in the company of nuns or priests. The latter, without exception, had thick Irish accents and had obviously escaped from a John Ford production. It was always a problem arranging visits on a Sunday because of the number of times Ruth felt the need to attend mass. Despite her deep religious attitude, Ruth did not shy away from negative comments. Actress Mae Clarke was a very difficult human being, both at the Motion Picture Country House and on frequent visits to our house. When she died, Ruth delivered an appropriate epitaph: "Spiteful to the last." When Ruth Clifford died, on November 30, 1998, she was as old as the century, and only a few days earlier she had commented, "It's time for me to move on."

Bibliography

Aleiss, Angela. "Hollywood Memories." *The Tidings*, August 22, 1997, pp. 16–17.
Delvigne, Doris. "Flying to Success." *Motion Picture*, May 1919, pp. 58–59, 106.
Gebhart, Myrtle. "The Girl Who Waited." *Picture-Play*, November 1925, pp. 27–28, 100.
"The Knot-Hole Astronomer." *Photoplay*. April 1918, pp. 87–88.

Elmer Clifton in a theatrical, pre-cinema role.

ELMER CLIFTON

Elmer Clifton has never received the recognition he deserves as a director. Active as both a director and screenwriter up until his death in Los Angeles on October 15, 1949, Clifton was reliable, efficient, speedy, and creative, despite the films seldom being worthy of much effort. He had the immense good fortune to learn the craft of filmmaking from D.W. Griffith and, also, to be featured in two very disparate roles in the director's masterworks, *The Birth of a Nation* (1915) and *Intolerance* (1916).

Born on one of the islands in the St. Lawrence River on March 15, 1890, Clifton was educated in Chicago before embarking on a theatrical career. He appeared in stock with Hobart Bosworth, Lewis Stone, and others, and in 1913, he was touring California in Richard Bennett's company. At this time, he was approached by Hobart Bosworth and offered the leading role in his 1914 production of *John Barleycorn*, based on the Jack London novel. It was followed by two further Bosworth productions, also adapted from the works of Jack London, *Martin Eden* and *Burning Daylight*. D.W. Griffith saw the young man in *John Barleycorn* and invited him to join his company.

In *The Birth of a Nation*, Elmer Clifton plays Phil Stoneman, the eldest son of the Northern family, whose sister, Elsie (played by Lillian Gish), is loved by Ben Cameron, the "little colonel" (Henry B. Walthall). It is Phil Stoneman who recognizes the "little colonel" leading a heroic charge against the Union soldiers and drags the wounded officer into the trench. Later, Stoneman rescues Cameron's father and is besieged, with the Cameron family, in an isolated cabin, from which they are rescued by the Ku Klux Klan.

As Phil Stoneman, Elmer Clifton displays a masculinity and heroic virility virtually unknown in silent films up to this point and, in all honesty, seldom seen in later silent productions. In the performance, there is a natural manliness unhampered by mannerisms and makeup. His love scenes with Miriam Cooper (as Margaret Cameron) are in perfect counterpoint to similar scenes between Walthall and Lillian Gish.

It is an amazing transformation from the heterosexuality of Phil Stoneman to the innate effeminacy of the Rhapsode in the Babylonian story from *Intolerance* (1916). The Rhapsode may be in love with Constance Talmadge as the Mountain Girl, but there is no hint of masculinity in the performance, and the Mountain Girl's rejection of her would-be suitor seems more than understandable. Without Phil Stoneman's moustache, and in a costume displaying a body that is singularly devoid of muscular appeal, Elmer Clifton has recreated himself. He is a man humiliated and held up to ridicule by the woman he loves. These two performances—Phil Stoneman and the Rhapsode—demonstrate a range of emotions and acting styles that no other actor up to this time had attempted and, more likely, was incapable of attempting. They are also two performances that generated not the slightest interest from contemporary critics or commentators.

There were other films under Griffith's supervision, if not direction, at Fine Arts, including *The Sable Lorcha* (1915), *The Lily and the Rose* (1915), *The Missing Link* (1916), and *The Little School Ma'am* (1916), but it was very obvious that Clifton wanted to direct. He had worked as an assistant director on both *The Birth of a Nation* and *Intolerance*, and in 1917, Griffith allowed him to direct, in collaboration with Joseph Henabery, *Her Official Fathers*, starring Dorothy Gish.

Clifton directed a couple of further Dorothy Gish vehicles at Fine Arts before departing to a directorial position at Universal (where he is sometimes credited as having discovered Priscilla Dean). He returned to Griffith in 1918 to direct a series of Dorothy Gish comedies that his mentor was supervising for Paramount-Artcraft. Clifton also worked very closely with Griffith and, without credit, on *Way Down East*. He shot some of the scenes on the ice and, in all probability, doubled for Richard Barthelmess in the rescue from the ice floe of Lillian Gish. Clifton also worked in an unidentified capacity, but probably as an associate director, on Griffith's next production, *Dream Street* (1921). In 1922, Clifton told Gladys Hall of his respect for Griffith,

"It isn't a question of influence. I simply believe in Mr. Griffith's methods, because they are truths. His great points are young love and the 'run to the rescue.' They will be mine. Young love and the romance of youth, whether it be love or adventure, is the primary, the all-important thing. Who wants to see age depicted? We all know that it exists, and that it is coming to us, but it is youth we wish to watch, youth we wish to recapture, if only in a vision."

Elmer Clifton left Griffith to begin work on his only major contribution to the cinema as a director; his only independent production. *Down to the Sea in Ships* is an epic of whaling, shot on the open sea and on location in New Bedford, Massachusetts, over a one-year period. It made a star of its juvenile lead, Clara Bow, and was highly praised on its 1922 release. It is commendable for the sheer documentary quality that Clifton has created, but it is overlong and at times loses the attention of the viewer. The only advice Griffith gave Clifton, according to the latter's wife, was "never put your own money into your own productions." Clifton heeded Griffith and raised funding for *Down to the Sea in Ships* from the citizens of New Bedford.

From the independence of *Down to the Sea in Ships*, Elmer Clifton moved on to the politics of studio production with William Fox and Cecil B. DeMille. He had a grandiose scheme to take two Bell & Howell cameras and shoot scenes and backgrounds around the world for a group of feature films that would be completed in Hollywood, but the Wall Street Crash put an end to the project. With the coming of sound, Clifton kept busy, often associated with B Westerns but never working on anything comparable to *Down to the Sea in Ships* and never returning to acting. He was to have directed *The Vicious Years* (1950) but died shortly before filming began and was replaced by Robert Florey, another director worthy of further study.

Note: Elmer Clifton's scrapbook is at the Los Angeles County Museum of Natural History.

Bibliography

"Clifton Tells Why He Made 'Down to the Sea in Ships.'" *Moving Picture World,* February 17, 1923, p. 644.

Hall, Gladys. "The Prince of Whales." *Motion Picture,* June 1922, pp. 75, 106.

Underhill, Harriette. "Out from an Old Album." *Motion Picture,* October 1921, pp. 60, 90.

Service, Faith. "The Democrat at the Dinner Table." *Motion Picture Classic,* August 1921, pp. 58–59, 80.

MIRIAM COOPER

Miriam Cooper has never received the attention lavished on other D.W. Griffith actresses, and yet she provides one of the most modern and naturalistic of silent film performances in *Intolerance* (1916). Only Mae Marsh is her equal in the film, but the styles are too different to be worthy of comparison. As the Friendless One, Cooper is driven to murder her lover, the Musketeer of the Slums (Walter Long). After the killing, she is so stricken with guilt and revulsion that she actually bites her lower lip and draws blood. This is method acting carried to its ultimate level! Griffith keeps the camera on Cooper's face as she registers a variety of emotions—horror, anger, self-pity. The combined physical and emotional depth of the performance is incredible and unmatched on screen before or since. The sequence is as memorable and as stylistically impressive as the much later close-ups of Mae Marsh in the courtroom scene as she listens to her husband being found guilty of Cooper's crime. In many respects, although far removed by real and filmic time, the two sets of close-ups serve as counterpoint.

Equally worthy of respect is Cooper's earlier performance as Margaret Cameron in *The Birth of a Nation* (1915). Here, Cooper is a quiet presence, her role lacking the melodramatic force of the Mae Marsh and Lillian Gish characterizations. Yet it is the very soberness of Cooper's performance opposite her would-be lover, played by Elmer Clifton, that serves to hold the audience's attention. "I think I must have been sort of a natural actress," explained Cooper, without pretension or, for that matter, understanding of her accomplishments: "You know, my idea of a good time was to lie in a cemetery, either yelling into the tombs or lying on the graves and looking up at the trees, saying I was going to be something great. Mr. Griffith said I was a natural-born actress. It wasn't difficult to direct me. The only time I can remember he spent a lot of time with me was when he was trying to get me to cry. I couldn't cry to save my soul. He sent everyone off the set and he pulled a chair up. 'Miss Cooper, I didn't want to tell you this, but your mother has just died.' Well, I burst into tears, and he said, 'Camera.'"

The remainder of the career of Miriam Cooper (Baltimore, Maryland, November 7, 1894–Charlottesville, Virginia, April 12, 1976) is relatively unimportant. She began her career with D.W. Griffith, although it is doubtful he would have remembered her performance as an extra in the 1911 American Biograph short, *A Blot on the 'Scutcheon*. It was with the Kalem Company in 1912 and 1913 that Miriam Cooper developed as a leading player, often featured in one-reel Civil War dramas shot in Jacksonville, Florida. She could swim and ride a horse, and her films emphasized action over characterization. "I was a stunt girl; I didn't do any acting," asserted Cooper. Even in those primitive Kalem subjects, the actress's inherent natural good looks are apparent—the simply cut black hair and the large and dreamy eyes—but Griffith hired her more because to him she represented Southern beauty. After a handful of 1914 Reliance-Majestic productions directed by Christy Cabanne, Griffith first directed her in *Home, Sweet Home* (1914) in the minor role of Robert Harron's fiancée. Then came *The Birth of a Nation* and *Intolerance*.

As her post-film career indicates, Miriam Cooper must have been shrewd and sophisticated when it came to financial matters, but as far as her work as an actress was concerned, she had no concept of why she was good and how she could turn in such good performances. She lacked refinement, and thus her comments on Griffith and her sister actresses were less inhibited:

"One morning I came in and I said, 'Good morning, Mr. Griffith.' And he didn't answer me. I thought he was very common, very rude. I told Mae Marsh—I was rooming with Mae—and she told him. I had to get up and rehearse in front of all the other actresses, a lot more experienced that I. 'Now we will have the queen.' I was furious. I didn't know why he was treating me so awful. Later, he said, 'I understand you think I'm very ordinary, very common, very rude, ill-bred and ill-mannered.' I got mad and told the truth. I said, 'Yes.' I wasn't fired. He never called us by our first names, always Miss Cooper, Miss Gish, Miss Marsh.

"In those days, you had in-a-door-bed apartments. Lillian had one, Dorothy had one and their mother had one, all on the same floor. Dorothy was the hoyden type, and Lillian was very elegant. The girls did not like Lillian, frankly, because she felt she was really something. She had a beautiful bed and beautiful furniture, and they all used to go and do the cooking in her apartment. We had a girls' club that met every Tuesday, the Hens' Club. The hens drink beer once in a while and maybe puff on a cigarette. Lillian was too high-toned. One night, Dorothy said, 'Let's go in and have some fun.' We burst in on Lillian, and she was in bed in her gorgeous wrap, and we were so jealous because she was so elegant.

"Mr. Griffith was a gentleman, but even gentlemen have affairs with ladies," noted Cooper. "One night Lillian would be out with him to dinner. The next night Mae. I was dead tired and he said he'd take me home. Griffith had a chauffeur. Griffith and Raoul Walsh were the only two that had their own cars, 'cause Raoul's father was quite wealthy. I was in the back seat and Griffith was in the back seat. I just lay back, and I felt someone kissing me. I was furious because I was in love with Raoul. I pushed him so hard, he landed on the floor of the car. I guess he thought I wasn't so hot. I'll never forget his expression. He was shocked! He sat there on the floor and looked at me, 'Don't you want me to kiss you?' I said, 'No.'"

Miriam Cooper and director Raoul Walsh married in 1916, and the actress starred in a series of William Fox productions directed by her husband, including *Betrayed* (1917), *The Prussian Cur* (1918), and *Should a Husband Forgive?* (1919). The most important of the group are *Evangeline*, released in September 1919, based on the Longfellow poem and with Cooper in the title role, and *The Honor System*, released in February 1917.

The latter was filmed on location at the Arizona State Prison and, in fictional terms, examines the attempts of Governor George W.P. Hunt to improve prison conditions in the state. The central character, played by Milton Sills, is convicted of murder after killing a man in self-defense and looses his eyesight as a result of the treatment he receives in jail. Cooper's rambling comments on the film are indicative of a liberal spirit:

"I became quite interested in some of the things I learned. I lived with the Indians, South Sea Island people and with the prisoners. Then I thought how lovely they were in comparison with the white man. 'The White Savage.' Then I thought of the Civil War, and how we beat the hell—pardon the French—out of the colored people to make them slaves. 'White American Savage.'

"A couple of Mexicans tried to swim across the Rio Grande and just for fun they'd shoot at their heads. They'd say, 'You can escape.' And the guards would just stand there and shoot at their heads. I thought that was the most awful thing, the most saddest thing, I've ever seen in my life—and I've seen some pretty sad things."

Both Walsh and Cooper left Fox when the director entered independent production with *The Deep Purple* (1920). Cooper ended her professional association with Walsh in 1922 with *Kindred of the Dust*. The couple separated and was divorced in 1925. Their two adopted sons both ended up living with their father, and, in old age, Cooper had no idea (and no interest in knowing) if they were dead or alive. In 1923, there were five films for other directors, none of them important, and then the actress simply retired. She negotiated an ample divorce settlement with Walsh, took up golf, and retired, eventually, to Charlottesville, Virginia. In 1973, she published her autobiography, *Dark Lady of the Silents*, which relied heavily on the research of her collaborator, Bonnie Herndon, a local resident whose husband, Booton, had authored a number of biographies. In old age, the black hair had turned white and Cooper did not seem to care too much about her appearance in the nursing home where she ended her days, but there was still a strength of character there, an outspokenness that must have both appealed to and confounded D.W. Griffith.

Note: Miriam Cooper's papers are at the Library of Congress

Bibliography

"Before They Were Stars: Miriam Cooper." *New York Dramatic Mirror,* May 15, 1920, pp. 1008, 1029.

Cheatham, Maude. "Fifty-Fifty." *Motion Picture,* August 1921, pp. 36–37, 88.

Cooper, Miriam, with Bonnie Herndon. *Dark Lady of the Silents: My Life in Early Hollywood.* Indianapolis: Bobbs-Merrill, 1973.

"Dual Lives." *Photoplay,* September 1920, pp. 57–58.

Fletcher, Adele Whitely. "Miriam the Constant." *Motion Picture,* March 1920, pp. 32–33, 106.

O'Dell, Paul. "Miriam Cooper: Forgotten Star." *The Silent Picture,* no. 4, autumn 1969, pp. 5–9.

Tucker, Jean E. "Voices from the Silents." *Quarterly Journal of the Library of Congress,* summer/fall 1980, pp. 387–412.

Pauline Curley

Pauline Curley always had a childlike appearance even after she had graduated from child star to leading lady. Her screen career ran from the start of the
silent feature film era in 1915 until its end in 1928, and yet few of her films are
remembered today, and she remains a relatively unknown performer. Prior to
her film career, Pauline Curley had been on stage from the age of seven, touring the U.S. and Canada in vaudeville and playing a remarkable 159 performances in a long-forgotten Broadway melodrama, *Polygamy*, which opened
in December 1914. Born in Holyoke, Massachusetts, on December 19, 1903,
Curley was always the entertainer:

"I started when I was three years and nine months old, singing and dancing. When I was seven, mother decided to take me to New York and I was
going to have a career. We went there and I started working—and she did too.
My dad didn't go with us. He wasn't in favor of it at all. Eventually my father
came to New York. He knew what I was doing, and it was no use staying
there, because my mother wasn't about to come home. I was twelve years old,
and my mother put me in long dresses, and I became an ingénue. My mother,
of course, lied about my age, said I was sixteen.

"I always had long curls. That's the one thing I hated. I had to get down in
front of my mother, and she had a glass and a comb. She'd take her finger and
put the curl around it. Then I'd have to stay straight until they dried, so the
curls would stay in place."

Curley starred for director Allan Dwan in two films, *A Case at Law* (1917)
and *Bound in Morocco* (1918), in which she is much too young an actress to
be the love interest for Douglas Fairbanks. She was Antonio Moreno's leading man in two 1920 serials produced by the Vitagraph Company, *The Invis-
ible Hand* and *The Veiled Mystery*. Harold Lockwood is usually associated as
a leading man with May Allison, but he and Curley co-starred in three films
together, two comedies, *The Square Deceiver* (1917) and *Lend Me Your Name*
(1918), and one drama, *The Landloper* (1918): "I was fourteen years old when
I was working with him. Well, I got home from work early—we had a house on
Lexington Avenue—and I knew all the kids on the block. When I had a chance
I'd go out and play with them. I was a child still. We were playing 'statue' and
all these things and I was perspiring, and who drives up but Harold Lockwood.
I was humiliated, because I had a crush on him. And when he saw me, he said,
'My leading lady!' I felt so humiliated because I was such a mess, but you see,
I still wanted to be like a child out there playing.

"When I first started working with Harold, we got along just fine. When
we went on location, his girlfriend used to go along with him in his limousine.

Then she didn't come in, and he said, 'Pauline why don't you come with me. I was just thrilled about that. I was like an adult. Then at lunchtime, Harold and I would go out to lunch, not with the company. We were getting along famously. Then this one morning, I thought why isn't he taking me today. My mother said, 'He didn't take you, did he?' I said, 'No, I wonder what happened.' She said, 'I showed him your birth certificate.'"

The most prominent of Pauline Curley's films is perhaps *The Fall of the Romanoffs*, released in January 1918, in which she portrays Princess Irena under Herbert Brenon's direction: "That was a beautiful film. Rasputin [Edward Connelly] tries to rape me. I'm in this bedroom and I jump out of this window. It was very dramatic. I came down pretty hard when I landed. I never forgot it!" As for Herbert Brenon, "Let's say he was a difficult director if you didn't do it right. You'd really hear it from him. But if you did it right, he was a very nice man. I didn't have any problems with him. I didn't want to!"

Pauline Curley is also the leading lady in King Vidor's first feature-length production, *The Turn in the Road*, released in March 1919: "How I got that part, there was a man owned a theatre down in Los Angeles. He had seen *Bound in Morocco*, and I got to meet him. When King Vidor wanted to make his picture, he went to this man about getting a release. He said, 'I'll tell you what will help you a lot. Use Pauline Curley in it.' That's how I got the part."

To Curley, filmmaking was easy: "You read your script. Then the director tells you what the scene is. 'Now here I want you to do this.' You said your own words—you didn't have lines. What you thought is what you said. It was always very simple. You know the situation of the story, why wouldn't you know what to say? It's what you would say if it was real."

The actress was married for 66 years to cinematographer Kenneth Peach: "I was married very young. We were both underage. We eloped. We went to Santa Ana, and we were married by Judge Cox. I went home and told my parents that we had got married, and my mother said, 'If you want to stay married, you have to live here.' I didn't like that, but we'd do anything so we could stay together. Then to punish me, when we moved, she wouldn't let me have my car. Fortunately at that time, we had an apartment on Gower Street, right near Sunset Boulevard, and the independent studios were on the next block. So one block and I was at work."

In the 1920s, Pauline Curley was primarily a Western leading lady, appearing in a total of twelve, many with Kit Carson. She was Tom Mix's leading lady in *Hands Off* (1921): "Of course, what he didn't do in the show was to make love to me, because he was too old." She recalled an interview with William S. Hart, who rejected her with the words, "I don't care what you do with her hair, what you do with anything. There's no way she could play opposite me. I'm too old."

After two final and unimportant films in 1928, *Power* and *Devil Dogs*, Pauline Curley retired. After her husband's death, she continued to live on alone in their Calabassas home. Just before I met her in 1993, she had been attacked by an intruder who broke a heavy chair across her face. The physical damage had mended, but she was still traumatized by the event, refusing to enter the part of the house where the attack took place. It was a tragic end for a woman who grew up on screen and discovered late in life that reality is not as pleasant an experience as depicted on screen. Pauline Curley died in Santa Monica on December 16, 2000.

Bibliography

Cheatham, Maude S. "Rose-Colored Glasses." *Motion Picture*, October 1919, pp. 52–53, 127.

Remont, Fritzi. "The Sixteenth Curley." *Motion Picture Classic*, March 1919, pp. 34–35, 74.

VIOLA DANA

There is a much-praised sequence in the 1980 *Hollywood* television series, in which Viola Dana tells of the crash that killed her lover, stunt pilot Ormer Locklear, during the filming of *The Skywayman* in Los Angeles on August 20, 1920. As she recounts the moment that the plane hit the ground, the camera moves in for a close-up of her face, Dana's eyes brimming with tears. There is an immediacy to the moment, exemplary of fine documentary filmmaking, write the critics. Nobody bothers to consider that Viola Dana is a great actress, that she is playing a role and that perhaps the praise belongs to the star not the situation. Long before she became a light comedienne in the 1920s, Dana had been a great tragedienne. She knew how to "milk" a scene in 1915 and she knew how to "milk" a scene sixty years later.

The Viola Dana crying at the death of her long-dead lover is far removed from the individual who was a frequent guest at the dinner table. She might have held many extreme rightwing views, but she had no belief in God or an afterlife, she knew many a risqué story and, above all, Vi (as everyone called her) had a healthy interest in sex. "She laid everything in Hollywood except the linoleum," commented Kathryn Perry. According to Vi, her only regret in life was the men she said no to. The years did not diminish her interest in sex. Once, she and Priscilla Bonner were discussing a recently publicized police raid on a Beverly Hills brothel. Priscilla was concerned at its proximity to her apartment. Vi's first reaction was whether there might be an opening there for a woman of her years.

Viola Dana had three husbands. The first was director John Collins, who died in the 1918 Spanish flu epidemic. The second was Maurice "Lefty" Flynn, who had the body of a weightlifter and an acting talent to match. The third was a professional golfer, with whom Vi can be seen in her last screen appearance, a 1933 *Hollywood on Parade* short. Perhaps because of her sense of humor, she was sexually attracted to comedians and enjoyed affairs with both Roscoe "Fatty" Arbuckle and Buster Keaton, who, if Vi is to be believed, was living with her during part of the time he was married to Natalie Talmadge.

Vi had a wicked sense of humor. She always claimed that Frank Capra had chosen her for his first Columbia feature, *That Certain Thing* (1928), because, when she walked, she had the "cutest little wiggle." She might have been outraged that a director had more interest in her sex appeal than her acting ability, but Dana had no hesitation in showing off her wiggle to appreciative dinner guests. One summer afternoon, at the Motion Picture Country House, she and actress Mae Clarke impersonated the Duncan Sisters in *Topsy and Eva*, with Vi as Little Eva and Mae, in blackface, as Topsy. She once sent a note to Herb Sterne, accompanied by the most unattractive photograph that she could find, with glasses and her hair in a bun, asking, "Do you think I have a future in the movies? I'll do *anything* to get my foot in," and signed Viola Flugrath.

Flugrath was the family name, and Viola was the second oldest of three sisters, all of whom became screen stars. Shirley Mason (real name Leonie, 1901–1979) was almost as big a star as Vi and made a great Jim Hawkins in *Treasure Island* (1920). Vi once told me that director Maurice Tourneur tried to get Metro to loan Vi as a replacement for Mason but the studio refused. Shirley Mason and Vi both began their careers with Edison and appear as sisters in *The Show of Shows* (1929), the last feature film for both of them. There was some antagonism between Vi and her oldest sister, Edna Flugrath (1893–1966); she would not talk of her and did not even know if she was alive or dead. Edna's career was primarily in the United Kingdom, where she was a prominent leading lady from 1914 to 1915 and from 1920 to 1921. She married her director Harold Shaw in Johannesburg, South Africa, in January 1917, while the two were filming *Die Voortrekkers* there.

Born in Brooklyn, New York, on June 28, 1897, Vi began dancing at the age of three at Coney Island eating-places. Patrons would throw coins at her, and Vi would "pick up the money for momma," as she would say. From Coney Island, she became a legitimate child actress, appearing with the likes of Dustin Farnum and William Faversham. Her first major stage role, and it was a most important one, was as Gwendolyn in Eleanor Gates's *The Poor Little Rich Girl*, which opened at New York's Hudson Theatre on January 21, 1913, and ran for 160 performances. It led to Vi's being billed as "Broadway's Youngest Star." The play was filmed in 1917 as a starring vehicle for Mary Pickford.

Long before *The Poor Little Rich Girl*, Vi and her mother had discovered the Edison Company, and the actress first worked there in 1910, making her debut in *A Christmas Carol*. She was to remain with the company through 1916, playing primarily in the short subjects that Edison emphasized over features long after the advent of the long format production:

"It was the closest [studio] to where we lived. We would be on the stage, in a road company, in the winter, and in the summer, in order to pick up a few dollars, for some reason my mother thought she would register us at the Edison Company. Shirley and myself, we were the kids there. And there, of course, I met my first husband. As a matter of fact, I fell in love with him when I was eleven years old. I was so scared I wouldn't grow up in time to marry him! I finally did. I was sixteen.

"You had to walk up the hill from Webster Avenue [to the studio], and it was a little-bitty entrance. As you walked in through the door, there were benches that actors sat on. All the women dressed in one room and the men in another, and that included children. A long dressing room with a john at the end. I think there were a few personal dressing rooms that Gertrude McCoy and Mabel Trunelle had. They were the big stars when I was a child. Afterward I graduated to one of those rooms. They would serve box lunches, ham and cheese sandwiches, that were terrible. Horace Plimpton was the manager. He didn't know the first thing about pictures. He had been in the carpet business.

"I had the pleasure of meeting Thomas Edison at one time. He was very hard of hearing—you had to shout at him—and I don't think he was vitally interested in the motion picture end, because he seemed kind of vague. I thought it was just great to be able to shake the hand of Thomas Edison."

The final major films that Viola Dana made at Edison were five-reel features, *Children of Eve* (1915) and *The Cossack Whip* (1916), both directed by John Collins. She was also the star of the 1915 two-reel production, *The Stoning*, directed by Charles Brabin (who later married Theda Bara): "The story was about a little girl that had gone astray and went to the big city. Harry Beaumont was the man that led the poor girl astray. She came back to her hometown and everybody turned against her. She finally threw herself in the river, and it was quite sensational, because I got into a little black coffin. That was very sensational, somebody getting into a coffin!"

The emphasis at Edison was on drama, and Viola Dana gained a reputation as a dramatic actress, with the ability to cry often and on cue. It was a reputation that led to a contract in 1916 with Metro, with whom the actress remained through 1924, starring in some 51 feature films. Vi's first major production at Metro was *Blue Jeans*, released in December 1917, again directed by John Collins, and based on a popular melodrama of the 1890s. By the early 1920s, earning $1,750 a week, Viola Dana was the highest paid female star at the studio. Only Bert Lytell, at $2,000 a week, earned more.

At the studio, the actress played both drama and comedy. For example, in 1924, she could be seen in the French melodrama, *Revelation*, which earlier had starred Nazimova, and as a manicurist who wins a beauty contest in the comedic *The Beauty Prize*. Her diminutive stature and good looks made Vi easy to cast, but by the 1920s, she was tired of serious drama. "I ran dry of tears," she was fond of remarking, and her saucy grin—and it was saucy—was ideally suited to comedy. Two of the best, also from 1924, were made by Paramount. In *Merton of the Movies*, she is a slapstick comedienne, helping the hero gain access to the studio where she works. In *Open All Night*, she is a bored Parisienne housewife who is attracted to a circus bicyclist, played by Dana's second husband, Maurice "Lefty" Flynn. (The couple married the following year and divorced in 1928.) All Vi recalled of the film was that the other leading lady, Jetta Goudal was "a stinker. She tried to upstage me, but she didn't realize she was dealing with a professional."

Vi always gave the impression that she became bored with films. She gave up on them not the other way around. With her stage background, she could easily have continued in talkies but choose to retire comfortably. She would serve as a volunteer at the Motion Picture Country House and eventually retired there, not from a lack of funds but in search of a sense of security. The final illness was thankfully speedy; Vi hated to be bed-ridden and was horrified that visitors could enter her room and see her without makeup. She died on July 3, 1987.

Bibliography

Bartlett, Randolph. "A Melody for the Viola." *Photoplay*, October 1917, pp. 69–72.

Bodeen, DeWitt. "Where Did All the Fun Go?" *Films in Review*, March 1976, pp. 141–165.

Brooks, Russell. "A Maid There Was." *Motion Picture Classic*, June 1921, pp. 56–57, 83–84.

Gateson, Elizabeth. "Vivacious Vivid Viola." *Motion Picture Classic*, October 1919, pp. 43–44, 64.

James, Arthur. "The Girl Who Never Grew Up." *Picture-Play*, July 1918, pp. 46–49.

McKelvie, Martha Groves. "Good Gracious, Viola!" *Motion Picture Classic*, July 1918, pp. 41–42.

St. Johns, Ivan. "It's No Laughing Matter." *Photoplay*, July 1925, pp. 58, 119.

Service, Faith. "The Poor Little Rich Star." *Motion Picture Classic*, January 1919, pp. 52–53, 67.

Shelley, Hazel. "Peter Pan Dana." *Motion Picture Classic*, November 1920, pp. 44–45.

Spensley, Dorothy. "They Go on Smiling." *Photoplay*, June 1926, pp. 38–39, 132–133.

Strong, Ralph. "Just Viola Dana." *Picture-Play*, May 1916, pp. 246–249.

The wedding of Bebe and Ben.

BEBE DANIELS AND BEN LYON

Both were American silent stars, but Bebe Daniels and Ben Lyon also hold a unique place in the history of British entertainment. They were the only major U.S. stars to sit out World War Two and the blitz in London and the only American performers to have starred in long-running BBC radio shows. From 1940 to 1942, Bebe and Ben were heard on *Hi Gang!*, which was also revived as a postwar series in 1949. They devised and wrote the comedy-variety series and also starred in a 1942 film version. Bebe Daniels also provided the script for the situation comedy *Life with the Lyons*, heard on the BBC from 1950 to 1961, and in which Bebe and Ben were joined by daughter Barbara and adopted son Richard. *Life with the Lyons* also made the transition to television and was the basis for two feature films, *Life with the Lyons* (1954) and *The Lyons in Paris* (1956).

The Spanish ancestry is evident in Bebe Daniels's physical appearance, her exotic look, and her first name, Spanish for baby. The wicked grin, however, is quite unique. In comparison, Ben Lyon, a Southerner of Irish ancestry, is very much American. Indeed, there was a while in the mid-1920s when he was promoted as the all-American equivalent of the Latin lover.

Bebe Daniels was born in Dallas, Texas, on January 14, 1901, and was a child actress on stage before making her film debut in two 1910 Selig Polyscope shorts, *The Wonderful Wizard of Oz* and *The Common Enemy*. In 1915, she joined the Rolin Company, appearing in the "Lonesome Luke" comedy shorts opposite Harold Lloyd. She was the comedian's first acknowledged leading lady, and he could not have been more fulsome in his praise of Bebe Daniels when we talked in London in 1970:

"She's a wonderful individual, and I can understand why she's tremendously revered here. She has so many friends in the United States. Bebe makes friends very easily. She's very warm-hearted and she has a habit of giving. I've always loved Bebe, and, of course, she worked with me in so many pictures. I felt terrible when I lost her. But I was the featured individual in our pictures, so Bebe had to be content with the next important role. In the C.B. DeMille films, it gave her a chance to do a little bit of dramatic art."

Despite her later talent as a screenwriter, Bebe did not contribute creatively to the Harold Lloyd shorts: "I don't say that Bebe wouldn't occasionally think of something funny. But she wasn't a part of that end of it. I think she had all she could to get her costumes, do what she had to do, and carry on with her personal life."

One evening, Bebe was having dinner with Lloyd and Hal Roach when Cecil B. DeMille came over and asked if she would like to work for him. "I said,

'I'll wait till my contract expires,' which I did," recalled Bebe. "Then I called up and asked if he was still interested, and he said, 'Very much so.' So I borrowed my mother's suit and my grandmother had brought a lot of egrets back from South Africa, and I had this hat with all these egrets on it. I went to his office and he said, 'Well, I'm signing you up, but please throw that hat away.'" DeMille first featured Daniels in the small role of the favorite of the Babylonian king (Thomas Meighan) in the flashback sequence in *Male and Female* (1919). She was signed to a Paramount contract, became a leading lady to Wallace Reid in *The Dancin' Fool* (1920) and *Sick Abed* (1921), and was starred by DeMille with Gloria Swanson in *Why Change Your Wife?* (1920) and *The Affairs of Anatol* (1921). In all, Bebe Daniels appeared in more than fifty Paramount releases of the 1920s.

Bebe remembered Wallace Reid and Rudolph Valentino as "two of the nicest men I've ever known. I have never met a more modest man in my life than Rudy was. I remember we used to go horseback riding together, and I'd say, 'Come on Rudy, let's take this fence.' And he'd say, 'No, Bebe, they'll think I'm showing off.' He went back to Italy, and when he came back, I said, 'Rudy, what happened? They must have mobbed you.' He said, 'Nothing happened, because I look like every other wop on the street.' He didn't know what conceit was."

Bebe was one of the stars featured by Paramount in its Realart brand, and there the actress first demonstrated her creativity outside of her original profession:

"When I was working at Realart, it was very difficult to get the right kind of writers, so I would write most of the stuff myself. I didn't take credit for it. At Realart, I used to work in the cutting room as well. They didn't seem to mind. I used to go in and splice films and work on them. Somebody had cut it, and I would say, 'you've cut it in the wrong place,' and they would say, 'Well you better go and cut it yourself.' So I would. We worked sort of as a unit, nothing like it today."

There are at least two of Bebe's Paramount films containing male-female reversal of roles. The George Barr McCutcheon comedy *Brewster's Millions* became *Miss Brewster's Millions* (1926), with Bebe's trying to spend a million dollars within one year. In *She's a Sheik* (1927), Bebe is the granddaughter of an Arab sheik who kidnaps French Legionnaire Richard Arlen. Unfortunately, the film is not quite as funny as the situation suggests.

One of Bebe's best known films of the 1920s is *The Speed Girl* (1921), based on her own personal experiences in the Santa Ana, California, jail, where the actress spent time for speeding:

"I was riding in my car with Jack Dempsey and my mother, and this speed cop came along and said, 'You know we put people in jail for going that fast.' And I said, 'Oh don't be silly, my uncle won't let me go to jail.' I phone Uncle Jack up and he said,'Where are you Bebe?' I said, 'Santa Ana.' He said, 'Bebe, you're in the wrong county.' So I had to go to jail, had a trial by jury, and had to go to jail for nine days, one off for good behavior. My cell was furnished by the best decorator in town, my meals were served by a waiter in full dress, and every time anyone called to see me, the jailor would come in and say, 'Miss Daniels, so-and-so to see you.' And I'd say, 'Tell them I'm out.'"

Bebe Daniels had been driving through Tustin, Orange County, over the 56-miles-per-hour speed limit when arrested on January 11, 1921. She was sentenced by Judge John Cox and began her sentence in the county jail on April 15th. In all, she had 792 visitors, including the judge. The story was written up in *Photoplay* (July 1921) and has all the earmarks of a publicity stunt. At the time, this deception was denied, and Bebe continued to deny it in old age. However, Paramount publicist Barrett Kiesling assured me that it was a stunt, which he created.

With the coming of sound, Paramount should have kept Bebe Daniels under contract, but the studio did not even offer her a voice test. Happily, RKO producer William Le Baron offered Bebe the lead in the screen adaptation of *Rio Rita* (1929). "He didn't even make a test of me," said Bebe. The film was a tremendous success, leading to an abysmal second film, also shot in Technicolor, *Dixiana* (1930): "That was terrible. It was dated then, believe me. The leading man [Everett Marshall] was awful."

Bebe appeared in more than a dozen other American sound features, including the original 1931 version of *The Maltese Falcon* (in the Mary Astor role), a sorry adaptation of the Irving Berlin musical *Reaching for the Moon* (1931), and William Wyler's *Counsellor at Law* (1933). Most audiences know Bebe as the leading lady who breaks her ankle and thus allows Ruby Keeler to become a star in *42nd Street* (1933), but Bebe is even more entertaining in another show business-oriented film, *Music Is Magic* (1935). Here, billed below Alice Faye, she is a screen star pretending that her daughter is really her sister, unable to come to terms with her age. There is incredible humor in Bebe's performance, a natural sense of fun. *Music Is Magic* should have marked the start of a Hollywood career, not its close.

Ben Lyon was born in Atlanta, Georgia, on February 6, 1901. His first two film appearances were most unusual. In 1918, he starred for the Catholic Art Association in *The Transgressor*, playing the son of steel mill owner who gets involved in labor agitation. In *Open Your Eyes* (1919), a co-production of Warner Bros. and State Health Films, Ben contracts syphilis from a prostitute and infects his hometown sweetheart:

"It was produced, directed and acted by a fellow named Jack Warner. We didn't know who he was. We took shots all over the streets of New York. I remember the big scene, the big shock to the audience. I was the good boy, led astray by five or six bad boys, and the big kick of the picture was when I was taken before the doctor for examination and the doctor looks me straight in the face and he says, 'Young man, you have syphilis.' I always say I survived and got over it.

"Now Jack Warner came over to London for the opening of *My Fair Lady*, and we met at the Claridges Hotel. I said, 'Jack, you remember that time you engaged me to work with you in *Open Your Eyes*? You know, I wish I'd been as bad an actor as you.' He said, 'What do you mean?' I said, 'Well, if I'd been as bad as you, I might have been the head of a big company today.'"

Many an actor would have ended his career after films such as these, but Ben Lyon soldiered on and eventually signed a longterm contract with First National in 1923. Colleen Moore was first attracted to his dark hair, blue eyes, and clean-cut, all-American look, suggestive of a college football player. He was the perfect leading man for the likes of Aileen Pringle, May McAvoy, Lois Wilson, and Billie Dove.

Despite so many films, silent and sound, the only memorable one in Ben's career is Howard Hughes's production of *Hell's Angels* (1930), in which Ben is Monte Rutledge, the cowardly brother of James Hall. Ben's hysteria after the two are captured by the Germans, in the sinister form of Lucien Prival, is quite laughable. Ben always displayed a sense of humor about his performance, and there are frequent references to it in *Life with the Lyons*:

"I don't think it was the reading, the speaking of the dialogue. I think it was the writing. We over-acted terribly. Don't forget in silent films you had to mime, you were gesticulating with your hands, and you over-acted. It was a transition. We hadn't become accustomed to talkies. You'd come in and register surprise with a terrific facial expression, maybe with a gesture with your hands and your arms.

"When I was first engaged for *Hell's Angels*, I was a leading man in films, making five or six pictures a year, and consequently my fan mail was terrific. We used to get 800 to 1,000 letters a day. Now, after I completed *Hell's Angels*, 104 weeks on the silent and talking versions, I was completely forgotten. My fan mail was down to 28 to thirty letters a day."

Ben and Bebe met in 1925. Ben recalled, "I think it was at a big dinner party in New York. I stepped from the New York stage into leading roles in films. Everything was going so marvelously for me so that evening I met Bebe, I was so enthused, I spent my evening telling her about the films I had done and she thought I was the most egotistical man she'd ever met." "Couldn't stand him," chimed in Bebe. "It wasn't ego or anything," insisted Ben. "It was just enthusiasm. I didn't see her again until about 1928 in California, when we met at another dinner party, and then, about late 1928, we became engaged."

The couple married on June 14, 1930. Bebe's bridesmaids included Adela Rogers St. Johns, Constance Talmadge and Lila Lee. Howard Hughes was one of the ushers, and the aged matron of honor was gossip columnist Louella Parsons, a close friend of whom Ben and Bebe were highly defensive. After a honeymoon in Santa Barbara, the couple resumed their respective film careers.

Bebe Daniels had visited England in 1933 to star in a minor musical, *The Song You Gave Me*, directed by Paul Stein, with Hungarian and sometimes Hollywood leading man Victor Varconi. In 1936, she returned with Ben to star in a variety act at the London Palladium; they became concerned at a kidnap threat against daughter Barbara, and according to Ben, "the district attorney advised us to get out of the country until it blew over."

This was not the first time the couple had appeared on stage. They had both starred in a 1934 comedy *Hollywood Holiday* that never made it to Broadway. "We were booked for New York, but I got measles," explained Bebe. "My mother was always proud of the fact that I didn't get any children's diseases, so I got them all after I was grownup." "Yes," responded Ben. "Mother used to say, 'My baby never had mumps, never had measles, chicken pox, any of those things.' After we got married she had everything."

It was this sort of natural, verbal sparring that made Ben and Bebe so entertaining. It was the basis for the radio show, and, much earlier, it led to their being booked, after the London Palladium appearance, for a tour of British music halls. "We were hams, we loved it, walking out on stage, getting laughs and applause, which you didn't get in the studio," explained Ben.

In the summer of 1939, with the threat of war looming, most Americans exited Europe. Ben and Bebe flew to Los Angeles in June of that year, not to resume life in America but to leave their children in the safe keeping of Bebe's mother. In August, the couple returned to England; "We accepted what England had to offer us in good times," they explained, "and so we think we should not run out when there is trouble."

With America's entry into the war, Ben became a lieutenant colonel in the Army Air Force; he had held a pilot's license since 1928 and been a member of the air force reserve since 1931. The couple organized the American Overseas Artists to entertain the troops and broadcast the radio program *The Stars and Stripes*. Bebe was the first female civilian to land in Normandy after D-Day and was awarded the Medal of Freedom for service under fire. As Ben recalled,

"She went over and recorded the American wounded, showing the speed and efficiency of the chain of evacuation. How a man could be wounded in Normandy in the morning, and be in a hospital in England in the afternoon. It gave great comfort to mothers and fathers and sweethearts back in America. Later in Italy, she recorded the British wounded, as well as Americans down there."

And Bebe still had time to star on stage in 1943 and 1944 in the musical *Panama Hattie!*

After the war, Ben and Bebe returned to the United States. Bebe accepted a producing job with Hal Roach: "*The Fabulous Joe* [1947] was the story of a talking dog. You know we had auditions for dogs, and there was one that came in [who] could really talk. He could say several things, but he wasn't the type." Ben became talent director for 20th Century–Fox, and just as he had discovered a blonde name Jean Harlow for *Hell's Angels*, he discovered another legendary blonde, Marilyn Monroe. Ultimately, neither Bebe nor Ben was completely happy in Hollywood, and they came back to England in 1949.

Bebe and Ben again took up residence at 18 Southwick Street, London, where they spent much of their life in England and which was familiar to most Britishers as the home of their favorite American stars. When I met Bebe and Ben, they had moved to a small service flat in Dolphin Square, and the former had suffered a stroke. She was still the older familiar Bebe with the streak of silver across her black hair, and her humor remained intact. She and Ben planned to attend a November 1970 screening of *She's a Sheik* that I had arranged at London's National Film Theatre, but Bebe was unable to face an audience again. She died on March 16, 1971.

Ben Lyon returned to the United States and married former silent leading lady Marion Nixon, whom he had known since the 1920s. The couple took up residence in a spacious apartment on Wilshire Boulevard in the Westwood area of Los Angeles. Ben became considerably disenchanted with the British, noting a racist attitude that had developed with the influx of immigrants from India and Pakistan. He was back for a visit to London in December 1975 and told me how dirty everyone looked. He was saddened by what was happening to the country, but the English were entirely to blame and needed "a kick in the ass." While on a cruise of the South Pacific on the Queen Elizabeth II, Ben suffered a heart attack and died on March 22, 1979.

Note: Prior to his departure for the United States in July 1972, Ben Lyon presented his and Bebe Daniels's memorabilia to the British Film Institute.

Bibliography

Allgood, Jill. *Bebe and Ben*. London: Robert Hale, 1975.
Cannon, Regina. "I Can Handle Ben—I Can Handle Bebe." *Modern Screen*, May 1934, pp. 56–57, 86, 88.
Daniels, Bebe, and Ben Lyon. *Life with the Lyons*. London: Odhams, 1963.
Lang, Harry. "Bebe and Ben." *Photoplay*, July 1930, pp. 73–74, 114–115.

Bebe Daniels Bibliography

"Bebe." *The Silent Picture*, no. 11–12, summer-autumn 1971, unpaged.
Cheatham, Maude S. "Bebe, the Oriental." *Motion Picture*, November 1919, pp. 32–33, 123.
Goldbeck, Willis. "In Black and Scarlet." *Motion Picture Classic*, September 1921, pp. 16–17, 82.
Gordon, Ralph. "On Pomander Walk." *Motion Picture*, April 1922, pp. 22–23, 97–98.
Hall, Gladys. "Confessions of the Stars: Bebe Daniels." *Motion Picture Classic*, January 1929, pp. 16–17, 82–83.
Handy, Truman B. "Bebe's Behavior." *Motion Picture*, September 1920, pp. 36–37, 103.
Johnson, Carol. "A Good Little Sport." *Motion Picture Classic*, December 1928, pp. 51, 78.
Jordan, Joan. "A Belle of Bogota." *Photoplay*, January 1921, p. 46.
Kingsley, Grace. "On Bebe's Beach." *Screenland*, December 1927, pp. 46–47, 94, 96–97.
Morris, Mary, "Bouncing Bebe." *PM*, May 19, 1946, pp. M13–M15.
Naylor, Hazel Simpson. "Sunlight on Black Lacquer." *Motion Picture*, November 1921, pp. 28–29, 82.
Remont, Fritzi. "A Daniels Come to Judgment." *Motion Picture Classic*, May 1919, pp. 42–43, 74.
St. Johns, Adela Rogers. "The Most Popular Girl in Hollywood." *Photoplay*, November 1922, pp. 33, 95.
Spensley, Dorothy. "The Evolution of Bebe." *Photoplay*, November 1925, pp. 34–35, 107–108.
Ben Lyon Bibliography
"A Great Come-Back." *Photoplay*, September 1930, pp. 41, 86.
Hall, Harold R. "Blame It on the Ladies." *Motion Picture Classic*, February 1927, pp. 54–55, 83, 87.
Parsons, Harriet. "Matrimony Made Him an Actor." *Movie Mirror*, September 1932, pp. 34–35, 93.
Redway, Sara. "Just Like Your Brother." *Motion Picture Classic*, January 1926, pp. 56–57, 82, 85.
St. Johns, Adela Rogers. "Hollywood's New Heart Breaker." *Photoplay*, January 1925, pp. 42, 106.

PHILIPPE DE LACY

After the death of Barbara La Marr, Philippe De Lacy (who was sometimes billed as Philippe De Lacey) and his adopted mother moved into her home, leading at least one fan magazine writer to note that "The boy who is too beautiful" now occupied the same address as had "The Girl who was too beautiful." While one might question La Marr's right to the title—Corinne Griffith easily surpasses her—there is no doubt that De Lacy is deserving of his title. Was there ever a more beautiful boy on screen, and was there ever a child star with such a tragic yet romantic background?

When De Lacy was born in Nancy, France, on July 25, 1917, his father was already a victim of World War One; his mother died two days after his birth. The boy was discovered in a shell hole by an American Red Cross nurse, Edith De Lacy, who brought him to the United States. Back in Los Angeles in 1920, she and her adopted son were invited to watch a scene being shot for *The Riddle: Woman*. The film's star, Geraldine Farrar, noticed the three-year-old and featured him in a scene. With his dark, smouldering looks and his girlish locks, De Lacy was obviously destined to become a darling of female filmgoers. There were other child stars of the 1920s, Baby Peggy, Junior Coghlan and the like, but they were primarily featured in short subjects or in minor features; Philippe De Lacy appeared in one major production after another.

He was Mary Pickford's brother in *Rosita* (1923) and Michael in the original 1924 screen adaptation of *Peter Pan*, directed by Herbert Brenon. Esther Ralston told me,

"We were doing a big close-up of me as Mrs. Darling, and 'Michael' got a little bored. He came just to my waistline, and put his arm around my waist. And just as Mr. Brenon said, 'OK, camera,' I let out a yelp. Mr. Brenon said, 'Stop, cut, what is the matter?' I said, 'Michael bit me in the stomach.' He came over to Michael and he said, 'No matter how tired you get Philippe or bored you get, you are not to bite Miss Ralston again. Now we'll take the scene.'"

De Lacy was Neil Hamilton as a child in *Beau Geste* (1926) and *Mother Machree* (1928), John Barrymore as a child in *Don Juan* (1926) and *General Crack* (1929), Emil Jannings as a child in *The Way of All Flesh* (1927), Barry Norton as a child in *Four Devils* (1929), and Richard Arlen as a child in *The Four Feathers* (1929). Among the major directors with whom he worked are Herbert Brenon, Victor Fleming, John Ford, Ernst Lubitsch, and F.W. Murnau. He ended his acting career on a high note in 1930, playing opposite Lillian Gish in *One Romantic Night*.

That same year, De Lacy was Ruth Chatterton's son, Bobby, in Dorothy Arzner's production of *Sarah and Son*. Back in November 1985, I asked Philippe about the film:

"I was twelve years old, and it did not seem any different or unusual to me to be directed by a woman rather than a man. And don't forget I had been with a lot of top directors. I do remember that I wanted the part desperately, and that another young boy was much more favored. However, Dorothy called me and told me she had selected me for the part.

"She was extremely capable, quiet, and she had to deal with a very forceful and temperamental actress in Ruth Chatterton. My mother had great admiration for her, and for her kindness to me. There was a scene where I was in cold water, and she was very concerned that I was kept warm with blankets and so forth. I was enjoying it—it was all a game to me. But then, of course, I enjoyed all my motion picture life, unlike so many people that you read about today."

Yet De Lacy's life in Hollywood was not as happy as he chose to remember. The child actor's looks might be most appealing to those women in the audience with a motherly instinct, but they also held appeal for a certain class of males. In 2000, one of my projects was the editing of director Bernard Vorhaus's autobiography. In the course of the book's production, we talked about many matters, and it was a shock when he revealed to me that director/designer Ferdinand Pinney Earle had more than a friendly interest in the young De Lacy. Even after 75 years, Vorhaus was unwilling to discuss details, but there was no doubt that De Lacy had been sexually molested by Earle.

Was it that De Lacy became too "old" for Hollywood roles, or was something more sinister involved? The young man tried unsuccessfully for a stage career and then in 1936 joined Louis de Rochemont's staff on the newsreel production "March of Time." De Lacy remained with de Rochemont through the mid-1950s, co-directing the second Cinerama feature, *Cinerama Holiday* (1955). From de Rochemont, the former child star joined the advertising agency of J. Walter Thompson Co., where he remained until his retirement in 1980.

It was in 1980 that Filmex, the Los Angeles International Film Exposition, screened *Peter Pan*. I escorted Mary Brian, who had played Wendy, and also there was Philippe De Lacy, no longer young and beautiful and, very obviously, nervous at being in the limelight again. When I talked with him some years later, he offered to introduce a program on "March of Time" but had no interest in a nostalgic tribute to his career as a child star. He asked that his address in Northern California be kept secret, and when he died, in Carmel, California, on July 29, 1995, not one newspaper carried his obituary.

Bibliography

Carr, Harry. "Bombed into the Movies." *Motion Picture Classic*, September 1923,
pp. 26, 82.
Don, Val Jo. "War Orphan." *Photoplay*, July 1928, pp. 40–41, 120–121.
Jansen, Larry. "A Child of Destiny." *Photoplay*, September 1924, pp. 81, 134.

CAROL DEMPSTER

Neither audiences nor her colleagues liked Carol Dempster very much. "I never cared for her," said Lois Wilson. "She had sharp features, you know, and I always used to say she was as sharp offscreen as she was on. She was working at the Paramount, Long Island, studios, and I was working there with Bebe Daniels. Bebe would say, 'Do you get on with that Carol?' And I'd say, 'No,' and she'd say, 'Same here.'" The sole reason for Carol Dempster's career was D.W. Griffith, her mentor and, in all probability, her lover. "He [Griffith] was mad at me for telling Carol Dempster not to get mixed up with old men. She'd destroy herself. I used to give imitations of her, and he caught me at it once," recalled Dempster's leading man in *Dream Street*, Ralph Graves. In reality, it was Griffith who was ultimately destroyed by Carol Dempster and his insistence on starring her.

Carol Dempster was not, of course, the first mistress to be promoted as a film star. Publisher Eugene V. Brewster discovered the untalented Corliss Palmer (1909–1952) when she was the winner of the 1920 "Fame and Fortune" contest sponsored by his magazine, *Motion Picture Classic*. In quick succession, Brewster made her a star and married her. William Randolph Hearst's elevation to stardom of Marion Davies is common knowledge, but she, at least, had talent, personality, and good humor, items lacking in Carol Dempster's repertoire. "Carol Dempster was such a bad actress and such a stupid girl, she certainly didn't do him [Griffith] any good," opined Anita Loos. Herb Sterne recalled Republic studio head Herbert J. Yates printing matchbooks with a photograph of his wife, Vera Hruba Ralson, encircled with a horseshoe and the phrase "The Most Beautiful Woman in the World." Herb gave Griffith one; he looked at it and said, "Christ, I was never that stupid about Carol Dempster."

In later years, Griffith was more than happy to acknowledge his mistake with Carol Dempster. Herb Sterne screened one of her films, *The White Rose* (1923), for the director, Mae Marsh, and Lillian and Dorothy Gish: "Dorothy had a dog, Rover, and whenever Dempster came on the screen—she didn't have a hell of a lot of footage—the dog would go mad and bark. Griffith went into convulsions, because he insisted the Gish girls had trained the dog to do this. It was very humorous."

The Gish sisters and Mae Marsh had every reason for disliking Carol Dempster: her appearances in Griffith's films tend to be nothing more than shoddy impersonations of them, adoptions of their nervous mannerisms and body language. Lillian Gish can get away with hysteria, but Carol Dempster's hysterical running around in *The Love Flower* (1920) is nothing more than poor melodrama. "As an actress Miss Dempster is an excellent high diver," wrote Burns Mantle unkindly but correctly in *Photoplay* (November 1920).

Born in Duluth, Minnesota, on December 8, 1901, Carol Dempster moved with her family to California, where she came to the attention of Ruth St. Denis and joined her dance school. She is apparently one of the dancers in the Babylonian sequence of *Intolerance* (1916), but whether Griffith noticed her at this point is unknown. Within three years, she was featured in Griffith's productions of *A Romance of Happy Valley*, *The Girl Who Stayed at Home*, and *True Heart Susie*, all released in 1919, in which she is adequate, in large part because because the roles are not big enough to permit too much of a failure.

The impersonation of Griffith's better leading ladies begins with the woefully poor *The Love Flower* (1920), the first film in which Dempster is starred, and continues with *Dream Street* (1921), with an amateurish attempt to mimic Dorothy Gish, and *One Exciting Night* (1922), the weakest of all Griffith features, containing one ludicrous scene in which the star is tied to an altar, "Youth sacrificed on the altars of greed and passion." She gave one performance in a non-Griffith production, *Sherlock Holmes* (1922), starring John Barrymore, and Dempster is, to a certain extent, charming in the minor characterization of Alice.

Carol Dempster ended her career starring in four of Griffith's last films. Two from 1925, *Sally of the Sawdust* and *That Royle Girl*, are unworthy of comment. "Some day I am sure we shall see her make a fine picture," wrote Delight Evans of Carol Dempster in 1922. It took a couple of years, but *Isn't Life Wonderful* (1924), with its grim portrait of postwar Germany, boasts a drab and emotionally strong Carol Dempster as Inga. *The Sorrows of Satan* (1927) opens slowly, and some might argue that the early scenes between Dempster and leading man Ricardo Cortez are dull. This is a trite, old-fashioned melodrama by a mistress of the genre, Marie Corelli, but it provides Carol Dempster with her one great screen role.

Here, as Mavis Claire, she is truly an actress, as she sits across from Cortez, listening to the poem he has written as a tribute to her beauty; here is the girl who believes in the morning that the night of love with Cortez is not the beginning but the end of romance; here is the hysterical child who chases after her lover as he drives away in the car of Satan (Adolphe Menjou), standing still for one long, wistful close-up when she realizes she has lost him.

There were no more films for Dempster, perhaps in large part because producers were unwilling to tolerate Griffith's insistence on the presence of an inadequate leading lady. In 1929, the actress married New York banker Edwin S. Larsen, and the couple eventually settled in La Jolla, an affluent community just outside of San Diego, from where the actress assured her fans that "in real life Carol Dempster had a happy ending." Some years prior to her death in La Jolla, on February 1, 1991, she traveled to New York to present her photographs to the Museum of Modern Art. At the last minute, she became scared at showing her face before the staff there and sent in her husband, alone, to make the presentation.

Bibliography

Biery, Ruth. "I Don't Care If I Don't Make Another Picture." *Photoplay*, August 1928, pp. 55, 118–119.

Carr, Harry. The Case of Carol Dempster." *Motion Picture Classic*, December 1925, pp. 38–39, 70.

Dorr, John. "The Movies, Mr. Griffith & Carol Dempster." *Cinema*, vol. VII, no. 1, fall 1971, pp. 23–34.

Evans, Delight. "Griffith's Newest Heroine." *Photoplay*, February 1922, pp. 31, 116.

Hall, Gladys. "One of Us." *Motion Picture*, July 1922, pp. 40–41, 93.

———. "The Gentle Gypsy." *Motion Picture Classic*, October 1926, pp. 53, 86, 88.

Herzog, Dorothy. "The Mystery Girl of Pictures." *Photoplay*, July 1925, pp. 54, 123.

———. "A Victim of Prejudice." *Photoplay*, March 1926, pp. 36–37, 127–128.

Kingsley, Grace. "A Dancing Star." *Picture-Play*, February 1920, pp. 61–62, 91.

Klumph, Helen. "You Can't Ignore Her." *Picture-Play*, December 1925, pp. 47, 98.

Robbins, E.M. "The Two Strange Women." *Photoplay*, August 1917, pp. 87–89.

Schonert, Vernon L. "Carol Dempster." *Film Fan Monthly*, November 1971, pp. 22–29.

Smith, Frederick James. "Carol and Her Car." *Motion Picture Classic*, October 1920, pp. 16–17, 83.

DOROTHY DEVORE

Petite and pretty and with a very homespun American charm, Dorothy Devore was one of the major second-league screen comediennes. She had neither the personality nor the commercial appeal of Mabel Normand, but as the leading female star of the Al Christie comedy company, her films had a guaranteed audience.

Born Anna Inez Williams in Fort Worth, Texas, on June 22, 1899, Dorothy Devore began her professional career as a singer at Al Levy's Café in Los Angeles at the age of fourteen, at which time she changed her name, and in 1918, she was signed to a contract by Al Christie, a major producer of what might be termed polite comedy. As she recalled, "There were two brothers, Charles and Al. Charles handled all the business, and Al was producing and directing. When I started, it was just very small, but, of course, naturally, daily or at least yearly, it grew and grew and grew. The studios were small, on the corner of Gower and Sunset Boulevard, and it was like a family."

The familial relationship at the studio between Christie and Devore was not that of father and daughter but of mentor and mistress. The actress had something of a reputation for promiscuity. She and Priscilla Bonner had been friends—Priscilla appears as her sister-in-law in *Hold Your Breath* (1924) and was cast in a small role in Christie's *Charley's Aunt* (1925) thanks to Devore's efforts—but once Priscilla had married, she was forbidden by her husband ever to communicate with Dorothy.

Dorothy Devore was unusual for a light comedienne: she undertook quite a lot of physical comedy in her films. In one comedy, opposite Earle Rodney, she had a horse sitting in her lap for a couple of hours. Dorothy could take a fall with the best of them. Nowhere is this more apparent than in her 1924 star vehicle, *Hold Your Breath*, which might well be described as a feminist response to Harold Lloyd's *Safety Last*, although sadly without the comedic genius of the latter. The bad puns in virtually every title prove tiresome to a modern audience, and while Harold Lloyd has an attractive leading lady in *Safety Last*, Dorothy Devore's romantic interest comes in the plump form of mediocre comic Walter Hiers (the poor man's Roscoe "Fatty" Arbuckle). Here Dorothy Devore is Mabel, who gets a job with the *Daily Bulletin* and is forced to chase after an organ grinder's monkey, who has stolen a $50,000 antique bracelet from reclusive millionaire Tully Marshall. She follows as it progresses up the side of the office building (located on East Hill Street in Los Angeles) and obviously uses a stunt double for some of the escapades, but, in all probability, little more than did Harold Lloyd. There can be no doubt that Devore does crawl along an outside ledge on the third and fourth floors of the building, climbs up higher on the façade, and swings and hangs from a canopy several stories up. It is not, as advertised in 1924, "one of the greatest super-comedies of all time," but it is fun.

"That was one of the good features I made," recalled the comedienne. "This monkey was on wires, and he would get excited and bite—the poor little thing. I felt so sorry for the monkey, but quite often I was all cut up and bitten."

Hold Your Breath was not Devore's first feature. In 1920, Al Christie had loaned her out to Charles Ray to be his leading lady in his first independent production, *Forty-Five Minutes from Broadway*, based on the George M. Cohan musical.

Hold Your Breath also features a comedic device of which Al Christie was most fond, that of dressing his leading ladies in male attire. Here, Devore disguises herself as a male messenger boy in order to approach Tully Marshall. This penchant for male attire on mistresses seems an obsessive one among middle-aged American males of the period; William Randolph Hearst loved to put Marion Davies into a pair of trousers. In *Know Thy Wife* (1918), Al Christie has Devore disguised as her boy friend Earle Rodney's best man, Steve, in order to confuse his parents at an arranged marriage. "You boys are certainly fond of each other," comments Rodney's mother when she discovers the two "men" kissing. Yes, there is something cute and charming about Dorothy Devore in young man's attire with her shoulder-length brunette hair hidden by a wig and her breasts unpronounced, but it is all a bit kinky.

Hold Your Breath notwithstanding; the Christie films were basically situation comedies, rather like today's television productions—and about as funny. Al Christie directed some, but many were directed by Norman Z. McLeod, Scott Sidney, William Beaudine (who later directed Dorothy at Warner Bros.) and his younger brother Harold, all of whom learned their craft at Christie.

Dorothy Devore's departure from the studio came one year before her marriage to Honolulu businessman A.Wiley Mather in San Francisco on December 18, 1925. (She divorced him on the grounds of cruelty on August 16, 1933.) It was obvious that both the sexual and the professional relationship with Christie had run its course. The actress signed a contract with Warner Bros., starring first in *The Narrow Street* (1924); the engagement was supposed to run seven years, but Devore bought herself out of the contract rather than play a supporting role to Rin Tin Tin in *The Night Cry* (1926). From 1927 to 1929, she had her own series, the Dorothy Devore Comedies, for Educational Pictures ("I had complete charge of them, cast and everything") and was also featured in some poverty row productions but basically retired with the coming of sound.

Dorothy Devore died on September 10, 1976, at the Motion Picture Country House exactly ten years after becoming a resident there. She had obviously always looked after herself, professionally and financially, and even at the end of her life she was something of a businesswoman. I met her first in December 1971, at which time she showed me Christie synopses and scripts she had kept. A year or so later, when I pointed out to her that these might be useful in compiling the 1912–1920 edition of the *American Film Institute Catalog*, she arranged to sell them to the Institute.

Bibliography

Cheatham, Maude. "A Toiling Lily." *Motion Picture*, March 1921, pp. 54–55, 112.
Denbo, Doris. "The Versatile Dorothy Devore." *Picture-Play*, August 1925, p. 83.
Slide, Anthony. "Dorothy Devore." *The Silent Picture*, no. 15, summer 1972, pp. 16–
    17.

RICHARD DIX

With his footballer's build, the square-jawed Richard Dix (St. Paul, Minnesota, July 18, 1893–at sea, September 20, 1949) is very much a man's man, standing apart from the Latin lovers and the seemingly effeminate leading men who make up the roster of male silent stars. The hulking Francis X. Bushman saw Dix on stage in Montreal and recommended him for screen work after noting how much the actor looked like him. Dix does have an undeniable screen presence. Jane Wyatt was an unlikely Western heroine opposite Dix in *Buckskin Frontier* and *The Kansan*, both released in 1943, distressed as much by the subject matter of the films as the aging leading man. However, as she recounted, once Dix had put on his toupée, his corset, and his high-heeled boots, he really did sit tall in the saddle.

Mary Brian was Dix's leading lady in three 1927 films—*Knockout Reilly*, *Man Power*, and *Shanghai Bound*—and she recalled him as "a very dynamic man, very masculine and very strong, not exactly a matinée idol. I was very impressed with him because he was quite a big star at the time. He was kind of escorting me around, and I thought he was wonderful." Returning by train from location filming on the Sacramento River for *Shanghai Bound*, the somewhat smitten Mary Brian was devastated when she heard coming from the next compartment the sounds of lovemaking between Dix and the film's second female lead, Jocelyn Lee: "There was quite a thing that night, which was so disillusioning to me. Broke my heart. That was such puppy love. I was just heart-broken, which didn't last long. It opened my eyes to many things. In this business, it's not very easy to shock you about the things that go on."

Richard Dix was the personification of the noble savage, thanks to his portrayals of native Americans in *The Vanishing American* (1925) and *Redskin* (1929); the last with its offensive title song of "Redskin, Redskin, Boy of My Dreams." But, of course, he is a fake, offering politically incorrect characterizations in terms of both the performance and the concept. There is no truth in portrayal here in that the ancestors of Ernest Carlton Brimmer Jr. (Dix's real name) came over on the Mayflower. Nevertheless, in 1930, the actor was inducted into the Kaw tribe and given the name of "Big Heart," in honor of his "true" characterizations of native Americans.

On screen from 1916, after a lengthy stage career, Richard Dix came to fame in 1923 with *The Christian*, directed by Maurice Tourneur and shot on location in England. He is well cast as the deeply religious John Storm, who falls in love with an actress in this second screen adaptation of the popular Hall Caine novel. A Paramount contract followed, resulting in 33 films between 1923 and 1929. Dix is the star of the modern story of Cecil B.

DeMille's *The Ten Commandments* (1923), but no matter how good or weak his performance, it is the Biblical sequences that dominate and hold the audience.

On screen, Richard Dix is a man of action: a racing car driver in *Racing Hearts* (1923), an aviator in *Sinners in Heaven* (1924), a would-be prizefighter in *The Shock Punch* (1925), a football player in *The Quarterback* (1926), a world heavyweight boxer in *Knockout Reilly* (1927), a sea captain in *Shanghai Bound* (1927), and a baseball pitcher in *Warming Up* (1928). He made an easy transition to sound in *Nothing But the Truth* (1929), remade by Bob Hope in 1941. In 1929, Dix left Paramount and moved over to RKO, appearing in 23 feature films there through 1940, beginning with an adaptation of the George M. Cohan mystery, *Seven Keys to Baldpate* (1929).

In 1935, he visited the United Kingdom, starring opposite Madge Evans in *Trans-Atlantic Tunnel*, directed by the untalented Maurice Elvey. The best of Dix's RKO features is *The Ghost Ship* (1943), directed by Maurice Tourneur's son, Jacques, in which the actor is a dictatorial captain and psychological killer. He ended his career in 1947 with Columbia's *The Thirteenth Hour.*

Richard Dix died suddenly as a result of a heart attack while on board a ship returning from France. Following his death, Dix's second wife married Walter Van de Kamp of the baking family in 1950. His two sons were hellraisers in the tradition of their father. In 1951, fifteen-year-old Richard Dix Jr. was named in a paternity suit; he died three years later in a logging camp accident. The second son, Robert, was arrested in 1953 for participation in "a wild sex party." By 1963, he had twice been married and divorced.

Bibliography

Bell, Caroline. "The Real Richard Dix." *Picture-Play*, April 1924, pp. 84–85, 104.
Bodeen, DeWitt. "Richard Dix." *Films in Review*, October 1966, pp. 487–504.
Byers, Leslie. "D'yeknow Mr. Dix?" *Motion Picture*, January 1922, pp. 50–51, 86.
Coleman, Jane. "He Was Not Afraid to Die." *Photoplay*, July 1928, pp. 31, 133.
Dix, Richard. "How It Feels to Become a Star." *Photoplay*, January 1925, pp. 51, 125.
Herzog, Dorothy. "Mr. Columbus Dix." *Photoplay*, July 1926, pp. 69, 118–119.
Irwin, Murray. "Richard Dix: The Man Who Found Himself." *Cinema Art*, July 1926, pp. 55–56.
Johaneson, Bland. "That Saving Sense of Humor." *Photoplay*, May 1924, pp. 67, 141.
Kingsley, Grace. "Coming Star—and Why." *Movie Weekly*, April 29, 1922, pp. 11, 18.
Martin, Elliot. "I'm No Ladies' Man!" *Photoplay*, January 1930, pp. 55, 117.
Masters, E. Lanning. "All That His Name Implies." *Picture-Play*, April 1923, pp. 65, 92.

Montalvo, Carmencita. "Introducing a Casual Mr. Dix." *Cinema Art*, March 1927, pp. 24, 42.
Oettinger, Malcolm H. "Thoughts on Attaining Stardom." *Picture-Play*, December 1924, pp. 43, 108.
York, Cal. "Still the Most Eligible Young Man." *Photoplay*, September 1926, pp. 74, 92.

Best wishes,
Billie Dove.

BILLIE DOVE

Billie Dove's last film, *Blondie of the Follies*, released by MGM in August 1932, is an example of art imitating life. Like her screen character, Dove had been a showgirl and dancer in the Ziegfeld *Follies* (in 1917 and 1918), as had the star of *Blondie of the Follies*, Marion Davies. (Of course, they were both looking a bit long in the tooth by this time.) And just as their screen personae have sugar daddies, so did Dove and Davies. The latter, of course, was the mistress of William Randolph Hearst. Billie Dove was the wife of director Irvin Willat, when in July 1930, he divorced her upon receipt of $350,000 from Howard Hughes. As Hughes's mistress, Billie Dove was starred in two films, *The Age for Love* (1931) and *Cock of the Air* (1932). She was not particularly good in either film, and Hughes lost interest in her. Davies's lover, William Randolph Hearst, also starred her and she proved to be an exceptional comedic talent whose career was more damaged than helped by Hearst's insistence on starring her in unsuitable parts.

Born Lillian Bohney, Billie Dove (New York, May 4, 1901–Woodland Hills, California, December 31, 1998) was an exceptional beauty, and her brown hair lightly streaked with grey added to the dramatic effect. She was sometimes described as delicate, but her features and body language indicate strength and fortitude. In 1927, Dove starred in a feature titled *The American Beauty* and became known by the sobriquet. But if she was an American Beauty rose, she was one that could weather many a storm. Her breasts were much admired by Hollywood's male fraternity, and art director Harold Grieve remembered that director Marshall Neilan would stare at them, remarking, "Look at those Billie Doves!"

Billie Dove worked as an extra at Fort Lee, New Jersey, before receiving her first screen credit in *Get-Rich-Quick-Wallingford* in 1921. She was a Follies girl opposite Constance Talmadge in *Polly of the Follies* (1922) and came to prominence with *All the Brothers Were Valiant* (1923). Dove was featured in two early Technicolor features (utilizing the two-strip process), *Wanderer of the Wasteland* (1924), directed by her husband, Irvin Willat, and *The Black Pirate* (1926), in which, like other leading ladies before her, she does nothing more than support Douglas Fairbanks. In both Technicolor features, she wears a wig. In *The Black Pirate*, she is "doubled" in the final love scene by Mary Pickford, who perhaps did not want her husband too close to the sultry Billie Dove.

By 1926, Billie Dove had become a star, but, as she would be the first to admit, she was not a great actress. Dove was a recluse in later years, but she was always willing to talk with me about the woman who taught her to act, director Lois Weber: "She was a wonderful person. John Ford was a man's director. This was a woman's director. She had a woman's feeling for everything. She would talk about it, and then do it. So simple, so easy." For Weber, Billie Dove starred in *The Marriage Clause* (1926) and *Sensation Seekers* (1927). Neither is a great film and does little to enhance Weber's reputation as the major directorial talent that she was. As Egypt Hagen, Dove is certainly entertaining as she vamps the new minister, played by the singularly untalented Raymond Bloomer, in *Sensation Seekers*, but there is little more can be written of her characterization. Thanks to Weber, Billie Dove maintained, she was offered a contract "by every studio in town—it wasn't me, it was the director."

In all Billie Dove made in excess of 45 feature films, starring in 23 after she left Lois Weber. She was neither a difficult nor a temperamental actress. "We all worked for the picture—we wanted the picture to be good," she insisted.

Following the breakup with Howard Hughes and completion of *Blondie of the Follies*, Billie Dove married wealthy rancher Robert Kenaston in 1933 and settled down to a life of luxury with homes in Pacific Palisades and Palm Springs. (In 1970, she divorced Kenaston and briefly married for a third time.) In 1962, she returned to the screen under amusing circumstances. Dove was a great entrant in competitions, and in one, organized by Columbia Pictures, she wrote a jingle to promote *Gidget Goes Hawaiian*. The prize was a trip to Hawaii and a walk-on in *Diamond Head*. The actress accepted the prize, after revealing her past to the studio. Of course, it was great publicity for Columbia, so much so that one cannot help but wonder if it was not all a publicity stunt. Anyway, Dove is not identifiable in the film—she is apparently in a luau scene— and for all intents and purposes, the actress bid the screen a triumphant farewell with *Blondie of the Follies*.

Bibliography

Bodeen, DeWitt. "Billie Dove." *Films in Review*, April 1979, pp. 193–208.
Gassaway, Gordon. "Dove's Eyes." *Motion Picture Classic*, November 1922, pp. 36–37, 76, 100.
"Miss Billie Dove New Metro Star." *Moving Picture World*, April 9, 1922, p. 932.
Wagner, Bruce. "Annals of Hollywood: Moving Pictures." *The New Yorker*, July 20, 1998, pp. 54–61.

CLAIRE DUBREY

Claire DuBrey was not an easy woman to know. She was outspoken, arrogant, and unwilling to listen to others. Her career was long and basically undistinguished, but, as she grew older, she saw herself as one of the last pioneers of the cinema. She was born in Bonners Ferry, Idaho, on August 31, 1892, and died, almost 101 years later, on August 1, 1993. Thus, she could claim—quite legitimately—to be the oldest living actress of the silent era. As such, she was determined to offer her opinion, wanted or not, on anything related to the era. She did not see Peter Bogdanovich's "tribute" to the period, *Nickelodeon* (1976), but still denounced it, fuming, "The Good Old Days—May they never come back!" Perhaps she didn't need to see it. Director Allan Dwan, who was a consultant on the film, complained to me that nobody involved in the production had any interest in hearing what he had to say about what was wrong with the film.

After time in minor theatrical stock companies, Claire DuBrey entered films with the Lubin Company around 1913. She spent four years with producer Thomas H. Ince from 1915 through 1917, initially at Inceville, the studio complex he had created where today Sunset Boulevard runs into the ocean at Pacific Palisades, but where I don't believe he ever actually shot a production in which the ocean was visible. Claire's remembrances of Ince and Inceville were vidid:

"The studio itself, which was a rough board, unpainted affair, with stables and wigwams for the Indians, was on the ocean front. There was a road between the water and the stables, and it was fairly level down there. They did their Westerns up there, with the Indians chasing the settlers.

"But Ince wanted to get away from this, and so he resolved to engage New York stars, and he put this ad in the paper for society women to work in pictures. I was married to a doctor, I was young, not too unattractive, I was told, and I had time on my hands. So I went up to Inceville, and I got a job immediately. It wasn't much of a job. It was ten dollars a week, but that was the going price. He had about thirty girls and twenty boys in what was called stock at ten dollars apiece. One of the boys was Jack Gilbert, and one of the girls was Alice Terry. There we were, working for Ince six days a week, playing settlers in the morning and possibly Indians in the afternoon.

"A new class of women was needed. He was no longer using the cowgirls or the Indian squaws. He was using society women, because we had independent means. We had to furnish our own clothes, makeup, etc., and a girl could hardly live on her salary, so we had to have a family.

"Mr. Ince was absolutely charming. He never issued orders. He had a man to do that, as one should. He had a stooge, who was called a studio manager, and he was rude. His name was E.H. Allen, an ignorant and foul-mouthed Irishman. He would come on the set and bawl the director out, or the actors or anyone else. Ince issued these orders, but he was always charming. We thought he was a dear. Ince never, never, never directed. He just appeared on the set on rare occasions. Once or twice a week, he'd come around and smile and say hello, but do nothing on his part to make himself unpleasant."

There was, however, one film that Claire remembered Ince directing, and that was *Peggy* (1916), in which Billie Burke (Mrs. Florenz Ziegfeld) made her screen debut and in which DuBrey doubled for the star: "He kinda liked the girl, built her a whole stage, including a piano, down on level ground 200 feet from the ocean road. She didn't need to climb the steep wooden stairs as did Bill Hart, Louise Glaum, etc." Ince also built Billie Burke her own personal toilet, creating considerable animosity among the fellow actors and actresses, who had to share a single faucet. Like so many actresses from the silent era, Claire DuBrey had a fixation over problems relating to studio toilets—a strange phenomenon unnoticed by other historians. Later at Universal, she complained that the dressing rooms had no toilets, no matter the preeminence of the occupant. Soap was available only in the communal washrooms, but no toilet paper!

Claire DuBrey left Ince in 1917 to join Universal, where she was offered $25 a week: "I rushed home to tell Alice Terry. She had a crush on someone at the beach—we all lived at Santa Monica—and said she didn't want to go all the way to Universal and be there all day. So I went alone." At Universal, she was Harry Carey's leading lady in Western features and short subjects:

"Olive Fuller Golden, who was always on the set, who he was engaged to at the time, and whom he eventually married, liked me. She felt that I was safe with Harry. Harry had had four wives and he wasn't quite divorced from the last one. I had a dreadful time getting away from him. I'd go to the front office and scream and yell to be taken out of these Westerns. I'd say I'm not a Western type. I look ridiculous in these Western clothes. And they'd say, you may be right, but Harry won't let you go."

Claire also played minor roles in Lon Chaney features and was the second female lead in Dorothy Phillips vehicles. Because she was tall and dark, she began to be cast more and more in exotic roles, such as the anarchist in *The World Aflame* (1919) and the Bolshevik agitator in *Dangerous Hours* (1920). She also gained recognition as a vamp, luring away from wives and sweethearts such minor leading men as Franklyn Farnum in *The Winged Mystery* (1917), Dustin Farnum in *A Man in the Open* (1919), Robert Ellis in *The Spite Bride* (1919), and Hallam Cooley in *A Light Woman* (1920):

"I did mind it, because I thought it was ridiculous. There was only one really great vampire, and that was Theda Bara. I didn't know how to act as a vampire. I was very self-conscious about it, because I was brought up in the day when women didn't fling themselves around. I was dignified. I always was. But by that time I was intent on working, earning a living. I realized a time would come when I would need every bit of money I could get. So I wanted to work, and I did whatever I was told. However, if I had been acting in today's times when they tell you to take off your clothes, I'm afraid I'd have found myself another job!"

In the 1920s, Claire DuBrey was generally featured in second leads, usually playing well-dressed women. As the decades came and went, the parts became considerably smaller, but the work was always available, and she made more than sixty screen appearances in the 1930s and more than forty in the 1940s. It was not until 1967 that Claire DuBrey officially retired from the screen. In later years, her features became harder and she had the look of an unappealing, aging spinster. She is particularly good as the governor's wife who sees herself as much-maligned in *The Sin of Nora Moran* (1933), which is surely one of the best and most original B pictures ever to come out of Hollywood.

In the early 1930s, the actress became "secretary" to Marie Dressler. There has been much speculation as to the relationship between the two women, but there can be little doubt that they were lovers. Later, Claire established a minor talent agency with another lesbian from the silent era, Anna Q. Nilsson, and it seems possible that the relationship was also a personal one.

Claire DuBrey lived for many years at a house on Miller Drive in West Hollywood. Her neighbor and friend on one side was actor Richard Cromwell, who sometimes disguised his homosexuality by using her as a "beard" at various gatherings. The Law family, living on the other side, was close to both DuBrey and Cromwell, and in later years, one of the two Law sons, actor John Phillip Law, took care of Claire DuBrey and was her eventual heir.

Note: Claire DuBrey's papers are at the American Film Institute.

Bibliography

"Claire DuBrey: Film Pioneer." *Screen Actor*, summer 1979, pp. 28–29.
Slide, Anthony. "Claire DuBrey." *The Silent Picture*, no. 14, spring 1972, pp. 7–8.
"A Want-Ad Vampire." *Photoplay*, August 1919, p. 66.

DOUGLAS FAIRBANKS. *See* **MARY PICKFORD AND DOUGLAS FAIRBANKS**

VIRGINIA BROWN FAIRE

Leisure World is an upscale senior citizen retirement community close to the California resort town of Laguna Beach. It was also for many years the home of Tinker Bell or, to be more precise, the actress who played J.M. Barrie's fairy creation in the original 1924 screen adaptation of *Peter Pan*, Virginia Brown Faire. Since the 1920s, she, Priscilla Bonner, and Mary Brian had been good friends, and, happily, the friendship of Robert Gitt and I with Priscilla and Mary was extended to include Ginnie. For a while in the mid- through late 1970s it became a routine for the four of us to drive down from Los Angeles to Leisure World. After dropping off Priscilla and Mary, Bob and I would spend the afternoon in Laguna Beach, returning late afternoon or early evening for dinner and, on occasions, a screening of one of Ginnie's films that we had brought along.

We looked at *The Cricket on the Hearth* (1923), which was somewhat unappealing in its lack of dramatic action and which its star recalled was filmed in a house on Beverly Boulevard and in woods behind Cahuenga Boulevard. One can tell that producer Paul Gerson is straining with his concept of an English location. The Morris R. Schlank production of *Queen of the Chorus* (1928), directed by Charles J. Hunt, is hardly a major production, but it does manage to relate a complex story of a chorus girl's love for a millionaire's secretary in six tight reels. Schlank's wife, Bess, was a prominent Los Angeles modiste, and her occupation presumably helped the producer decide to open the film at a couturier's showroom, where the chorus girls have their men take care of their outer bodily needs. Here, as elsewhere in the film, the use of pig Latin and contemporary slang in the titles adds to the realism. Rex Lease, whom Priscilla Bonner remembered as "always very nice and courteous," makes a pleasant, lightweight hero, and Virginia Brown Faire is an equally pleasing heroine. All ends happily for the pair, and, as Priscilla Bonner commented, "Virtue triumphs—or at least it did in 1928."

Virginia Brown Faire does not do too much in *Tracked by the Police* (1927), but it is one of the best Rin Tin Tin features. "He supported Bill Desmond and me [in *Shadows of the North*, 1923], and then, later, I supported him. Rinty was a darling animal, a wonderful animal. I'm sure he understood every word. He was better than most humans. He climbed a ladder, which is a thing most dogs don't do. He came down a ladder, which is unheard of. I remember Lee Duncan, his owner, just holding his breath, because if anything happened to that dog...He didn't have a stand-in. He had a mate, Gloria, a beautiful white dog. Rinty could be very friendly and loveable, but you didn't dare go near him unless Lee said it was all right. There was no recognition of anyone unless his owner said OK."

Ginnie was disappointed in *Peter Pan*, asserting that the original "cut" had contained more scenes with Tinker Bell. It seems unlikely, but she did vividly recall a scene inside a drawer with Peter Pan's shadow. At the same time, the actress also remembered that cinematographer James Wong Howe had determined how he could shoot close-ups of Tinker Bell but that J.M. Barrie had insisted, "No close-ups, because it would spoil the illusion." Both Esther Ralston (Mrs. Darling) and Mary Brian (Wendy) became close friends:

"We had to work together to get the feeling of the picture, but we weren't photographed together. The director of special effects at Paramount at that time was Roy Pomeroy, and I got to know him and his wife. I found out he'd been carrying my head around with him for years. In New York, before I left there, Djinsky, a Russian sculptor, had started to sculpt me, and never quite finished because I was signed up and sent out here. But Roy Pomeroy liked the head so much that he took it. I don't know what happened to my poor old head!"

Born Virginia La Buna in Brooklyn, New York, on June 26, 1904, the actress used her stepfather's name of Brown when she entered the "Fame and Fortune" contest organized in 1919 by the fan magazine, *Motion Picture Classic*. The organizers felt that "Brown" was too common a name, and so gave her the name of Virginia Faire. When she discovered that there was already an actress named Elinor Fair, Ginnie decided to reclaim Brown. The actress had already had some screen experience as an extra in New York, and when the judges, including Cecil B. DeMille, Richard Barthelmess, Olga Petrova, and James Montgomery Flagg saw a screen test, they determined she was the obvious winner:

"Then I was signed by Universal. The prize was the possibility of getting a contract. Of course, I wasn't sixteen yet, so I had to be apprenticed to Universal. I came out, and the first thing they did was stick me into Western two-reelers. I had learned to ride, English saddle of course, in Central Park, so they immediately put me in a Western in a Western saddle. The horse took off, I managed to get in the saddle, and the cowboys applauded. I didn't know it, but I had made a flying mount.

"They were mostly two-reelers. I did make one five-reeler [*Under Northern Lights*, 1920], but I don't remember the names. I guess I wanted to forget the names of those. I was there for not quite a year. My salary was going up too fast for them. They wanted to change the contract, and they also wanted me to do a serial. I guess maybe I had a lot of fight in me. I said no, I wouldn't do a serial and I didn't want to do any more Westerns. So we broke the contract just as it was."

Robert Brunton, who owned the Brunton Studios, became her personal manager, and he produced *Without Benefit of Clergy* (1921), in which Ginnie has the leading role of Ameera. The film is an adaptation of the Rudyard Kipling novel, and the author was sufficiently interested in the production to execute sketches for the props and sets. "That really started me in good parts," said Faire. "It was called an artistic triumph. Those artistic triumphs don't usually make money, but at least it did give me the recognition for better parts." The film's director, James Young, wanted the actress for the title role in *Trilby* (1923), but instead she foolishly agreed to star opposite Van Mattimore (who later changed his name to Richard Arlen) in *Vengeance of the Deep* (1923), because it was to be shot in Honolulu. "A very bad picture."

While she was occasionally under contract to major studios, including First National, Faire notes that she fared better as a freelancer: "We all used to do quickies in between [major productions] because it was good money, twice as much as you got for a big studio production. And nobody looked down on it because everybody did it. We worked fast in those days." There were lesser features such as *Thundergate* (1923), *The Lightning Rider* (1924), and *The Thoroughbred* (1925), as well as major productions, including *Monte Cristo* (1922) and *Romance Ranch* (1924) with John Gilbert at Fox, and *The Temptress* (1926) with Garbo at MGM:

"That was just her second picture in this country, and she had a difficult time with the English language. Mauritz Stiller was a big director in Sweden, but he, by this time, I guess was a pretty sick man, although nobody seemed to know it. And every scene she did, he'd make her do over twenty times at least. Her fingers and everything had to be exactly right. The veins used to stand up on his head. You could just see them. And all they were getting in the front office, in the rushes, were close-ups of Garbo. The poor girl was in tears most of the time. Finally, they took him off after two weeks. They put Fred Niblo on the picture, and he finished it.

"Garbo was difficult and remote. We all tried—Lionel Barrymore, Tony Moreno—everybody tried to make her feel at home, but she was upset that Stiller was taken off. She was in a foreign country. It was impossible to get close to her. I know I had one beautiful costume at the end, because I end up getting Tony. She had all these beautiful costumes, and I was in those gaucho things all the time. She was so mad. The only time I ever saw sparks fly. She didn't like that. That's kind of a catty thing to tell about her, but even the best of them have their peculiarities."

His People (1925) is, arguably, the best Jewish-themed film to come out of Hollywood in the 1920s, a vivid drama of Jewish life on New York's lower East Side and the problems that modern society can create for those rooted in orthodox Jewish life. Credit for the film's greatness belongs to director Edward Sloman, to leading Rudolph Schildkraut and also to Virginia Brown Faire as Ruth Stein, to whom Schildkraut's son has become engaged: "I remember Rudolph Schildkraut. He was so wonderful. His son and I were engaged, and he was not invited. His son was shunning him and apparently trying to keep him under cover. But he did come. I was supposed to talk to him, and I became so enthralled, just watching him, and the tears starting rolling down my face."

In all, Virginia Brown Faire made credited appearances in more than forty silent films. And there are uncredited roles. She recalls being in the Will Rogers vehicle *Doubling for Romeo* (1922) and playing "The Spirit of Portugal" in *The Lost World* (1925). The actress was also tested by D.W. Griffith, whom she described as "a cruel taskmaster," for a role in *Drums of Love* (1928), but her character was cut before the film began shooting.

As with her contemporaries, Virginia Brown Faire did not find the transition to sound easy, despite a most pleasing voice. There were vaudeville appearances and also a Los Angeles stage production of *The Dybbuk*. In the latter, the actress learned to talk with a baritone voice as the director would not allow the young male lead to talk off stage with her mouthing his words, a theatrical device utilized in the New York production. On screen, Virginia Brown Faire played the maid in Frank Capra's production of *The Donovan Affair* (1929): "I remember Agnes Ayres. They had to have some screams. She'd been taking elocution lessons, getting ready for talkies, but every time she'd scream, she'd blow something, one of the tubes. So I ended up doing the screaming. Apparently, I didn't scream quite as loud."

Virginia Brown Faire continued to act through 1934, generally in Westerns, returning to her screen roots, including three directed by Duke Worne, whom she married in 1930 (after an earlier marriage from 1927 to 1928 to cowboy actor Jack Dougherty). Her marriage to businessman William Bayer later in the 1930s marked an end to the actress's screen career, although she did some radio work in Chicago and also appeared in a number of industrial films produced in the city, along with former silent actors Cullen Landis and Allan Forrest.

The last time we saw Virginia Brown Faire, late in 1979, her face evidenced the cancer that was to end her life on June 30, 1980, but she was still very much a beautiful woman. One could well understand why director Preston Sturges, upon being introduced to her by Priscilla Bonner, had commented that she had "a face like an old Italian coin."

Bibliography

Allen, Barbara. "A Rose in the Bud." *Motion Picture Classic*, June 1920, pp. 46–47, 86.
Cheatham, Maude. "Fulfilment." *Motion Picture*, July 1921, pp. 28–29, 87.
Ogden, Helen. "A Star's Balance Sheet." *Picture-Play*, May 1925, pp. 49, 100.

Bess Flowers in *A Woman of Paris* (1923).

BESS FLOWERS

The number of Hollywood extras is probably in the hundreds of thousands. As early as November 1934, *Photoplay* reported some 17,541 individuals registered as extras with Central Casting. Among the number of small part and bit players available at that time were former stars, including Monte Blue, Betty Blythe, Mae Marsh, and Dorothy Phillips, and silent directors, including Francis Ford, Frank Reicher and George Melford. One-time stars might become extras, but the only extra ever to be accorded the celebrity and fame of stardom is Bess Flowers.

A statuesque beauty of silent films, with the coming of sound, Bess Flowers became the most famous of extras, billed as Hollywood's best dressed extra. Easily recognizable at five feet, eight inches, the actress was noted for the style, quality, and quantity of the gowns in her wardrobe, along with her ability to wear them with panache. "I was always clothes-conscious," she explained. "I wanted to be an individual always, never one of the horde. Mitch Leisen started making clothes for me at Paramount, when he was head designer there. He used to rave about my figure, and he introduced me to Walter Plunkett at MGM as a wearer of beautiful clothes." Through purchasing clothing made by the studios for her various roles, Bess Flowers was able to build up an impressive wardrobe. The casting director would telephone to ask if she had a particular costume, and, if she did, as was generally the situation, the part was hers.

The male equivalent of Bess Flowers was Paul Bradley, who pointed out to me that in order to get better work, one had to be very well dressed with a good wardrobe. He entered films in 1922 and soon boasted four suits, a topcoat, a tuxedo and tails. Prior to the advent of Central Casting, extras such as Bradley and Flowers would register with David Allen's Screen Service, located on South Broadway in downtown Los Angeles. The studios picked up the cost of the service and paid extras three dollars a day plus a boxed lunch. "Some people worked for five dollars and no box lunch," recalled Bradley. "The better extras worked for $7.50 and $10. That was the highest amount for extra work."

Bess Flowers was born in Sherman, Texas, on November 23, 1898, and the story of her entry into film reads rather like a movie plot: "My father was very strict, and when I had a date my poppa came in and just bawled the boy out. And I was furious with father. My momma used to keep extra money in the sugar bowl and I thought to myself, 'I'm going to take that money and I'm going to New York because I want to be an actress.' As I went to the station, I saw a great big sign with oranges growing which said California. 'What the devil,' I said, 'I'll go to California and get in pictures.' So I did. I got a job the first day I ever went on an interview."

The title of that first production is unknown, but it was at Metro and the year was 1922. It was the first of more than 350 feature films, ending with *Good Neighbor Sam* in 1964. Bess Flowers's first major appearance is in Chaplin's *A Woman of Paris* (1923). Here she is the model, naked except for a band of cloth wrapped around her body, which is slowly unrolled as she stands on a podium. The concept is not original; it was presented, in reverse, on the vaudeville stage in the 1920s through the 1940s by Alphonse Berg, slowly draping his model with a bolt of material that he would style into an elegant dress.

"I admired Chaplin so extravagantly," Bess told me, "Every morning in my dressing room was one American Beauty rose with a long stem. And the fire was on. He introduced me to Rupert Brooke's poetry. If he couldn't start a scene, he'd go back in the flaps and play the violin until he got an inspiration."

There were occasional performances as a leading lady to Lefty Flynn, John Bowers, and Fred Thomson in the 1920s: "They liked tall women, because they didn't have to bend down to kiss them and ruin their profile." But, basically, Bess Flowers settled for minor roles. Director Frank Lloyd had told her, "You'll be selected to work with principals because you're tall, but when you get older, you'll be a good character woman."

She made an easy transition to sound—her slight Texas drawl was very attractive—making her debut opposite Chic Sales in the 1928 Fox comedy short, *Ladies Man*. During the silent era, director James Cruze admired and used her in most of his films, from *Hollywood* (1923) onwards; with the coming of sound, she became a regular performer in the films of Frank Capra and Gregory La Cava. The actress was as much at home in comedy as in drama, playing Stan Laurel's wife in *We Faw Down* (1928) and a frequent foil for the Three Stooges in their Columbia shorts.

Unlike many of her contemporaries, she was not always willing to accept any part. She would not work at the Fox Western Avenue studio or at Universal in the early years, rejecting the latter, as she bluntly put it, because it had dirty toilets. (A complaint that I recall Broderick Crawford also making to me.) She remembered, "Once I rushed to go for an interview at some studio and the man had his feet up on the desk. Well, I walked out—I wouldn't even stay and talk to him, because I don't approve of a man meeting a woman with his feet up on the desk. I have principles and ethics for myself, and I didn't cut them one damn bit to work."

Looking through a Bess Flowers filmography, one is at first struck by the number of famous Hollywood titles here, from *Blonde Venus* in 1932 through *Mr. Deeds Goes to Town* (1936), *Holiday* (1938) and *Now Voyager* (1942) to *Singin' in the Rain* (1952). One is equally impressed by the lack of ego. Bess Flowers could play a major role with Colleen Moore in *Irene* (1926), and that same year appear as a walk-on in *Old Ironsides*. With typical good humor, she would lose a scene opposite Kathryn Grayson because her dress clashed with that of the star. She could handle dialogue scenes with Herbert Marshall in *Forgotten Faces* (1936) and Anne Baxter in *All about Eve* (1950), and then, in following films, appear as nothing more than an extra in the crowd without discomfort to her vanity.

Bess Flowers had been twice married: to Cullen Tate, who was for many years Cecil B. DeMille's much put-upon assistant director, and, later, to Columbia studio manager William Holman. After retirement, she briefly managed an apartment complex, and then moved to the Motion Picture Country House, where she required special storage facilities for her wardrobe, and where she died on July 28, 1984. We would meet there often, and on one such occasion, she responded philosophically about her career, "I never amounted to a row of pins in the picture industry, but I made a good living. I'm lazy, from the South, so I never took anything that was hard. I was always good to Bess."

Bibliography

Harris, Warren G. "Bess Flowers." *Film Fan Monthly*, January 1972, pp. 21–24.
Slide, Anthony. "Bess Flowers: Hollywood's Best Dressed Extra." *Films in Review* June/July 1984, pp. 365–368.

GRETA GARBO. *See* **THE LEGENDS**

HOWARD GAYE

Crucial roles in *The Birth of a Nation* (1915) and *Intolerance* (1916) are played by a statuesque actor who has never received any recognition in his lifetime or since. The actor is an Englishman, Howard Gaye (Hitchin, Hertforshire, May 23, 1878–London, December 26, 1955), and the characters he created on screen are General Robert E. Lee and Christ. Not a bad combination.

Gaye was a well-educated young man whose father co-owned London's Gaiety Theatre. He had been a newspaper reporter in England and decided to visit America in 1912. While staying at the Hollywood Hotel, he was introduced to actor Carlyle Blackwell and invited to join the Kalem Company. After appearing in a handful of Kalem productions, Gaye spoke with D.W. Griffith and was hired in 1914 as a member of the director's stock company. Actor and assistant director George Siegmann gave Gaye a portrait of Robert E. Lee and asked if he could make up exactly like the Confederate general. The actor spent three hours on the facial makeup, using putty to create high cheekbones and to alter the contours of his nose, together with white crepe hair for the beard and moustache.

Christ had first been portrayed on screen in a feature film by another Englishman, R. Henderson Bland, in the 1912 Kalem production of *From the Manger to the Cross*. It is, of course, obvious typecasting for an Englishman to play Christ in that God is known to be an Englishman, and so, by natural deduction, is his son. Howard Gaye was "nailed" to the cross for three hours during the filming of *Intolerance*, with shooting beginning at dawn. George Siegmann accidentally hit the actor's toe with hammer during the "nailing" and Gaye's blood added to the realism. It was Howard Gaye's opinion that the long shooting schedule for one scene was deliberate on Griffith's part in order that the director would "wear me out physically."

Howard Gaye again played Christ on screen in Metro's 1918 release of *Restitution*, which the actor also directed. It was a silly anti-German Biblical epic, with Satan helping Kaiser Wilhelm. The actor's performance as Christ certainly had an impact on those around him, and years later, Lillian Gish wrote to his widow that on a 1955 visit to Jerusalem she and sister Dorothy expected to see Howard Gaye coming down the street at any moment.

Aside from *The Birth of a Nation* and *Intolerance*, Howard Gaye was also featured by Griffith in a number of Fine Arts productions of 1916, including *Daphne and the Pirate*, *Flirting with Fate*, *The Devil's Needle*, and *Diane of the Follies*. He had supporting roles in half a dozen feature films of the teens, most notably in the 1917 William Fox production of *The Scarlet Pimpernel*, in which Sir Percy Blakeney is played by Dustin Farnum.

Gaye acquired many of his later roles because of his makeup ability. For example, he was paid $350 a week to play the Duke of Norfolk in Mary Pickford's 1924 production of *Dorothy Vernon of Haddon Hall*. Gaye is a French aristocrat in Rex Ingram's *Scaramouche* (1923), and he helped George Siegmann with his makeup as Danton, creating smallpox marks on the actor's face. Gaye's last U.S. feature is *Dante's Inferno*, in which a millionaire is given a tour of hell. Released by Fox in September 1924, with British actor Lawson Butt as Dante and Gay as Virgil, the film's chief claim to fame is the suggested nudity in several of the scenes.

Back in England, Gaye found little worthwhile employment in the British film industry, but he did lecture on his career in Hollywood and he also wrote an unpublished autobiography, *So This Was Hollywood*. The latter was given to me by Gaye's widow, who, like her husband, ended her days in a small apartment close to Wembley Stadium, the home of Britain's soccer Cup Final and, more recently, rock concerts. It was about as far removed from the glamor of Hollywood as it is possible to be.

Note: A copy of Howard Gaye's autobiography is at the Museum of Modern Art, and the original is on deposit at the Margaret Herrick Library of the Academy of Motion Picture Arts and Sciences.

LILLIAN GISH

There is a title that describes Lillian Gish's title character in *Romola* (1925) as "learned of books but of the world untaught." That probably provides the shortest, and best, word portrait of Lillian Gish as seen on screen and as she exists in the public psyche. She certainly loved books, and her apartment was crowded with titles, many first editions signed by their famous authors. The Gish characters were generally ethereal, unworldly and unsuspecting of the evils of society, of which they were often made abruptly and dangerously aware. Be it the mulatto Silas Lynch in *The Birth of a Nation* (1915), von Strohm, the Hunnish soldier in *Hearts of the World* (1918), a brutal father in *Broken Blossoms* (1920), the debauched Lennox Sanderson in *Way Down East* (1920), or the revolutionary mob in *Orphans of the Storm* (1922), Lillian Gish faced considerable danger on screen. She won out through a strength of character that is symbolic of Lillian Gish in real life. She was always strong, always a fighter, taking up causes as varied as the isolationist America First prior to World War Two, a commemorative stamp for her mentor D.W. Griffith, or the need to preserve America's newsreels. As a child, Lillian had been told by her mother to project her voice in order that it might be heard in the theatre by those seated in the furthest row. She never ceased projecting her voice and her image as a legendary actress on screen and on stage.

Lillian was always the consummate professional. As a young actress, she faced horrific working conditions, extreme cold, and extreme heat in *Way Down East* (1920) and *The Wind* (1928) and never complained. At a time of scandal in the film industry, Gish told *The Moving Picture World* (March 4, 1922), "I have heard that there are terrible people in the movies, but I never see them. And there are terrible people everywhere for that matter. Why even the weather is not always what it should be." In later life, she never openly groused about a location or work demand, at times to the irritation of younger actors and actresses, who saw no reasons to extend the harsh circumstances of early filmmaking through to the present. She was always on time, always knew her lines—just as mother taught her. "Speak clearly and loudly otherwise another little girl will get the part," said Gish's mother, and I am sure that Lillian always worried about that other little girl waiting in the wings.

Jane Wyatt, who appeared with Lillian on Broadway in 1934 in Philip Barry's *The Joyous Season*, told me, "I remember coming to the first rehearsal. We were all in awe of her, and she was so mysterious. She came in with a great coat to the floor and a hood. And she knew all her lines! Then she impressed me because she didn't have a theatre maid, and everybody had a theatre maid."

There is no question that even contemporary audiences could sometimes find a Lillian Gish performance irritating. "Lillian Gish weeps like a fish," wrote one disgruntled fan. "The mood in which to go to the theatre is one of naïve vacuity, expecting nothing," opined Robert Benchley in the old *Life* humor magazine. "Try to look like a close-up of Lillian Gish." In the December 1926 edition of *Photoplay*, editor and publisher James R. Quirk wrote a most outspoken attack on an actress, whose salary at MGM was at the time the highest paid to any performer and, in reality, over $7,000 a week:

"Lillian Gish continues to demonstrate that virtue can be its own reward to the tune of six thousand bucks every week. Even as Hester Prynne in *The Scarlet Letter*, she proves conclusively that babies are brought by storks. I'd pay triple admission to see her play *Madam Bovary*.

"In the last twelve years she has been saved just in the nick of time from the brutal attack of 4,000 German soldiers, 2,000 border ruffians and 999 conscienceless men about town. Some day I hope the American hero breaks a leg and fails to get there before the German soldier smashes in the door."

I first met Lillian Gish on August 30, 1969. She was in London to present her one-woman show, *Lillian Gish: The Movies, Mr. Griffith and Me*, and I had prepared the printed program handed out to the audience. We meet at the Connaught Hotel, where Lillian always stayed when in England, and she inscribed for me a copy of her autobiography, which has the same title as her show. She also spent a couple of hours talking about various aspects of her career, an interview in which she was surprisingly frank in view of our never having previously met, and one which is often quoted by other authors.

The Lillian Gish career scarcely needs recording here. There can be few who are not aware of her devastating performances for D.W. Griffith in *The Birth of a Nation*, *Hearts of the World*, *Broken Blossoms*, *Way Down East*, and *Orphans of the Storm*. Griffith must have first become aware of the unique quality of her acting when he directed her at American Biograph. Lillian and younger sister Dorothy made their debut there in *The Unseen Enemy*, released on September 9, 1912, a one-reel suspense drama featuring the pair. *The Mothering Heart*, a two-reeler, released on June 21, 1913, first demonstrated the emotional intensity of which Lillian was capable. As a wife who has discovered her husband's infidelity, and, later, lost her baby, Lillian's anguish is almost unbearable to watch as she walks in the garden, destroying all the flowers and plants around her. As she and husband (Walter Miller) are reunited, a title asks, "Forgiveness—Is there any greater act?" It would appear not from a viewing of this, arguably the most moving of the American Biograph shorts.

After leaving Griffith, Lillian continued as a major star of the silent screen, appearing in *The White Sister* (1923), *Romola* (1925), *La Bohème* (1926), *The Scarlet Letter* (1926), *The Wind* (1928), and others. With the coming of sound, her importance in the industry dwindled. She is good in *His Double Life* (1932), but not as good as Gracie Fields is as the same character in the 1943 remake, *Holy Matrimony*. Gish's comeback role in *Commandos Strike at Dawn* (1942) is hardly worthy of consideration, and many of her later films were not really worth the effort. In a way, she returned triumphantly to the screen not in the 1940s but in 1955 under Charles Laughton's direction in *The Night of the Hunter*. Here, Lillian is the mother figure, suffering the little children to come unto her, harsh at times, sometimes angry, but always loving and forgiving. Sensibly Laughton chooses to end the film with Lillian, symbolic of her burgeoning status as a legend, a link not only with the past in which the film is set but also the past as represented by a directorial and pictorial style heavily influenced by both D.W. Griffith and German expressionism.

Lillian, of course, was never a mother, and, as one perceptive female viewer pointed out to me, she was obviously uncomfortable with infants. In *Way Down East*, in which she baptizes her dying child, the actress has no idea how to hold the baby.

Followers of the Gish screen career might be concerned as to how it would end after watching her playing worthless roles in worthless films such as *Hambone and Hillie* (1984) and *Sweet Liberty* (1986). When in 1987 it was announced that she was to co-star with Bette Davis in Mike Kaplan's production of *The Whales of August*, enthusiasm was mingled with anxiety when Lindsay Anderson was hired as the director. How could the man responsible for such raw, naked drama as *This Sporting Life* and *If...* handle Lillian Gish? Surprisingly well. He controlled whatever troubling mannerisms Gish and Davis might have adopted during their long careers, kept both under control, and gave Lillian one last great movie scene. On the 46th wedding anniversary of her character, Sarah, she sits at a table, with a white rose "for truth" and a red rose "for passion," and with a glass of wine in hand talks to her long dead husband of the day's happenings. It is a screen moment as intense in its dramatic simplicity as anything D.W. Griffith could have contemplated.

Despite the paucity of great film roles in the sound era, Lillian Gish was able to continue her career and endure on stage. Also, with surprising speed, she gained legendary status, something that the actress most carefully nurtured. She was always someone special; as early as 1925, one fan magazine writer commented that to interview Lillian Gish was a privilege and a pleasure. Lillian played with the truth, even changing the year of her birth in Springfield, Ohio, on October 14, from 1893 to 1896. She would recount stories of the making of her films that were not perhaps always completely accurate but which entertained and enthralled her audience. She behaved in the manner of a legend but at the same time never lost personal touch with her fans. Lillian was always overly gracious in responding to fan mail, and after a performance of her one-woman show, she would never leave the auditorium until requests for autographs from every member of the audience had been granted.

Lillian Gish always knew what to say to make one feel special. I recall she and James Frasher, her longtime manager, friend, and companion, coming to my house to pick me up. Lillian's first words upon seeing my somewhat humble abode were, "Truly you live in beauty." I was completely entranced but later somewhat nonplussed to discover that she said exactly the same thing upon seeing where anyone lived.

Thanks in large part to Jim Frasher, it has been my good fortune to be with Lillian on a number of special occasions. Our mutual, close friend was Herb Sterne, who double-dated with Lillian, Griffith, and Griffith's wife Evelyn in the 1940s. Lillian and Herb correspondended on a regular basis, with most of the former's comments directed to Herb's cat, Squire Bartlett, and signed Anna Moore. (*Way Down East* was Herb's favorite film.) When Lillian did the Blackglama advertisement, "What Becomes a Legend Most?," she sent a copy to Squire with the inscription, "My fur vs. yours. How's this for the cat's meow?" It was that sort of relationship that Herb enjoyed with Lillian.

Whenever she was in town, Lillian would have lunch with Herb, and I was also lucky enough to be invited. Herb was a resident of the Motion Picture Country House and another resident, Mary Astor, also joined us on at least one occasion. At the time she directed her only feature film, *Remodeling Her Husband* (1920), starring sister Dorothy and her husband James Rennie, Lillian also devoted an entire Sunday to directing Mary Astor's screen test.

Mary Astor was one of the few film performers with whom Lillian was close. She really did not know many of her contemporaries. Once we stood talking in the parking lot at the Motion Picture Country House, and Mary Brian and Harriet Nelson came by. Knowing them both, I introduced them to Lillian, who obviously had no idea who they were. Lillian also had an inability to understand that other actresses were not like her. Herb Sterne remembered that once at Pickfair, Gish chastised Mary Pickford for giving a pension to an American Biograph actress. "She had the same opportunites as us," argued Lillian. "No, we had talent," responded Pickford.

I have a tenuous link to Lillian's last and seldom noted contribution to film. In 1988, I was commissioned by Boss Film Corporation to write a treatment for a ten-minute epilogue to *Intolerance*, which was to be filmed in 70mm and screened after a Japanese presentation of the feature. The music for the epilogue was played live by a symphony orchestra, and the only recorded words heard were those of Lillian Gish. The comments were "lifted" from various interviews, but there were a couple of potential quotes that could not be found in such sources. I wrote these in the style of Lillian Gish, as represented in her autobiography, and she recorded them in her New York apartment. A year after making *The Whales of August* and five years prior to her death on February 27, 1993, Lillian sounds old, but there is still strength to her voice, and, I have to admit, she did choose to add a couple of words of her own to my dialogue. What becomes a legend most asked the Blackglama advertisement. Immortality. And Lillian has certainly earned that.

Note: Lillian Gish's papers are in the Billy Rose Theatre Collection of the New York Public Library.

Bibliography

Affron, Charles. *Lillian Gish: Her Legend, Her Life.* New York: Scribner, 2001.

"Before They Were Stars: Lillian Gish." *New York Dramatic Mirror,* April 3, 1920, pp. 642, 661.

Bodeen, DeWitt. "Lillian Gish: The Movies, Mr. Griffith, and Me." *The Silent Picture,* no. 4, autumn 1969, pp. 2–4.

Brownlow, Kevin. "Lillian Gish." *Griffithiana,* October 1993, pp. 4–11.

"Conversation with Lillian Gish." *Sight and Sound,* Winter 1957/58, pp. 128–130.

Frasher, James, ed. *Dorothy and Lillian Gish.* New York: Charles Scribner's Sons, 1973.

Gish, Lillian. "Beginning Young." *Ladies' Home Journal,* September 1925, pp. 19, 117–118, 120.

―――― with Ann Pinchot. *The Movies, Mr. Griffith and Me.* Englewood Cliffs, N.J.: Prentice-Hall, 1969.

Hall, Gladys. "Lights! Says Lillian!" *Motion Picture,* April-May 1920, pp. 30–31, 102–103.

――――. "The Dreamer Undismayed." *Motion Picture Classic,* June 1921, pp. 26, 73.

――――. "The Grave and Guileless Gish." *Motion Picture Classic,* July 1927, pp. 53, 85.

Hall, Gladys and Adele Whitely Fletcher. "We Interview the Two Orphans." *Motion Picture,* May 1922, pp. 47–49, 97.

Hall, Leonard. "Lillian Fights Alone." *Photoplay,* April 1929, pp. 63, 128–130.

Hergesheimer, Joseph. "Lillian Gish, *The American Mercury,* April 1924, pp. 397–402.

Johnson, Julian. "The Real Lillian Gish vs. the Imaginary." *Photoplay,* August 1918, pp. 24–26.

"Lillian Gish." *Moving Picture World,* June 20, 1914, p. 1702.

"Lillian Gish....Director." *The Silent Picture,* no. 6, spring 1970, pp. 12–13.

Loos, Anita. "Lillian Gish—A Tribute to a Trouper." *New York Times,* September 14, 1980, Section 2, pp. 1, 19.

Oderman, Stuart. *Lillian Gish: A Life on Stage and Screen.* Jefferson, N.C.: McFarland, 2000.

Paine, Arthur Bigelow. *Life and Lillian Gish.* New York: Macmillan, 1932.

Quirk, James R. "The Enigma of the Screen." *Photoplay,* March 1926, pp. 63, 129–130.

Silver, Charles, ed. *Lillian Gish.* New York: Museum of Modern Art, 1980.

LOUISE GLAUM. *See* THE VAMPS

DAGMAR GODOWSKY

With her jet black hair drawn tightly to the nape of the neck, Dagmar Godowsky had an exotic look, ideally suited to Spanish roles—or even pseudo-Chinese or Javanese. She was heavily reliant on makeup for her image on screen in the 1920s and throughout her life, but makeup could not conceal the effects of a love for good food. In later years, she did not weigh a ton, as she claimed, but she was certainly not the svelte actress who had portrayed Dona Florencia opposite Rudolph Valentino in *The Sainted Devil* (1924).

When I met her in London in December 1969, she was staying at the Strand Palace Hotel. It had special rates for "stars," she explained. She also noted, with a Continental accent that one fan magazine had likened to a rare combination of Lenore Ulric, Nazimova, and Anna Held, "I don't remember much, which is very good, because I don't remember to be unhappy."

Born in St. Petersburg (later known as Petrograd and then Leningrad), Russia, on November 24, 1896, Dagmar Godowsky was the daughter of pianist Leopold Godowsky, and with her father, she traveled to the United States, where she became a prominent New York socialite. (Her brother, Leopold, married George Gershwin's sister, Frances.) She became a screen star not through talent but rather because of an innate sense of the dramatic and because her family's place in society guaranteed prominent publicity for any endeavor with which she was associated: "Because my father was famous, I had the door opened, and I knew how to walk in."

Between 1919 and 1926, Dagmar appeared in some 24 feature films, starting at Universal. "I wanted to see the studios," she remembered, "So Pa, Charlie Chaplin and I went to Universal, and I don't think there was an hour before they put me in a film—I was so beautiful. A Western...."

"When I was with Universal, I go in to see my general manager, and there was a very young man with a desk who took messages, and I would sit on the desk and talk to him. I thought he'd get places. He was intelligent and nice. We became great friends. He got ill, and I used to send my chauffeur over with chicken broth. When he got better, Nazimova and her husband, Mae Murray and her husband, my husband and I went to the theatre, and I said to this chap, 'Why don't you come afterwards, around eleven. We will have late supper.' As we were coming from the theatre, I told these two great stars that I had asked this boy. Well they thought that was horrible. 'You asked an office boy with us!' This office boy happened to become one of the great men in Hollywood—Irving Thalberg. Irving saw their coldness and he never forgave them."

Nazimova was one of Godowsky's closest friends in Hollywood, and she cast Dagmar in her 1920 feature *Stronger than Death* but then cut the part from the film. Dagmar maintained that her first role on screen was in a Tom Mix Western, but as Mix was not making films with Universal at the time, it seems unlikely. Her first credited role is as a Russian in the 1919 Sessue Hayakawa feature *Bonds of Honor*.

At Universal, Dagmar Godowsky met Frank Mayo (1889–1963) and appeared with him in four 1920 features. She described him and Wallace Reid as "the handsomest men I've ever seen," which would imply that Mayo's photographs do not do him justice. The couple was married in Mexico in October 1921, and the marriage lasted through 1928. Godowsky again played with Mayo in Universal's 1922 production of *The Altar Stairs*. He is featured in Goldwyn's all-star production of *Souls for Sale* (1923), and Dagmar is also in the film, not in a character part but as one of thirty or more celebrities, including Chaplin, Erich von Stroheim, and Blanche Sweet, providing star appeal. The juxtaposition of her contribution to *Souls for Sale*, compared to that of Mayo, is indicative of the real reason that Dagmar Godowsky enjoyed a lengthy film career. Her role in society was a primary and well-publicized one, while her roles on screen were generally secondary—and in secondary productions. When she made her last film appearance in 1926, she was seventh billed in a feature, *In Borrowed Plumes*, from an obscure production company named Welcome Pictures and directed by Victor Halperin.

That is not to suggest that the actress was without talent, although with so few of her films extant it is difficult to make a valued judgment. She was a satisfactory "vamp," be it opposite Lionel Barrymore in *Meddling Women* or Valentino in *A Sainted Devil*, both released in 1924. The role in *A Sainted Devil* is her best-remembered performance but one that only came about because Jetta Goudal, who was to have played the part, refused to wear costumes designed by Valentino's second wife, Natacha Rambova. The first night she ever went to a nightclub, Dagmar recounted, was with her father and Enrico Caruso—"he was a singer," she adds for fear he might be unknown to me.

"Suddenly, Caruso got up and waved to someone frantically to come over. It was a fellow Italian, and he introduced him to us as Mr. Guiglielmi. And Mr. Guiglielmi was engaged to dance with unescorted and escorted women with whom their husbands didn't want to dance. Anyway, maybe a year or two afterwards, I was in Hollywood at Ships Café, and there were all the Metro stars standing around. I'm looking across the floor, and I can see Rudolph Valentino. Hello I say, and I introduced him to Nazimova and the others. None of them would say hello to him. When he went away, Nazimova said, 'How could you introduce that'—I won't mention what she said, I leave it to you.

"Valentino was a shy man, very retiring. He'd come to the house and make spaghetti. We danced a lot together, and I introduced him to both of his wives. I saw him when he was poor, I saw him when he got rich. I think he was one of the nicest, kindest persons. There wasn't an ugly thought about him."

With memories like that, Dagmar Godowsky did not really need much of a film career to ensure her popularity at social events. She published an auto-biography in 1958 and was threatening a second volume when her death put an end to the project on February 13, 1975 (in New York).

Bibliography

"Dagmar Wins a Part with Valentino." *Photoplay*, October 1924, pp. 36, 117.

Evans, Delight. "Kiss Me Frank." *Photoplay*, June 1922, pp. 41, 99.

Godowsky, Dagmar. "I Want to Be the Wickedest Woman on the Screen." *Photoplay*, May 1924,p.86.

———. *First Person Plural: The Lives of Dagmar Godowsky*. New York: Viking Press, 1958.

Oettinger, Malcolm H. "Dagmar the Wanderer." *Picture-Play*, November 1920, pp. 18, 85–86.

Peltret, Elizabeth. "Enter the Snake Woman." *Motion Picture Classic*, January 1921, pp. 32–33, 75.

KITTY GORDON. *See* **THE VAMPS**

JETTA GOUDAL

"Get the boy some cheese, Daddy." The boy is me, Daddy is the former silent art director Harold Grieve, and the speaker is his wife Jetta Goudal. The date is July 6, 1974, and the temperamental silent star is seated in a wheelchair and wearing a black veil. Despite the wheelchair, Jetta is every bit as domineering as she was on the set in the 1920s. She has just read my comments on her in *The Griffith Actresses* and announced that she should spank me. Based on the manner in which she addresses Harold Grieve, I have every reason to believe she is quite capable of putting me across her knee and dealing with me most severely. But Miss Goudal is forgiving. She is more than anxious to share her many glowing reviews with me, and some six hours later, I emerge from her apartment, dazed, exhausted, and more than a little bored.

Jetta had that effect on people. She did not tell a story once but would repeat it at each meeting. Any attempt at a change of subject was quickly stifled. Any conversation involving Harold Grieve's career was speedily halted. And woe betide to Daddy should he choose to interrupt. At one memorable gathering, Harold spoke up once too often and a furious Jetta ordered, "Daddy, go to your room."

I utilized the material obtained from Jetta for a chapter in my 1976 book, *Idols of the Silence*. From fear of retribution, I did not bother to send her a copy, but in May of 1978, Jetta wrote that she had seen the piece and that, perhaps not surprisingly in view of her ego, she had had the pleasure of reading and re-reading it. "I'd like to compliment you as well as thank you. It certainly covered my film career nobly." As a result, a friendship developed, conducted, of course, on Jetta's terms.

There would be dinners at the Tail o' the Cock, an old-fashioned and dignified restaurant on La Cienega Boulevard in Los Angeles. Some lunches took place at the Beach Club in Santa Monica, which Jetta and Harold had helped found. There would be occasional afternoon and evening visits to the apartment at Park La Brea, where Jetta and Harold had knocked together two one-bedroom units and created an elegant setting somewhat out of place in such a middle-class housing development. Telephone conversations were frequent and lasted an hour or more. During one such conversation in October 1978, Jetta talked nonstop for one hour and ten minutes. An actress was defined as "Someone who feels everything a thousand times deeper than anyone else....I'm 2,000 years old. I've gone through enough in life to fill 2,000 years."

Jetta was perhaps at her most outrageous when Volkswagen announced its latest vehicle, the Jetta. Little did the car manufacturer know that there really was a Jetta, who was furious that her name had been used without permission. It was bad enough that Jetta was now the name of a non-luxury car, but, even worse, it was the name of a car made by Germans! Miss Goudal spent many fruitless hours on the telephone to Volkswagen explaining her prominence in the Hollywood community, but all to no avail.

Friction arouse when Jetta demanded that I organize a tribute in her honor at the Academy of Motion Picture Arts and Sciences. Joan Crawford had had to wait until she died before receiving such a tribute. Jetta had no intention of waiting so long. I tried to explain to Jetta that it was not in my power to arrange such an event. I did persuade the Academy to agree to a Saturday afternoon presentation of one of Jetta's films and with commentary by whatever celebrities could be persuaded to pay her tribute. Jetta dismissed a Saturday afternoon screening as an insult to a star of her magnitude. It must be an evening program. Her friends had better things to do on a Saturday afternoon. Because I could not deliver an appropriate Academy tribute, I was dismissed apparently forever from her presence. Similarly, the Academy was struck from her will; her papers would no longer reside in its library but instead would be presented to the Library of Congress.

Jetta Goudal was born Henriette Goudeket, into a wealthy Orthodox Jewish family, in Amsterdam on July 12, 1891. Her origins were no secret in the Netherlands; in 1930, the Dutch magazine *Nova* noted that Jetta described herself as a "Parisienne," but that she was actually born in the shadow of the Westertoren, the tower of a church in the Jordaan district of Amsterdam. A sister, Bertha, was born three years earlier. Her father, Moses, was a diamond merchant who died in his Amsterdam home in 1942; her mother died in 1921. I once plucked up the courage to ask if she had been born in Holland. The answer was, "No, not really. I lived there....If I needed help from anyone in Holland, I can assure you I would not have gotten it."

When Jetta completed an information sheet for the Paramount Publicity Department, she gave her date of birth as July 12, 1901, her birthplace as Versailles, and her father's name as Maurice Guillaume Goudal, a lawyer. Jetta's accent was long a mystery to her friends. It was a curious mix of French, Italian, and Spanish. At times, one had the suspicion, there was a bit of German in there but that seemed unlikely in view of her outspoken hatred of anything Germanic. There was always something cosmopolitan, something continental, about her. With her jet black hair and those dark eyes, even in old age as sharp as steel, one could understand how some contemporary writers might have wondered if she was of Javanese ancestry. Whatever her ethnic background, whatever her accent, both were somehow most appropriate to her name.

Jetta's determination to hide her background was most certainly approved of by her producers. In 1927, one publicist, Sig Schlager, wrote to her of the importance of shrouding what went before her motion picture career in utmost mystery, declaring it a splendid policy that should be rigidly maintained. Not only did Jetta turn her back on the Netherlands, but also she rejected her Jewish roots. She was a self-loathing Jew, for whom anti-Semitism became a part of her private image.

I recall one horrendous evening in 1981 when she invited me to join her and Harold at a private screening of George Cukor's latest (and last) film, *Rich and Famous*, at MGM. I should have been forewarned. The last time Jetta had been known to view one of Cukor's films was back in 1930. She had allowed the director to drive with her to the premiere of his *The Royal of Broadway Family*, but en route he had started smoking and he had promptly been expelled from the car. Once seated in the MGM theatre, Jetta surveyed the audience and she and Harold both noted the presence of a "hook-nosed Jewess" who just happened to be a leading Los Angeles socialite. The atmosphere got cold around our seats and began to freeze over as the film commenced and each four-letter word and, above all, a male nude scene was greeted by Jetta with a baleful stare at either me or her husband. At the film's close, Goudal announced very loudly that had she not been in her wheelchair, she would have stalked out of the theatre in disgust

Called either Juliet or Jetje by her family, Jetta was well educated. One of her uncles, Maurits, was the third husband of Colette, and so, perhaps, it is not surprising that Jetta should have been fluent in French. She came to the United States in 1917, following a man with whom she was in love but who would have nothing to do with her. A sensible guy. In New York, she worked in an office and then tried her luck in the theatre. The parts were relatively small, and the plays—*The Hero, The Elton Case, Simon Called Peter*—forgotten, but they did bring Jetta to the attention of director John S. Robertson, who tested and cast her for the role of Pilar in the screen adaptation of Joseph Hergesheimer's novel, *The Bright Shawl*, about to begin filming on location in Cuba. Jetta joined a cast of major names—Mary Astor, Richard Barthelmess, Dorothy Gish, Edward G. Robinson—in a production that made good use of costumes and location but was short on dramatic impact.

Prior to the April 1923 release of *The Bright Shawl*, Jetta took on the role of the tubercular woman of the slums in Sidney Olcott's *Timothy's Quest*, a charming drama of a young boy and girl in search of parental love. Jetta is surprisingly effective as the pathetic and waif-like mother, who dies early in the proceedings but receives no screen credit. Later in 1923, Olcott again cast the actress, this time as the Ayah in the George Arliss vehicle *The Green*

Goddess. Jetta's exotic looks caught the attention of the critics and led to the 1924 signing of a three-picture contract with Paramount.

Open All Night (1924), *The Spaniard* (1925), and *Salome of the Tenements* (1925) were not great films, but they did give Jetta the opportunity to display a modicum of acting talent. She was particularly proud of *Salome of the Tenements*, in which she plays a ten-year-old child from New York's East Side tenements. Anyone who knew the actress would find the casting somewhat hard to contemplate, and I, certainly, would not disagree with Jetta's claim that the performance was her "tour de force." She would often retell the story of children from the slums being utilized as extras in the production: "Even the street children, all brought in from the ghetto, did not realize that I was not one of them, which was and which I considered one of the greatest compliments."

Open All Night, which tries desperately to be sophisticated but finishes up being merely gauche, was Jetta's first production in California. Driving to the premiere with director Paul Bern, the actress noted the various eating establishment displaying signs stating "Open All Night." She turned to Bern and congratulated him on the excellent publicity the film was receiving.

It was during the Paramount period that producers and directors became aware of Jetta's spirited disposition. Her temperament was legendary; she was the the most successful "storm and strifer" in film history who once kept an entire company waiting while she contemplated the need for a $200 or a $175 lace handkerchief that she was required to drop in a scene. Her arguments with costume designers were almost surreal. For one scene in *Three Faces East* (1926), costume designer Adrian had designed a white evening gown for the actress. Miss Goudal decided a black dress would be more appropriate. After much argument, as Jetta retold the story (again and again and again), she stayed up all night hand-sewing a black gown and triumphantly appeared on set in it the next day.

Legend has it that Jetta would visit costume designer Howard Greer, who would work with one seam on a dress for six hours. When the work was completed, Goudal would sigh, "Well, if this is what you call a dress, I'll wear it." And then she would wear it—in just that tone of voice.

When the Hollywood Walk of Fame was created by the Hollywood Chamber of Commerce in 1960, Jetta was "honored" with a star on Vine Street. The actress was outraged; not only was her star not on the main thoroughfare of Hollywood Boulevard, but it was in front of Home Savings and Loan, a bank with which Goudal had argued. In short order, the Jetta Goudal star was moved to Hollywood Boulevard, and the actress became the only honoree to have her star resited.

The Goudal temperament appears to have been displayed as early as *Salome of the Tenements*. While making the film, the studio sent her to dress designer Lucille to purchase some gowns. Despite the warm, sunny day, Jetta demanded the fire be lit immediately. After an hour of rejecting every gown on display, the actress declared an immediate need for dry toast and tea. The staff showed her the door.

Often with venomous rage, Jetta would deny that she was ever temperamental. Her claim always was that her temperamentality had been thought up as a publicity stunt by Paramount's publicity department and that it was not long before the studio and others began believing in it. "They have accused me of many things, but never of being dumb," Jetta angrily retorted.

No matter, Paramount did terminate her contract, claiming, in March 1925, that Goudal was too temperamental, entirely unmanageable, and that she delayed production for trivial reasons. Goudal sued for breach of contract but went ahead and signed a new contract with Cecil B. DeMille. It was a partnership both would regret. Perhaps DeMille more than Goudal, who made only one film actually directed by DeMille, *The Road to Yesterday*, released in November 1925. Joseph Schildkraut and Jetta are one of two couples hurled back in time as a result of a train crash. The wreck was the best thing in a very silly film. At one point, Jetta was to have appeared in DeMille's *King of Kings*. She was first cast as Mary Magdalene, but that role eventually went to Jacqueline Logan. Perhaps with a certain amount of wry humor, DeMille next cast her as "the afflicted woman" on the Via Doloroso but then, probably with great delight, deleted Jetta's footage from the production.

Under the DeMille contract, Jetta was primarily starred in films produced by DeMille but directed by others: *The Coming of Amos* (1925), *Three Faces East* (1926), *Her Man o' War* (1926), *Paris at Midnight* (1926), *White Gold* (1927), *Fighting Love* (1927), and *The Forbidden Woman* (1927). Thanks in large part to the direction of William K. Howard, *White Gold* presents the actress in a role with some substance, but basically Jetta was little more than a clotheshorse in the other films. In *Her Man o' War*, she looks very pretty in a fetching assortment of Alsacian peasant dresses, including a ludicrous hat in the form of a gigantic bow. Goudal sufficiently dominated the making of *Three Faces East* and *The Forbidden Woman* that she was able to write new endings for both films. While working on these films, Jetta would write to "Papa de Mille," as she called him. "The cameraman is very wonderful and likes to photograph me," she assured him. "He is very funny: no matter how big the close-up, he always wants to take a bigger one."

Jetta was to have appeared in three more DeMille-produced features, beginning with *The Leopard Woman*, but, on September 13, 1927, the *Los*

Angeles Times announced that the contract had been terminated by mutual consent. In reality, the consent was anything but mutual. DeMille claimed the actress had frequently walked off the set and demanded new directors. Jetta claimed only that she wanted to do everything to the best of her ability and that DeMille had demanded she take a fifty percent cut in salary. The actress was eventually awarded $31,000 in damages.

From DeMille, Jetta moved to MGM, appearing as the second lead in the 1928 Marion Davies vehicle *The Cardboard Lover*, directed by Robert Z. Leonard. The highspot of the film is a biting parody of Miss Goudal by Miss Davies, which the former claims was done with her full approval and with her designing the costume. Goudal was less happy with an impersonation of her performed by Lupe Velez, as part of a personal appearance tour the latter participated in to promote *Lady of the Pavements*. The film, released in February 1929 and directed by D.W. Griffith, has Goudal as a French countess who takes a woman of the streets, played by Velez, and trains her to win the love of the man, William Boyd, who has rejected her advances. There were stormy scenes on the set as Goudal displayed as much grandeur and hauteur as her character and insisted, yet again, on designing her own clothes.

Design, be it of clothes or interiors, was increasingly of interest to Jetta Goudal. She was invited by Paul Bern to help in the interior decoration of his home, and here she met Harold Grieve. Grieve had worked as art director on a number of major silent films, including *The Prisoner of Zenda* (1922), *Scaramouche* (1923), *Lady Windermere's Fan* (1925), and *So This Is Paris* (1926), and worked, in a secondary capacity, on *The Thief of Bagdad* (1924) and *Ben-Hur* (1926). The couple married on October 11, 1930, and Jetta became a dominant force in Harold's career. As she once commented, "People do not realize that behind Mr. Daddy is Mrs. Daddy." Probably Daddy was very aware of her presence as he designed the homes of Bing Crosby, Walt Disney, Cecil B. DeMille, John Gilbert, Edith Head, and others, as well as Colleen Moore's famous Doll's House and the Eisenhower White House.

It was a strange marriage but also presumably a happy one. If not outright gay, Harold Grieve was certainly bisexual. Jetta obviously tolerated her husband's lifestyle, provided he kept secret any sexual liaisons. She was happy to have a good-looking and successful man as a companion and, in all probability, expected no sexual contact in their marriage.

Jetta did make two last film appearances. She starred in the French-language version of *The Unholy Night* (*Le Spectre Vert*) for MGM in 1929 and was featured opposite Will Rogers in David Butler's 1932 production of *Business and Pleasure*. The teaming here might appear odd, but, in reality, Jetta was as much a stereotypical Midwesterner as Rogers. Her favorite television program was *The Lawrence Welk Show*, and, often, she would reject social engagements in favor of staying at home to listen to Welk's champagne music.

Miss Goudal and I did have one last meeting. Jetta invited me to dinner at the Tail o' the Cock. It was a horrific evening. Jetta wanted to sit at a round table but only a booth was available. A temper tantrum of titanic proportion followed. Dinner was ordered, but Miss Goudal refused to order anything for herself. She was simply too upset to eat. I was just glad to get away from there.

Jetta died on January 14, 1985. Her death certificate states she was born in France of unknown parentage. In 54 years of marriage, Harold Grieve never knew of Jetta's secret past. Harold asked that I come to the apartment and help pack up her papers for the Library of Congress. Despite Jetta's wishes, I did put aside duplicate still photographs, clippings, and other items for the Margaret Herrick Library of the Academy of Motion Picture Arts and Sciences.

Harold's health steadily declined, but he did come over to the house for a few parties. He also invited Robert Gitt and me to join him at the Beach Club for lunch. After the meal, he would insist that we accompany him to the volleyball court, where he would sit entranced, watching the scantily clad youths going after the ball. It was a pleasure obviously denied to him while Jetta was alive.

In old age, Harold became increasingly confused. At the same time, one had the distinct impression that he was not entirely unhappy no longer to be Mr. Jetta Goudal. He died at the age of 92 on November 3, 1993.

Bibliography

Bodeen, DeWitt. "Jetta Goudal." *Films in Review*, October 1974, pp. 449–466.

Busby, Marquis. "Sunday Night at Jetta's." *Photoplay*, May 1930, pp. 60, 94.

Carr, Harry. "Jetta and Her Temperament." *Motion Picture Classic*, October 1924, pp. 20–21, 78.

Clark, Francis. "Jetta Lives Down Her Past." *Photoplay*, August 1927, pp. 34–35, 131.

Cruikshank, Herbert. "I Was Never Temperamental." *Motion Picture*, July 1929, pp. 40, 98–99.

Donnell, Dorothy. "The Mistress of Mystery." *Motion Picture Classic*, February 1929, pp. 22, 84.

Durantz, Charles J. "Jetta Goudal—Aloof and Mysterious." *Cinema Art*, November 1926, pp. 18–19, 47.

Howe, Herbert. "A Parisian Chinese Lily." *Photoplay*, August 1923, p. 50.

Oettinger, Malcolm H. "Sapristi!—How Foreign!" *Picture-Play*, November 1923, pp. 22–23, 97.

ETHEL GRANDIN

In the mid- to late 1970s, a routine developed, with Robert Gitt and I screening films in the library at the Motion Picture Country House for Herb Sterne and for another resident, Ethel Grandin. I don't know quite how Ethel became involved, but she was relatively lonely and enjoyed the opportunity to talk, perhaps to have dinner, and then to look at films, including some of her own. She had no close friends at the facility, and as the years progressed, she lost the ability to speak. The problem was more psychological than physical, and it was if she had literally regressed to being once again a silent star. One would feel so helpless as she would break down and cry, but efforts to interest other residents in her plight seemed useless. "She's crying 'cause she's lonely," Rose Hobart told me dismissively. "Aren't we all?" Here was an institution for members of the film community, but Ethel was so old, her career so long ago, that she had nothing in common with performers or technicians whose film careers dated from the 1930s.

It was hard to accept Ethel Grandin as a film star. As winsome and diminutive in old age as she had been on screen, Ethel had little personality or character. It was easy to imagine her visiting, as she did, with the wife of Universal's Carl Laemmle, and the two of them enjoying their knitting as they sipped cups of tea. The memories of her career were never too specific or detailed, and film titles meant nothing: "They were all alike, and I've forgotten them. They're in the back of me."

Ethel Grandin was very old-fashioned; she was born—in New York on March 3, 1894—into another age of course, with different values. I had written about her in my 1978 book, *Aspects of American Film History Prior to 1920*. When I showed Ethel the text, she had one strong objection. I could not imagine what it might be as I was particularly laudatory to her. It transpired I had made reference to her being pregnant. She felt this was much too explicit a term and that I should change it to "with child." The whole world was perhaps a little frightening, and she welcomed the security—"I have a safe feeling, I feel safe out here"—provided by the Motion Picture Country House. She had moved there with her husband, when he became ill in 1958 and had become its longest-surviving resident.

At her mother's urging, Ethel had gone on stage in 1900 at the age of six. She appeared with Joseph Jefferson in *Rip Van Winkle* and toured with Chauncey Olcott, along with Lottie Pickford, Mary's sister. Mrs. Charlotte Pickford kept an eye on the young actress and probably urged her to enter films. In 1910, with her mother, Ethel went down to the American Biograph studio on East fourteenth Street and was interviewed by D.W. Griffith. The director pulled up her dress and inspected her legs. When Ethel began to pout and sulk, Griffith explained to her that he wanted to make sure she did not have bowlegs, as did so many of the actresses there. Despite knowing this to be true, Ethel was so outraged by Griffith's behavior that she refused to return to the studio the next day. Instead, she and mother went to Carl Laemmle's IMP Company; she was seen by Thomas H. Ince, who had just returned from directing Mary Pickford in Cuba, and was signed to a contract.

Mary Pickford was about to leave the company, and Ince saw something of a similarity between Ethel and Pickford; although she obviously lacked the latter's personality, Ethel had such physical Pickford attributes as long curls and dark hair. Coincidentally, Ethel played Pickford's sister in IMP's *The Toss of the Coin*, released on August 31, 1911. The studio was located on New York's fifty-sixth Street: "I think it was over at Ninth and Tenth Avenue, a terrible district then. There was just one big stage. Separate dressing rooms. I remember mine was right on the stage, and I lost a purse full of jewelry. It was taken. I have bad feelings about that!"

When Ince decided to enter independent production with the New York Motion Picture Company, he invited Ethel to come to California with him as his leading lady. Also in the group was cinematographer Ray Smallwood, who would later become a director and whom Ethel married in 1912. Ince wanted to make "real" Westerns, and the first such production was *War on the Plains*, a two-reel drama released on February 23, 1912, of which Ethel Grandin was the star. Production techniques were primitive: "They'd build a set and he would get the locations. You'd come in and do this and do that. We never read a script. Ince would tell us before each scene, and maybe once in a while we'd know the idea of the story."

In 1913, Carl Laemmle asked Ethel to return to his company, along with Ray Smallwood. So prominent a star was the actress at this time and so close was she to Laemmle that he paid her salary for three months while she went back east to visit her dying mother. She was the company's leading star, billed as "The Imp of the IMP Company." For Laemmle, Ethel starred in both Western and comedy shorts, and she played the title role in IMP's two-reel adaptation of *Jane Eyre*, released on February 9, 1914, with Irving Cummings as Edward Rochester.

Ethel also starred, along with Matt Moore and Jane Gail, in George Loane Tucker's 1913 production of *Traffic in Souls*, a melodrama of white slavery, produced in semi-secrecy without Laemmle's approval: "I was on salary of course, but they hadn't worked out my schedule. I was waiting for pictures to be written. They saw me in the studio and they said, 'Ethel, would you like to do a few scenes for us?' They said they had to finish very quickly, and I said,

'I'm available.' I had worked with George Loane Tucker many times as an actor. I didn't even read that story. I had no idea what it was, and so I worked one day, skipped a couple of days and did another scene, and so forth. I think I put in three or four days. I wasn't in very much of the story. I wasn't the star.

"I was very busy in those days. I had just returned from California, and I was busy getting a house in order and buying furniture. Also worrying about my little baby and the nurse. I didn't pay much attention. I thought I was doing them a favor.

"I think it was the Daly Theatre in New York, they had a prevue of it, and, of course, the picture people all came to see this. I was there with my husband, and I was so excited. I hadn't been to one of these showings ever before, because I was just a little girl really. Everyone that knew me came up and congratulated me, and I thought, 'Why?' I didn't know I was in an exceptional film. I didn't realize it was so big. It made a lot of money. And had they known it was going to be a success as it was, they would have collaborated on it more, put more story and more money in it."

The total budget for the film was less than $6,000, raised by Tucker, director Herbert Brenon, and others. In his *A Million and One Nights*, Terry Ramsaye claims that with *Traffic in Souls* the screen discovered sex. And how odd that Ethel Grandin, of all actresses, should have been a party to such a find. But, in reality, aside from the white slavery theme and what that implies, there is nothing sexual here. *Traffic in Souls* is important as one of the America's film industry's first feature-length productions, opening in November 1913, for its semi-documentary quality with exteriors on the streets of New York, and for an innovative, if intrusive, panoramic shot. Ethel recalled the "canvas sets, when you closed the door, they would shake like this, " and she also remembered that famous shot: "That was the first picture that had a panorama; they did it on a dolly, rolled the dolly along with the camera on it."

In the summer of 1914, Grandin and Ray Smallwood left Carl Laemmle and formed their own production company, the Smallwood Film Corporation, operating out of a rental studio at Central Park West and Amsterdam Avenue in New York: "It was the top of a building, and it had been a Turkish bath. It had a glass roof that let in a certain amount of light. It had a really large stage, and the dressing rooms downstairs." The first of the independent productions was the three-reel *The Adopted Daughter*, released on December 21, 1914, in which Ethel plays a dual role.

The company was relatively short-lived, and in 1915, Ethel Grandin retired from the screen in order to take care of her infant son. A year later, she agreed to return to the screen, and co-starred with Maurice Costello in the serial *The Crimson Stain Mystery*, produced by Erbograph and directed by

T. Hayes Hunter. The serial made good use of New York locations, and interior scenes were filmed at a studio on 135th Street.

Ethel claims to have enjoyed making *The Crimson Stain Mystery*, but it does not seem to have persuaded her to return permanently to the screen. When Ray Smallwood was hired by Metro to head its camera department, she came with him back to Los Angeles. Smallwood turned to direction in the early 1920s, and Ethel returned briefly to the screen in two 1921 films with Gareth Hughes, *Garments of Truth* and *The Hunch*, and the Charles Ray feature *A Tailor-Made Man* (1922).

Ray Smallwood died in 1964, and Ethel lived on for 24 years at the Motion Picture Country House and died there on September 27, 1988.

Bibliography

Bell, James. "Maurice Comes Back; So Does Ethel." *Photoplay*, January 1917, pp. 136–137.

Condon, Mabel. "Rain—and the Radiant Ethel Grandin." *Photoplay*, June 1914, pp. 91–95.

Katterjohn, Monte M. "A Film Star at Twenty." *Green Book Magazine*, August 1914, pp. 255–258.

RALPH GRAVES

Ralph Graves's goofy face and grin did not exactly match his muscular, boxer's body. On screen, his clothes never seemed quite to fit. He was a likeable character but not a great actor. He never seemed to know what to do with his hands. As he admitted, "I was no actor," and so perhaps the progression to writing, directing, and producing was natural, a career change that coincided with the end of the silent era.

In old age, Graves had a healthy contempt for a society that could relegate a great man such as D.W. Griffith to the gutter and that could denigrate a Rudolph Valentino because he was a foreigner. "We always look down on black people and uneducated people," fumed Graves. "Make yourself try and discount the Richard Nixons and the John Waynes. Just thinking about them makes me want to throw up."

The alcohol that he had consumed during the course of our interview might also have forced a lesser man to throw up. We were talking at his Santa Barbara home in the summer of 1973. I had arrived at 11:00 A.M. to find Ralph already drinking heavily. By dinnertime, I was amazed that he could still stand, let alone continue our meandering conversation.

The vodka certainly paved the way for an uninhibited discussion. With his current wife at his side, Graves spoke of a wedding night—"some other wife," insisted Mrs. Graves—when "this young, beautiful and wonderful girl found Mack Sennett, W.C. Fields and Gene Fowler all in bed with her. Four of us on the bed with this chaste, lovely girl who had just been robbed of her virginity." Amazingly, Graves also revealed homosexual liaisons ("I'd been in bed with a couple of fairies, no involvement"), intimate relationships with Noel Coward and Somerset Maugham, and, most extraordinary of all, a long-term gay affair in the 1920s with Mack Sennett: "I had an unholy relationship with Mack Sennett; two years of my life, every day, every night, were spent with Mack Sennett."

Born in Cleveland on July 23, 1900, Ralph Graves came from a wealthy family—"a good father and a questionable mother"—but jumped a freight train to get away from his parents and soon found himself up in Chicago. Here, he entered a contest organized by Universal to find a new leading man for actress Violet Mersereau. "A fat-faced, good-looking kid," Graves won the contest but instead of coming to Hollywood was found a position with the Chicago-based Essanay Company by Louella Parsons, who was then a newspaperwoman in the city. His first major screen role was as leading man to Mary MacLane in *Men Who Have Made Love to Me* (1918), based on the lurid sexual adventures of its star.

In 1919, Graves was signed by D.W. Griffith. "I was a good-looking man to Griffith," he recalled. "I was a little above the movies. My father left some money, I used to buy my clothes at Brooks Brothers, so I looked different to Griffith. He used to wear horrible clothes and murder the King's English, which I didn't. So he took an interest in me, and immediately signed me up to a contract at $200 to $300 a week." Griffith featured Graves in two 1919 productions, *Scarlet Days* and *The Greatest Question*, and starred him opposite Carol Dempster in the 1921 feature *Dream Street*.

Certainly not a great film, *Dream Street* is primarily of interest because of the director's spoken introduction and the inclusion of a title song, recorded on a sound-on-disc process, Kellum's Talking Pictures. "I recorded the song—it wasn't a bad song—and they cut the film into it," Graves told me. "I was amazed at my beautiful voice; I have a gorgeous voice, but nobody else knows it."

After *Dream Street*, Graves received a number of offers from other producers. The actor went to consult with Griffith and, as he had done with Blanche Sweet, Lillian Gish, and others, the director told him to go. "He kissed me and said, 'Go on, take it.' I wish I hadn't now."

The features in which Ralph Graves appeared in the 1920s were not memorable, but they did provide him with the opportunity to play opposite Colleen Moore, Miriam Cooper, Marjorie Daw, Marguerite de la Motte, Bessie Love, and Blanche Sweet. From 1923 through 1926 he was under contract to Mack Sennett, playing opposite Mabel Normand in *The Extra Girl* (1923) and starring in a series of two-reel comedy shorts.

Claiming that he was losing his hair and his sex appeal, Graves decided to become a director, initially for Harry Cohn at Columbia, although, in fact, he did continue acting until as late as 1949. For Columbia, in 1927, Graves directed himself and Shirley Mason in *Rich Men's Sons*, himself and Mildred Harris in *The Swell-Head*, and Marguerite de la Motte in *The Kid Sister*. Also in 1927, he wrote and directed *A Reno Divorce*, with May McAvoy, at Warner Bros.

At Columbia, Ralph Graves became associated with actor Jack Holt, the two generally playing tough military types, and with director Frank Capra, whom the actor had become familiar with at the Mack Sennett studios. "He was one of my gag-writers—a delightful guy. I brought him over to Harry Cohn," claimed Graves in a comment not supported by Capra's autobiography. Capra did star Ralph Graves in five features: *That Certain Thing* (1928), *Submarine* (1928), *Flight* (1929, for which the actor also provided the story), *Ladies of Leisure* (1930), and *Dirigible* (1931).

In the 1930s, Ralph Graves became an assistant at MGM to Irving Thalberg, "the most honest and straightforward person I ever met," and his presence on screen diminished. By the 1950s, he was retired but living well in Balboa, Holmby Hills, and eventually Santa Barbara, where he died on February 18, 1977.

Bibliography

Boone, Arabella. "Griffith's First Blonde Hero." *Photoplay*, October 1919, pp. 54–55.
Naylor, Hazel Simpson. "Half Priest." *Motion Picture*, April 1922, pp. 27, 86.
Remont, Fritzi. "The Grave Mr. Graves." *Motion Picture Classic*, November 1919, pp. 18–19, 86, 90.

ARCHER'S
STUDIOS
Hollywood

GILDA GRAY

"That was a very interesting picture," said Percy Marmont, discussing *Aloma of the* South Seas. "The snag was it had the shimmy dancer Gilda Gray. She was the star of the picture in the same way that they would make a star of Rex, the king of wild horses, or Rin Tin Tin. She was a dancer, and she was well known all over America, so they starred her in pictures, and in support they gave her Warner Baxter, William Powell, me, and another old film star, Harry Morey. We all supported Gilda Gray."

Percy Marmont's comment is a little unkind, but true. Gilda Gray had only one claim to fame. She shook her chemise, or, as she first explained it in a Polish accent, her "shimee." As a result, she became the most famous exponent and originator of the shimmy, a dance that symbolized the jazz age as much as the Charleston, the flapper, Clara Bow, or Texas Guinan. She was not particularly beautiful, but Gilda Gray was known not for her face but for her legs and her figure. "A ripple here, a quiver there, a shudder or two—and then I shake all the way up from my feet with everything," said Gray. While most men watched and lusted, Carl Van Vechten described her as "the girl with the most beautiful soul," and Heywood Broun called her "a sophisticated hoyden."

Gilda Gray was also a woman with a tragic past. Born in Krakow, Poland, on October 24, 1897, she was adopted by Wandy and Maximilian Michalska and raised in Milwaukee. At the age of twelve, she was forced to marry one John Gorelki, and a year later, a son, Michael, was born. There would be two further marriages and divorces. The shimmy was introduced in 1919, and that same year Sophie Tucker gave her the name of Gilda Gray. There is a record of her shimmy in the 1931 Paramount short, *He Was Her Man*, which is more illustrative of the technical virtuosity of its director-writer, Dudley Murphy, than the brilliance of its star. Ziegfeld starred her in his 1922 *Follies*, and she made a triumphant tour of Europe. As early as 1923, Gray was featured as a nightclub dancer in the feature *Lawful Larceny*, a vehicle for the untalented Hope Hampton, but it was *Aloma of the South Seas* in 1926 that brought Gray to the screen as a star. Under the direction of Maurice Tourneur, she plays a dancer on Paradise Island, living with her lover, Warner Baxter, and loved, in turn, by the villainous William Powell and the decent Percy Marmont. The last recalled, "It was a South Sea Islands story and the South Sea from California is about a seven day's sail. So, we went across America and took ship for the West Indies, because Maurice Tourneur knew the South Seas, but he hadn't been to the West Indies and he wanted to see them. We went to Puerto Rico and made it there. Tourneur was a very good director, a wonderful compositioner. Every setup of the camera was a picture. He didn't bother his actors. He got actors who knew their job, and he left them to it. Of course, the picture...Well, I don't know. I thought it was rather peculiar."

Peculiar or not, the film did well and led to Gray's casting in two further silent features, both of which emphasized her talents as a dancer rather than an actress. In *Cabaret*, released in March 1927, she is a nightclub dancer loved by detective Tom Moore. In *The Devil Dancer*, released in November 1927, she is Takla, the title character, loved by another decent Englishman, Clive Brook. Gilda Gray seems to have a penchant for English leading men, so much so that in 1928 she came to the United Kingdom to star as the mistress of nightclub owner Jameson Thomas in E.A. Dupont's production of *Piccadilly*. (Chinese-American Anna May Wong is also featured as a dancer in a production, released in 1929, that garnered considerable critical praise at the time but today seems overburdened with technical pretension.)

In 1936, Gilda Gray played herself in *The Great Ziegfeld* but was cut from the film prior to its premiere; she had the substantial role of Belle, a tavern entertainer in the Jeanette MacDonald-Nelson Eddy adaptation of *Rose-Marie*. From then on, it was downhill, until the dancer filed for bankruptcy in 1941. In 1946, she filed suit against Columbia Pictures, making the outrageous claim that *Gilda* was based on her life story. The case was eventually settled out of court. Her final involvement in film came in December 1954, when she was hired, presumably as a publicity stunt, in the role of "sex appeal consultant" on *Kiss Me Deadly*.

In the 1950s, Gray was living with Denver Juvenile Court Judge Mary Rose. She ended her days in a tiny apartment on Hollywood Boulevard, and died, en route to the hospital on December 22, 1959. She received more publicity at her death than she had received in all the years since her stardom in the 1920s.

Bibliography

Carlisle, Helen. "Gilda Does the Devil Dance." *Motion Picture*, January 1928, p. 45.
Cruikshank, Herbert. "The Girl Who Closed Broadway." *Motion Picture Classic*, June 1928, pp. 37, 86.
"Golden Girl." *Time*, January 4, 1960, pp. 43–44.
Smith, Agnes. "The Girl Danced and Made the Piper Pay." *Photoplay*, October 1925, pp. 38–39, 94.
Thorp, Dunham. "Gilda Gray Tells How She Does Her Stuff." *Motion Picture*, September 1926, pp. 40–41, 88, 101.
"We Interview Gilda Gray." *Paris and Hollywood*, September 1925, pp. 10–13.
York, Cal. "The Girl on the Cover." *Photoplay*, March 1926, p. 84.

OLGA GREY. *See* **THE VAMPS**

Corinne Griffith, with Victor Varconi, in *The Divine Lady* (1929).

Corinne Griffith

Silent stardom and beauty are often linked, at least in regard to female performers. (Although both Ramon Novarro and Rudolph Valentino might both be considered top contenders in the beauty stakes if one is to adopt a pansexual approach.) Barbara LaMarr is described as the actress who was too beautiful. Renée Adorée is also promoted as a major screen beauty. And the early deaths of both actresses help to sway the emotional vote among silent film enthusiasts. Both are a little too Rubinesque for my liking, Adorée in particular always seems to have a weight problem, and both seem overreliant on looks rather than acting ability.

Corinne Grififth was not one of the most popular of silent stars within the Hollywood community. Valeria Belletti was the private secretary to Samuel Goldwyn, for whom the actress made *Six Days* (1923) just prior to her First National contract. In 1925, Belletti wrote, I am sure accurately, of Griffith, "Very haughty and disdainful. She looks at no one but her dogs, and is generally disliked by all." She is, however, in my opinion, the most beautiful of all silent stars, talented or otherwise. Griffith became known as "The Orchid of the Screen," and in the 1920s, Gloria Swanson described her as the only real beauty in Hollywood. The phrase "the camera loves her" was written for Corinne Griffith. She has a face for which the close-up was created. She entered films in 1916 after winning a beauty contest in Santa Monica, California, and, in reality, she is the only beauty contest winner who entered films and not only remained but developed as a major beauty.

If the age of the American silent film had to end, it is argued, it is well it concluded with the blending of German expressionism and technical virtuosity of F.W. Murnau's *Sunrise*. I would argue it is even better that silent film came to a close with the brilliant romanticism of Corinne Griffith's *The Divine Lady*, which is exemplary of the best in direction (by Frank Lloyd), scripting (by Agnes Christine Johnston), cinematography (by John Seitz), and, above all, is dominated by a lyrical performance from its star.

Lady Emma Hamilton, the mistress of Admiral Nelson, was one of the most famous beauties of history (at least in legend), and who is more appropriate to play her on screen that the most famous beauty of the silent screen? The love affair between Emma Hamilton and Lord Nelson is perfect for screen adaptation. Vivien Leigh and Laurence Olivier proved it with Alexander Korda's production of *That Hamilton Woman* (1941). Corinne Griffith proves it with *The Divine Lady*, even if she must overcome a somewhat wooden performance from her leading man, the Hungarian-born Victor Varconi, miscast as England's naval hero. Varconi is not the only problem, as Marie Dressler, playing Emma's mother, overacts and mugs furiously as if she is appearing in a nineteenth Century farce.

There is an overpowering sense of drama to the love scenes between Griffith and Varconi, with the camera lingering on the former's features. The love here between Hamilton and Nelson is nothing compared to the love between Griffith and the camera, and the film frame and the audience. The actress handles drama with total competence When Hardy comes to take Nelson away from her, she asks, through the subtitle, "So England has sent you to me for Nelson—to me." Responding to herself, "Well—go back and tell them he's mine—and I'll never let him go." But, ultimately, both Hamilton and the audience know what she must do. As Hardy explains, "You can't keep him! His country is in peril—you can't stand between England and Nelson." Nelson leaves her for his destiny, and Corinne Griffith suffers quietly and with dignity. Magnificent!

The Divine Lady boasts battle scenes as formidable as Griffith's performance. The film was budgeted at $885,000, and cost in excess of $1,111,000. First National might not have agreed—and did not—but it was money well spent. The problem was that while *The Divine Lady* was being filmed in 1928, sound had very much taken command in Hollywood. When the film premiered at the Carthay Circle Theatre in Los Angeles on January 29, 1929, the accompanying short was an all-talkie comedy with Edward Everett Horton. *The Divine Lady* had only sound effects and a song, "Drink to Me Only with Thine Eyes," supposedly sung by Griffith while accompanying herself on the harp. It was doomed, just like the silent era and just like Corinne Griffith's career.

Corinne Griffith (Texarkana, Texas, November 21, 1894–Santa Monica, California, July 13, 1979) was a leading lady with Vitagraph from 1916 to 1922, appearing in more than forty films. Percy Marmont played opposite Griffith at Vitagraph in *The Climbers* (1919) and *What's Your Reputation Worth?* (1921). At First National, he was her leading man in *Infatuation* (1925), adapted from Somerset Maugham's play, *Caesar's Wife*: "I was certainly infatuated by Corinne. She was an adorable person and a lovely woman."

From Vitagraph, Corinne Griffith moved on to First National, where she headed her own production unit and where she was to remain until 1930, except for one film, *The Garden of Eden* (1928), released by United Artists. Of the more than 25 First National films, three stand out, aside from *The Divine Lady*. In *Lilies of the Field* (1924), which Griffith remade as her first full-talkie in 1930, she is a divorced woman who loses custody of her child to husband Conway Tearle. Tearle is again the leading man in *Black Oxen* (1924), based on a popular novel by Gertrude Atherton, with Griffith as a New York socialite who rejuvenates herself. In the 1925 screen adaptation of the Zoe

Atkins's play *Declasée*, Griffith is Lady Helen, the last of the mad Varicks, who falls in love with a young American played by Lloyd Hughes.

The Divine Lady was to have had talking sequences, but for whatever reason, they were either not filmed or not included in the released picture. Griffith did appear in a couple of 1929 features with sound sequences, followed by two complete talkies, *Lilies of the Field* and *Back Pay* in 1930. With those films, her First National contract ended. At the height of her fame at First National, Griffith had complete control of the choice of director, leading man, cinematographer, and story. After *The Divine Lady*, she was informed by First National that in the future she would act in films assigned to her and that all personnel decisions would be made by the studio.

After First National, Griffith's career was really at an end. She did make the obligatory trip to England, as did so many faded silent stars, appearing in an adaptation of Michael Arlen's *Lily Christine* for Paramount-British in 1932. In 1957, she financed production of *Stars in the Backyard*, starring herself and directed by Hugo Haas, but the film was never released.

Corinne Griffith was multi-married, first to her Vitagraph director Webster Campbell (1920–1923), then to producer Walter Morosco (1924–1934). In June 1936, she married George Marshall, owner of the Boston Braves, and became a baseball fan. She wrote of her experiences in a 1946 *Saturday Evening Post* article, "My Life with the Redskins," and a year later expanded that into a book with the same title. It was the first of half a dozen books that Griffith was to author, including *Eggs I Have Known* (1955), *Hollywood Stories* (1962), *This You Won't Believe* (1972), and *Papa's Delicate Condition* (1952), which was filmed in 1963 as a vehicle for Jackie Gleason.

The actress and George Marshall divorced in 1958, and in 1965, Griffith married a realtor and singer named Dan Scholl. He was 38 years old, and the couple separated after six weeks. In an extraordinarily messy and vitriolic divorce proceeding, Corinne Griffith dropped a bombshell. Much was made by Scholl of Griffith's claiming to be 51 years old when she was really 71. On May 5, 1966, Corinne Griffith took the stand and, after announcing "I don't give my age because it is part of my religion [Christian Science] not to," she denied that she was Corinne Griffith. The actress claimed she had become Griffith's stand-in in the early 1930s, that the real Corinne Griffith had died in Mexico, and that she had replaced her. Two silent screen stars, Betty Blythe and Claire Windsor, were brought into court, and both insisted that the Corinne Griffith in the courtroom was the same Corinne Griffith they had known in the 1920s. Actor Tom Tryon was later to use Corinne Griffith's "story" as the basis for his novella *Fedora*.

Six days later, Griffith was granted a divorce from Scholl, who was now reported to be 44 years old, ordered to pay his attorney fees but relieved from any alimony payment. The judge mysteriously noted that the marriage was not consummated because the conduct of the parties "was not conducive to amorous activities."

The bitterness of the divorce proceedings should have surprised no one— in that Griffith was obsessed with money and with keeping it. Throughout the 1950s, she waged a campaign against income tax. The only money she is known to have given to any charity or political entity is a $10,000 contribution in 1972 to Governor George Wallace of Alabama. By 1926, it was reported she owned in excess of $500,000 in real estate holdings. At her death, Griffith's estate was valued at $150 million, making her one of the wealthiest women in the world.

Bibliography

Bruce, Betsy. "Corinne Herself." *Motion Picture*, March 1920, pp. 64–65, 123.

Busby, Marquis. "Exit—Corinne Griffith." *Photoplay*, May 1930, pp. 33, 131.

Craig, Marion. "Frappéd in Flatbush." *Photoplay*, January 1919, pp. 80–81.

Evans, Delight. "The Girl on the Cover." *Photoplay*, January 1922, pp. 38–39, 105.

Fletcher, Adele Whitely. "Instead of the Orchid." *Motion Picture Classic*, March 1921, pp. 18–19, 74.

———. "A Portrait of Corinne Griffith." *Cinema Art*, September 1927, pp. 21, 46.

Little, Barbara. "A Hothouse Star." *Picture-Play*, May 1922, pp. 73, 95.

St. Johns, Adela Rogers. "Why Men Go Crazy over Corinne Griffith." *Photoplay*, December 1923, pp. 36–37, 116.

Schallert, Edwin. "The Age of Corinne." *Picture-Play*, April 1924, pp. 43, 91.

Smith, Frederick James. "Corinne, Chocolate Cake and a Deep, Dark Secret." *Motion Picture Classic*, April 1919, pp. 20–21, 80.

———. "Beauty and the Interviewer." *Motion Picture*, January 1922, pp. 36–37, 88.

Weitzel, Edward. "Corinne Griffith on Police Beat Meets a Courteous Taxicab Driver." *Moving Picture World*, February 28, 1920, pp. 1491, 1521.

ROBERT HARRON

Audiences in the teens watched Robert Harron grow and mature from a teen-age boy into an appealing young man. Ultimately, they also watched him die. Harron was an actor associated with only one director, D.W. Griffith, an actor of whom no unkind word was spoken, and an actor responsible for two of the greatest male performances on silent film. "A darling boy" is the expression both Miriam Cooper and Blanche Sweet used to describe him to me.

Born in New York on April 24, 1893, Robert Emmett Harron was the second oldest of nine children, a son of poor Irish-American, Roman Catholic parents. At the age of fourteen, one of the Brothers at St. John's Parochial School sent him, along with a friend, James Smith, to the American Biograph studio. Both boys were hired to work in the cutting room. Smith would become D.W. Griffith's personal editor, cutting both *The Birth of a Nation* (1915) and *Intolerance* (1916), while Harron was destined to "star" in both of those productions. "He was always standing around and watching," remembered Blanche Sweet. "If he didn't have to be off somewhere doing something, he was watching."

As early as November 1907, Harron can be seen in an American Biograph production, *Dr. Skinum*, and by January 1908, the company was featuring Harron in a one-reel short bearing his name, *Bobby's Kodak*. Wallace McCutcheon directed the latter, but it was D.W. Griffith, joining the company in the spring of 1908, who recognized and nurtured Harron's acting talent. The young man's first leading role for Griffith was probably in *Bobby the Coward*, released on July 13, 1911, "a story of the streets of New York" in which Harron stands up to two bullies who break into his grandfather's home.

It is very obvious that Robert Harron was a natural actor, unhampered by the theatrical influences governing other screen performers of the time. He played from the heart and could easily be manipulated and molded by his director. "He was restrained," noted Blanche Sweet, "but I think he was very intense also. Bobby felt. He had sensibilities. He was quite sensitive, but I've never known him to carry on in any way nervously." To Harron, Griffith was both a mentor and a father figure, and to the director, who actively disliked children, Bobby Harron was a son with whom he might have felt comfortable. "Griffith was old enough to be his father," recalled Blanche Sweet. "I think he probably had that attitude without any complex. There was no complex there. I think Griffith loved him....Bobby Harron would have gotten down and let Griffith jump up and down on him if that had been necessary."

When Mae Marsh joined American Biograph in 1912, she and Harron were teamed in *Man's Genesis*, released on July 11, 1912, and the on-screen partnership of the two was further enhanced with *The Sands of Dee*, released on July 22, 1912. When Griffith left American Biograph, he took Bobby Harron with him and continued to feature him opposite Mae Marsh. In *The Birth of a Nation*, the actor plays Lillian Gish's younger brother, Tod Stoneman. He also has at least three other minor roles in the film. Little attention has been paid to Griffith's parallel casting in *The Birth of a Nation*, perhaps nothing more than a private joke. For example, Harron is billed as Tod Stoneman, the younger son of a Northern family, friendly with the Southern Cameron family. He is also the Negro soldier, in blackface, who arrests Dr. Cameron and arranges his humiliation. Similarly, Jennie Lee, who plays the Cameron's faithful Negro retainer, is also the white matron at the abolitionist's meeting; and George Siegmann, who as Silas Lynch seeks to destroy "white" Piedmont, is also the leader of the Confederate soldiers who rescue Piedmont from attack by a renegade Negro band.

Harron's greatest performance, and the finest male performance in silent films, is that of "The Boy" in the modern story of *Intolerance*. As a result of the realities of life, he matures from a poor yet relatively happy boy into an innocent but convicted murderer, who has earlier served time for theft. The innermost feelings of the character are revealed through Harron's close-ups and body language. He is young and vulnerable, trying desperately to prove himself first to the sophisticated crime lord and then to his equally innocent sweetheart and wife. He loses his self-respect, his child, and comes close to losing his life. Even if at times the plotline might seem overly melodramatic, there is a modern naturalism to Harron's performance that holds the audience to rapt attention.

Robert Harron and Mae Marsh continued to act together in nine Fine Arts productions supervised by Griffith. When Mae left Griffith to sign with Goldwyn in 1917, the director allowed Harron to play opposite her in *Sunshine Alley*. As early as *The Misunderstood Boy* (1913), the actor had played opposite Lillian Gish. After Mae Marsh left, Griffith teamed the two in seven features: *Hearts of the World* (1918), *The Great Love* (1918), *The Greatest Thing in Life* (1918), *A Romance of Happy Valley* (1918), *The Girl Who Stayed at Home* (1919), *True Heart Susie* (1919), and *The Greatest Question* (1919). There is a mix here of major and minor productions but to all Harron brought a sense of dignity, demonstrating that consummate ability to portray young men of an awkward age. The actor was declared 2A by his local Los Angeles draft board but avoided military service because of his involvement in the propagandistic *Hearts of the World*.

The October 1919 issue of *Motion Picture Magazine* carries a gossip item that "Robert Harron and D.W. Griffith have had sort of a falling out and that Bobbie [*sic*] is going to shift for himself." Those familiar with the director and leading man at this time question the validity of the claim, but Griffith did choose Richard Barthelmess over Robert Harron as the star of his next major production, *Way Down East*, and it was announced that Harron's new film, *Coincidence*, directed by Chet Withey, was to be made by his own company, for release by Metro. Despite past memorable roles, it was not until *Coincidence* that Harron was actually acknowledged as a star rather than a leading man.

Robert Harron came to New York for the premiere of *Way Down East*. Screenwriter-director Victor Heerman had lived with Harron at the Los Angeles Athletic Club and shared the hotel room with him in New York: "We went to see a preview of his picture and it didn't go very well, but I said, 'Don't worry, it will be all right.' I was over at the studio at Fort Lee, working on a story for Owen Moore, and the telephone rang. 'This is the hotel. Mr. Harron has just shot himself.' I dashed down to the hospital and I said, 'Christ, Bobby, why didn't you say something to me?' He looked up at me and said, 'You don't think I did this? I was getting the trousers out of the trunk. When I left [Los Angeles], Johnnie [his younger brother] was getting a little hard to handle. There was a gun in the house, and I said, I don't want that around, and wrapped it up in the trousers. I said, I better get those trousers out and have them pressed, and as I did this thing dropped and the gun went off.' Then the police came in and we talked and talked, and I stayed the rest of the day and that night."

Miriam Cooper recalled, "We heard that Bobby had this accident, and my husband [Raoul Walsh] went over—it was Sunday morning—and Bobby was sitting up in bed reading the papers. He came back and he said, 'He's fine.' About four hours later, we got the news that Bobby was dead."

Reasons for his suicide ranged from Griffith's rejection of him to the breakup of a relationship with Dorothy Gish. Victor Heerman told me that almost every night he and Harron would double-date Dorothy Gish and Constance Talmadge, but, with tears in his eyes, he recounted that the saddest thing of all was that Harron was still a virgin: "That fellow had never been with a woman. Never in his life. He'd go out to the drunkenest parties, and he would laugh and have a good time with just a glass of ginger ale. He smoked, but he never took a drink in his life, and, as I say, he had never been with a woman—and plenty of opportunities, by golly!"

Even before his death on September 5, 1920, four days after the shooting, there were rumors that Harron had committed suicide, suggestions rejected by Heerman, Miriam Cooper, and Lillian Gish, in large part because Harron was a devout Catholic and the breadwinner for his family. Further, he was about to start shooting a second film under Elmer Clifton's direction.

As the Harron tragedy unfolded in New York, his mother was on a train heading to the city for the premiere of *Coincidence*. Actress Teddy Sampson, also on the train, kept the story of her son's death from her, and Heerman arranged for him, Lillian Gish, and Griffith to meet Harron's mother on arrival, take her to a nearby hotel, and break the news.

With Robert Harron's death, the film industry for the first time had to deal with the release of a film whose star had just died under mysterious circumstances. Today, the tragedy would be treated as publicity for the film. In 1920, Metro was so stunned by the death of its young star that it arranged a low-key release of *Coincidence* without reference to Harron, preferring not to associate such a sad situation with a comedy feature. "Where many things were cheap, he never was," wrote Gladys Hall. And for once the industry displayed the same respectful attitude as its star.

There is a strong element of tragedy surrounding the entire Harron family. Sister Tessie, who worked as an extra, died at the age of nineteen, a victim of the Spanish flu epidemic of 1918. Twenty-three-year-old brother Charles died in 1915 in an automobile accident in Los Angeles. Harron's father, John, was murdered on October 16, 1930, when the Los Angeles gas station he operated was robbed, his body found burning in an incinerator. (Incredibly, a coroner's jury ruled the death a suicide.) Brother John, who was active as a somewhat mediocre actor on screen in the 1920s and 1930s, died at the age of 36 in 1939, while filming on location in Seattle.

Bibliography

"The Boy Whom Everybody Liked." *Picture-Play*, December 1920, p. 30.

Dunham, Harold. "Bobby Harron." *Films in Review*, December 1963, pp. 607–618.

———. "Mae Marsh, Robert Harron and D.W. Griffith." *The Silent Picture*, no. 4, autumn 1969, pp.10–14.

Fox, Fred W. "The Five Tragedies of the Harrons." Los Angeles *Mirror*, part II, August 12, 1960, p. 6.

Hall, Gladys. "Unchanging." *Motion Picture*, December 1920, pp. 66, 116–117.

Handy, Truman B. "Buoyant Bobby." *Motion Picture*, September 1919, pp. 60–61, 109.

North, Jean. "Digging up the Acorn." *Photoplay*, October 1920, pp. 51–52.

Peltret, Elizabeth. "Griffith's Boy." *Photoplay*, April 1918, pp. 20–22, 115.

Smith, Frederick James. "Bashful Bobbie." *Motion Picture Classic*, July 1920, pp. 16–17, 71.

Witzel
L.A.

WILLIAM S. HART

William Surrey Hart (Newburgh, New York, December 6, 1865–Los Angeles, June 23, 1946) was already a major stage actor when he entered films in 1914 with the two-reel short *His Hour of Manhood*. He had originated the role of Messala in *Ben-Hur* in 1899 and played Cash Hawkins in the original 1905 production of *The Squaw Man*. Hart's screen characterizations were always well-considered, serious types. He lacked and rejected the flamboyance of Tom Mix or the comic antics of Hoot Gibson. No cowboy dressed like these two or had as much fun as they did. It is odd that Mix was the real cowboy that Hart was not, and yet Mix's screen persona was entirely one of make-believe.

Hart's concept was to depict the West as he sincerely believed it to be, and he viewed his films as much as an art form as the paintings of Frederick Remington. Hart genuinely loved the West, and he took the Western movie away from the painted backdrop and showed the Western environment as it really was. It was very much a friendless place, with Hart as the man who walks alone. His piercing eyes saw all and rejected most of it. The Hart character is no better described than in a subtitle from his 1916 production of *Hell's Hinges*, "The embodiment of the best and worst of the early West."

Producer Thomas H. Ince brought Hart to the screen, but the two men quarreled and Hart operated as an independent production unit with his own studio. Under the Ince banner, Hart starred in 55 films, ending with *John Petticoats* in 1919. Hart was an Aztec in *The Captive God* (1916) and visited modern-day New York in *Branding Broadway* (1918), chasing a taxi on horseback through Central Park. But the Ince films and the later eleven productions from 1919 onward for Paramount-Artcraft were generally Westerns. Hart did not appear comfortable in non-Western attire, despite an earlier non-Western stage career, and audiences accepted him only as a Western hero. He would not compromise on production values or cost and, in the end, left Paramount, independently producing his last film, *Tumbleweeds*, for United Artists. It succeeds not so much because of its hero but because of the energetic, opening land rush sequence. It is ironic that William S. Hart should have been a star of silent Westerns, and yet his last film is moving only thanks to the sound introduction that the star added in 1939: "My friends, I loved the art of making motion pictures. It is as the breath of life to me...the rush of the wind that cuts your face, the pounding hooves of the pursuing posse. And then, the clouds of dust through which comes the faint voice of the director, 'OK Bill, great stuff! And say Bill, give old Fritz a pat on the nose for me, willya?'

And so William S. Hart spoke a final farewell to the screen. In many ways, he was a giant brought down by a change in audiences' tastes. At one point, in the late 1920s, he considered a comeback with Hal Roach, but nothing came of the proposal.

William S. Hart's leading ladies served generally as plot devices. They helped to make or keep him pure. Again, *Hell's Hinges* serves as a perfect example of this ploy, as Hart meets the new minister's sister, played by Clara Williams; "One who is evil, looking for the first time upon that which is good." Hart was certainly a ladies man. Margery Wilson told me he proposed to five of his leading ladies, including her and Jane Novak. Neither his deportment on a horse nor his moral stance was his best attribute; according to Margery Wilson what was far more appealing were "the most beautiful legs you ever saw."

Jane Novak was Hart's leading lady in five films between 1918 and 1921, and did not care for his screen image at all: "A friend of mine was making a picture with him, and she said, 'Oh, you must go and see one of his films.' So I did, and I made the comment, 'I never want to meet that man.'" After her first performance as Hart's leading lady, Novak had to admit, "he wasn't the ogre I thought he was on screen." At the same time, she did reveal a disturbingly sadistic streak in Hart's character: "They used to do all sorts of horrible things to me. One day, they tied my hands behind my back. Then they put whiskey bottles all around me. They said, 'Look over here,' and I wouldn't look at the camera. I wasn't going to be photographed in this horrible position. So they took a piece of rope, tied it to the back of my hair, and pulled my head until they got my head into position." John Ford's widow Mary dismissed Hart to me as "just a dirty old man" while praising Tom Mix for the "wonderful things" that he did.

The major female figure in Hart's life was his sister, Mary Ellen. He escaped briefly from her clutches when he married his leading lady from *John Petticoats*, Winifred Westover, in Los Angeles on December 7, 1921. He was 56 years old. A son, William S. Hart Jr., was born on September 6, 1922, and shortly thereafter, the couple divorced. Hart returned to his sister, and Westover took the child. At the end of *On the Night Stage* (1915), Hart laments to his horse, "I ain't got nobody but you Midnight, nobody at all." And that pretty much summed up Hart's final years.

Hart's faithful horse, Fritz, died in 1938 at the cowboy's Newhall ranch. Hart willed that ranch to the people of Los Angeles County. It was initially administered by the Los Angeles County Museum of Natural History, and John Dewar became its first curator. Dewar is one of those unsung heroes of film history, who, in 1970, set up a Movie Gallery at the Museum, displaying many of its motion picture treasures from Lon Chaney's makeup kit to Buster Keaton's pork pie hat. It was always fun to visit the Hart ranch with John, as he pointed out how he had rearranged the furniture and added hanging blankets and rugs, making the place, as he put it, far more tastefully decorated than when William S. Hart lived there.

Note: The William S. Hart Park and Museum is located at 24151 Newhall Avenue, Newhall, Ca. 91355; Hart's scrapbooks and other papers are there.

Bibliography

Cheatham, Maude. "And They Live Happily." *Motion Picture*, June 1922, pp. 36–37, 88–89.

Crowell, Merle. "Famous Two-Gun Star of the Movies." *American Magazine*, July 1921, pp. 18–19.

Duffy, Gerald C. "Cupid Thought he Could Out-Shoot Hart." *Motion Picture Classic*, October 1918, pp. 43–44, 70.

Firestone, Bruce. "A Man Named Sioux: Nostalgia and the Career of William S.Hart." *Film & History*, vol. 7, no. 4, December 1977, pp. 85–89.

Fletcher, Adele Whitely. "Out from the West." *Motion Picture*, February 1922, pp. 22–23, 84.

"Fritz and His Hired Man." *Photoplay*, May 1917, pp. 78–79.

Fuir, Charles W. "The Most Popular Horse in Films Is William Hart's 'Fritz,'" *Motion Picture*, January 1918, pp. 95–98.

Gordon, Gertrude. "William S. Hart, the Man of the West." *Motion Picture*, November 1916, pp. 117–123.

Hart, William S. "Living Your Character." *Motion Picture*, May 1917, pp. 71–72.

———. "How I Got In." *Motion Picture*, December 1917, pp. 78–79.

———. "And They Are All Beautiful." *Motion Picture*, August 1919, pp. 38–39.

———. *Told under a White Oak, by Bill Hart's Pinto Pony.* Boston: Houghton, Mifflin, 1922.

———. *My Life East and West.* Boston: Houghton, Mifflin, 1929.

Kokszarski, Diane Kaiser. *The Complete Films of William S. Hart: A Pictorial Record.* New York: Dover Publications, 1980.

Langford, Marion Howe. "An' Oh, the Heart of Him!" *Motion Picture Classic*, August 1918, pp. 50–51, 76.

McKelvie, Martha Groves. "Adventures of a Cub." *Motion Picture*, April 1917, pp. 71–72.

Mitchell, George J. "The Wm. S. Hart Museum." *Films in Review*, August-September 1962, pp. 401–406.

Moore, William. "On Tour with Bill Hart." *Motion Picture*, January 1918, pp. 41–42.

Naylor, Hazel Simpson. "On a Tour with Bill Hart." *Motion Picture Classic*, November 1917, pp. 32–33.

———. "The Hungry Hart." *Motion Picture*, March 1919, pp. 32–34.

Patterson, Ada. "Bill Hart's True Love Story." *Photoplay*, January 1921, pp. 36–37, 109.

———. "The Screen's Saddest Hero." *Photoplay*, September 1925, pp. 48–49.

"The Stage Career of William S. Hart, 1898-1912." *The Silent Picture*, no. 16, autumn 1972, pp. 17–20.

Vosges, Hilary. "What Bill Hart Told Them in the Maid's Room." *Photoplay*, September 1917, pp. 81–82.

"William S. Hart." *Moving Picture World*, November 14, 1914, p. 920.

"William S. Hart Tells Why He Prefers Stories Written Expressly for the Screen." *Moving Picture World*, May 29, 1920, p. 1184.

ALICE HOLLISTER. See **THE VAMPS**

ALICE HOWELL

When I first met George Stevens Jr. at the American Film Institute, I was aware of his father's contribution to cinema as a major director, but I did not realize there was another, more unusual, family connection through George Junior's mother. Yvonne Stevens, who married George Senior in 1930, was the daughter of one of the most entertaining, unusual and underrated of silent screen comediennes, Alice Howell. A former vaudevillian, Alice Howell was born Alice Clark in New York on May 20, 1886, and took her stage name from a vaudeville act, Howell and Howell, that she and her husband, Dick Smith, replaced.

The couple entered films in 1913 with Mack Sennett, appearing together as party guests in *Tillie's Punctured Romance* (1914); Alice can be seen in a number of Chaplin's Keystone shorts, most notably as the dentist's wife in *Laughing Gas*, released in July 1914. She became a comedy star with Henry "Pathé" Lehrman's Knock-Out Komedies, made by his L-Ko Motion Picture Company in 1915. At L-Ko, Alice Howell hid her natural beauty and developed a unique, eccentric style of dress with ill-fitting clothing, the hair piled into a mess of golden curls and topped with the most unsuitable of hats. The eyebrows were overemphasized, the eyes set in a vacant stare and the walk more like the shuffle of a penguin. Howell constantly uses her hands and body language for emphasis. Her feet are as eloquent as her expressive hands. She is no light or polite comedienne, no leading lady simpering beside the male comedy star, but a physical comic who can handle a pratfall better than any male. It is no exaggeration to describe Howell as the female counterpart of Charlie Chaplin.

Chaplin had his tramp costume. Alice Howell had her scrub lady outfit. Chaplin developed his comedy for the feature-length motion picture, while Howell was stuck in short subjects for most of her career, moving from L-Ko to Reelcraft, to Universal in the early 1920s, and, finally, to Fox for a couple of titles in 1926 and 1927. The few feature film appearances she made in the early 1920s are little more than cameos and often uncredited. Unlike Chaplin, it seems that Alice Howell never really cared that much about her career. She made films in order to make money, and she invested her money in real estate. By the 1920s she had no need to work. "All she wanted to do was make money," explained Yvonne. "She didn't care about being an actress. All she cared about was real estate."

Alice Howell died, a wealthy woman, in Los Angeles on April 11, 1961. Her passing went unrecorded in both the trade and the popular press. There is not even a complete record of her films, and many went unnoticed in contemporary trade papers. There are well in excess of eighty, with intriguing titles such as *Silk Hose and High Pressure* (1915), *Lizzie's Lingering Love* (1916), *Tillie's Terrible Tumbles* (1916), and *Beauty and the Boob* (1919). She was not a creative comedienne in the sense that she wrote or fine-tuned her films—at L-Ko, she relied much on the talent of her director, John G. Blystone—but she knew how to get laughs, and, if someone would screen her films today, she would generate far more genuine laughter and applause than Mabel Normand.

Bibliography

"The Funniest Woman in Pictures." *Pictures and the Picturegoer*, June 16, 1917, p. 11.
"She's a Rough Gal." *Photoplay*, August 1917, p. 133.
Slide, Anthony. "Alice Howell" in *Eccentrics of Comedy*. Lanham, Md.: Scarecrow Press, 1998, pp. 75–79.

ALICE JOYCE

Gracious and charming the way young matrons should be in silent films, with a reserve that is not condescending but rather indicative of good breeding and good manners, Alice Joyce (Kansas City, Missouri, October 1, 1890–Los Angeles, October 9, 1955) was also a pioneering actress. She was a New York hotel switchboard operator when she joined the Kalem Company in 1911, after twice being rejected by D.W. Griffith. Asked to explain her placid disposition, she would joke that it was because Griffith remarked that she reminded him of a cow. Joyce was often partnered with Carlyle Blackwell or Tom Moore (who became her first husband), and her films at Kalem, many of which were action dramas and Westerns, give little hint of the quiet, patrician beauty that she was to become. She left Kalem in 1915 and the following year embarked on a five-year residency with the Vitagraph Company, slowly but surely developing an appealing screen persona.

At Vitagraph, Alice Joyce's leading man in four films—*The Winchester Woman* (1919), *The Vengeance of Durand* (1919), *Slaves of Pride* (1920), and *The Sporting Duchess* (1920)—was Percy Marmont (with whom she also co-starred in Zoe Akins's *Daddy's Gone a-Hunting* at MGM in 1925). Marmont had fond memories of her: "Talking of sweet women, when I first met Alice Joyce, actually before I'd even been introduced to her, I played a scene in which I kissed her about ten times. We kept taking and retaking, and I remember saying to her, 'I'm awfully sorry to introduce myself in this manner,' and she said, 'Oh, I rather like it.' When I went home in the evening I said to my wife, 'I've been kissing the most lovely woman all morning.' They finished up being the greatest of friends, they were terrific pals."

In 1920, Joyce married wealthy New Yorker James Regan Jr. and made fewer film appearances as she devoted her time to her two daughters and to the life of a wealthy socialite. She and Regan divorced in 1932, and the following year the actress married MGM director Clarence Brown. They divorced in 1945.

Perhaps it was because she knew she did not have to work or perhaps it was good common sense, but in the 1920s, Alice Joyce made a remarkably intelligent choice of films to which to lend her talent. She was Lucilla Crespin in both the 1923 silent and 1930 sound versions of the popular stage melodrama *The Green Goddess*, an English major's wife captured by the Rajah of Rukh, played in undemonstrative and charmingly villainous style by George Arliss. You believed her as an English lady, and, not surprisingly, the actress came to the United Kingdom to star in two features, *The Passionate Adventure* (1924) and *The Rising Generation* (1928).

There were starring roles in prominent features, including *Stella Dallas* (1925), *Beau Geste* (1926), *So's Your Old Man* (1926), and *Sorrell and Son* (1927), but the two films that stand out most are King Baggot's *The Home Maker* (1925) and Herbert Brenon's *Dancing Mothers* (1926), both of which are prominent and little discussed feminist dramas from an age not noted for such fare. In the latter, she is a housewife who hates housework. When her husband, Clive Brook, is unable to work, confined to a wheelchair as the result of an accident, the conventional marriage roles are reversed. He enjoys staying at home and taking care of the three children, while she finds satisfying employment in the department store where he had worked. A surprising plot twist has the husband discover that he is once again able to walk and work, but choosing not to let his wife know and thus spoil her newfound happiness. Obviously, credit for the storyline belongs to the author of the original novel, Dorothy Canfield, and the screenwriter Mary O'Hara, but credit should also go to Alice Joyce for yet another understated performance that manages to emphasize the characterization so well. *Dancing Mothers* is better known and very "modern" as Joyce plays a commanding yet singularly unobtrusive role as the wife whose husband is having an affair and who falls in love with her daughter's boyfriend. The conventional silent film ending would have wife and husband reconciled, but here she goes off to Paris, deserting both her husband and potential lover for a new life. Both of these roles might have led a lesser actress to give a strident performance, but Alice Joyce remains the personification of class. As Frederick James Smith so aptly put it, she is "a madonna listening to a jazz band." There is an inner repose here that no mere male can disturb. Just as her character in *The Home Maker* has no problem becoming a successful wage earner, in *Dancing Mothers*, she will have no difficulty establishing a new life in Europe.

A wealthy woman, Alice Joyce had no need to act for a living. After the second version of *The Green Goddess*, she made two last talkies in 1930, *Song o' My Heart* and *He Knew Women*, and was happy to retire.

Bibliography

Bodeen, DeWitt. "Alice Joyce." *Films in Review*, December 1976, pp. 599–618.
Bruce, Betsy. "Alice a la Mode." *Motion Picture*, April-May 1920, pp. 42, 110.
Durling, E.V. "Alice Where Have You Been?" *Photoplay*, May 1924, pp. 72–73, 199.
Hall, Gladys. "The Honeymoon and Sixpence." *Motion Picture*, July 1920, pp. 52–53, 102.
———. "Alice the Enigma." *Motion Picture Classic*, January 1927, pp. 53, 84.
Martin, Minerva. "Alice Joyce Advises." *Photoplay*, July 1914, pp. 71–74.
Patterson, Ada. "The Lady of Vast Silences." *Photoplay*, March 1920, pp. 85–86, 95.
Redway, Sara. "This Business of Being a Screen Lady." *Motion Picture Classic*,

March 1926, pp. 32–33, 77.

Smith, Frederick James. "Alice for Short." *Photoplay*, October 1917, pp. 77–79.

———. "Alice in Quest of a Temperament." *Motion Picture Classic*, December 1918, pp. 18–19.

Van Horn, Elizabeth. "A Priestess of Poise." *Picture-Play*, November 1926, pp. 71–72, 98.

York, Cal. "The Girl on the Cover." *Photoplay*, October 1926, p. 74

BUSTER KEATON. *See* **THE LEGENDS**

MADGE KENNEDY

It was hardly unusual to come across former silent stars in Los Angeles. It was more uncommon to find former stage performers retired in the city. It was virtually unique to encounter someone who had not only been a great silent star but an equally prominent performer on the Broadway stage, but Madge Kennedy was such an actress. Now living in a small apartment in a rundown, largely immigrant neighborhood of the city a few blocks north of the Ambassador Hotel, which was also showing its age and soon to close, was an actress who should have been a major celebrity but who was merely forgotten, relying upon a pension from the Actors Fund to pay the bills.

Madge Kennedy belonged to the era when gentlemen drank champagne from the shoes of Broadway leading ladies. Madge's longtime friend, Herb Sterne, always wanted to drink from the high-heeled shoes she had worn in her 1915 comedy *Fair and Warmer.* When she died, Madge left those shoes to Herb, and they now reside in my closet. They are incredibly tiny—can any woman have had feet so small?—and yet despite their provenance, I feel a little queasy about drinking from them.

Through those shoes, one feels a psychic link to the Broadway stage of seventy or more years ago. Their owner was the star of the 1923 hit *Poppy,* in which she was supported (and not the other way around) by W.C. Fields. In 1931, Madge Kennedy took over the role of Amanda Prynne from Gertrude Lawrence in Noel Coward's *Private Lives.* Earlier, in 1925, Coward had wanted her as his American leading lady in *Fallen Angels.* In the teens, she was the leading purveyor of farce on the American stage, thanks in large part to Salibury Fields and Margaret Mayo's *Twin Beds,* which ran for an incredible 411 performances in 1914 and 1915. The play contains all the elements associated with farce, including a drunken man undressing in a young lady's room that he has mistaken for his own and hiding in the closet when the jealous husband appears on the scene. The title is taken from the decision by the young married couple to adopt twin beds, the latest novelty, rather than sharing a double bed. The play demonstrated, as *Everybody's Magazine* commented at the time, "the American way of flirting with a risky situation and then dodging it."

Although born in Chicago, on April 19, 1891, Madge and her family moved to California and then to New York, where the actress began her professional stage career in 1910: "I'm sure actors are born with an instinct. You can't teach it. You have it or you don't. It's like the color of your hair or your eyes. I have an instinct for timing, and I was usually let alone. The best thing that ever happened to me when I was young was a wonderful critic said of me—it was

Little Miss Brown, my first play in New York City—'Madge Kennedy would keep the show going, but before she can keep anything going she will have to get rid of that accent from the shores of Lake Michigan.' So I went to diction teachers."

When Samuel Goldwyn (or Samuel Goldfish, as Madge would still insist on calling him) formed his own production company in 1917, she was the third star he signed, following Mabel Normand and Mae Marsh: "I was engaged for films as a funny girl, a combination between Norma Talmadge, who was the beautiful dramatic actress, and the comic ones like Marie Dressler." In his 1923 autobiography, *Behind the Screen*, Goldwyn wrote of her, "Madge Kennedy was always prompt on the set and was most conscientious in her efforts to do good work....No moods, no sharp edges obtruded themselves into any business relation with her."

Between 1917 and 1920, Madge Kennedy starred in 21 five-reel features for Goldwyn, beginning with *Baby Mine*, based on the 1910 theatrical comedy by Margaret Mayo. Farce was Madge's forté at the studio, with her dark brown, gentle eyes and bronze hair as attractive on screen as they had appeared to theatre audiences.

"In those days, there were five women stars: Mabel Normand, Mae Marsh, Geraldine Farrar, Pauline Frederick and me. We had our dressing rooms in a big hall that had just like board [walls], so everybody's dressing room was public property. Geraldine Farrar was just a darling, and she had this male secretary, and he would always say, 'Miss Farrar, where are you?' A voice from the back—'I'm in the toilet'—and that was Mabel Normand."

When Kennedy's contract with Goldwyn expired in 1921 after her last films, *The Girl with a Jazz Heart, The Highest Bidder,* and *Oh Mary Be Careful,* she decided to return to the stage: "I got on with him [Goldwyn] very well. I was heartbroken because of the things they were giving me to do. I had been a stage actress and I wanted to do things a little more important than a little wife, newly married, and that sort of thing. I went to him one day and I said, 'Mr. Goldwyn, I'm terribly unhappy, couldn't you let me do a biography of Marie Antoinette.' Oh I thought of so many things, including *The Hunchback of Notre Dame*. Well, he said, 'You are just crazy. Costume pictures are out.' And not six months after that Pola Negri did a fantastic one, *Passion*."

Madge's return to the stage was in *Cornered* (1920), and although she was to make six independent feature films between 1923 and 1926, she primarily devoted her energy to theatrical work. *Poppy* with W.C. Fields, which opened at New York's Apollo Theatre on September 3, 1923, is, in retrospect, the most famous of those stage productions: "Bill was very frightened about the length of his part, so he kept saying to me, 'Daughter, make them take away some of those lines. And I'd say, 'Pop, wait 'til the opening night and you'll see how good you are.' Well, he was a sensation of course. And there was a moment at the end of the second act, a very touching scene, where they arrested him, and I used to say to the sheriff, 'You can't take him away, he's like a child.' I would go to Bill, he'd take me in his arms, and it was a touching moment, because it had been a very funny act up to that time. Well, a month went by, and I said to the sheriff, 'You can't take him away, look at him, he's only a child.' And from under his overcoat, Bill took out a lollipop that was the size of a cartwheel. Of course, the audience and the cast were convulsed, but the play went out the window. I said, 'Now Pop, if you will just play that one scene straight, from then on it doesn't matter what you do.' He said, 'Daughter, you're absolutely right.' And the next month, it would be a trumpet which he blew. He never missed a performance. He was never late but once, and that was when he had my mother in his dressing room, mixing her a new kind of cocktail."

Madge Kennedy also had amusing memories of another theatrical event of the 1920s, when legendary stage actress Mrs. Minnie Maddern Fiske had organized a benefit to protest the use of animal furs for women's adornment. The tickets were so expensive that Douglas Fairbanks remarked that it would be kinder to buy a horse. Madge was to play Katharine Parr opposite critic Alexander Woolcott's Henry VIII. Because the latter was a far from popular commentator on theatrical matters, the moment the curtain ascended there were sustained hisses and boos from the audience. Woolcott turned to the assembled company and commented, "I didn't know Madge Kennedy was so unpopular." When later I described the scene to George Cukor, he added, "Woolcott was the original stagestruck amateur and Madge was a professional."

With her first husband Harold Bolster, a former Goldwyn executive who died in 1927, Madge formed an independent film production company, Kenma Corporation. She had wanted to adapt *Dorothy Vernon of Haddon Hall* for the screen, but the rights were acquired by Mary Pickford, and so she produced and starred in *The Purple Highway* (1923) and *Three Miles Out* (1924), both filmed at the Astoria Studios on Long Island and both relatively unsuccessful.

In the 1930s, Madge's career began to falter. She made her last Broadway appearance in *Bridal Wise* in 1932, toured in revivals, did some radio work, and basically served as a good wife to her second husband, William Hanley, to whom she was married from 1934 until his death in 1959. That might have been the end of Madge Kennedy's career had it not been for three fans, namely Ruth Gordon, Garson Kanin, and George Cukor. In the summer of 1951, the trio was involved in pre-production on *The Marrying Kind*, which the Kanins had scripted and George was to direct. Judy Holliday and Aldo Ray had been cast in the starring roles, but the three were looking for someone to play Judge Carroll, in whose divorce court Holliday and Ray would air their marital differences. After rejecting Ina Claire, Florence Bates, Dorothy Gish, and Frieda Inescourt, Cukor tested Madge Kennedy and reported, "She acts absolutely beautifully, with authority and intensity." Later George told me, "She was easy to direct, very conscientious, very intelligent. She behaved the way an intelligent star behaves."

The Marrying Kind was followed by fourteen film roles in "talkies," as Madge still insisted on calling them ("I was just like Rip Van Winkle"), including *The Rains of Ranchipur* (1955), *Lust for Life* (1956), and *North by Northwest* (1959). She is great as the elderly resident of the San Berdoo Arms in *The Day of the Locust* (1975); Cukor suggested her to director John Schlessinger because, he told me, "She became a pal of mine." Critics singled out her performance as the elderly spectator of the dance marathon in *They Shoot Horses, Don't They?* (1969), despite the lack of a screen credit: "The dancers in the film became friends and they'd come over to me and have a visit. One of them said, 'what did you do with all the money you earned?' I said, 'I enjoyed it!'" In her last film, *The Marathon Man* (1976), Madge is the old lady who makes weekly visits to her safe deposit box at the bank: "When you're no longer the love interest, you can play anything. If you have a good seat on a broomstick, you can make a good witch."

I saw Madge Kennedy a great deal taking Herb Sterne to visit her often, but after her death at the Motion Picture Country Hospital on June 9, 1987, I realized how little I had really appreciated her. She was too big a talent to ignore, and yet her stage roles meant so little almost 75 years later. She was a little old lady in whose presence there was an almost overwhelming smell of rose water. The stories were often long and convoluted, and the pink champagne that she insisted on drinking and serving was always, I realize in retrospect, of necessity, cheap.

Writing of her in the old humor magazine, *Life* (April 29, 1926), Robert Benchley described Madge as "the gentlest and most effective of our comediennes." She was gentle and kind, but there was an edge to her humor. She once commented that she had wanted to play Lady Macbeth "because in my early, early days, I thought she was a kind of a charmer, and she should be played rather arch." There was an archness there behind the sweet and innocent façade.

Her later years cannot have been easy. There was little if any money, and the roles she played in many of those "talkies" were small and insignificant. Yet, despite it all, Madge would always insist, "I have no tale to tell about difficult times. I had nothing but joy."

Bibliography

Allison, Dorothy. "Nee Madge Kennedy." *Photoplay*, January 1919, pp. 63, 102.

Bruce, Betsy. "The Keeper of Her Gift." *Motion Picture*, January 1922, pp. 52-53, 87.

Fletcher, Adele Whitely. "The Great Career." *Shadowland*, July 1921, pp. 28, 71.

Gray, Allison. "Madge Kennedy is Lucky, But She Doesn't Trust to Luck." *American Magazine*, February 1925, pp. 34-35.

Lamb, Grace. "Madge Kennedy." *Motion Picture Classic*, October 1918, pp. 28-29, 72.

Slide, Anthony. "Madge Kennedy." *Films in Review*, March 1984, pp. 131-141.

Squier, Emma-Lindsay. "Angel Bloom—Plus Madge Kennedy." *Picture-Play*, April 1920, pp. 30-31, 80.

Doris Kenyon and Milton Sills show off their new son, Kenyon.

DORIS KENYON

An intelligent, well-educated actress, Doris Kenyon had little time for reminiscing about her career as a silent star. In fact, she had no recollection of her work in silent films. She was happy to look through her scrapbooks and report on what she found therein, but when it came to any personal commentary, there was little she chose to recall. "I have put all my films to one side, and forgotten about them," she told me in 1977. Doris was happier remembering her first husband, Milton Sills (1882–1930), with whom she had co-starred in her first released film, *The Rack*, in 1915, and who became the first of her four husbands on October 12, 1926. She recalled that when she and Sills were visting the redwood forests of Northern California, probably during the filming of *Valley of the Giants* (1927), they were spotted by a group of tourists and mobbed. Prophetically, Sills commented, "Don't they realize that people will be coming to admire these trees long after I'm gone and forgotten. The silent stars won't be remembered. Our fame is only brief."

Despite a strong and virile presence in silent films and a handful of talkies from 1914 through 1930, Milton Sills is very much forgotten today. It was that lack of permanence in the history of popular entertainment, plus the death of their only son, Kenyon, in 1971, that most distressed Doris Kenyon.

Born in Syracuse, New York, on September 5, 1897, Doris Kenyon began her career as a chorus girl in the 1915 New York production of Victor Herbert's *Princess Pat*. She was spotted by producer William A. Brady and offered a contract with his World Film Corporation, located at Fort Lee, New Jersey. It was the start of a film career that ended with the role of the French queen in *The Man in the Iron Mask* (1939) and included some 60 screen appearances. In 1918, Doris had her own production company, DeLuxe Pictures, for which she starred in *The Street of Seven Stars, The Inn of the Blue Moon,* and *Wild Honey*. In 1928, she made her sound debut in *The Home Towners*, and the following year she was the star of Paramount's first talkie, *Interference*.

She was the favorite star of Alma Sophia Kappelhoff of Cincinnati, and when Alma gave birth to a daughter in 1924, she named her Doris in honor of Doris Kenyon. Doris Kappelhoff also made a name for herself on screen—as Doris Day.

There is one film of Doris Kenyon's that stands out, and that is *Monsieur Beaucaire* from 1924. It is generally dismissed as rather a weak vehicle for its star, Rudolph Valentino, who, unfortunately, looks more than a little effeminate in eighteenth century French garb. Doris co-stars as Lady Mary, and the screen positively sizzles in the love scenes between her and Valentino.

They are arguably some of the most erotic moments captured on silent film—particularly with both players fully clothed.

In 1947, Doris Kenyon had married the Polish composer and conductor Bronislaw Mlynarksi (who died in 1971), and the marriage cemented her reputation at the time as one of the leaders of Los Angeles society. She had become close to director Jean Renoir and his wife, Dido, and it was through Jean and Dido that I came to view *Monsieur Beaucaire* with Doris. The actress had long refused to watch any of her films, but when Jean asked Robert Gitt and I if we would screen *Monsieur Beaucaire* for him on October 15, 1978—he had never seen Doris Kenyon on screen—she felt an obligation to be present at Jean's Beverly Hills home.

Once the screening was over, the memories were rekindled. Doris dismissed Sidney Olcott as a useless director. She admitted that Valentino was "a little flirty" but added that nothing could go too far because his wife, Natacha Rambova, was constantly seated at the side of her set, indicating with the movement of her hands how Valentino should act out a scene. Doris was cast for the role not because of her talent as an actress but rather because the producers wanted an English-looking beauty with blonde hair to appear opposite Bebe Daniels, as Princess Henriette, with her dark hair and complexion.

When I first met Doris, she was living in a high-rise apartment building on Wilshire Boulevard in the Westwood area of Los Angeles. When I last saw her, she had moved to a small, and very expensive "cottage" a block south of Wilshire Boulevard in Beverly Hills. With her at both locations was a closet-size cage of doves, representing both her companions and her hobby. That last visit, August 11, 1979, Dido Renoir was with me, and the three of us walked to the Beverly Hills Brown Derby for dinner. Doris was not happy with the service, which had certainly deteriorated from the days when the restaurant was frequented by the community's stars and socialites. Doris Kenyon died a few weeks later, on September 1, 1979.

Bibliography

Bodeen, DeWitt. "Doris Kenyon." *Films in Review,* April 1980, pp. 203–217.
Burgess, Bess. "Result: Doris Kenyon, Star!" *Photoplay,* October 1916, pp. 104–105.
Fletcher, Adele Whitely. "Of the People." *Motion Picture Classic,* September 1921, pp. 50–51, 90.
Little, Barbara. "Fortune Smiles on Doris." *Picture-Play,* October 1924, pp. 74–75, 107.
Montanye, Lillian M. "Doris Kenyon." *Motion Picture Classic,* June 1917, pp. 47–48.
———. "Doris Kenyon, Little Miss Happiness." *Motion Picture,* December 1918, pp. 43–44.

Montanye, Perry. "The Little Girl in the Parsonage." *Photoplay*, October 1920, pp. 34–35, 133–134.

Squier, Emma-Lindsay. "Doris—Twice Over." *Picture-Play*, September 1922, pp. 43–44, 102.

J. WARREN KERRIGAN

It is perhaps difficult to understand just how popular was J. (Jack) Warren Kerrigan and how much he fell out of favor at the height of his career. Harold Lloyd was an extra at Universal when Kerrigan was the studio star: "Kerrigan was a tremendous figure in those days. He was a wonderful individual, big, handsome, had a Roman-type nose. I think he would be good today with the appearance he had. He was certainly the star of that lot." Kerrigan had an open, round-face, a good physique, hazel eyes, and black hair, and he attracted female audiences. When the October 1917 issue of *Motion Picture Classic* carried his image on its cover, the fan magazine suggested that a year earlier Kerrrigan had been the most popular player in the world.

J. Warren Kerrigan (Louisville, Kentucky, July 25, 1879–Balboa Beach, California, June 9, 1947) was an unlikely character to be a hero. His father, who died in 1914, wanted him to be a businessman. Kerrigan wanted to be a minister. His eldest brother—he had seven brothers and one sister—suggested he should be a prizefighter. Ultimately he became an actor, making his first stage appearance in *Sam Houston*, directed and co-authored by his brother-in-law Clay Clement, at New York's Garden Theatre on October 16, 1906.

While on tour in Chicago in 1910 with *The Road to Yesterday*, Kerrigan was invited to join that city's Essanay Film Manufacturing Company. Aside from cowboy star Broncho Billy Anderson, who was also co-owner of the company, Kerrigan was Essanay's most popular male star. When the American Film Manufacturing Company was established in Chicago in October 1910, it quickly lured Kerrigan and others away from Essanay. With newly appointed director Allan Dwan, Kerrigan went with American to La Mesa, California, and then to Santa Barbara, where the company built its permanent studio. As his popularity soared, and after appearing in more than 150 one- or two-reel shorts subjects, Kerrigan moved on from American to Universal in 1913.

At Universal, the actor continued in short films until 1915, when he began to star in features. Early in 1917, he founded his own production company in association with Paralta and began a long relationship with leading lady Lois Wilson. She was often romantically linked with him but told me that he was more a big brother to her. Some of Kerrigan's films were rather odd. In *One Dollar Bid*, released in June 1918, Lois Wilson purchases him for a dollar. In *Three X Gordon*, released in October 1918, he sets up a farm for the regeneration of sons of millionaires. But generally Kerrigan played honest, decent men in a world peopled with villains, and quite often he was a wealthy man duped out of his fortune. Stories were generally written to permit the actor to wear a shirt open at the throat, hinting at a hairy, masculine chest about to be exposed, even if Kerrigan appears to have been clean-shaven—at least on screen.

All went well with J. Warren Kerrigan until he began believing too much in his fan mail. He received literally thousands of letters a week from female fans. When his contract with Universal came up for renewal, he used the fan mail to prove his popularity and justify a pay raise. Universal executive Pat Powers responded by organizing a flurry of negative mail that destroyed Kerrigan's self-confidence.

The actor's reputation was further hurt by an interview in the May 11, 1917, issue of the *Denver Times*, in which he announced he would not respond to the World War One draft until necessary, believing that his country should take "the great mass of men who aren't good for anything" before calling up actors, musicians, writers, and artists. "Isn't it a pity when people are sacrificed who are capable of such things—of adding to the beauty of the world." In its August 1917 editorial, *Photoplay* denounced Kerrigan as "one of the beautiful slackers." In an effort to make amends, in 1919 Kerrigan adopted a six-year-old Polish war orphan, about whom nothing is ever heard again.

Kerrigan's career declined rapidly, and between 1920 and 1923 he starred in no films. His return to the screen as Will Banion in *The Covered Wagon*, again with Lois Wilson as his leading lady, assures him a place in film history, although the classic epic Western is basically a bore. The actor ended his career in 1924, playing the title role in Vitagraph's *Captain Blood*, which was not the great costume drama it should have been and garnered poor reviews.

In later years the actor remained aloof from Hollywood society, maintaining homes in Sunland, on the outskirts of Los Angeles, and south of the city at Balboa Beach. His private life remained private.

Behind J. Warren Kerrigan's public life lurked a dark secret that even today most Hollywood stars would prefer to keep secret. J. Warren Kerrigan was homosexual, carefully hiding his sexual orientation behind a devotion, almost an obsession, to his mother. A 1919 fan magazine writer noted that Kerrigan led a double life, the home life with his mother being the opposite of his screen characterizations. The double life was far less innocent. Whatever Kerrigan did, it was for his mother. He entered films because he wanted a permanent home with his mother. He was the first film star to author an autobiography, in 1914, and the thousand copies of the book are dedicated to "My Mother." (The book is somewhat anti-Semitic in that Kerrigan finds it necessary to make it clear that he is not a Jew.) He built a home in the Cahuenga Pass between Hollywood and the San Fernando Valley, and here Kerrigan lived with his mother, his sister and his twin brother Wallace. The arrangement was "clean-lived," as Kerrigan pointed out to the fan magazines. "I don't believe a screen star should be married....It doesn't seem quite fair...besides I have my Mother." In all conversations with Kerrigan, the "M" of Mother is capitalized, rather like the "G" of God.

Kerrigan's problem was that his World War One remark did not sound like that of a red-blooded, heterosexual American male. And by 1924, and *Captain Blood*, Kerrigan's image on screen was much too effete. The period costumes with lace-trimmed sleeves and the long-haired wigs did not help. Even producer Albert E. Smith, who had originally wanted John Barrymore for the role, had to admit that his star was much too effeminate.

Many of Kerrigan's colleagues must have known of his homosexuality. Once he was a star, no one would dare to confront him, but early in his career, at American, it does appear that he was subjected to some ridicule and "gay bashing." In at least one film, Kerrigan is forced into a humiliating situation to the obvious amusement of the crew. The May 1912 killing of his dog, Puddles, in La Mesa, is suggestive of a possible anti-gay act.

J. Warren Kerrigan was the first in a line of silent leading men who are known to have been gay. Other gay actors from the early years of American film include J. Jiquel Lanoe, who plays the eunoch in *Judith of Bethulia* (1913), his lover Harry Hyde, and Edwin August. Ironically, when Kerrigan left Universal the studio replaced him with another gay actor, Harrison Ford (no relation to the current star of the same name). Other gay leading men include the diminutive Glenn Hunter and Gareth Hughes, who later became a priest and billed himself as Father David. Nils Asther was gay, and an arranged marriage with Vivian Duncan of the Duncan Sisters was a disastrous failure. Eugene O'Brien's homosexuality proved an asset when he became Norma Talmadge's leading man. The actress's husband-producer Joseph Schenck worried that she might have an affair with her co-star and actively promoted the homosexual O'Brien to play opposite his wife.

The two major gay stars of the silent era, the fame of both of whom eclipsed that of J. Warren Kerrigan are William Haines (1900–1973) and Ramon Novarro (1899–1968). According to his biographer, William J. Mann, Haines was Hollywood's first openly gay star, which is something of an exaggeration. While friends and colleagues knew of the actor's sexual orientation, which he made no effort to hide, it was kept carefully obscured from contemporary audiences. A rugged leading man, William Haines was never a great actor, and by the end of the silent era he had developed something of a paunch. Ramon Novarro is the better actor, thanks in large part to early training under Rex Ingram's direction in *The Prisoner of Zenda* (1922), *Trifling Women* (1922), *Where the Pavement Ends* (1923), *Scaramouche* (1923), and *The Arab* (1924). There is a sensitivity to many of his performances that marks Novarro as one of the best male actors of the silent era, although he is obviously mis-cast in *Ben-Hur* (1926), lacking the physique necessary to portray such a hero. Like Kerrigan, Ramon Novarro bought a home in which he might live with his family. He would often justify his unmarried status with plans to become a priest or a monk. Ramon Novarro's post-stardom life was a tragedy of alco-holism and a search for rough sex that ended with his murder. J. Warren Kerrigan appears to have ended his days in quiet seclusion with an unknown lover, undeterred by the demise of his career. "I don't miss it really. I've had my day," he told an inquiring journalist in 1928.

Note: I have written on homosexuality and the silent film in "The Silent Closet," *Film Quarterly*, summer 1999, pp. 24–32.

Bibliography

"Autobiography of J. Warren Kerrigan." *Universal Weekly*, June 27, 1914, p. 12.

Baker, Hettie Gray. "What Warren Kerrigan Isn't." *Motion Picture*, May 1915, pp. 99–103.

Chapman, Jay Brien. "Leading a Double Life." *Motion Picture*, October 1919, pp. 64–65, 121.

Henry, William M. "The Great God Kerrigan." *Photoplay*, February 1916, pp. 33–36.

Kerrigan, J. Warren. *How I Became a Successful Motion Picture Star*. Los Angeles: The Author, 1914.

Petersen, Elizabeth. "Warren Kerrigan's Home Life: His Mother Is His Best Com-panion." *Motion Picture Classic*, December 1916, p. 21.

Remont, Fritzi. "Sonny." *Motion Picture*, May 1918, pp. 70–71, 124.

Robinson, Carlyle. "If Dreams Come True." *Motion Picture Classic*, October 1917, pp. 62–64.

"Trials of the Star-Makers." *New Movie*, November 1933, pp. 36–37, 79–81.

LAURA LA PLANTE

The natural, down-home beauty of Laura La Plante was matched by an easy-going charm and personality. Her characterizations were generally whole-some and refreshingly light, a welcome relief from the exoticism of other leading ladies of the 1920s.

Following a divorce, Laura's mother moved her and her sister from St. Louis, where the actress was born on November 1, 1904, to California. In the summer of 1920, Laura was sent to stay with her aunt in Los Angeles and obtained work with the Christie Comedy Company: "I was living about a block-and-a-half away from the studio, and someone suggested that I go over there. Dorothy Devore was being married to Neal Burns, and they wanted six brides-maids. They dressed me up as a bridesmaid and I went to work straight away. Of course, the first thing I did was to walk back into a scene that was being shot, because I had no idea what the inside of a studio looked like. I was for-given after being sharply scolded for it.

"They put me in stock, and that meant I would get $35 a week if I worked seven days. Of course, they never needed me for seven days. I couldn't make less than $20. If I didn't work at all I would still get the $20."

As early as September 1920, Christie promoted Laura La Plante as one of its players, but the biggest role she ever had there was as the daughter, Nora, in a couple of 1921 films based on the Jiggs and Maggie cartoon strip. Her big break came when Charles Ray cast her as the love interest, Myrtle, in his 1921 screen adaptation of James Whitcomb Riley's *The Old Swimmin' Hole*. After three minor films at Fox, La Plante moved over to Universal, where she was to spend the rest of the decade: "I was taken out there to try for a film with Hoot Gibson. He was lots of fun, a very nice person. I made a test be-cause they wanted to see me on a horse. Sometimes a young lady would come out and say, 'Oh yes, I ride,' but when they got them on the set, they were frightened to death of getting on a horse. I was frightened, but apparently it didn't show. I got away with it. From that part, I got another part, and it wasn't long before someone asked me to come to the front office. They talked me into signing up for five years.

"I went just to be working. Every time I did a film I enjoyed it. I really didn't know where I was headed, because I didn't know what my capacities were. I had had no training of course. I just tried to follow direction, and I seemed to be doing it in passable fashion. I didn't know whether I was a dra-matic actress or what. I was adequate for the things they were giving me. Eventually I proved in my performances that I was more suited to comedy, and I think I developed into a quite good comedienne."

From Westerns, action shorts, and two serials starring William Desmond, Laura La Plante graduated to feature films at Universal. Bobbed hair that added to her beauty and today gives her a pleasing modern look replaced the long curls that had been a dominant feature in the early films. Bleached a pale yellow, the hairstyle gives La Plante a slightly mannish appearance, yet it allows her to retain her feminity. (The similar style adopted by Leatrice Joy makes her look like a young man in drag.)

Beginning with *Sporting Youth* (1924), La Plante was cast opposite Reginald Denny in a series of light romantic comedies, the best of which is *Skinner's Dress Suit* (1926). "He was an absolute darling," she said of the English-born and very English-looking Denny, who later ran a hobby shop on Hollywood Boulevard. "I don't think I ever worked with anyone who was a nicer man. I did not do a film with him thinking I was going to do a series. In fact, it was never called a series."

Despite her obvious ability as a light comedienne, Laura La Plante was featured in a surprising number of dramas. The best is Clarence Brown's *Butterfly* (1924), in which she plays the almost inadvertently selfish younger sister of Ruth Clifford. Playing as a world-class violinist in the film, her early training on the instrument came in handy. The actress is again a younger sister in another major Clarence Brown production, *Smouldering Fires* (1925). Pauline Frederick is the older sister who makes the mistake of marrying a younger man: "She was to me a great actress; I felt like an amateur with her." Modern audiences tend to know Laura for the horror classic *The Cat and the Canary* (1927) and for a second film from the same director, Paul Leni, *The Last Warning* (1928). As Gothic melodrama, *The Cat and the Canary* is ultimately rather disappointing and is better played as farce by Bob Hope a dozen years later.

A director with whom Laura La Plante worked on two features, and with whom she remained close, was Edward Sloman, a prominent contract director at the studio. Of the first production, *The Beautiful Cheat* (1926), in which shopgirl La Plante poses as a Russian actress, he recalled, "She came on the set late. We were sitting around, waiting for her. As she walked on the set, I said, 'Look here young lady, when we say nine o'clock, made-up, we mean nine o'clock made-up, not nine-thirty or ten-thirty.' She started crying, and from then on, we were good friends. I couldn't see a girl cry. It was one of those stories that I had to make up as I went along. It wasn't very good I can assure you. I'd write at night for what I was going to shoot the next day. There was a young boy [Alexander Carr] in it that they put opposite Laura, a very good-looking chap, but he couldn't act for sour apples. He was terrible. It wasn't a good picture. It was a bad picture."

The second film, *Butterflies in the Rain* (1926), a romantic comedy in which La Plante plays an Aristocratic Englishwoman, was a far happier experience for Sloman: "I realized what a good actress she was when she did this [thing] with her nose as she tried to wake herself up. James Kirkwood was the leading man, and he worked with her beautifully. I was out on location, where we were supposed to put a horse over a fence and this guy was going to double for Laura. I was telling the boy about the things he had to do, and I turned and there she stood. The most perfect English riding lady I ever saw with a black hat, a cutaway coat and riding britches. To me, the perfect embodiment of an English woman-rider.

"The old man [Carl Laemmle] didn't know how big a picture he had. He was going back to Germany, every year he would go back there, and this time he took along *Butterflies in the Rain*. He had someone show it on the ship, and everyone raved over the picture. When he got to London, he gave them a picture show, and the picture became a big hit in London. I think that was the beginning of Laura becoming a real star. I want to say without doubt that Laura was the nicest, the loveliest, the sweetest girl I've ever worked with."

Edward Sloman was not the only Universal director interested in Laura La Plante. Another was William Seiter, who directed five of her films at the studio. In 1926, the couple was married. She had no problems working with Seiter as her director: "I had worked with him before we were married. It never occurred to me to argue with anyone over a scene. I thought the man directing ought to know what he was doing or he wouldn't be a director. I do remember I got the giggles once. I was doing a scene with Hedda Hopper and two or three other players on a stairway, and we got to a certain point and we all giggled. Bill finally got so cross with me that he took off his hat and threw his hat at me. That's the only time I can remember he ever got cross with me."

The only director who did give the actress a problem was William Wyler, with whom she had already worked on one of his first productions, *The Love Trap* (1929): "They were already up North some place in the wilderness on location, and they had already shot some scenes. I had not gone because I was working on another film. During my work in the other film, I was using my noon hours to get my clothes for the part I was to step into. I asked Willie Wyler if he could possibly come up on his noon hours to see if I was going in the right direction as far as the clothes went, but he never found the time. That made me feel a little funny. I thought if he didn't have interest enough to do that, maybe he didn't want me in the film, and maybe I was being forced on him.

"The first day I appeared on the set, on location, he said, 'What on earth are you made up for? That won't do at all. You better go down to the village and see what you can find.' I turned around and went back to the hotel, and as I thought about it, I thought it was very unfair. Now I was going to have to go to the one store in the village and see what I could find that would suit me, whereas in Los Angeles I had everything available. I never, ever, ever had any problems with the director, the producer, the cameraman, a player. I never crossed swords with anyone. I loved doing what I was doing, and I had been doing one film after another, all films that I was not particularly well suited to. I phoned my husband and said, 'I don't think I want to do this film.' He said, 'Tell them to go to hell and come home.' Well, I didn't tell them anything of the sort, but I did let them know I thought I would go back.

"That was the reason I left [Universal]. They didn't ask me. They didn't build up an altercation or anything. They were making at the same time a film called *King of Jazz* [1930] and they wrote a couple of skits in it for me to do. I did those. No one said anything to me at all. I went into the front office to explain and I said if it was all right with them, let's just call it even Stephen. You don't have to pay me anything. I don't have to pay you anything. And I'll go my merry way. I didn't see any weeping, but I learned afterwards they were in a very uncomfortable financial position. I think it was a kind of blessing to not have to go on paying me, because my salary had got up around $3,500 a week."

The Love Trap had included talkie sequences, and Laura La Plante had starred in two full sound features at the studio, as well as the first version of Jerome Kern's *Show Boat* (1929). The latter was a curious production, shot as a silent film but with musical excerpts from the Broadway production utilized as a prologue. At its release, Universal added sound to the second half of the film: "There was an intermission, and when we went back, it was in sound. They didn't reshoot it, but they dubbed voices in. They did the best they could. It was impossible to reassemble the cast. Alma Rubens [who had a drug problem] was in a mental hospital. The man who played Captain Andy [Otis Harlan] was in some other country. Joseph Schildkraut was already working in something else. I was there because I was under contract."

After leaving Universal, La Plante made no major effort to find work: "I didn't call anybody, but they weren't calling me either. No one had any time for me. That pleased my husband. He didn't want me to work anyway." She made five inconsequential features and a couple of shorts, and then decided to visit Europe. William Seiter had no interest in making the trip, and Laura went with a friend, the wife of composer Max Steiner. In England, she met up with Irving Asher, whom she had known in Hollywood and who was heading Warner Bros. British production at Teddington Studios just outside of London. La Plante made two subsequent trips to Europe, including a 1934 visit to

Riga, Latvia, where La Plante divorced Seiter. That same year, she married Irving Asher in Paris.

The actress had not intended to make films in England, but, at her new husband's suggestion, she starred in five: *Her Imaginary Lover* (1933), *The Girl in Possession* (1934), *The Church Mouse* (1934), *Widow's Might* (1935), and *Man of the Moment* (1935), the last opposite Douglas Fairbanks Jr. The couple might have remained in England had it not been for World War Two: "We had two children and I had a baby who was about three months old, and we planned a trip back to the States to show off the new baby. We simply moved the sailing up because of the possibility of war. The American Embassy had already suggested that any American residents who intended returning to the States should do so now. While my husband did not intend going back, he did want us to get to California."

Back in the United States, Laura made a few films through 1957, but she had no real interest in reviving her career. She and Irving Asher retired to Rancho Mirage near Palm Springs. Laura retained the distinctive hairstyle and was as pretty and appealing as she had been in the Universal days. She last visited us in the early 1980s, when we screened *The Cat and the Canary* for her. As had Ethel Grandin, Laura lost the power of speech. Irving Asher died in 1985; Laura died at the Motion Picture Country Hospital on October 14, 1996.

Bibliography

Bodeen, DeWitt. "Laura La Plante." *Films in Review*, October 1980, pp. 449–465, 490.

Drew, William M. "Laura La Plante" in *Speaking of Silents: First Ladies of the Screen*. Vestal N.Y.: Vestal Press, 1989, pp. 88–109.

St. Johns, Ivan. "Minus the Wand." *Photoplay*, May 1927, pp. 37, 116.

Summers, Murray. "Laura La Plante in Her Reel Life." *Filmograph*, vol. 2, no. 3, 1971, pp. 22–25, 28–43, 51.

Tully, Jim. "Laura La Plante." *Vanity Fair*, January 1928, pp. 71, 100.

THE LEGENDS

Lon Chaney, Charlie Chaplin, Greta Garbo,
Buster Keaton, and Rudolph Valentino

Fame may last somewhat longer than Andy Warhol's fifteen minutes, but it seldom lasts a lifetime. Film buffs, students and, yes, even a few scholars may recall actors and actresses of the silent screen who were once household names, but even those members of the audience who are still living would be hard-pressed to identify many of them. To be a star, it was once necessary to have one's name billed above the title, in theory to be more important than the film itself. To be a legend, it is necessary to be remembered only by one's last name, and from the silent era, the only players with legendary status—*pace* fans of Gish, Novarro, Pickford, and others—are Lon Chaney, Charlie Chaplin, Greta Garbo, Buster Keaton, and Rudolph Valentino. Pearl White's name may be synonymous with the serial genre, but she is not a legend. Gloria

Swanson's name verges on legendary status, not because of her work in silent films, but because, as Norma Desmond in *Sunset Blvd.*, she represents to generation after generation how a silent star was supposed to be.

RUDOLPH VALENTINO (Castellaneta, Italy, May 6, 1895—New York, August 23, 1926) was not a great actor and nor was he a particularly great lover on screen or apparently off. He is symbolic of a type of leading man in silent films who never really existed outside of a Valentino film, the heavily made up, wildly histrionic romancer. He looks good, stripped to the waist and whipped in his last film, *The Son of the Sheik* (1926). You did not believe him as *The Sheik* in 1921 and you do not believe in the reality of his character here, just as you know he is not really fighting the bulls in *Blood and Sand* (1922). Rex Ingram made Valentino a star in 1921 with *The Four Horsemen of the Apocalypse* and *The Conquering Power*, actually prying performances from his leading man, but once Valentino gained that certain mystique, began to take himself too seriously, and allowed his wife, Natacha Rambova, to handle his career, any acting talent that the star had quickly disappeared. Valentino's leading lady, Alice Terry, once told me, "The biggest thing Valentino ever did was to die." True, and the timing was equally important. He died before the public had the opportunity to hear him speak and to laugh him off the screen as it did John Gilbert. As it was, audiences actually believed in retrospect that he was great. Valentino was the first silent star whose films were reissued after the coming of sound with no suggestion that they were being shown for comic relief. In 1938, both *The Sheik* and *The Son of the Sheik* played nationwide to enthusiastic response. The films were presented with respect and with dignified music scores. unlike poor Elmo Lincoln's *The Adventures of Tarzan* (1921), released in fifteen one-reel chapters with comic narration and musical effects.

Unlike Valentino, **CHARLIE CHAPLIN** (London, April 16, 1889—Corsier-sur-Vevey, Switzerland, December 25, 1977) did not die soon enough. It was too bad he was around to make *A King in New York* (1957) and *The Countess from Hong Kong* (1967). *Limelight* (1952) could have been a fitting conclusion to a film career that began back in 1914 with Mack Sennett's Keystone Company and includes features such as *The Kid* (1921), *The Gold Rush* (1925), *City Lights* (1931) and *Modern Times* (1936), which transcend the art of comedy and become works of art.

Chaplin is singularly out of favor with modern audiences. His films generate little response and few, if any, laughs. Rather like Laurel and Hardy, to whom he is in no other way comparable, his films are too quietly measured, too carefully planned and executed to appeal to audiences that find the Three Stooges or any of the MTV-generated comedians funny. The only silent comedian whose popularity has grown with time is **BUSTER KEATON** (Piqua,

Kansas, October 4, 1895—Woodland Hills, California, February 1, 1966). Keaton was as much a perfectionist in terms of creating gags and routines as Chaplin, but his comedic style is more acrobatic, fast moving, and violent. Chaplin had his origins in British Music Hall and Keaton in American vaudeville. In the creation of the Little Tramp character, Chaplin turned his back on his roots, whereas Keaton brought everything he learned from the family acrobatic act and transformed it for the screen in films such as *Our Hospitality* (1923), *The Navigator* (1924), *Seven Chances* (1925), *The General* (1927), and *Steamboat Bill, Jr.* (1928).

Buster Keaton's films were not particularly popular with contemporary audiences and would sometimes be received quite negatively by the critics. Today, he is the most popular of silent comedians, often generating stronger audience response than do many comedians of the sound era, quite a few of whom were helped by Keaton's unbilled contributions to their films. Buster Keaton developed a problem with alcohol that made him unemployable and resulted in financial difficulties in later years. He lived long enough to receive an enthusiastic ovation at the 1965 Venice Film Festival, but he did not live long enough to accept honors and applause from the new audiences that have come along and embraced his comedic style.

Like Valentino, **LON CHANEY** (Colorado Springs, Colorado, April 1, 1883—Los Angeles, August 26, 1930) career wise had a sensible life span. He was a journeyman actor on screen from 1913 who did not make his mark until *The Miracle Man* (1919). Here, he demonstrated what was a unique mastery of makeup, and he was "The Man of a Thousand Faces" (the title of a 1957 biographical film with James Cagney) in such films as *The Penalty* (1920), *The Hunchback of Notre Dame* (1923), *The Phantom of the Opera* (1925), *The Unholy Three* (1925), *Mr. Wu* (1927), *London after Midnight* (1927), and *Laugh Clown Laugh* (1928). In reality, a more appropriate title, in view of the range of his characterizations, both good and bad, would be, as Herbert Howe suggested, "the Dr. Jekyll and Mr. Hyde of pictures."

Chaney's films are not horrific, but are rather masterworks of the macabre genre. They are very much vehicles for him, and directors (even Tod Browning, who never quite lives up to expectations) are as irrelevant as are the leading ladies. In retrospect, Chaney had the good fortune to star as the Hunchback and the Phantom in films that found their way into public domain, thus becoming staples of any form of cheap entertainment in auditoria or on television. Chaney's only talkie, a 1930 remake of *The Unholy Three*, works well, but it is very obvious that had he lived the Man of a Thousand Faces would have become just another aging character actor, perhaps a villainous version of Henry B. Walthall.

The secret of the success of **GRETA GARBO** (Stockholm, Sweden, September 18, 1905–New York, April 15, 1990) is not that she lived too long or too short a space of years, but that she knew when to retire and how to fashion herself into a mysterious and reclusive figure. Like Chaplin, she is out of favor. There is no real audience for the 25 feature films she made at Metro-Goldwyn-Mayer between 1926 and 1941. She is devastatingly beautiful in the silent works, although quite frankly in *The Kiss* (1929) Lew Ayres is almost as attractive. In the talkies, she is often wooden and sometimes gives the appearance of a leaden lump of a woman. Can one really believe this character of hers in *Grand Hotel* (1932) is a ballerina as she thumps, thumps, thumps her way across the set?

Even Garbo memorabilia has lost its appeal. In 1995, when Christie's offered for sale the soiled knickers that she had given her lover, Gilbert Roland, in 1943, there were no potential buyers. What becomes a legend most? Not apparently soiled panties. It is a Garbo signature that is and was as elusive as the actress herself.

If memorabilia, such as autographs, are indicative of legendary status, then, according to the *Price Guide to Autographs*, Garbo leads with the pack, with her signature selling for $1,575, compared to $1,150 for Lon Chaney's. Valentino's signature has a value of $950. Chaplin sells for a mere $353, and Buster Keaton for $210.

Bibliographies

Lon Chaney

Blake, Michael F. *Lon Chaney: The Man behind the Thousand Faces*. Vestal, N.Y.: Vestal Press, 1990.

———. *A Thousand Faces: Lon Chaney's Unique Artistry in Motion Pictures*. Vestal, N.Y.: Vestal Press, 1995.

———. *The Films of Lon Chaney*. Lanham, Md.: Vestal Press, 1998.

Bodeen, DeWitt. "Lon Chaney: Man of a Thousand Faces." *Focus on Film*, May-August, 1970, pp. 21–39.

Chaney, Lon. "My Own Story." *Movie Magazine*, September 1925, pp. 42–44, 108–110; October 1925, pp. 55–57, 86–89; November 1925, pp. 55–56, 74–75.

Denbo, Doris. "The Phantom of Hollywood." *Picture-Play*, April 1925, pp. 88–89, 100.

Howe, Herbert. "A Miracle Man of Make Up." *Picture-Play*, March 1920, pp. 37–39, 96–97.

St. Johns, Adela Rogers. "Lon Chaney: A Portrait of the Man behind a Thousand Faces." *Liberty*, May 2, 1931, pp. 16–20, 22, 24–25; May 9, 1931, pp. 28–36; May 16, 1931, pp. 28–34; May 23, 1931, pp. 36–37, 40–44; May 30, 1931, pp. 39–44.

Waterbury, Ruth. "The True Life Story of Lon Chaney." *Photoplay*, December 1927, pp. 32–33, 110–114; January 1928, pp. 36–37, 119–121; February 1928, pp. 56–57, 94, 112–113.

Charlie Chaplin

Chaplin, Charles. *My Autobiography*. New York: Simon and Schuster, 1964.
Huff, Theodore. *Charlie Chaplin*. New York: Henry Schuman, 1951.
Lynn, Kenneth S. *Charlie Chaplin and His Times*. New York: Simon & Schuster, 1997.
Maland, Charles J. *Chaplin and American Culture: The Evolution of a Star Image*. Princeton, N.J.: Princeton University Press, 1989.
Milton, Joyce. *Tramp The: Life of Charlie Chaplin*. New York: HarperCollins, 1996.
Mitchell, Glenn. *The Chaplin Encyclopedia*. London: B.T. Batsford, 1997.
Robinson, David. *Chaplin: His Life and Art*. New York: McGraw-Hill, 1985.

Greta Garbo

Billquist, Fritiof. *Garbo: A Biography*. New York: G.P. Putnam's Sons, 1960.
Biery, Ruth. "The Story of Greta Garbo." *Photoplay*, April 1928, pp. 30–31, 78, 102; May 1928, pp. 36–37, 127–128; June 1928, pp. 65, 144–147.
Paris, Barry. *Garbo: A Biography*. New York: Alfred A. Knopf, 1995.
Swenson, Karen. *Greta Garbo: A Life Apart*. New York: Lisa Drew/Scribner, 1997.
Walker, Alexander. *Garbo*. New York: Macmillan, 1980.

Buster Keaton

Blesh, Rudi. *Keaton*. New York: Macmillan, 1966.
Dardis, Tom. *Keaton: The Man Who Wouldn't Lie Down*. New York: Charles Scribner's Sons, 1979.
Keaton, Buster and Charles Samuels. *My Wonderful World of Slapstick*. New York: Doubleday, 1960.
Meade, Marion. *Buster Keaton: Cut to the Chase*. New York: HarperCollins, 1995.
Oldham, Gabriella. *Keaton's Silent Shorts: Beyond the Laughter*. Carbondale, Il.: Southern Illinois University Press, 1996.
Rapf, Joanna E. and Gary L. Green. *Buster Keaton: A Bio-Bibliography*. Westport, Ct.: Greenwood Press, 1995.

Rudolph Valentino

Bodeen, DeWitt. "Rudolph Valentino." *Screen Facts*, vol. 3, no. 5, 1968, pp. 1–27.
Huff, Theodore. "The Career of Rudolph Valentino." *Films in Review*, April 1952, pp. 145–163.
Morris, Michael. *Madam Valentino: The Many Lives of Natacha Rambova*. New York: Abbeville Press, 1991.
Ullman, S. George. *Valentino as I Knew Him*. New York: Macy-Masius, 1926.
Valentino, Rudolph. *My Private Diary*. Chicago: Occult Publishing Company, 1929.
Walker, Alexander. *Rudolph Valentino*. New York: Stein and Day, 1976.

HAROLD LLOYD

There are some images that are indelible. As I write, the May 28, 2001, issue of *The New Yorker* has just appeared, and on its cover is a sketch by Barry Blitt, showing Harold Lloyd hanging from a modern clock face surrounded by New York skyscrapers, with the title "Safety Last, Again." With Chaplin, it is the tramp costume, with Keaton the porkpie hat that are the tokens of their trade. Harold Lloyd has his trademark props of the glasses and straw hat, but it is the shot of him desperately hanging on to the clock face, high above a city street, that symbolizes not only Lloyd but also silent screen comedy.

Why is Harold Lloyd so good? The answer lies in performances and roles that are not strictly comic. There is an element of physical humor always present, of course, but one enjoys and empathizes with Harold Lloyd because he is an ordinary young man facing the problems that most young men encounter. Nothing more typifies a Harold Lloyd comedy than a subtitle in his 1917 short, *Bliss*, when he first meets Bebe Daniels: "Nice Boy, Nice Girl, Nice Day." These few words are comforting; they make one smile and look forward with pleasure to what is about to take place on screen. There is always something nice and reassuring about a Harold Lloyd film, and that is because of the comedian himself and because of the charm of his two best leading ladies, Bebe Daniels and Jobyna Ralston. In between the two came Mildred Davis, whom Lloyd married in 1923, but, in all honesty, she is not as good as Daniels or Ralston. Mildred Davis's best role is as a wife to the comedian until her death in 1969. "She had an opportunity to work for someone else," said Lloyd. "That's how I happened to marry her. I thought I was going to loose her and so I thought that was the best kind of contract I could make. It seemed to prove a very happy one, went on for many years. She went into another type of production—we had three children."

Harold Lloyd had already released two compilations of his work, *Harold Lloyd's World of Comedy* (1962) and *The Funny Side of Life* (1963), and was just about to reissue his feature films when I met him in London in the summer of 1970. It was an exciting experience to walk down Piccadilly, with Lloyd asking my advice as to the potential theatres in which his films might play. As we talked, he explained how his screen character appealed to the positive side of the audience's nature: "My character has a certain tenacity to succeed. In most of the pictures, he does overcome all obstacles and difficulties—defeats, we'll say, the big man. And it has a sort of Horatio Alger quality to it. Especially the early ones. Even in *Kid Brother* (1927), that I like quite well, he succeeds there in the end against tremendous odds. He has these two brawny brothers and this powerful father. He's the puny little one, and as far as strength is concerned, he hasn't a chance with them. I outwitted the brothers by my mind rather than my physical being, and I did succeed in the finish. There was a lot of negative quality in it until he accomplished the positive.

"You see, so many comedies are constructed on trouble, difficulties that you have to get into, and it's overcoming these difficulties that allows you to succeed. Here's the difference. My character, when I put on glasses, was able to look more like the normal boy you met on the street. The romance was believable. I could win the girl. Now, if you notice, Charlie was practically always the losing lover, unless he runs into a girl who has maybe the same screwy thoughts as he does. Charlie was the little tramp, and his character didn't give one the feeling that he should win the girl. When you speak of Chaplin in the negative and me in the positive, lots of people used to compare us in that way. Although we used basic slapstick gags, broad comedy, light comedy, we used a blend as we moved out of the pure slapstick field and into the feature field. *The Freshman* (1925) and *Grandma's Boy* (1922) are pictures that are composed of many different types of comedy. Charlie went in for the dramatic much more than I did, although I did it in two or three. *Grandma's Boy* had it. *The Freshman* had it. But as a rule, mine were more like *Safety Last* (1923)."

Born in Burchard, Nebraska, on April 20, 1893, Harold Lloyd was an assistant with a dramatic school in San Diego when the Edison Company came there on location in 1912. He worked as an extra in a Spanish costume drama and again for Edison in a Dutch film shot in Long Beach. After moving to Los Angeles and working with a couple of stock companies, Lloyd joined Universal, appearing first as an extra in *Samson*, starring J. Warren Kerrigan, released on April 30, 1914. At Universal, Lloyd met Hal Roach, who was about to start his own production company with $3,000 he had inherited, and, in 1915, the comedian joined him, playing the comic character of Willie Work: "I think Hal had respect for the stage experience that I had accumulated, because Hal had not been an actor. Hal asked me if I wanted to come along and be part of his activities, and so I did. He started his pictures, and I was with him on the first one.

"In the early days, it was up to us to think up ideas ourselves. Hal was a very creative mind. He was very good at thinking up gag ideas. The one thing that Hal always repeated was he could tell what was in my mind, the idea that I had, and he seemed to have the knack of knowing how to take that idea and put it on the screen. There was a great bond between Hal and myself, not that we haven't had lots of squabbles through the years.

"Let's move back to a period when we just assembled a cast of characters. We had a policeman as a rule, we had a heavy, we had naturally the leading lady. We had only just a slight semblance of ideas that we wanted to do, and then we just constructed the picture in that park, a beautiful lake, lovely surroundings, little benches. They lent themselves to ideas. We started with an incident, probably where I started to flirt with somebody's girl. He probably proved to be a big individual that you don't fool around with. In the finish, we'd create a chase or a fight or something of that nature. Then when we had nine hundred feet, we had a one-reeler, and we quit."

With Hal Roach, Lloyd created a new character, Lonesome Luke, and then, in 1917, added a pair of spectacles to his attire. The Harold Lloyd character of the next thirty years was created. In 1923, Lloyd and Hal Roach parted company, with the latter forming his own production unit: "It was Hal's idea. He said, 'You've got eighty percent in your pictures at the present time, and I don't feel that I'm earning even my twenty percent. I think you ought to take over and go on and manage your situation, and I'll carry on with mine.' We couldn't have parted in a more amicable way. With the exception of a few squabbles here and there, Hal and I have been the closest of friends, and I believe we both recognize that each of us contributed to the other person's well-being, both personally and career-wise."

With the exception of the unfortunately right-wing *The Cat's Paw* in 1934, which would have been more appropriate as a Cecil B. DeMille production, Harold Lloyd continued to make great films. He ended his working career in 1947 with *Mad Wednesday*, also known as *The Sins of Harold Diddlebock*, directed by Preston Sturges, which utilizes the final sequences from *The Freshman*, and in many respects takes Lloyd's career full circle. Harold Lloyd died in Los Angeles on March 8, 1971.

Bibliography

Brownlow, Kevin. "Preserved in Amber." *Film Comment*, March-April 1993, pp. 26–34.

Cahn, William. *Harold Lloyd's World of Comedy*. New York: Duell, Sloan and Pearce, 1964.

D'Agostino, Annette M. *Harold Lloyd: A Bio-Bibliography*. Westport, Ct.: Greenwood Press, 1994. [Contains a complete annotated bibliography]

Dardis, Tom. *Harold Lloyd: The Man on the Clock*. New York: Viking Press, 1983.

Garringer, Nelson E. "Harold Lloyd." *Films in Review*, August-September 1962, pp. 407–422.

Kaminsky, Stuart. "Harold Lloyd: A Reassessment of His Film Comedy." *The Silent Picture*, no. 16, autumn 1972, pp. 21–29.

Lloyd, Harold and W.W. Stout. *An American Comedy*. New York: Longmans, Green, 1928. [reprinted in paperback by Dover Publications]

Reilly, Adam. *Harold Lloyd: The King of Daredevil Comedy*. New York: Macmillan, 1977.

Schickel, Richard. *Harold Lloyd: The Shape of Laughter*. Boston: New York Graphic Society, 1974.

BABE LONDON

In the 1923 Christie comedy, *Kiddin' Kate*, the hapless bridegroom arrives expecting that his mail order bride is Dorothy Devore but is shocked to discover that he is to marry overweight Babe London, looking totally unappealing in a oversize woolen sweater, a dress that is too short, and ankle-length socks. It's a typically degrading role for Babe London, but one with which the actress must, presumably, have felt comfortable. At the height of her career, Babe London had boasted a weight of 255 pounds, and in one of her earliest screen appearances, in Chaplin's *A Day's Pleasure* (1919), she is literally walked over by the comedian as he tries to get on board a pleasure boat and lands in the water.

Jean London—like another overweight comedy performer, Oliver Hardy, she adopted the name of "Babe"—was born in Des Moines, Iowa, on September 28, 1901. When the family moved to Oakland, California, she began acting on screen with a company based at the former Essanay Studios in Niles. From there, Babe persuaded her parents to relocate to Los Angeles, and in 1918, she joined the Vitagraph Company, appearing with the comedy team of Montgomery and Rock. A year later, Babe had an uncredited role in Douglas Fairbanks's *When the Clouds Roll By*.

She spent most of her working life as a featured comedienne in films produced in the 1920s by Christie and Educational. Babe claimed to have been in practically every film Al Christie directed during the decade: "He got a kick out of me as a bum Mary Pickford; he'd put a Mary Pickford wig on me, you know, with the curls." Her few roles in silent features emphasized her size; she was a circus strong woman in *Golden Dreams* (1922) and *Tillie's Punctured Romance* (1928) and a hefty stenographer in *Is That Nice?* (1926). Often, as in Blanche Sweet's *Tess of the D'Urbevilles* (1924), Colleen Moore's *The Perfect Flapper* (1924), Harry Langdon's *Long Pants* (1927) and the Vilma Banky vehicle *The Awaking* (1928), she was uncredited.

After a stint in vaudeville with her first husband, Babe London returned to the screen with the coming of sound, but, again, primarily in uncredited parts. She had one memorable role as Ollie's hapless fiancée, Dulcy, in the Laurel and Hardy Comedy short *Our Wife*, released in May 1931 but basically spent the sound era as an extra or bit player, appearing as late as 1970 in *Dirty Dingus Magee*. "I used to weigh 255 pounds," she remembered for me back in November 1971. "I was typed as a fat girl. I used to do chases and pratfalls, and in vaudeville I danced very fast, high-kicking numbers. Then my doctor told me I had to take this weight off—my heart was tired—and I did. But it was like starting anew. I'd be called down to an interview. 'You aren't Babe

London.' 'Oh, yes I am.' But I wouldn't fit the script. You get typed in pictures and established, and when you change your type radically, it's very hard."

Babe London took up painting after attending night classes at Hollywood High School in 1958. He style was primitive, sometimes compared to Grandma Moses, and her subjects silent comedy players that she had known or worked with. She gave her work the collective name of "The Vanishing Age," calling it, "a painted saga of the old silent days." There was one professional exhibition in Hollywood in July 1964, but Babe's work generated little interest, and the film buffs who might have snapped up this type of memorabilia just were not around at this time. She married her third husband, musical director 79-year-old Phil Boutelje, on March 2, 1975, while both were residents of the Motion Picture Country House, and died there on November 29, 1980. Babe London lived at the facility almost adjacent to another Christie comedy player, Dorothy Devore, but such was the rivalry between them in old age that the two never communicated.

Bibliography

Slide, Anthony. "Babe London." *The Silent Picture*, no. 15, summer 1972, pp. 4–7.

BESSIE LOVE

For an apt and early description of Bessie Love, one should turn to a self-published 1926 monograph, *Who's Whose in Hollywood: A Sorta Saga of Screenland*, by B.W. Sayres (either a pseudonym or an anagram): "Lillian Gish with a Charleston complex...No sex appeal, but a lotta loose and lovely legs." It is not exactly a positive image of the actress, but there is much truth here. Bessie Love does have some of the ethereal quality of Lillian Gish, hence her start with D.W. Griffith. Thanks to her performance in *The Broadway Melody* (1929) and other early sound musicals, she does exemplify the jazz era. As early as October 1923, *Photoplay* chose Bessie Love to pose in a series of photographs illustrating how to dance the Charleston. And, despite a somewhat squat body, she does have two loose and lovely legs—again only really seen to advantage with the coming of sound.

Born Juanita Horton in Midland, Texas, on September 10, 1898, Bessie Love attended high school in Los Angeles and obtained work as an extra with D.W. Griffith's company. He cast her as the Bride of Cana in *Intolerance* (1916) and changed her name to Bessie Love. William S. Hart borrowed her from Griffith to be his leading lady in *The Aryan* (1916), casting her as a young girl who persuades the ruthless Hart to provide water for her fellow Mississippians and to prevent his men from molesting their women.

Bessie Love returned to D.W. Griffith's company and was Douglas Fairbanks's leading lady in two 1916 features, *Reggie Mixes In* and *The Good Bad Man*. Her first starring role was as the surrogate mother of her brothers and sisters in *A Sister of Six*, released in October 1916. Griffith tried unsuccessfully to strengthen Bessie Love's performance by promoting other actresses against her. It didn't work, and, as Bessie recalled, the director told her, "There's no cat in you; you'll never be as good an actress as Mae Marsh."

In all truth, she wasn't, but Bessie Love did become a star, first with Pathé in 1918 and then, later that same year, with Vitagraph. A wealthy uncle financed a production company for his niece in 1920, but the three films she made independently did nothing for her career. The actress starred in more than thirty silent features in the 1920s, but she failed to stand out from the crowd of actresses who were equally busy. She did develop a close friendship with actress Blanche Sweet after working for Sweet's director husband Marshall Neilan in *The Eternal Three* (1923).

Blanche had a way of dealing with her husband's many girl friends: she would invite them home for the weekend, knowing that two days in close proximinity to Marshall Neilan would destroy any affair. Blanche suspected that Bessie might be her husband's latest lover, and so she was invited for the weekend, and the two actresses became lifelong friends. Bessie and Blanche appeared together in *Those Who Dance* (1924). Toward the close of the film, Bessie has a scene in which, as the gangster's moll, she realizes she is lonely without her man. After the scene was shot, Blanche said to her, "Remind me to tell you how much I hate you for doing that scene so beautifully."

With the coming of sound, Bessie Love had her first stage experience, touring in a Fanchon and Marco show. Irving Thalberg must have sensed something special in Bessie's personality when he hired her to star, with Anita Page, in MGM's first all talking, all singing, all dancing production, *The Broadway Melody*, released in February 1929. It made Bessie Love a star all over again, but the new success was all too brief as the public quickly tired of musicals. By 1931, Bessie Love was reduced to appearing in a poverty row production, *Morals for Women*. She had married William Hawks, the brother of director Howard, in 1929, and a daughter, Patricia, was born in 1932. With the disintegration of both her U.S. career and her marriage, Bessie Love decided to take her daughter to Europe, and in 1935, they settled in London.

Bessie Love became a fixture in British films. Whenever a mature American woman was needed, Bessie Love was available. Among her most memorable roles are Isadora Duncan's mother in *Isadora* (1968) and the telephone operator in *Sunday, Bloody Sunday* (1971). She also starred in her own play, *The Homecoming*, in 1958, in Perth, Scotland, and played Aunt Pittypat in a 1972 musical version of *Gone with the Wind* at London's Theatre Royal, Drury Lane. Bessie Love made her final screen appearance in *The Hunger* in 1983, and died, in London, on April 26, 1986.

Bibliography

Curley, Kenneth. "The Idealist Speaks." *Motion Picture*, May 1922, pp. 70, 109.
Dunham, Harold. "Bessie Love." *Films in Review*, February 1959, pp. 86–99.
Gassaway, Gordon. "Bonnie Sweet Bessie." *Motion Picture Classic*, August 1922, pp. 38–39, 78.
Hall, Gladys. "Confessions of the Stars: Bessie Love." *Motion Picture Classic*, June 1929, pp. 20–21, 72.
Howe, Herbert. "The Girl Who Walked Back." *Photoplay*, May 1929, pp. 60, 150–151.
Love, Bessie. *From Hollywood with Love*. London: Elm Tree Books, 1977.
Peltret, Elizabeth. "Bessie Love." *Motion Picture Classic*, September 1920, pp. 16–17, 86.
Sayford, I.S. "Just a Little Love." *Photoplay*, August 1916, pp. 123–125.
Todd, Stanley. "The Rise of Bessie Love." *Motion Picture*, October 1917, pp. 33–37.
"Wrong about the Face." *Photoplay*, December 1919, p. 106.

BEN LYON. *See* **BEBE DANIELS AND BEN LYON**

DOROTHY MACKAILL

Hull or, to be more precise, Kingston upon Hull, is a grim seaport on England's West Yorkshire Coast. Dorothy Mackaill was born there on March 4, 1903. I began my working life there as a local government employee, in 1960. I have no particularly happy memories of the place, only the overwhelming, pervasive smell of fish hanging over the city day after day. Aside from Mackaill, the only celebrities that Hull has produced are flyer Amy Johnson (the British equivalent of Amelia Earhart) and poet Philip Larkin, who was librarian at the University of Hull. I am sure the city was much the same in Dorothy Mackaill's time as it was in mine, and despite an affluent family, one can well understand why she decided to run away from home at the age of thirteen and become a London chorus girl. Thanks to a natural blonde beauty and a pert personality, she quickly graduated to featured billing in revues in both London and Paris, and, in 1920, Mackaill made her film debut, uncredited, in the British feature *The Face at the Window*, starring C. Aubrey Smith and released in 1921.

On the advice of American dance director Ned Wayburn, she headed for New York and was hired by Florenz Ziegfeld. In 1921 she made her American film debut, again uncredited, under Marshall Neilan's direction in the John Barrymore vehicle *The Lotus Eater*. The actress had a natural light comedic touch, and while she certainly could, and did, play dramatic roles in many features of the 1920s, she was at her best in comedy, first as Johnny Hines's leading lady in the "Torchy" shorts, and, later, as Jack Mulhall's leading lady in a series of ten romantic comedies, including *Smile, Brother, Smile* (1927) and *Ladies' Night in a Turkish Bath* (1928).

Dorothy Mackaill was never a great star, but she was one of those reliable leading ladies who gave no trouble either to the director or to prominent leading men, such as Milton Sills (whom she played opposite in *The Making of O'Malley* [1925] and in her first talkie, *The Barker* [1928]) or Richard Barthelmess with whom she co-starred in *The Fighting Blade* (1923), *Twenty-One* (1923), *Shore Leave* (1925), and *Ransom's Folly* (1926). She was very much the modern girl on screen. Mackaill was neither the first nor the most prominent film flapper, but she is the one actress who most personifies that unique type of personality.

The Yorkshire accent is not a pleasing one, and Dorothy Mackaill must certainly have acquired such an accent as a child. Yet once in the United States, she became very much American and had no problem appearing as such in fifteen talkies from 1928 through 1937, when she ended her film career, where it had begun, in England, playing opposite John Lodge in *Bulldog Drummond at Bay.* "I was fortunate and happy in realizing a most interesting career and I must confess I terminated same too soon as I loved every minute of it," she recalled.

Mackaill married three times, the first in 1926 to director Lothar Mendes, and all ended in divorce. Her second and third husbands both had ties to Hawaii, where Dorothy Mackaill settled in the early 1930s. In 1955, she took up residence at the Royal Hawaiian Hotel in Honolulu, apparently serving as an unofficial greeter in return for complimentary accommodation. She died there on August 12, 1990. As she wrote to the teenage fan from Hull, "Now I live in these beautiful Hawaiian Islands with a host of friends, a beautiful hotel and I swim practically every day with loads of sunshine, and what more can I ask?"

Bibliography

Bodeen, DeWitt. "Dorothy Mackaill." *Films in Review,* December 1977, pp. 577–592.
Burton, Stanley. "Second Thoughts on Matrimony." *Photoplay,* March 1930, pp. 43, 106.
Klumph, Helen. "Not to Be Pigeon Holed." *Picture-Play,* July 1923, pp. 20–21, 98.
Sewell, Jameson. "A Cockney Beauty." *Photoplay,* August 1923, p. 51.
Squier, Emma-Lindsay. "Dinner with Dorothy." *Picture-Play,* September 1925, pp. 83, 103.

Finn Dudley

MARY MACLAREN

It might well be a Hollywood novel. There were two sisters. The younger, Katherine MacDonald (Pittsburgh, December 14, 1891–Santa Barbara, July 4, 1956) was not a great actress but a noted screen beauty. She died in luxury with a villa in the affluent Montecito suburb of Santa Barbara. She entered films in 1918, using the influence of her sister, Mary, who had changed her last name to MacLaren. Katherine MacDonald was renowed for her good looks, billed as "The American Beauty," and supposedly was the mistress of Woodrow Wilson. She dominated the career of her more talented sibling, forcing an end to a lucrative Universal contract and canceling a proposed Paramount contract. Even without the bad advice of her sister, there is every reason to believe that Mary MacLaren's life was destined to be a disaster.

Born in Pittsburgh on January 19, 1896, Mary MacLaren became a chorus girl at the age of thirteen and a Hollywood extra a year later. While working at Universal, she was spotted by Lois Weber, the most important director on the lot, who cast her in a small role in *John Needham's Double* (1916) and as the maid in the controversial anti-abortion, pro–birth control feature *Where Are My Children?* (1916). Weber found the young actress very malleable and easy to direct, and was impressed by the very ordinariness of her features. MacLaren was barely pretty, but she had the appearance of an average working-class American girl. As such, she was perfect for the lead in *Shoes*, released in June 1916. Here she is a shop girl who prostitutes herself in order to raise the money to purchase a new pair of shoes. It was a heartrending melodrama that might have been over the top were it not for Weber's controlled direction and the undemonstrative performance from MacLaren. "She was very strict, always telling me not to do this or not to do that," Mary told me.

Weber directed MacLaren again in *Idle Wives* (1916), *Saving the Family Name* (1916), *Wanted—a Home* (1916), and *The Mysterious Mrs. M.* (1917), in which the actress had the opportunity to play a lighter role. The director brought out in MacLaren a talent that others could not discern. David O. Selznick was particularly harsh, stating emphatically that she could not act and looked as if she needed a good sleep. Audiences enjoyed the actress's performances not so much for the depth of the characterizations but because she seemed able to weep profusely on camera.

Persuaded by her sister not to renegotiate a Universal contract, and unable to come to terms with Paramount, Mary MacLaren became an independent player in the late teens, but she was unsuccessful at finding adequate roles. Her last prominent appearance is as the queen of France in Douglas

Fairbanks's 1921 production of *The Three Musketeers*. MacLaren's last silent film is *The Dark Swan*, released by Warner Bros. in December 1924, in which she is seventh billed. In 1924, she married a British colonel George H. Young and moved with him to India. Neither the marriage nor the change of scene was successful. The couple divorced and MacLaren returned to Hollywood, complaining bitterly of India, a country unfit for a movie star! MacLaren used her husband as the basis for the leading character in a 1952 self-published novel, *The Twisted Heart*, which deals with a woman who fails to realize she has married a homosexual. A lurid and unconvincing tale, *The Twisted Heart* boasts that it is edited by James M. Cain, who, in view of his anti-gay stance in his 1937 novel *Serenade*, may well have found the plot appealing.

Mary MacLaren returned to the screen in 1933 as a bit player and can be glimpsed by discerning viewers in more than 75 films made over the next two decades. One of her first sound roles is as the woman who faints at seeing her husband's name on a list of the war dead in *Cavalcade* (1933). In the late 1940s, she began operating the home into which she had moved on April 17, 1917, at 127 North Manhattan Place in Hollywood as a rooming house. She sank slowly but surely into poverty. In February 1965, Mary married Robert S. Coleman, a blind amputee veteran of World War One. She described it as "a marriage of mercy."

She was accident prone, involved in automobile wrecks in 1946 and 1961. A fire in January 1981 destroyed the upper floor of the house. Mary wandered around, attired in a soiled dressing gown and slippers. She slept on a rotted mattress with her five dogs and four cats. The welfare of the animals was far more important to her than her own wellbeing. Whatever money was available, she spent on them. She despised her sister, telling me that Katherine and her friend J. Paul Getty were "twin souls—those misers."

A visit to Mary MacLaren was certainly an experience. One sat down gingerly on the decomposing couch on the front porch, wondering what it might contain that was still alive. It was difficult to get her to talk about films when her current interest was astrology. A trip inside the house could prove horrendous. The stench of cats was pervasive, and one stood by silently as Mary showed you a room whose sole and permanent inhabitants were three kittens. Stray dogs and cats and stray people gravitated toward Mary. The animals were relatively harmless. The people less so; she recounted stories of one female lodger who tried to force her to eat poisoned pancakes.

A strict vegetarian, lunch was a baked potato and a cup of tea at the local Sizzler, and afterward, Mary would stand outside and feed the pigeons, much to the irritation of the restaurant management. A tenant secured ownership of her home in January 1979 under confused circumstances. As early as

1979, Mary fought off efforts by the county to gain conservatorship over her, but in June 1983, she lost the fight. In December of that year, the house in which she had lived for 65 years was auctioned off. Mary MacLaren ended her life as a resident of the Virgil Convalescent Hospital and died on November 9, 1985.

Bibliography

Kingsley, Grace. "Sweet Sobber of the Celluloid." *Photoplay*, February 1917, pp. 27–28, 142.

Kingsley, Ruth. "How Mary Made Her Eyes Behave." *Motion Picture*, March 1919, pp. 38–39, 107.

Koszarski, Richard. "Truth or Reality: A Few Thoughts on Mary MacLaren's *Shoes*." *Griffithiana*, no. 40/42, October 1991, pp. 79–82.

Pepper, Peter. "The Strange Case of Mary MacLaren." *Moving Picture Weekly*, June 24, 1916, pp. 9, 34.

Shirley, Lois. "Sadder but Wiser." Photoplay, June 1928, pp. 39, 117.

Valentine, Sydney. "I—Mary MacLaren." *Photoplay*, December 1920, p. 36.

PERCY MARMONT

Watching Percy Marmont as the personification of the English gentleman on screen in more than thirty British films from 1928 through 1968—typified by his role as the Chief Constable father of Nova Pilbeam in Hitchcock's *Young and Innocent/The Girl Was Young* (1937)—it is difficult to imagine him as a silent star. Yet there he is in some fifty American features from 1918 through the end of the silent era. He always wore a dyspeptic and anguished look, as if he was not really enjoying himself. In *Mantrap* (1926), he picked up his leading lady, Clara Bow, and suffered a hernia, and so perhaps that expression was at times close to reality.

Percy Marmont was born in the West London suburb of Gunnersbury on November 25, 1883, into a comfortably upper–middle-class household. When I met him in 1969, he had risen from a middle-class to an upper-class environment, residing on a magnificent country estate a one-hour train ride outside of London. He was blind but got around with the help of his actress-daughter Pam and her husband, Moray Watson, who, like his father-in-law, is adept at portraying warm and friendly upper-class types. He had thoroughly enjoyed his career and the friendships he had formed in the film industry. There was no hint of bitterness or antagonism toward anyone, simply pleasure with a life well spent.

Long before he entered films, Marmont had been on stage, starring in a touring production of *The Only Way* in 1900, and working with Ben Greet, Cyril Maude, Granville Barker, and other legendary names of British theatre. He made his screen debut while touring South Africa (his second visit) in 1917 in *Die Voortrekkers*, directed by Harold Shaw and released in the United States in 1924 as *Winning a Continent*: "As the studio was quite near to Johannesburg I was able to work there in the daytime. I didn't take it very seriously. It was just fun. I did a lot of horse-riding in it, and I enjoyed it from that point of view." From South Africa, the theatrical tour moved on to Australia, where Marmont made his second film, *The Monk and the Woman* (1917), dealing with the controversial subject of a monk who renounces his vow of celibacy: "I think I must have been terrible, but by the time they released it, I was out of Australia and safely away in America."

Percy Marmont arrived in the United States as a tourist with every intention of continuing home to England. A chance encounter on Broadway with a producer led to his being cast in Edward Childs Carpenter's comedy *The Three Bears*, which opened at New York's Empire Theatre on November 13, 1917, and to an eleven-year stay in America. Marmont's second New York stage appearance—also at the Empire in 1917—was in Ethel Barrymore's production of *The Lady of the Camellias*, in which silent screen star-to-be Conway Tearle appeared as Armand. While working on stage, Marmont began to appear in films during the day, starring opposite Corinne Griffith and Alice Joyce at Vitagraph. The film that made Marmont a star was the 1923 adaptation of the A.S.M. Hutchinson novel *If Winter Comes*, which is unusual in that there are no principal female roles. The film was shot at a studio in New York, and its star went home to England to film scenes in London, Canterbury and Brighton, and at Leeds Castle.

"I was in the fortunate position of being able to pick and choose after that," said Marmont, but in order to consolidate his success, the actor did have to move from New York to Los Angeles: "One had a lovely home life, also one had a lovely home. It was particularly nice for us because we had our own little bunch of friends, Ernest Torrence, Ronald Colman, William Powell, Warner Baxter, and another Warner, a wonderful man, Warner Oland, Jack Holt, Tim McCoy. We used to use each other's houses and get together at weekends. When I say weekends, I mean it, because during the week one just could not be social. It was quite a usual thing if there was a party and you were on a film, you unostentatiously left the party before nine o'clock. You had to be up at half past five in the morning. All this nonsense about Hollywood parties didn't exist. You couldn't burn the midnight oil."

Percy Marmont's comments on specific films were always straightforward and no-nonsense. *The Marriage Clause* (1922): "A shocking picture, under the auspices of Thomas Ince, directed by John [Griffith] Wray. It was such utter drivel and such frightful nonsense. It was very hard for any of us to take it seriously. It was all set in some extraordinary island in the South Seas, which nobody had ever heard of, where everything was primitive and terrible. I, of course, was a missionary who converted the heathen to something. I don't know what I converted them to. I had my beautiful wife, Leatrice Joy, and in due course of time she became pregnant. The night the child was born, she was suffering, poor soul. You didn't see her suffering—you only saw me doing the suffering. Can you imagine a director wanting me to do this? He wanted me to go down on my knees to a heathen idol and pray to it. I said, 'John, you can't do that. It's too silly.' Suddenly I got a brainwave. I said, 'Let me go down on my knees and pray. There's a little native girl, and she comes and takes an idol and puts it in front of me while I'm praying. I don't know it's there.' Some of the things we had to do, I can't tell you how silly they were."

You Can't Get Away with It (1923): "The reason for that title was the hero and the heroine, there was a reason why they couldn't marry, so they lived together. Rowland Lee said, 'I shouldn't engage you at all for this, but I like your work very much.' I said, 'Well, that's very nice of you, but why are you engaging me?' He said, 'It's essentially an American man, must be American, but being silent, we can make you look American.' He came down into Los Angeles with me to a tailor that he knew of and ordered five or six suits, and they were all cut in the American line. The first day I appeared on the set, he looked at me and said, 'Just an Englishman in an American suit.' He was quite right. I didn't look a bit like an American."

The Shooting of Dan McGrew (1924): "That was dreadful, directed by Clarence Badger. The stars were Mae Busch and Lew Cody—such a nice man and such a beast on the screen."

The Legend of Hollywood (1924): "That was made by Victor Hugo Halperin. That was certainly a slow motion picture; because we played it in such slow tempo that it was almost like slow motion. This was the story of an author who went to Hollywood, hoping to make good, and he didn't. He flopped all the time. He got down to starvation point and decided to put an end to it. But being an author, he had a silly dramatic sense. He got a circular tray and put on it twelve drinks, and one of them was poisoned. Having done that, he spun the tray around and said, 'I'm going to take one each day and if a job doesn't come in before I come to the poisoned one....' Utterly ridiculous. I did it very seriously, much to my credit, because I thought lot of damned nonsense this is. ZaSu Pitts was the girl in the background who saved me, and we lived happy ever afterwards. What a sweet woman she was, a dear sweet woman."

The Street of Forgotten Men (1925): "I came back from California to New York to make that with Herbert Brenon. He directed. Brenon was very efficient, a very difficult man, very temperamental. We became very good friends, but you had to be very tactful with Herbert Brenon. He had a lot of Irish blood in him, and you had to be very careful that you didn't tread on the tail of his coat. I trod on it several times, but we got over it."

A Woman's Fate (1925): "That was interesting from the point of view that it was directed by a grandson of Carl Laemmle. Little Eddie Laemmle was a nice little man. He didn't know much about it, but he was learning all the time. It was one of those very serious pictures that we laughed our way through. The situations were so absurd that if was very difficult for Alma Rubens and for me, who both, if I may say so, had a certain sense of humor in common. I was blinded and I was cured by going to St. Anne de Beaupré, which was the American equivalent of Lourdes. It was called *The Stairway of Hope* in England, because I had to go up a long flight of stairs, grope my way up."

Mantrap (1926): "I enjoyed it very much because it was done by people that I liked so much, not only Clara Bow, who was a sweet woman, but my dear friend Ernest Torrence and one of my favorite directors, Victor Fleming.

He was a lovely director. We shot it all up in the San Bernardino Mountains. A very happy experience."

In 1928, Marmont returned to the United Kingdom, where his first film was *Yellow Stockings*, directed by Theodor Komisarjevsky: "I don't think it was very good." *The Squeaker* (1930), written and directed by Edgar Wallace, was his first talkie. After Hollywood, conditions at the British studios seemed very primitive: "For example, instead of having a nice restaurant with a decent dinner, you had bread, cheese and beer, and worked on till ten o'clock at night. It damned near killed me, but I stuck it. In America, I went into the top role, and stayed there for a bit. Then came back to England—into the bottom role."

The year 1936 was a momentous one in Percy Marmont's career. It began with the making of his favorite British film, *The Secret Agent*, directed by Alfred Hitchcock, in which, as Mr. Caypor, he is murdered by Peter Lorre. Marmont was then approached by producer James Fitzpatrick, for whom he had made *The Lady of the Lake* in 1928, to participate in the filming of a feature-length travelogue. Because of a clash in dates, Marmont had to approach Hitchcock with a view to an early completion of his filming: "And Hitchcock, dear fellow that he was, said, 'I don't see how we can possibly do it unless we work Sundays. I'm not going to ask John Gielgud to work on Sunday, but if you'd like to ask him well and good. I went Gielgud, and his reaction was, 'My dear fellow, we'll work all night, Sunday or any other day, of course we will.' Every member of the cast except one—don't ask me her name [Madeleine Carroll]—said yes. Fitzpatrick said, 'Never mind, tell you what we'll do. You join us at Capetown,' So they did their South American stuff, which I was sorry to miss, but I joined them in Capetown. We did a lot of work in Africa. From Africa, we went to Madagascar, the Seychelles, and on to India, Ceylon, Malaya, Singapore. Then up to Japan. From China, we went to Manilla, from Manilla to Honolulu, then back to Los Angeles, across to New York, and back to London. Some of the stuff that I personally directed, some of the African shots and all the Taj Mahal stuff in India, was shown as a travelogue. We were going to do a story, but we were defeated by the sound. We couldn't control the sound."

Out of the shot footage, Fitzpatrick crafted *David Livingstone* (1936), with Marmont in the title role. On return to England, the producer planned to film the crime drama *The Captain's Table* (1936), but, too busy to direct, he asked Marmont to take on the double duty of star and director: "I'm rather sorry I did because it wasn't very good. We did have a very good cast, but I wasn't much of a director. I hope I was better than I thought I was."

Percy Marmont was to remain active for another thirty years on stage and screen. He played opposite Vivien Leigh in her last British stage appearance, *La Contessa* (1965), and Orson Welles featured him in an abortive film project, *Blue Moon*, shot in Budapest: "I said, 'Why on earth did you pick me?' He said, 'Because I thought you'd be good in it.' I never even knew he knew of my existence." This grand old man of British and American cinema died in London on March 3, 1977.

Bibliography

Breedlove, Frederick. "Percy Marmont, a Reluctant Martyr." *Cinema Art*, December 1927, pp. 23, 49.

Manners, Dorothy. "As Others See Him." *Picture-Play*, June 1926, pp. 74, 105.

Service, Faith. "Living Down the Name of Percy." *Motion Picture Classic*, May 1919, pp. 31,72.

Slide, Anthony. "Percy Marmont's Hollywood." *The Silent Picture*, no. 7, summer 1970, pp. 15–17.

Tibbetts, John C. "Percy Marmont: Leading Man to More Stars Than Are in Heaven." *Films in Review*, September/October 1995, pp. 9–19.

MAE MARSH

When Mae Marsh died at her longtime home in Hermosa Beach, California, on February 13, 1968, Pauline Kael reminded us in one the finest modern tributes to silent film ever published in *The New Yorker* (February 24, 1968), "She is our dream not of heavenly beauty, like Gish, but of earthly beauty, and sunlight makes her youth more entrancing. She looks as if she could be a happy, sensual, ordinary woman. The tragedies that befall her are accidents that could happen to any of us, for she has never wanted more than common pleasures....the girl who twists her hands in the courtroom scenes of *Intolerance* is the image of youth-in-trouble forever."

Of all D.W. Griffith's actresses, Mae Marsh is the one who could so easily be transformed from the ordinary to the extraordinary. With Flora Cameron accepting death over rape in *The Birth of Nation* (1915) and the Dear One in *Intolerance* (1916), cradling her father and the Boy (Robert Harron) as much as she cradles "the hopeful geranium," Mae Marsh gives us two of the greatest performances in the entire history of American film, silent or sound. Born Mary Warne Marsh in Madrid, New Mexico, on November 9, 1895, Mae Marsh joined D.W. Griffith and the American Biograph Company in 1912. She and Robert Harron formed a romantic partnership on screen, seldom equaled since, and continued it, under Griffith's guidance, from American Biograph through the masterworks of *The Birth of a Nation* and *Intolerance* to the Fine Arts features of 1915 and 1916.

Mae Marsh left Griffith at the end of 1916 to join Samuel Goldwyn's company. According to Mary Pickford, and confirmed by Miriam Cooper, Mae had had an affair with the director, but he treated her very badly, forcing her to ride the streetcar home after spending the night with him. Griffith made an actress of Mae Marsh. Goldwyn made her a star. Unfortunately, the starring vehicles were not that great and their directors failed to elicit great performances from the new leading lady. A September 2, 1918, marriage to Goldwyn publicist Louis Lee Arms foundered when he became an alcoholic, spending his wife's money and treating her badly, and a planned retirement from the screen failed to materialize.

Producer Herbert Wilcox and director Graham Cutts brought Mae to England in 1922 to star in *Flames of Passion* and *Paddy-the-Next-Best-Thing*; "There must have been thirty to forty thousand people at Waterloo station to meet this little wisp of a girl," recalled Wilcox. Cutts brought Mae back to the U.K. in 1925 to star opposite Ivor Novello in *The Rat*, a film of considerable technical skill in which Marsh's passivity against the unlikely domination of the effeminate Novello is somewhat hard to take. Novello had written *The Rat* while appearing with Mae, under Griffith's direction, in the 1924 production of *The White Rose*, in which the actress suffers pitilessly. At one point Griffith does change Mae's image and makes her his approximation of a flapper, and he cannot resist, as Mae contemplates suicide, a close-up of the hands that had so moved us in *Intolerance*.

After *The Rat*, Mae Marsh retired, but she returned to the screen with the coming of sound, giving a brilliant performance as the weary and worn mother consigned by her son to the poorhouse, in Henry King's production of *Over the Hill* (1932). Like Ruth Clifford, Mae became a valued, and somewhat more featured, member of John Ford's stock company. She had a problem remembering lines and so never accepted any major role. Her last screen appearance was for John Ford in *Two Rode Together* (1961). A sister, Marguerite (1888–1925) also appeared in films, as did her niece Betty. The latter told me how Griffith had wanted a little girl who could pray on the set of *Home, Sweet Home* (1914). Betty piped up, "I know how to say my prayers," and with that began a brief film career.

In 1976, Blanche Sweet was invited to appear on a New York talk show on WNEW and decided that she would speak about Mae Marsh. Host Bill Boggs's mouth dropped and Lillian Gish's face froze, reported Blanche gleefully, as she launched into a tribute to Mae. Blanche subsequently sent her notes to me, asking that I publish them. A quarter century later, I am happy so to do: "We do so much I, I, I, me, me, me talk. I want to speak about someone else. Mae Marsh.

"She was so much a part of the Griffith years. She didn't have any theatre background, she didn't have any experience, she wasn't even beautiful, she had freckles. But she had a sensitive expressive face—and she was one of his finest actresses.

"I remember Apple Pie Mary [*Home, Sweet Home*, 1914], a delightful early comedy with Bobby Harron, *Man's Genesis* [1912], also with Bobby, and *Sands of Dee* (1912), and, of course, her outstanding performance in *The Birth of a Nation*. Then her beautiful work in *Intolerance*, the never to be forgotten courtroom sequence where her young husband, Bobby again, is being tried for a crime he had not committed.

"The end is more than you can bear. I saw it recently at Modern Art. A car racing with Mae and a pardon to stop the execution, and a woman in the audience, with trembling voice, called out, 'Hurry, hurry,' completely involved in the harrowing situation.

"Last time I saw Mae, about 1959, a fine young man was with her, her son. It was a cold and very windy day at a California ranch formerly owned by Griffith, and the present owner had placed a plaque honoring the great director, and we were to dedicate it. There was quite a gathering. I had on a high, jaunty hat and whenever the wind caught it I had to grab and then my bare midriff showed between my skirt and short jacket, but I went right on reading the dedication.

"Mae was to raise the flag. Of course the line tangled but she gave it a mighty jerk and got it aloft. The little Boy Scouts, their cold bare knees knocking, sang the National Anthem. We were a hapless but gallant lot.

"And then Mae went off with her tall son. But all I could see was Apple Pie Mary and the many loveable characters she and Griffith had created."

Bibliography

Bartlett, Randolph. "There Were Two Little Girls Named Mary." *Photoplay*, March 1917, pp. 36–41.

Bruce, Robert. "The Girl on the Cover." *Photoplay*, July 1915, pp. 57–60.

Carlisle, Helen. "Mae and the Early Days." *Motion Picture*, March 1924, pp. 25–26, 83.

Cheatham, Maude. "The Marsh Flower." *Motion Picture*, February 1921, pp. 54–55, 101.

Dunham, Harold. "Mae Marsh." *Films in Review*, June/July 1958, pp. 306–321.

Evans, Delight. "Will Mae Marsh Come Back?" *Photoplay*, March 1923, pp. 28–29.

Marsh, Mae. *Screen Acting*. Los Angeles: Photo-Star Publishing, 1921.

Naylor, Hazel Simpson. "Too Many Marys Make a Mae." *Motion Picture Classic*, June 1918, pp. 29–31.

Smith, Frederick James. "Mae, Mary and Matrimony." *Motion Picture Classic*, March 1920, pp. 16–17, 60.

"Where Is Mae Marsh?" *Photoplay*, July 1919, pp. 65–66.

Zeidman, Benjamin. "The Poppy Girl of the Films." *Motion Picture Classic*, October 1916, pp. 42–43, 69.

James Morrison and Jean Page in *Black Beauty* (1921).

JAMES MORRISON

Winsome, boyish James Morrison was the perennial silent screen juvenile, a leading member of the Vitagraph Company from 1911 through 1916, who returned to the company as a freelance player in later years. He was small in stature, good-looking in a boy-next-door fashion and was so passive in his performances that he also seemed to blend in with the scenery. Watching him act, one can well understand why he described silent film playing as "the thought behind the action." It is what we, the audience, do not see that matters, not the performance itself.

Born in Mattoon, Illinois, on November 15, 1888, James Morrison studied at the University of Chicago and later at the American Academy of Dramatic Arts in New York before visiting the Vitagraph studios in Flatbush and being hired at $25 a week. The first film in which he appeared was *A Tale of Two Cities*, a three-reeler, released in February 1911. Morrison is a young peasant who attemps, unsuccessfully, to save his lover, Lillian Walker, from the advances of a marquis: "The marquis carries her off. I come in in a rage, jump over a balustrade, try to kill the marquis and, of course, I'm killed. There was a little john off this studio into which [leading lady] Julia Swayne Gordon had gone. She heard a yell, came out, and said, 'Something's going on here.' It was me jumping over a pedestal. She always said, 'That was the first time I really saw you. You pulled me up short, and I had to come out and see what was happening.'"

Julia Swayne Gordon played Julia Ward Howe in *The Battle Hymn of the Republic*, released by Vitagraph on June 30, 1911, and Morrison recalled it well: "It followed the poem very specifically. They had the battle all set up in the Vitagraph tank, a big concrete pool. They were going to superimpose a lot of angels coming down the stairs. These were the days when anybody had to work at anything, and among the angels, the extras, were Norma Talmadge, Lillian Walker, and Mabel Normand. John Bunny was Nero and Maurice Costello was Sidney Carton, approaching the judgment seat as common figures. There was to be an earthquake and the temple was to be destroyed. The temple fell and the columns fell into the pool. And they all floated—they were all wooden!"

Morrison remembered the Vitagraph Company as it has been portrayed through the years, as a close group. "It was a family. It really was. The people there were very fond of each other. In the dressing room which I had were Earle Williams, Harry Morey, Leo Delaney, and, afterwards, Tom Powers joined us. I remember we used to get paid in cash, and we never knew when we were going to get a raise. We usually got a raise when the Paris office sent word. Yes, the Paris office. I was going home one evening, and Julia [Swayne Gordon] was behind some scenery, and she said, 'Jim, will you come over and count this for me.' I said, 'Sure, Judy.' She'd gotten a fifteen-dollar raise for some picture she'd done. That's the way the business went. We had no contract. Just word of mouth."

Tom Powers and Helen Gardner were brought to the studio by James Morrison. When Anita Stewart came for an audition, Morrison played opposite her. (Years later, Louis B. Mayer proudly boasted to Morrison, "I killed that girl with bad scripts.") Initially, the costumes provided by the company were ill fitting, and Earle Williams was the first to insist upon his own wardrobe. Clothing could not always help an actor, and as Morrison recalled of George Cooper, who always played toughs, "you couldn't dress George up."

The parting from Vitagraph in 1916 was reasonably amicable as Morrison signed a contract with Ivan Film Productions, Inc. Founded by Ivan Abramson, the company was noted for its lurid, exploitative melodramas. In all, Morrison starred in seven features for Ivan between 1916 and 1918. The first, *The Sex Lure*, released in November 1916, is a drama of kidnapping and revenge. *Enlighten Thy Daughter*, released in December 1917, is the most famous of the Ivan productions and has Morrison forcing his girlfriend to undergo an abortion. In the last of the Ivan films, *Life or Honor?*, released in March 1918, the actor has the dual role of a son accused of murdering his father and the father's valet who is the real murderer.

Morrison returned to Vitagraph early in 1918 to play the World War One deserter who became a hero in the screen adaptation of Arthur Guy Empey's book *Over the Top*. The actor had already been drafted into the military as a machine-gunner, most appropriate as Morrison's character in the production dies over his machine-gun. Empey has the lead in the film, which was the last to feature another Vitagraph player, Mary Maurice, who specialized in mother roles and died on April 31, 1918. *Over the Top* remained Morrison's favorite film, along with a 1919 Vitagraph feature *The Redemption of Dave Darcy*, in which he has the title role of a gang leader who tries to rehabilitate himself.

In the 1920s, Morrison was generally cast as the second male lead. His Vitagraph films during this period include *Black Beauty* (1921), *The Little Minister* (1922), and *Captain Blood* (1924). He retired from the screen in 1926: "I was fed-up with them. Everyone thought I was so old as I'd been in films so long. A Los Angeles newspaper called me 'the perennial juvenile,' and I decided that was my exit line."

Many of his early Vitagraph films had been produced by the company's co-founder J. Stuart Blackton. The latter's daughter, Marian, recalled Morrison as "a gentle, smooth-faced, handsome chap who never seemed to act He just was the sympathetic young man who wooed audiences with his quiet charm. He last played for my father in a ghastly film we made in the Flatbush studio about 1923, *On the Banks of the Wabash*. It was so earthy you could smell it. Not a nice smell really."

Leaving the industry, Morrison made a few Broadway appearances and wrote two novels for G.P. Putnam, *Road End* (1927) and *April Luck* (1932). For seventeen years, he taught speech and drama at the Parker Collegiate Institute in Brooklyn. I met Jimmy Morrison on a number of occasions between 1970 and 1973, always at his tiny Greenwich Village apartment. He was crippled with arthritis, used two sticks, and would spend most of our time together lying on his bed. He was not a happy man. Age and illness had made him waspish and bad-tempered. When I assured him that he had enjoyed a marvelous career, he responded, "I don't think so. Most of my pictures made me sick. I wanted to do more with them but the material wasn't there." He died in New York on November 15, 1974.

Bibliography

Herzog, Dorothea B. "In the Good Old Days." *Movie Weekly*, March 5, 1921, p. 17.
"James Morrison, Versatile Vitagrapher." *Moving Picture World*, May 6, 1916, p. 978.
Pollock, Arthur. "James Morrison and the Tricks of the Screen Trade." *Motion Picture*, November 1916, pp. 51–54.

JACK MULHALL

If you wanted to chat with Jack about his career, he was usually to be found, ready to entertain fans, at the Screen Actors Guild. There he told me that the secret for acting in silent films he found not from watching one of the great names of the screen but rather from House Peters and Lewis Stone: "Spacing—that's everything in life—spacing. If you space your life right, you'll be all right." Like House Peters, he was not a famous name in film history, but like Lewis Stone, he was a reliable and affable leading man who ultimately outlasted many of his female stars. With his broad smile, blue eyes, and genial demeanor, Jack Mulhall was a natural actor, not a poseur in the manner of, say, Valentino. He was breezy without being arrogant. He was not an irritant but a delight to the spirit. On screen and off, Jack Mulhall was a decent human being.

Mulhall was born on October 7, 1887, in a community with as delightful a name as was his nature, Wappinger Falls, New York. He entered films in 1913 with the American Biograph Company after a career as a café singer and a dancer in vaudeville. In all, Mulhall made major appearances in over 150 silent films, together with more than 200 supporting and bit performances in sound features over five decades. He was under contract to Universal as a juvenile lead opposite Cleo Madison in 1916, to Famous Players–Lasky in 1918, and to First National for seven years in the 1920s. The silent films are not well remembered, and the titles do not really matter: *Dulcy* (1923) with Constance Talmadge, *The Mad Whirl* (1925) with May McAvoy, *Classified* (1925) with Corinne Griffith, *Orchids and Ermine* (1927) with Colleen Moore, and ten features with Dorothy Mackaill, who perfectly matched him in charm and unpretentious performance.

For all his onscreen good humor, Mulhall's private life was relatively tragic. His first wife, Bertha Vuillot, died shortly after their marriage; his second, Laura Brunton, committed suicide in 1921. A third marriage in 1921 to Evelyn Winans outlasted Mulhall's life; she died in 1994. Mulhall once owned much of what is now Sherman Oaks, but he lost his real estate holdings and millions of dollars in the 1929 stock market crash.

Jack Mulhall may not have been a typical actor, but he was a longstanding member of the Screen Actors Guild, becoming a life member in 1934, and from 1959 through 1976, he served as a field representative for the organization. He died at the Motion Picture Country House on June 1, 1979.

Bibliography

Cheatham, Maude. "Because of a Dress Suit." *Motion Picture*, June 1921, pp. 45, 92–93.

Drew, Robert. "Once the Gibson Man." *Motion Picture*, April 1922,pp. 62–63, 95.

Elliott, Malcolm. "The Youngest Grand Old Man!" *Photoplay*, November 1930, pp. 71, 126.

Larkin, Mark. "The Pose-Killer." *Photoplay*, November 1928, p.75.

Peltret, Elizabeth. "The Romantic Irish." *Motion Picture*, July 1920, pp. 32–33, 103–104.

Sebastian, Inez. "Discovered—Jack Mulhall." *Picture-Play*, October 1926, pp. 74–75, 108.

Mae Murray is delighted with *The Merry Widow* waltz; director Erich von Stroheim less so.

MAE MURRAY

"I don't believe Mae Murray was temperamental," said Blanche Sweet. "I've never known a harder worker than she was. She could work any hour, any day, to accomplish something that she thought was right. Not that Mae was a great actress, but she was a beautiful person, beautiful body, danced lovely, and gave a fine performance in *The Merry Widow* [1925]." That is one contemporary's opinion, but, aside from agreeing with the description of Mae Murray as not a great actress, one is hard pressed to acknowledge she has much to recommend her to modern audiences. She doesn't act—she poses. Even her dancing style is antiquated. With her bee-stung lips and outlandish makeup, she was the personification of Norma Desmond. In later life, she had little understanding of what was taking place around her, and she lived off the charity of friends. She spent her time helping Jane Ardmore in the writing of a biography with little connection to reality.

A former showgirl and artists' model, Mae Murray (Portsmouth, Virginia, May 10, 1889–Los Angeles, March 23, 1965) came to films in 1915. She made few concessions to the realism that the film industry should have demanded of its players, and as early as *A Mormon Maid* in 1917, she is the daughter of Western pioneer, complete with bee-stung lips that are singularly out of place in Utah of the 1840s. In the 1920s, Swanson married a French marquis and Murray married David Mdivani, a Georgian prince of equally dubious ancestry. (She had earlier been married to New York playboy Jay O'Brien and director Robert Z. Leonard.)

No better proof of Murray's incompetence as an actress can be found than *Mademoiselle Midnight* (1924), directed by Robert Z. Leonard. Beginning in France at the time of the American Civil War and quickly moving to contemporary Mexico, the film has Murray as a blonde French lady doing the can-can in the first part and as a Mexican spitfire, the granddaughter of the earlier incarnation, for the rest of the film. "Reckless impulses" lead her character to acts of wild abandon at midnight, and at the height of the silliness, Murray "summoning every femine lure," outrageously vamps the villain, played by Robert McKim. Only a leading man as insipid as Monte Blue could play opposite her.

By the coming of sound, Mae Murray was reduced to working in a poverty row production of *Peacock Alley* (1930), which took its title (and nothing more) from the actress's 1922 hit film. Ironically, between 1922 and 1924, Murray had starred in eight films for Tiffany, a production company formed by her and Robert Z. Leonard, whose name was indicative of the highest quality. A company called Tiffany but one whose films were representative of anything but quality also produced the 1930 *Peacock Alley*.

The tales of Mae Murray's later life are heartrending and include time in a Salvation Army shelter in St. Louis, but the actress herself was basically unaware of her surroundings, hearing only the waltz from *The Merry Widow*, in which she had co-starred with John Gilbert and been directed by Erich von Stroheim decades earlier. Of her forty films, *The Merry Widow* is the only one worthy of respect—and not because of the presence of Mae Murray.

Bibliography

Ardmore, Jane. *The Self-Enchanted, Mae Murray: Image of an Era*. New York: McGraw-Hill, 1959.

Bennett, Alice. "Mae Murray Makes-Believe." *Motion Picture Classic*, February 1919, pp. 25–26.

Bodeen, DeWitt. "Mae Murray." *Films in Review*, December 1975, pp. 597–618.

Briscoe, Johnson. "A Child of Fortune." *Motion Picture*, March 1917, pp. 95–97, 156.

Cohn, Alfred A. "The Girl with the Bee-Stung Lips." *Photoplay*, November 1917, p. 53.

Corliss, Allen. "Motoring with Mae." *Photoplay*, March 1917, pp. 29–31.

Evans, Delight. "The Truth about Mae Murray." *Photoplay*, August 1920, pp. 40–41.

Lee, Carol. "A Bit of Fluff from Folly Land." *Motion Picture Classic*, June 1917, pp. 35–36.

"Mae Murray—the Star Who Danced to Fame." *Theatre*, June 1919, p. 395.

Morgan, Mary. "Secrets of Mae Murray's Success." *Photoplay*, January 1922, pp. 31, 112.

St. Johns, Adela Rogers. "Mae Murray—A Study in Contradictions." *Photoplay*, July 1924, pp. 43, 124.

Conrad Nagel and Edith Roberts in *There You Are!* (1926).

CONRAD NAGEL

Conrad Nagel (Keokuk, Iowa, March 16, 1897–New York, February 24, 1970) was president of the Academy of Motion Picture Arts and Sciences from 1932 to 1933 and received a special Oscar at the twelfth Academy Awards presentation for "outstanding services to the industry." He probably deserves more praise for his work founding the Academy and as a spokesman for Actors' Equity than as an actor, for he was a decidedly bland performer, so innocuous as to almost blend in with the sets on many of his features. In a forty-year film career that began in 1919 with *Little Women* and ended 109 features later with *Stranger in My Arms* in 1959, he did not appear in one production in which he leaves a memorable impression. Nagel was very much the perfect leading man for "strong" female stars such as Pola Negri (*Bella Donna*, 1923), Blanche Sweet (*Tess of the D'Urbevilles*, 1924), Marion Davies (*Quality Street*, 1927), and Garbo (*The Mysterious Lady*, 1928, and *The Kiss*, 1929). Perhaps the most ludicrous casting of Conrad Nagel was as the hero of the film version of Elinor Glyn's searing melodrama *Three Weeks* (1924). Although initially opposed to such casting, Madame Glyn apparently liked Nagel's performance; unfortunately (or perhaps fortunately) the film is no longer available for re-evaluation.

One might have supposed that the coming of sound would hurt an actor as devoid of glamor as Nagel, but, in reality, it helped him, thanks to the actor's stage background. He was reliable, perfect as one of the on-screen hosts for MGM's *Hollywood Revue of 1929* or as the unseen and unbilled narrator of Warner Bros.' early talkie *The Terror* (1928). Nagel's diction was superb, and his demeanor such that he could play both light comedy and drama.

Conrad Nagel's characterizations in later years were those of gentlemen husbands or lovers (a role that he played off screen to everyone's satisfaction, according to Joan Fontaine's autobiography); he was never the virile leading man. It would be unthinkable to imagine Nagel in a fistfight or dealing with the great outdoors. Just as he had made the transition to sound, so did Nagel make an easy crossover to television, appearing as a regular on *Broadway to Hollywood: Headline Clues* (DuMont, 1953–1954) and hosting *The Silver Theater* (CBS, 1949–1950) and *Celebrity Time* (CBS and ABC, 1949–1952).

Curiously, despite the length of his career, the number of features in which he appeared, and the major studios for which he worked, Conrad Nagel did not appear in one film that might be regarded as a classic.

Bibliography

Allison, Dorothy. "Conrad in Quest of Age." *Photoplay*, July 1919, p. 67.

Boone, Arabella. "A Nice Boy, etc." *Photoplay*, February 1921, p. 38.

Cheatham, Maude. "Conrad in Quest of Adventure." *Motion Picture*, March 1922, pp. 30–31, 96–97.

Holland, Larry Lee. "Conrad Nagel." *Films in Review*, May 1979, pp. 265–282.

Larkin, Mark. "Conrad in Quest of a Voice." *Photoplay*, January 1929, pp. 58, 113–114.

Peltret, Elizabeth. "The Convictions of Conrad." *Motion Picture Classic*, October 1920, pp. 46–47, 74.

Trepel, Beth. "The Importance of Being Earnest." *Motion Picture*, March 1921, pp. 24–25, 100–101.

NITA NALDI

Nobody played Nita Naldi better than Nita Naldi. She lived the outrageous vamp character that she had become on screen. With her high cheekbones, jet black hair, strong nose, large, piercing eyes, and a sensual mouth that cried out for the bee-stung lips effect of Mae Murray, she was the screen personification of a wicked woman. She was wildly melodramatic, loving every minute of it as she vamped Rudolph Valentino in *Blood and Sand*. Off screen, her behavior was equally outrageous, and Kathryn Perry recalled that Naldi and Lilyan Tashman were discovered enjoying sex together in the ladies room at the Vernon Country Club in Los Angeles.

Photoplay (May 1924) makes veiled reference to Naldi's relationship with a woman named Mary Rinaldi, whom the actress claimed was her sister. In reality, it seems the two met at school in New York, and the actress adapted her last name from her friend.

This female Valentino, as she liked to refer to herself, was born Donna Dooley in New York on April 1, 1897, and grew up in a Fort Lee, New Jersey, convent, where her great-aunt was the mother superior. Fort Lee was, of course, the East Coast center of film production, and Naldi tried unsuccessfully to gain work there before becoming a model and a showgirl and member of the chorus in *The Passing Show of 1918* and Morris Gest's *Midnight Whirl* in 1919. She also played Touni in *Aphrodite* at the Century Theatre in 1919. John Barrymore and director John Robertson saw her in the *Midnight Whirl*, and, as a result, she was hired for *Dr. Jekyll and Mr. Hyde* (1920), which was currently being filmed at the New York studios of Famous Players–Lasky. Although Barrymore rudely described her as his "Dumb Duse," in reference to the great Italian actress, Nita Naldi certainly leaves an impression as Gina, the dancer who tries to seduce Dr. Jekyll and becomes the mistress of Mr. Hyde.

Also in 1920, Naldi was featured in *The Common Sin*, again as a mistress, and in *Life*, in which she began her vamping career in earnest. The latter is of interest in that theatrical producer William A. Brady briefly handed over the directorial reigns to a young actor named Humphrey Bogart, who proved unequal to the task.

Aside from *Blood and Sand*, in which she is outrageously campy but for which she was selected by novelist Vicente Blasco-Ibanez, Nita Naldi also vamped Rudolph Valentino in *A Sainted Devil* (1924) and *Cobra* (1925). Gertrude Olmstead, who was in the latter, remembered Naldi as "adorable. She was so sweet to me and she was very interesting. I didn't see any problem at all. But look, people can find problems if they want them. I seem to have escaped a good many."

The actress was in Europe in 1926 and is the star of Alfred Hitchcock's second film, *The Mountain Eagle*, released in the United States as *Fear o' God*, playing Beatrice, a Kentucky schoolteacher forced into marriage with the local justice of the peace. For many years, it has been wrongly claimed that the actress has the small role of the native girl who seduces leading man Miles Mander in Hitchcock's first film, *The Pleasure Garden*.

Wisely, Nita Naldi ended her film career with the coming of sound, making her last screen appearance—again as a vamp—in *What Price Beauty* (1928), written and produced by Valentino's ex-wife, Natacha Rambova. It was a most fitting conclusion to her film career. Millionaire J. Searle Barclay, whom she married in 1930 and who died broke, may not have been her first husband; in a 1924 fan magazine article, "What Is Love," she makes reference to a marriage at the age of seventeen to an Italian officer who refused to give her a divorce. Naldi returned briefly to the New York stage in *The Firebird* (1932) and *Queer People* (1934). She was back in the public eye in 1941, appearing alongside Betty Compson, Carlyle Blackwell, and Lila Lee with an act called "Silver Screen" at Billy Rose's Diamond Horseshoe nightclub in New York. Naldi's contribution to the show was the recitation of Rudyard Kipling's "A Fool There Was" under a deep blue spotlight and backed by a row of males in evening attire. "You amaze me, the way you hold that audience," said Rose. "Don't be a fool," Naldi replied. "They all think I'm dead." Her final New York appearance was as an Italian aristocrat with Uta Hagen in the 1952 stage comedy *In Any Language*.

In her final years, Nita Naldi became a recluse. She died on February 17, 1961, in a shabby room at New York's Wentworth Hotel on West 46th Street. She had been dead 48 hours before the body was discovered.

In the fall of 1955, she had been hired to advise Carol Channing in her portrayal of a vamp in the John Latouche musical initially called *Delilah* and subsequently retitled *The Vamp*. The actress provided a far from glamorous view of vamping to a reporter from *Daily Variety* (October 5, 1955): "Silent screen sirens had one thing in common, we were all blind as bats. Theda Bara couldn't see a foot ahead of her and poor Rudy groped his way through many a love scene, and I really mean groped....They all used big reflectors to get extra light from the sun. It was so blinding we all had to squint—that's how we acquired that interesting Oriental look....We never took ourselves seriously, at least I didn't and I know some of my best friends and rivals didn't either."

Bibliography

Goodman, Ezra. "Nita Naldi, Vamp Again, Finds Kipling a Sort of Herring Now." New York *Herald Tribune*, December 28, 1941, part VI, p. 5.

Montanye, Lillian. "As by Fire." *Motion Picture Classic*, July 1921, pp. 22–23, 87.

"Nita Naldi a Star." *The Moving Picture World*, July 29, 1922, p. 352.

Oettinger, Malcolm H. "An Optical Illusion." *Picture-Play*, December 1922, pp. 34, 100.

"A Rag and a Bone and a Hank of Hair." *Theatre Arts*, October 1952, p. 17.

Smith, Agnes. "Morris Was Right." *Picture-Play*, October 1922, pp. 72–73.

Talese, Gay J. "Then and Now." New York *Times Magazine*, October 16, 1955, p. 20.

"What Is Love?" *Photoplay*, November 1924, pp. 28–29.

MABEL NORMAND

Mabel Normand. The name has a distinctive and euphonious quality to it, a pleasing ring summoning forth an attractive presence. One immediately thinks of later cinematic beauties—of Marilyn Monroe—whose images are symbolic of both beauty and an undercurrent of fun. At the same time, there is a sense of lower-class unpretentiousness, almost a cheapness, to the name of Mabel. It evokes images of a back street urchin with a hint of tomfoolery, a working girl that knows the score. Mabel Normand. The name provides a complete definition of the woman. It is beauty. It is humor. And ultimately, just like Marilyn Monroe, it is tragedy.

The life story of Mabel Normand (Staten Island, New York, November 9, 1892–Monrovia, California, February 23, 1930) reads like an early-twentieth-century Hollywood novel, perhaps written by Theodore Dreiser—or Fannie Hurst. A quick recounting of its content dispels any suggestion that Mabel Normand was the twenty-first Century concept of a stereotypical silent star, overendowed with innocence, sweetness, and light. Like most of her contemporaries, Mabel Normand was tough. Being so was the only way to succeed in an industry where, literally, an actor or actress might have to fight his or her way to the top. Or, as with Mary Pickford, Mary Miles Minter, and others, one had a mother to do it.

Mabel Normand's film career began in 1910 after an earlier vocation posing as a model for some of the best-known illustrators of the day. At the Vitagraph Company, at the beginning of her film career, she even had her own screen character, Betty, but soon her on-screen character would be known simply as Mabel. She was the only silent star indelibly linked by name to the heroine she portrayed on film. To the public, on screen and off, Mabel Normand was one and the same personality.

As Normand came to fame, she worked with two of the cinema's greatest pioneers, D.W. Griffith and J. Stuart Blackton, but neither has left any indication that they were particularly impressed with the actress. It took a rough, tough, and by some accounts crude Irish-Canadian named Mack Sennett to recognize Normand's comedic talents—in 1911—and from then on, no matter for whom she worked, Mabel Normand's name was always to be associated with that of Mack Sennett, the so-called King of Comedy. When he formed his Keystone Company, Mabel Normand was with him, and when Charlie Chaplin joined the company, Mabel was his earliest leading lady. She was was also his director, an occupation with which she is not generally associated and which Chaplin chooses not to acknowledge in his autobiography. This area of her career deserves far more research and study. In all, in 1913 and 1914,

Normand directed twelve comedy shorts, in all of which she was the star, and in five of which she was supported by a young Charlie Chaplin.

The breakup of the Mabel Normand–Mack Sennett relationship came in the summer of 1915, when a purported engagement fell apart, supposedly after Normand found Sennett in a compromising situation with another actress, Mae Busch. True or false? Who can tell? Sennett never married, and this bachelor's private life remains shrouded in mystery. Certainly, the end of Normand's early years with Sennett did not restrain her career, and there appear to have been no hard feelings when the comedienne returned to his employ in the early 1920s.

But the 1920s was not a good decade for Mabel Normand. There were two scandals—involving her relationships with director William Desmond Taylor and oil tycoon Courtland S. Dines—and, of course, there was an over-indulgence and overreliance on drugs. It was the last that killed her, four years after her only marriage to actor Lew Cody. The marriage was probably one of convenience, but one can hope that it brought some happiness to the pair.

Had she lived, had her life been scandal-free, would Mabel Normand's career have prospered with the coming of sound? Would she have been reduced to playing supporting roles in those dreadful Al Christie Educational comedies? Or would she have followed in the footsteps of sister Mack Sennett graduate Louise Fazenda, married a major producer, and become a reliable supporting comedienne in feature films, a familiar face to American moviegoers and a beloved figure within the Hollywood community?

It is ironic, but the premature death of a movie star always guarantees a form of immortality. Look at Patsy Kelly and Thelma Todd. Both were equally popular, appearing together in Hal Roach comedies. Thelma Todd died a mysterious death while at the height of her fame and is a relatively familiar name to the general public. Patsy Kelly died of old age and is generally forgotten. It is unfair, as is life, that because Mabel Normand died so young and because of the unsolved William Desmond Taylor murder she is assured a prominent place in film history.

Was Mabel Normand ever funny in and of herself? Not really. The situations in which she was placed might be amusing, even hilarious, as in her two best feature-length films, *Molly O'* (1921) and *The Extra Girl* (1923), but the central character is not. There is nothing remotely funny about her 1920 Goldwyn feature *What Happened to Rosa*. Mabel Normand was a contradiction in terms, a light comedienne whose forté was physical comedy.

The facts of Mabel Normand's life are well documented in William Thomas Sherman's *Mabel Normand: A Source Book to Her Life and Films*. Her life story is not so well presented in Betty H. Fussell's *Mabel: Hollywood's*

First I Don't Care Girl, which is less a biography and more a study of the problems involved in trying to compile a biography of the comedienne.

Mabel Normand has her place in history as an original and distinctive actress of the cinema's infancy and as the most influential woman in the early career of Charlie Chaplin. What is needed is a revisionist study of her films, her characterizations, and her comedic presence. What perhaps scares away anyone contemplating such an examination is the fear that it might well result in a downgrading of the actress and a loss from the upper echelon of silent film stars of one of the few women whose name has remained constant in the collective public memory. Ironically, a biography of Mabel Normand might destroy not only its subject but also the readership for such a book.

Bibliography

Bartlett, Randolph. "Would You Ever Suspect It?" *Photoplay*, August 1918, pp. 43–45.

"Before They Were Stars: Mabel Normand." *New York Dramatic Mirror*, March 20, 1920, pp. 534, 557.

Fussell, Betty H. *Mabel*. New Haven: Ticknor & Fields, 1982.

———. "The Films of Mabel Normand." *Film History*, vol. 2, no. 4, November/December 1988, pp. 373–391.

Gaddis, Pearl. ""The Dream That Came True." *Motion Picture*, December 1916, pp. 83–86.

Goldbeck, Willis. "Wordly But Not Weary." *Motion Picture*, September 1921, pp. 46–47, 85.

Lusk, Norbert. "The Girl on the Cover." *Picture-Play*, February 1918, pp. 262–265.

"Mabel Normand, Key to Many Laughs in Keystone Comedies." *Moving Picture World*, July 11, 1914, p. 230.

Quirk, James R. "The Girl on the Cover." *Photoplay*, August 1915, pp. 39–42.

———. "Mabel Normand Says Goodbye." *Photoplay*, May 1930, pp. 36–37, 130–131.

Rex, Wil [sic]. "Behind the Scenes with Fatty and Mabel." *Picture-Play*, April 1916, pp. 46–53.

St. Johns, Adela Rogers. "Hello, Mabel!" *Photoplay*, August 1921, pp. 24–25, 94.

———. "The Butterfly Man and the Little Clown." *Photoplay*, July 1929, pp. 38–39, 123.

Sherman, William Thomas. *Mabel Normand: A Source Book to Her Life and Films*. The Author, 2000. [contains major bibliography, but pages numbers are not provided]

Smith, Frederick James. "Mabel in a Hurry." *Motion Picture*, November 1918, pp. 31–33, 119.

JANE NOVAK

Blonde, blue-eyed Jane Novak was a starstruck teenager who became a star almost overnight at a time when stardom was a commodity neither really known nor understood. Born in St. Louis on January 12, 1896, to parents of Hungarian ancestry—her father actually came from Prague—Novak arrived in Los Angeles in the summer of 1913 at the suggestion of her aunt, Anne Schaefer, who had been with the Vitagraph Company since 1909 and was at the time its principal Western leading lady. Schaefer had a photograph of her niece in her dressing room, and it had caught the eye of director Rollin Sturgeon.

The day after she arrived, Novak was taken by her aunt for breakfast at the Kalem studio. Ruth Roland saw her and asked her to be a member of a party scene that was being filmed. Frank Newberg was the leading man, and within two years, he and Novak were married; they divorced in 1920. After a day with Kalem, the seventeen-year-old became a member of the Vitagraph Company, appearing in more than 25 films for the studio through 1915. When Vitagraph did not need her, Novak went over to Hal Roach, where Harold Lloyd and Roy Stewart were the principal players: "Roy and I would do a drama one week, and Harold would play anything, and the following week, Roy would play anything, and Harold and I would play the leads. We never had a script. We would start out in the morning, and they would say, 'Where shall we go?' So this day when I went into the studio, they said, 'We're going out to Universal City today.' Universal City was opening that day, and we went in to join the celebration. I met Pat Powers and Carl Laemmle, who were the owners. To the day they died, we were very dear friends. Carl Laemmle was a little, tiny man. He looked at me and said, 'How would you like to work for me?' I said I couldn't, 'I'm working for Mr. Roach.' So Hal said, 'While I'm in New York selling the pictures, you work for Uncle Carl.' Of course I stayed with Uncle Carl. He wouldn't let me go after that."

In reality, Novak appeared in few Universal films and in 1918 signed a contract with producer Thomas H. Ince: "I liked Thomas Ince. I'm saying that about all of them. But I did! He was not a very big man either. He could be very, very kind and gentle, and he could be a very mean person. That side of him I never knew. I only knew from hearing about it. The same with Harry Cohn. To me, Harry Cohn was a sweet, gentle, kind, wonderful person. I said that in this room one day in front of a number of studio people, and they all looked at me and said, 'What!' I said, 'Well, that is the Harry I knew.'"

The actress was Charles Ray's leading lady at Ince, appearing in *The Claws of the Hun*, *A Nine O'Clock Town*, and *String Beans*, all released in

1918. Jane Novak always had a rather weary, put-upon look, which perhaps made her an ideal leading lady to the domineering William S. Hart in a total of five feature films: *The Tiger Man* (1918), *Selfish Yates* (1918), *The Money Corral* (1919), *Wagon Tracks* (1919), and *Three Word Brand* (1921). A younger sister, Eva (1898–1988) followed Jane to Los Angeles in 1919, and she became Hart's leading lady in *The Testing Block* (1920) and *O'Malley of the Mounted* (1921).

Jane Novak had fond memories of Lewis Stone, with whom she appeared in *Man's Desire* (1919), which Stone also produced, *The River's End* (1920) and *The Rosary* (1922), produced by pioneer William N. Selig and co-starring Wallace Beery: "Lewis Stone and Wallace Beery were clowns, and they would try to outdo each other. If they had to touch hands, Lewis Stone always had putty or something in his hand, and if he took your hand, he left it there. When they had scenes together, if there was a piece of candy or some fruit around, Wallace Beery would immediately pick one up and start eating. That would distract Lewis Stone."

The River's End, based on a James Oliver Curwood novel, is a beautiful film to view, with sensitive performances from Jane Novak, Marjorie Daw, and Lewis Stone in the dual role of a Canadian Mountie and the accused murderer who assumes his identity. Filmed on location at Big Bear, Jane Novak recalled it also as "a fun picture," thanks in large part to the antics of Stone and director Marshall Neilan. "I always did very emotional and dramatic things, and when you were having a closeup, Mickey Neilan would say, 'Now look at me.' I would look at him, and then he'd look cross-eyed or he'd be mouthing things at me or he'd hold up some ridiculous sign, and, of course, I would break up. After a few days, I would look over his head, never at him. Always clowning, always fun. One day, we [Stone and Novak] were sitting and talking, and I said, 'You know, I was baptized Joanna, and I had a sister and she thought that was such a plebeian name.' So he never called me anything but Jo after that. To Lewis Stone, until the day he died, I was Jo. He was not a big man. He was tallish. He was a military man you know. I've forgotten how many years he was in the military service. He had that bearing. He was slim and he did give the impression of being very frail. However he wasn't. He was a very hardy man, a wonderful actor, a beautiful actor. He was a very fine man.

"You had to know him to work with him and really work well. You would be having a very close scene, maybe it was a love scene, and under his breath—he was like a ventriloquist—he was saying something else to you. You had to just get to the point where you ignored all those sort of things. You could howl with laughter when it was over, but you couldn't keep spoiling scenes.

"We worked in the snow up in Big Bear, and I remember wearing a coat that was made of bearskin—and the odor that came from that coat. Every time I wore it and had scenes with Lewis Stone, you can imagine all the things he was saying under his breath."

Jane Novak is the leading lady of two remarkable features, neither of which are great films but both of which have taken on almost mythic proportions. With Wallace Beery, along with Hobart Bosworth, she co-stars in the Ince production of *Behind the Door* (1920), described by one critic as "an opus of brutality" and in which she is a young wife captured by a German submarine crew and gang-raped (or as one contemporary critic had it, "outraged beyond the power of words to express it"). When the crew is finished with her, the heroine is dispatched via the torpedo hatch, but the husband has his revenge by skinning the submarine captain alive. "That was a darling little film," recalled Jane.

Equally exploitative is *The Spirit of '76* (1917), an anti-British drama of the War of Independence, for the production of which Robert Goldstein was imprisoned for violation of the Espionage Act. The film opened concurrently with America's entry into the First World War, and the government did not take kindly to this "libel" of America's new ally, Great Britain. To her credit, Jane Novak did not participate in the witchhunt against Goldstein: "Everyone in the company was constantly excited and thrilled by what we expected to be one of the greatest films. Mr. Goldstein was very gentle and softspoken, kind to everyone." I have recounted the full story of the making of *The Spirit of '76* and its aftermath in *Robert Goldstein and The Spirit of '76* (Scarecrow Press, 1993).

As we talked, Jane Novak made only glowing references to her directors, including Frank Borzage ("so kind and so gentle and so everything") and Harry Beaumont ("a very sweet person"), with one exception, Maurice Tourneur, who directed the actress in a very silly 1923 melodrama involving gypsies, *Jealous Husbands*: "He used to have a habit. He never spoke softly, never used a normal tone of voice to anyone. He always screamed. I said, when I met Mr. Tourneur, 'I respect you and I like what you do. I would love to work for you, but I have to tell you one thing. If you ever scream at me, I will walk off the set and you will never get me back. My disposition is so that if you scream at me, everything is lost. I have to feel what I do, and if you scream, then you have broken that connection or whatever you call it.' He never did. He'd scream at everybody else, but when it was my turn or he had to say something to me, he was quiet. He was mostly concerned with Maurice Tourneur. He was a wonderful director, a marvelous director, but he was bombastic, loud and only thought of the big Maurice."

Chester Bennett directed Jane in four feature films between 1922 and 1923 and became her business partner. Successful as she was financially in the 1920s, the Wall Street Crash wiped out her assets, and by 1937, she was forced to file for bankruptcy. She had been off screen from the end of the silent era, when she made a triumphant and Technicolored farewell to the screen in *Redskin* (1929), until 1936, when she made a couple of minor films. A decade earlier, Jane Novak had starred in two British productions directed by Graham Cutts, both of which were relatively unsuccessful. The first, *The Prude's Fall* was shot in 1923 and not released until 1925. The second, *The Blackguard*, was filmed in 1925 and was the first Anglo-German co-production, a project of Gainsborough Pictures and Ufa. The assistant director, screenwriter, and art director of both films was Alfred Hitchcock, and when he began work on *Foreign Correspondent* in 1940, he remembered the former leading lady and gave her the small, uncredited role of Miss Benson. It led to appearances in small roles in four more films of the 1940s and three in 1950. Jane Novak's last film was *About Mrs. Leslie* (1954).

When I met her, Jane had been living for many years in Sherman Oaks with her daughter and her son-in-law, producer Walter Seltzer. Seltzer had planned a 1955 production in which both Jane and Eva Novak would appear—it would have been their only film together—but the project fell through. The actress was not totally retired from public life, and in 1974, she published *A Treasury of Chicken Cookery* based on recipes she had collected and fans had sent to her. Jane Novak, an actress with a fun-loving, almost foolish, approach to her career, died at the Motion Picture Country Hospital on February 1, 1990.

Bibliography

"From the Convent to the Film Studios." *Moving Picture World*, November 3, 1923, p.102.

Gassaway, Gordon. "The 'Punch the Clock' Girl." *Motion Picture*, April 1922, pp. 42–43, 94.

McKelvie, Martha Groves. "Just Jane." *Motion Picture*, October 1918, pp. 59, 127.

Slide, Anthony. "Jane Novak." *The Silent Picture*, no. 14, spring 1972, pp. 9–11.

Winship, Mary. "That Chin." *Photoplay*, January 1922, pp. 58, 107.

GEORGE O'BRIEN

With his good looks, outgoing personality, and athletic credentials, George O'Brien (San Francisco, April 19, 1900–Broken Arrow, Oklahoma, September 4, 1985) was a natural for Westerns, a genre in which almost all of his sound career was spent. He became a star in John Ford's semi-Western *The Iron Horse* (1924) and ended his career as a character actor in two Ford Westerns, *Fort Apache* (1948) and *She Wore a Yellow Ribbon* (1949). At the same time, O'Brien was able to immerse himself so totally in the character of the husband in Murnau's *Sunrise: A Song of Two Humans* (1927), becoming first pliable and then emotionally adrift, that one cannot help but wonder why an entirely different career did not open up for him. For example, he would have been perfect in the title role of Frank Borzage's stylistic *Liliom*, a part that went to another Fox contract player, Charles Farrell, who had earlier taken the role of Chico in *7th Heaven* away from O'Brien.

The problem with *Sunrise* was probably that it moved O'Brien a little too far away from the strong, masculine image that the studio had created for him. Perhaps there was concern that the homosexual director, F.W. Murnau, had too much of an influence over the young star. At the time and certainly in recent years, there were rumors that O'Brien was bisexual, an unfounded suggestion. In conversation, O'Brien never failed to speak honestly of his platonic love for Murnau, his respect and admiration for the director. He, Murnau and other members of the cast and crew lived on location at Lake Arrowhead for *Sunrise* "like one big family," and Murnau and O'Brien spoke of moving permanently to Tahiti. O'Brien told me, and I have no way of knowing if it is true, that he and his father put up $9,000 for the music score to Murnau's last film, *Tabu* (1931), and that the director was returning from a visit to O'Brien's father and repayment of the loan when he was killed in an automobile accident.

George O'Brien was married from 1933 to 1948 to actress Marguerite Churchill. His son, Darcy O'Brien (1939–1998) was a writer, responsible for the 1991 novel *Margaret in Hollywood*, based on his mother and father. O'Brien's closest male friend from the 1930s until his death was handsome Fox leading man John McGuire, who would usually be found in his company in later years.

The actor was very much the answer to the Latin-lover type, a well built, all-American who could ride and fight. He was a former boxer, who had initially wanted to be a cameraman, and he starred in two boxing features, *The Roughneck* (1924) and *Is Zat So?* (1927). He looked good stripped to the waist, as he usually was in most of his early films, although by 1930 and *The Lone*

Star Ranger, it is obvious that O'Brien is desperately holding in his stomach to impress both the leading lady (Sue Carol) and the audience.

Sunrise radically changed O'Brien's image; it proved that he was also a very fine, sympathetic actor, but it went contrary to his studio-created personality. It did, however, obtain for the actor the starring role in *Noah's Ark* (1928), which again brought out a strong performance from O'Brien, playing both a Biblical and a modern hero. George O'Brien's sound films, virtually all action pictures, are fun, thanks in no small way to the actor's cheery disposition, but they all hint at lost opportunities.

Bibliography

Donnell, Dorothy. "A Child of the Frisco Earthquake Is George O'Brien." *Motion Picture Classic*, August 1925, pp. 24–25, 81.
Martin, David. "George O'Brien." *Films in Review*, November 1962, pp. 541–551.
Irwin, Murray. "Chief Dan O'Brien's Boy George." *Cinema Art*, April 1926, pp. 26, 48.
Maltin, Leonard. "FFM Interviews George O'Brien." *Film Fan Monthly*, no. 119, May 1971, pp. 19–27.
Pierce, Scott. "The O'Brien Boy Gets a Kick out of Life." *Motion Picture Classic*, August 1926, pp. 56, 86.
St. Johns, Ivan. "The Catch of Hollywood." *Photoplay*, March 1925, pp. 48, 94.

GERTRUDE OLMSTEAD

Lunch in the early 1970s with Jetta Goudal's husband, Harold Grieve, was always a pleasant experience. The meal would generally be held by the swimming pool at the Beverly Hills Hotel—presumably in the hope that Harold might spy a few attractive young men in the water—and followed by a visit to Gertrude Olmstead (whose name is sometimes erroneously written as Olmsted). Gertie lived in a large Beverly Hills home, only one-story but still a mansion by most standards, and resembled a plump and jovial housewife. She was relaxed and had no illusions about the worth of her career. On screen, she was a frizzy-haired, pretty, and unsophisticated heroine with much the same anonymous look favored by Western leading ladies of later decades.

I use the Western analogy deliberately in that Olmstead's career began in cowboy films. On June 13, 1920, she won the *Herald-Examiner* Elks' beauty contest in Chicago, where she was born on November 13, 1904. Erich von Stroheim, all of people, was brought to Chicago to test the fifteen participants, and when Gertrude Olmstead was declared the winner, Carl Laemmle immediately signed her to a contract at Universal. Less than a month later, she and her mother were on their way to Los Angeles and the studio: "They were very kind, and I learned a lot, including how to vault a horse. Artie Ortego, a cowboy whom I liked a lot, taught me to perform a flying mount. I didn't know how to ride, yet he showed me how to run and fly on the horse. I couldn't get off but I did that!

"I just simply was there and did my job. I did the best I could, and then went home to mother. I wasn't at any time stagestruck. I simply won the contest, my father had died, we came out here, I did my job, and I enjoyed it."

Another individual at Universal who helped the young actress was Lon Chaney: "I was a young girl—everybody who gets to be an old girl was a young girl—and Lon Chaney taught me to make up. In my first pictures I must have looked quite like Lon Chaney. He showed me because I didn't know the slightest thing about it. I still don't. Mother would sit and watch him, because she came with me each day, and she just looked—because she didn't know anything about it either. She never put on lipstick. She got so good at it that when I would try to do it myself, she would say, 'Honey, you are smudging. Now Lon would never put it on like that.'"

Later, Gertie was to be Lon Chaney's leading lady in *The Monster* (1925), wearing a blonde wig, and she was to play a lesser role with him in *Mr. Wu* (1927).

In the early 1920s, Gertrude Olmstead left Universal and embarked on a career as leading lady to many of the major male stars of the day. She played opposite John Gilbert in *Cameo Kirby* (1923), Tom Mix in *Ladies to Board* (1924), Reginald Denny in *California Straight Ahead* (1925) and *The Cheerful Fraud* (1927), Milton Sills in *Puppets* (1926), Charles Ray in *Sweet Adeline* (1926), George K. Arthur in *The Boob* (1926), and Richard Dix in *Sporting Goods* (1928). "I worked all the time," she told me, "many, many pictures in one year."

Two of the most memorable, if not the most important, films of Gertrude Olmstead's career are *Cobra* (1925) with Valentino and *The Torrent* (1926), on which she was billed third below Greta Garbo and Ricardo Cortez. "Valentino was a delightful person, and so was his wife, Natacha Rambova," Olmstead recalled. "I was selected to do the picture, and they wanted me to be blonde, but unfortunately God didn't want me to be blonde. I wore a blonde wig. Mr. Valentino offered me a cigarette, and I just had never smoked a cigarette—I must have been retarded—but I took it, because I thought it was polite to accept. I took it home to mother and said, 'What shall I do with it?' Mother had never smoked a cigarette before, and we both sat down and learned how to smoke." With Garbo, the role was reversed: "I showed her—this is something—how to wax her lashes. At that time, we waxed the lashes, and she had lashes two yards long, but they were just straight lashes. I was so proud of that because she looked utterly beautiful. Not like Lon Chaney at all!"

Gertrude Olmstead reached the peak of her career in September 1924, when she was signed by MGM, a studio with which she was to remain through 1927. She was not among the upper echelon of MGM players, earning only $250 on signature of her contract, rising to $500 by 1926. Prior to the MGM contract, Gertrude Olmstead had been selected by June Mathis to play Esther (a role subsequently assigned May McAvoy) in *Ben-Hur*. "June Mathis was very anxious for me to do it. They were well under way, and I never did get to Rome. I think it was eight months. I didn't even have any salary. They didn't contract with money in those days. They contracted with honor. You gave your word. I gave my word I would wait to be sent to Rome, and I didn't work for eight months. Finally, I went to the studio, and asked Mr. [director Fred] Niblo who had been put in charge. George Walsh had been sent home, and Ramon Novarro had been given the part of Ben-Hur. I couldn't play with Ramon Novarro because he was too small. I was simply out. It was as simple as that. There was nothing to be said."

One positive result from the MGM contract was Olmstead's playing *Time, the Comedian* (1925), on the set of which she met director Robert Z. Leonard (1889–1968). "He chose me for the part, and I was just probably the world's worst actress," joked Gertie. "I'm sure he thought he better marry me to save the industry." Leonard had earlier been married to the temperamental and tempestuous Mae Murray, and relaxed, easy-going Gertrude Olmstead must have been a pleasant change. The couple were married in Santa Barbara in June 1926 and remained together until Leonard's death.

Gertrude Olmstead continued to work through 1929. Her first talkie was *Hit of the Show* (1928), opposite Joe E. Brown, followed by four further sound productions, all in 1929, the last three of which were for Warner Bros.: *The Lone Wolf's Daughter, Sonny Boy, The Time, the Place, and the Girl*, and *The Show of Shows*.

Did her husband object to her continued career? "He didn't mind. Of course, he was delighted when I decided not to. He was a most easy-going person. He had no definite opinions, a lovely disposition. He didn't care what I did. He was just delighted when I didn't. I did continue because I had a lot of commitments lined up, and I worked like an absolute badger, very hard."

After 1929 Gertrude Olmstead was happy to retire: "I was married, and I decided that was job enough. That's all. I don't think I had a favorite film. I just went along day-to- day, and enjoyed all of them. The only thing I objected to was bleaching my hair. I just got the part, and went out and did it. I went to work, and came home. It's a very colorless career, and very short." She died in Beverly Hills on January 18, 1975.

Note: Gertrude Olmstead's scrapbooks are at the Margaret Herrick Library of the Academy of Motion Picture Arts and Sciences.

Bibliography

"Carl Laemmle's Offer to Star Winner Helped Chicago Elks' Beauty Contest, *Moving Picture World*, July 3, 1920, p.73.

Seena Owen, with Alfred Paget, in *Intolerance* (1916).

SEENA OWEN

"Do you remember Seena Owen in *Intolerance* with those long eyelashes?" asks Margery Wilson, who plays Brown Eyes in the Griffith feature. Who could forget Seena Owen, not only in *Intolerance* but also at the end of her acting career in *Queen Kelly?* She is as memorable as her name and one of the great exotic character beauties of the screen, a natural blonde goddess. One contemporary critic may have described her as "a vigorous, athletic, clear-skinned and clear-eyed baby Viking," but she is no cold Scandinavian beauty. There is strong passion in her screen performances. "I'm not particularly eager to be a great moral influence—I'd rather be entertaining," she explained. Morality is happily missing from some of the screen characterizations but that they still remain entertaining through the present is indicative of a stylish and intelligent performer.

Born Signe Auen of Danish-Norwegian ancestry in Spokane, Washington, on November 14, 1894, Seena Owen spent her formative years from 1896 to 1912 in Denmark. After a very brief sojourn with the Alcazar Theatre troupe in San Francisco, she joined the Kalem Company under the direction of Marshall Neilan, and then, quickly, became a member of D.W. Griffith's company, making her feature film debut in 1915 in *Bred in the Bone*, as the "star" of a traveling theatrical troupe. As a member of the D.W. Griffith stock company, Seena Owen was given the nickname of "Singy" by George Siegmann—and that may well have determined the actress to change her screen name from Signe to the more easily pronounceable Seena. Her first major performance was as Douglas Fairbanks's first leading lady on screen in *The Lamb*, the first production of the newly formed Fine Arts Company, released on November 7, 1915. If these three "firsts" appear impressive, it should also be noted that Seena Owen also starred in the last production from Fine Arts, *Madame Bo-Peep*, released on May 27, 1917.

The characters in *Intolerance* may, perhaps, be divided into two types. There are those of quiet, intense personality, such as Mae Marsh and Robert Harron in the Modern Story and Margery Wilson in the French Story. Then there are the characters whose personalities fill the screen: Constance Talmadge as the Mountain Girl and Seena Owen as Attarea, the Princess Beloved in the Babylonian Story. It is impossible to imagine anyone other than Seena Owen as Belshazzar's favorite. She has just the right amount of sauciness in her character—you know she has to be good in bed—but she also evokes a spirit of love that is eternal. To her, Alfred Paget as Belshazzar delivers flowers in a chariot pulled by two white doves, and there is no doubt that the Princess Beloved is deserving of such a display of unadulterated love.

Little wonder that Belshazzar pays no attention to the Persians massing for an attack on Babylon when he has Seena Owen in the palace. (I remember taking Margery Wilson to a screening of *Intolerance* at the Los Angeles County Museum of Art on January 23, 1976; she asked me who played Belshazzar and when I told her Alfred Paget, she firmly commented, "He was a nice man.")

While she was making *Intolerance*, according to cinematographer Billy Bitzer, Griffith instigated a romance between Seena Owen and George Walsh in an effort to stir emotion within the actress and thus make her more of a lovesick Princess Beloved. It worked in that Owen and Walsh were married, and although the union produced a daughter, Patricia, it was a decidedly unhappy one, ending in divorce in 1924.

Once she left Fine Arts and D.W. Griffith, Seena Owen was featured in a string of unadventuresome melodramas. She was out of character as William S. Hart's leading lady in *Branding Broadway* (1918) and *Breed of Men* (1919). The 1921 Cosmopolitan production of *The Woman God Changed*, directed by Robert Vignola, in which Owen is a dancer accused of murder and whose story is told in flashback through courtroom testimony, was hailed by contemporary critics as the film that elevated the actress to stardom. In reality, no production could lift the actress out of the rut of second-rate fare.

There is fun to be found in the 1922 Cosmopolitan production of *Back Pay*, directed by Frank Borzage, with Seena Owen as the small town girl who dreams of big city life while her boyfriend, Matt Moore, enjoys being a small town boy. He likes her in gingham dresses, but, as she explains to him, "I've got a crepe-de-chine soul." Owen goes off to New York and becomes the mistress of a wealthy businessman. Moore goes off to war, is blinded, and returns to be nursed by Owen. When he dies, she gives up her wealth and position as a mistress to return to a $25 a week office job, working to pay off Moore's funeral expenses. The latter portion of the film gets a little tedious as entertainment so often does when morality takes over, but it is obvious that Seena Owen, Frank Borzage and Fannie Hurst, responsible for the original short story, make a good team.

How perceptive of director Erich von Stroheim to cast Seena Owen as Queen Regina V in Gloria Swanson's ill-fated 1928 production of *Queen Kelly*. Nothing in which the actress had previously appeared hints at the over-the-top performance she gives here, be it parading around the palace naked with a large white cat clutched to her bosom or furiously whipping Swanson after discovering she is a rival for the queen's fiancé in the form of Walter Byron (who is adequate if a trifle wooden in a role that a few years earlier would have been played by von Stroheim himself). Although uncompleted and originally released in truncated form, it would appear that Seena Owen's performance survives pretty much intact. She is a magnificent, overpowering presence, beside which Gloria Swanson pales into insignificance.

Despite or perhaps because of *Queen Kelly*, Seena Owen made only one other silent film, *Sinners in Love* (1928), and only a couple of talkies, *The Marriage Playground* (1929) and *Officer 13* (1932). In the mid-1930s, she embarked on a new career as a screenwriter, with the most important of her credits being the co-script and co-story for the Dorothy Lamour vehicle, *Aloma of the South Seas* (1941) and the original story idea (which cannot have been too much of an effort) for *Carnegie Hall* (1947), her last credit. The career change may have been influenced by Owen's older sister Lillie Hayward (1892–1978), who was active as a screenwriter and script editor from 1919 to 1960. Seena Owen died in Los Angeles on August 15, 1966.

Bibliography

Astor, Truth. "A Daughter of Denmark." *Motion Picture Classic*, August 1921, pp. 66, 83.

Evans, Delight. "The Camera Is Cruel to Her." *Photoplay*, May 1920, pp. 69–70.

Little, Barbara. "A Picture Puzzle." *Picture-Play*, September 1923, pp. 43, 98.

"'Owen' or 'Auen,' 'Signe' or 'Seena,'" *Photoplay*, March 1916, p. 143.

St. Johns, Adela Rogers. "Do You Believe in Dimples?" *Photoplay*, June 1921, pp. 57, 97.

Service, Faith. "Seena Seen Scenically." *Motion Picture Classic*, June 1920, pp. 34–35, 69.

Underhill, Harriette. "Rollo's Wild Oat." *Picture-Play*, December 1921, pp. 22–23, 99.

JEAN PAIGE

Some actresses marry their leading men, some their directors. Norma Shearer married Irving Thalberg, the head of production at MGM. Jean Paige worked for only one company, Vitagraph, and she married the head of the studio, becoming the only silent screen performer to make such a major transition. It could not have happened to a sweeter, less pretentious actress. The Vitagraph Company was always family-like, and Jean Paige became its young mother.

Born Lucille Beatrice O'Hair in Paris, Illinois, on July 3, 1895, Jean Paige's background does not hint at a film career. Her family was deeply religious and had no interest in the theatre. Her mother had wanted to be a missionary but had been denied the opportunity by her father. After her daughter had taken private acting lessons and studied acting at the Kings School of Oratory, Elocution and Dramatic Culture in Pittsburg, a family friend, director Martin Justice, offered the actress a screen test. Her mother determined not to stand in her daughter's way. With her Aunt Emmy, Jean Paige came to New York on July 25, 1917, made a test at the Vitagraph studios, and was immediately cast in a series of two-reel comedies based on O. Henry's short stories. She made her debut in *The Discounters of Money*, released on July 26, 1917, and within a year, Jean Paige was a Vitagraph star.

She came out to Los Angeles on Christmas Eve 1919 and never wanted to live anywhere else. There she met Vitagraph's co-founder and current owner, Albert E. Smith: "Mr. Smith's wife passed on the in the [1918 Spanish] flu epidemic, and Mr. Smith came out with the children and the nurse. We all went to meet him and he said, 'Well, Miss Paige, how do you like California?' I said, 'I simply love it. I get to ride horseback and do all the things I love to do.' He said, 'I ride every morning and maybe you could ride with me sometime.' I went home and told my aunt, and she said, 'I've always understood Mr. Smith was a very fine gentleman, and there's no reason why you shouldn't.' That was the way it started."

Albert E. Smith and Jean Paige married at her parent's home in December 1920, but the actress continued with films she had agreed to make. Placid and untemperamental, Jean Paige did whatever was asked of her. She played in the lurid melodrama *The Prodigal Son*, released in February 1922, "the only picture that I never cared for." She co-starred in the screen adaptation of Anna Sewell's *Black Beauty* (1921) opposite James Morrison, who was born only thirty miles away from her in Mattoon, Illinois: "She was a very sweet and charming person—we always had a bond in Illinois." When asked to explain the genesis of his interest in film, Swedish director Ingmar Bergman recalled that *Black Beauty* was the first production he ever saw, and he claimed that he could still remember the fire sequence. The feature is equally important as the first to be shot entirely with panchromatic film (by Reggie Lyons).

Jean Paige ended her Vitagraph, and her screen, career with the studio's last major production, the swashbuckling epic *Captain Blood* (1924), in which J. Warren Kerrigan has the title role and James Morrison is cast in the secondary male lead as Jeremy Pitt. Jean Paige wears the costumes to perfection but has little need to act. "I really wasn't interested in pictures anymore," the actress told me. "As I look back on my life, here I was a young girl in Illinois, whose family was not interested in the theatre. I land in New York and my aunt is pushing me. Then, when Mr. Smith needed me, I was there. And we had such a wonderful and happy life. As you look back on it, it sort of falls into place." Jean Paige died in Los Angeles on December 15, 1990.

Note: Jean Paige's still books from *Captain Blood* and *Black Beauty* are at the Los Angeles County Museum of Natural History, along with her costume from *Black Beauty*.

Bibliography

Fletcher, Adele Whitely. "Sick-a-Bed Lady." *Motion Picture*, April-May 1920, pp. 48–49, 108.
———. "Nee Jean Paige." *Motion Picture*, June 1921, pp. 22–23.
Forthe, Wales. "Of the Sub-Deb Squad." *Photoplay*, December 1920, p. 42.
Howe, Selma. "A Regular Home-Town Girl." *Picture-Play*, February 1920, pp. 17–18.
Little, Barbara. "When Dreams Came True for Jean." *Picture-Play*, March 1922, pp. 23, 95.
Squier, Emma-Lindsay. "Miss Paige from Paris." *Picture-Play*, January 1921, pp. 30, 93–94.

Kathryn Persey

KATHRYN PERRY

A visit to the Motion Picture Country House in the 1970s was never complete without a social call on Kathryn Perry, who was a longtime resident of the Lodge out there. She had aged from a sophisticated brunette to a gray-haired old lady with risqué sense of humor. She was no longer "The Most Beautiful Girl in New York," as she had been named in 1921, but she was obviously someone who still enjoyed life and was not willing easily to slip easily into senility. She had been married only once, to actor Owen Moore, who had previously been the first husband of Mary Pickford (from 1911 to 1920), and because of this Kate proudly referred to herself as Pickford's wife-in-law.

Born Katharine Perry in New York in 1897, Kate had begun her professional life as a dancer on the New York stage with Gertrude Hoffman and from there had been enlisted as a showgirl in the Ziegfeld *Follies*. "When I got in the *Follies*, I was a good girl," she giggled. "All the people I met in the show were kinda looking out for me, including Ziegfeld. Ziegfeld was always nice to me. I was always going with the girls that he was going with, and he was always telling me to change my companions." Life in the *Follies* was certainly no morality play. The showgirls would display their "service stripes," meaning the bracelets given to them by admirers: "So help me, I got three of the prettiest bracelets. I got a little ruby one, a little diamond one and a little sapphire one."

What did she have to do to get them? "Not a damn thing. When those boys drove me home and kissed me goodnight, they kissed me on the cheek. I went to this one man's house alone one night for dinner. He didn't get fresh with me, but he asked me if I'd like to stay there overnight and sleep at the foot of his bed. I said I didn't think so and I never went back. So he went from me to Billie Dove, and he put her in a terrific apartment with gorgeous furniture. [Theatrical impresario] Charles Dillingham is the only guy that tried to get after me. We only went around the desk once, and he didn't catch me. He looked so damned dignified."

Her memories of those she worked with in the Ziegfeld *Follies* were more interesting and perceptive than anything she had to say in regard to her film career. Legendary African-American entertainer Bert Williams "was cute and he was very smart." Eddie Cantor "was a nuisance; he had a dressing room next to us, and our dressing room had no door on it, and he was always looking in." Composer Buddy DeSylva "was a lot of fun; he talked dirty but he was funny." Of the tenor who introduced the song "A Pretty Girl Is Like a Melody": "Poor John Steele. He was such a sap—pretty singing voice, but it got a little wavery in spots."

"I didn't like Will Rogers. I was probably the only one in the world who didn't like him. While the other stars went out to lunch different places, he would mingle with the prop men and all those people. And he did it in such a way that you knew it was just on the surface. To me, he was a phoney.

"Billie Burke was around. None of us liked her very much. You can't blame her for behaving the way she did [having affairs with women], because Ziegfeld was playing around with a lot of different girls."

A showgirl as beautiful as Kathryn Perry was a natural for a screen career, despite an obviously limited talent as an actress. She came to D.W. Griffith's attention and with her mother visited his Mamaroneck Studios on Long Island on a bitter winter's day to be tested for a role—she had assumed it was the character subsequently played by Mary Hay—in *Way Down East* (1920). She was disappointed when her participation was limited to that of one the attractive young ladies partying with Lowell Sherman in the character of Lennox Sanderson. Griffith did, however, give her one close-up, and that may have lead to Kate's making her first credited screen appearance as Miss Hollander in Lewis J. Selznick's production of *Sooner or Later* (1920).

The leading man in *Sooner or Later* was Owen Moore. Kate did not play opposite him—that honor went to Seena Owen—but in her second film with the actor, *The Chicken in the Case*, released in January 1921, she was his leading lady. The couple were married on July 16, 1921, and embarked on a domestic life that was every bit as comic as the farces in which the two appeared on screen. Owen Moore died at the couple's Beverly Hills home on June 9, 1939. Contemporary newspaper reports suggested that his body remained undiscovered in the kitchen for some considerable time. Kate Perry assured me this was far from true. She had visited the kitchen on frequent occasions and would have noticed if he was lying dead there. It must have been their bedroom, to which she was a less frequent visitor, in which he was lying.

Owen Moore was brother to Matt and Tom, all of whom hailed from County Meath, Ireland, and all of whom were stocky leading men, not exactly handsome but each a commanding presence on screen. They were more in the mold of George Walsh than, say, Wallace Reid. Aside from *The Chicken in the Case*, Kathryn Perry also co-starred with Owen in *A Divorce of Conscience* (1921) and *Love Is an Awful Thing* (1922) for Lewis J. Selznick, and in *Husbands for Rent* (1927) at Warner Bros. She starred opposite Matt Moore in *The First Year* and *Early to Wed*, both released by Fox in 1926. And her first talkie was *Side Street*, a crime drama released by RKO in 1929, starring all three of the Moore brothers but with Tom rather than Owen as her romantic interest.

After *Side Street*, there were no more featured roles. Kate continued to act on screen through 1951, but her roles were always uncredited "bits" such as that of a socialite in *My Man Godfrey* (1936). She died at the Motion Picture Country Hospital on October 14, 1983. "It was a great life, a different world," as she once told me. "I had a wonderful time, and life doesn't owe me a thing. I don't think I did anything very well, but I was happy all the time."

Bibliography

"Will Owen Moore (Selznick Star) Marry Kathryn Perry?" *Movie Weekly*, April 20, 1921, p. 11.

©1915

OLGA PETROVA

Olga Petrova was a major performer on stage, onscreen, and in vaudeville; she also wrote plays and advice columns. She was an extraordinarily strong and determined female who seized upon the entertainment industry as a means not only to wealth but also for the propagandization of her beliefs. She was patrician, stubborn, self-centered, and eccentric. In the history of American popular culture of the twentieth century, Olga Petrova is quite unique, but because her films are not known to exist, her plays and writings long out of print, she is virtually forgotten. "You have never seen a film in which I took part," she commented. "Fate willing you never will."

"What is little? What is great?" she asked me. "Let me put it this way. I did achieve what I set out as a child to get, my own bread, my own butter, my own house in which to enjoy it. That—to me—is the height of what I will accept and acknowledge as greatness."

Just as she created a unique career, Petrova also created her own background and family history. She was born Muriel Harding on May 10, 1884, perhaps in Liverpool, England, or perhaps somewhere in Wales or on the Welsh border, and was of Welsh ancestry. Generally, she claimed Polish or Russian ancestry and a first husband, who may or may not have existed, named Boris Petrov. Throughout her public and private life, Petrova had a semi-Russian accent, that, if one listened very closely, contained a Welsh burr. Critic Janet Flanner once made reference to Petrova as "an exotic, bewilderingly vocal actress," and there was something very bewildering about the accent that seemed to get stronger with age and the more years the actress spent in the U.S.

As Muriel Harding, Petrova began her stage career in London, where a theatrical booker suggested the name change. With her red hair, temperament, and regal bearing, she did not look like a Muriel Harding. On April 5, 1911, Petrova became a star at the London Pavilion. She was seen by Jesse L. Lasky and Henry B. Harris and booked for their new Follies Bergere cabaret in New York. Modeled after the French establishment, the Follies Bergere was the first major attempt in the U.S. to create a nightclub with sophisticated entertainment, but neither it nor Petrova was a success. In order to promote herself, Petrova accepted a leading role in the Lionel Monckton musical comedy *The Quaker Girl*, which ran for 240 performances beginning on October 23, 1911. Petrova's success in *The Quaker Girl* led to a New York vaudeville engagement and a performance on the legitimate stage in 1914, opposite Milton Sills, in Monckton Hoffe's much-filmed *Panthea*.

Between 1914 and 1918, Petrova starred in 26 films, the first sixteen of which were produced by Popular Plays and Players for release by Metro. The last four were produced by the Petrova Picture Company. Petrova shot all of her films on the East Coast, and she never set foot in Hollywood. Her first film, *The Tigress*, three others from 1915, *The Heart of a Painted Woman*, *My Madonna*, and *The Vampire* and the 1916 production of *What Will People Say?* are directed by the screen's first female filmmaker, Alice Guy Blaché, and the two women were obviously well suited both in terms of temperament and creativity.

In many of the films, Petrova portrays a vamp, a woman who is generally little more than a high-class prostitute but often with an ulterior motive for her profession. For example, in *The Soul of a Magdalene*, released in May 1917, the actress becomes the mistress of a libertine in order to raise money for an operation on her mother. She is a vamp in her first production, *The Tigress*, and in the second and third films directed by Blaché, Petrova is a vamp with a pure heart, using money from a wealthy lawyer to found a hospital for orphans in *The Heart of a Painted Woman* and working with the poor in *My Madonna*. In *The Vampire*, released in August 1915, she is simply a ruthless vamp wreaking vengeance on mankind. In the last of the Blaché-directed features, *What Will People Say?* (1916), Petrova portrays a society girl.

Petrova is generally a representative of the upper or upper middle classes on screen. She is an opera singer in *The Black Butterfly* (1916), a screenwriter in *Extravagance* (1916), an Irish noblewoman who takes up social work in *Bridges Burned* (1917), the daughter of a U.S. ambassador in *Daughter of Destiny* (1917), and the wife of the governor of a Portuguese colony in *Exile* (1917). *The Eternal Question*, released in July 1916, boasts a Pygmalion theme with Petrova as a peasant girl transformed into a society woman.

The Petrova characters are usually feminists, if not always in the modern sense, and often fighting for justice. In *The Secret of Eve* (1917), Petrova protests the working conditions in her husband's factory. In *More Truth than Poetry* (1917), Petrova is the daughter of a steel magnate who argues in court that justice is often denied a woman. In *The Light Within* (1918), she is a bacteriologist developing a cure for anthrax, and in her penultimate film, *Tempered Steel* (1918), she is an actress who does not believe that a woman's place is in the home.

Aside from starring on screen, Petrova found time to write articles, interviews, and advice columns for various film magazines, including *Shadowland*, *Motion Picture*, and *Photoplay Journal*. She returned to vaudeville in 1919, giving recitations, singing, and sometimes simply standing there and crying real tears (in a scene from the 1906 play *The Shulamite*). It wasn't what Petrova did that was unique but rather the manner in which she did it, which, unfortunately, we will never be able to comprehend.

Audiences had never seen anything quite like Madame Petrova on stage or screen. Robert North was associated with Petrova on her films and he told me, "She wouldn't listen to any talk about women being inferior at all. She raised hell about it." Petrova's attitude was that women had basic rights: "These rights I voiced through various channels, including my stories, plays and so on. I merely put them into the mouths of fictional characters. If this was construed otherwise as encouragement, propaganda, etc., I repeat it was not intentional nor conscious on my part."

Petrova wrote a number of verses, including "Thus Speaks Woman," with its proclamation, "Clarion clear it shrieks and howls / From world to world. Ave *Woman Reigns.*"

In 1919, she appeared at New York's Palace Theatre with a new verse, "To a Child That Enquires," in which she explains to a young child that babies are the result of "a wonderful love, a love that was Daddy's and mine," ending,

I carried you under my heart, my sweet,

And I sheltered you, safe from alarms,

Till one wonderful day the dear God looked down –

And I cuddled you tight in my arms."

This was racy stuff for 1919 audiences, and vaudeville mogul E.F. Albee declared it obscene. Undaunted, Petrova went on to write and star in three popular plays, *The White Peacock* (1921), *Hurricane* (1923), and *What Do We Know?* (1927), the last two dealing with birth control and spiritualism.

In the late 1920s, Petrova retired from professional life and moved to the South of France. She lived in a farm at St. Raphael, and there, once a year, her husband, Dr. John Dillon Stewart, would visit her. As Petrova explained it, the marriage was a very sensible one, "the happy mean that should be maintained." She and the prominent New York surgeon had married in 1913, and they occupied separate residences until his death in 1938. With the outbreak of World War Two, Petrova returned to the United States, and in 1951, she moved permanently to Clearwater, Florida. In 1942, she published an autobiography, *Butter with My Bread*, telling of her tyrannical father, which she explained to me as "a tale of my struggle as a female child to break away from that life, a struggle to obtain by devious means—the screen happening to be one of them—a home, bread, and butter of my own."

Madame Petrova and I corresponded for many years. She also tape-recorded some of her original verses for me. The letters are all badly typed and heavily marked with additions and corrections in thick black ink. As our friendship developed, I was told that it should take on a less formal aspect; she would address me as Tony and I might address her as Petrova. She insisted that we had much in common despite our considerable difference in ages. "Do you think that curious waves, electrical of course, touch certain individuals?" she wrote. We spoke only once on the telephone—on February 28, 1977—and then we discussed the weather. It was raining in Clearwater.

As the years went by, Petrova asked me to try and help transform her life story into a *Masterpiece Theatre* presentation, from which I tried to dissuade her. It was very obvious that she needed money and was desperately seeking any opportunity. When she died on November 30, 1977, she left the rights to her writings to me, unaware that all were in the public domain. Reading pieces of mine that I had written on her through the years, Petrova noted, "You have not only written my ave but now my vale as well."

Bibliography

Bartlett, Randolph. "Petrova—Prophetess." *Photoplay*, December 1917, pp. 7, 112.

Hall, Gladys. "Purple Overtones." *Motion Picture*, March 1919, pp. 70-71, 106.

James, Neville. "Olga Petrova." *The Silent Picture*, no. 18, 1973, pp. 5-12.

Mullett, Mary B. "Ugly Duckling Who Became the White Peacock." *American Magazine*, December 1924, pp. 34-35.

"Olga Petrova." *Moving Picture World*, December 12, 1914, p. 1507.

Petrova, Olga. "How I Got In." *Motion Picture*, October 1917, pp. 106-107.

———. *Butter with My Bread*. Indianapolis: Bobbs-Merrill, 1942.

Russell, L. Case. "The Mona Lisa of the Screen." *Motion Picture Classic*, February 1917, pp. 54-56.

Severance, Constance. "Our Lady of Troubles." *Photoplay*, October 1916, pp. 56-58.

Smith, Frederick James. "Petrova and Her Philosophy of Life." *Motion Picture Classic*, September 1918, pp. 18-19, 77, 81.

Mary Philbin, with Norman Kerry, in *The Phantom of the Opera* (1925).

MARY PHILBIN

One silent star noted as a recluse was Mary Philbin (Chicago, July 16, 1903–Huntington Beach, California, May 7, 1993), who had lived in the same house on Fairfax Avenue since the early 1920s. If she was out working in the garden, film buffs might stop and ask for an autograph, but she did not grant interviews and did not attend screenings of her films. It was, therefore, a major and delightful surprise when, on April 24, 1989, she suddenly arrived at our house, in the company of Carla (Rebecca) Laemmle, the niece of Universal founder Carl. Robert Gitt and I had agreed to screen footage of the Laemmle family shot in the 1920s and 1930s, and Carla had given no indication as to the identity of her companion.

The surprise quickly changed to disappointment as it became obvious why Mary Philbin never gave interviews. She had nothing to say. Ask her about D.W. Griffith or Erich von Stroheim or Lon Chaney, or any other major figure with whom she worked, and the response was always the same. They were nice, they were pleasant, and they were kind. This was a woman without a brain in her head and, sadly, perhaps she was always that way. Compliant, undemonstrative, and, ultimately, dull.

Like Gertrude Olmstead, Mary Philbin had entered the 1920 *Herald-Examiner* Elks' beauty contest in Chicago. As Carla Laemmle explained it, her father, Joseph, sent a photograph of Mary to his brother Carl with a note that read, "This is a beauty." The actress was immediately signed to a contract and was to remain with Universal through 1929. She made her debut in the 1921 melodrama *The Blazing Trail* and had the good fortune to be cast in a number of the studio's best-known productions of the 1920s. She was Erich von Stroheim's leading lady in *Merry-Go-Round* (1923). She unmasked Lon Chaney in *The Phantom of the Opera* (1925). She tried unsuccessfully to emulate Mary Pickford in the 1925 remake of *Stella Maris*. She was Conrad Veidt's co-star in *The Man Who Laughs* and *The Last Performance*, both released in 1927. And in *Surrender* (1927), she was the leading lady to the great Russian actor Ivan Mosjoukine in his only Hollywood film.

In 1928, Philbin was loaned to D.W. Griffith for *Drums of Love*, one of the director's lesser works. Cinematographer Karl Struss described her as "a very beautiful girl," and spent two weeks testing different wigs for her. Karl considered *Drums of Love* "one of the best pictures I ever photographed," despite having to share cinematography credit with Billy Bitzer, who was never on the set but had an iron-bound contract with Griffith guaranteeing him screen credit.

One of the few comments that Mary Philbin made related to her affinity with Viennese roles: "I loved Vienna. When I went with my father over to Europe, we went to Vienna. They seemed to always pick me for little Viennese girls. I have a very dear, heartfelt feeling for Vienna."

The reference to her father, a former Chicago railroad engineer, is significant. He totally dominated her life and her career. Priscilla Bonner and Virginia Brown Faire were members, along with Mary Philbin, of a 1920s social group called the Regulars. They recall picking her up at the Fairfax Avenue home and promising to return her by eleven. One night the trio returned at 11:15, and Philbin's angry father dragged her into the house refusing to allow her out again. It was probably her father who prevented her marriage to agent Paul Kohner, who had co-written Philbin's 1928 film *Love Me and the World Is Mine*, directed by E.A. Dupont. There were no further suitors, and the actress died a spinster.

As early as 1925, Carl Laemmle had written an open letter declaring that Mary Philbin "has the potentialities of becoming one of the greatest actresses on the screen." She was once foolishly compared to Sarah Bernhardt! In reality, Philbin was a pretty face and little more. She was compliant; she could be molded, and that was good when she worked for a major director such as Griffith or von Stroheim, both of whom were obviously substitute father figures. The actress appeared in three sound films in 1929 and could have continued her career but instead retired. Thanks to her reclusivity, she became a minor Garbo in the eyes of fans of silent film.

Bibliography

Donnell, Dorothy. "The Girl Who Had No Childhood." *Motion Picture Classic*, October 1925, pp. 40–41, 85–86.
Gebhart, Myrtle. "A Candle Flame,' *Picture-Play*, November 1923, pp. 74, 92.
Gilmore, Frances. "The World Is Her Convent." *Motion Picture Classic*, April 1928, pp. 42, 84.
Littlefield, Constance P. "The Hand of Destiny." *Picture-Play*, June 1925, pp. 16, 98.
St. Johns, Ivan. "The Girl on the Cover." *Photoplay*, October 1924, pp. 39, 116.
Smith, Agnes. "Mary Herself." *Photoplay*, November 1926, pp. 30–31, 132.

MARY PICKFORD
AND DOUGLAS FAIRBANKS

They were the king and queen of Hollywood, more beloved and respected by their peers and their fans than most constitutional monarchs. Neither had the virginal qualities expected of royalty when they married in 1920 and moved into the royal residence of Pickfair. Both had been previously married and divorced, she to actor Owen Moore and he to socialite Beth Sully. It would be wrong to claim that either Pickford or Fairbanks was a great actor, but both were great personalities with followings unprecedented in the history of popular entertainment. For at least a decade—the 1920s—Mary Pickford and Douglas Fairbanks were the most famous couple in the world.

Both Pickford (Toronto, Canada, April 8, 1892–Santa Monica, California, May 29,1979) and Fairbanks (Denver, Colorado, May 23, 1883–Santa Monica, December 12, 1939) came from the stage, and both began their film careers with D.W. Griffith. Mary Pickford joined the American Biograph Company in 1909, under Griffith's direction, and in 1915, Fairbanks became a member of the Fine Arts Company, where his films were supervised but not directed by Griffith. In 1919, Griffith, Pickford and Fairbanks, along with Charlie Chaplin, formed the United Artists Corporation, the first major personality-based distribution entity. The company not only assured creative freedom for Pickford and Fairbanks, but, equally important, confirmed their unique position as Hollywood's leading stars.

Mary Pickford emphasized youth in her films. She always played under age in silent features, and the long, blonde curls that she sported well into the 1920s helped give the illusion of youth. She was primarily a light comedienne, but she could, if necessary, turn in a dramatic performance equal to that of any other silent actress. Most notably, in *Stella Maris*, released in January 1918, under the direction of Marshall Neilan, she delivers a brilliant dual performance as the deformed and ugly orphan Unity Blake and the wealthy, sweet, and somewhat spoiled title character. Both are childlike roles, but both are very different both in exterior look and inner concept.

Stella Maris is just one of the 52 feature films in which Pickford starred between 1913 and 1933. In retrospect, it is impressive but her performances here are far removed from the norm—the mischievous, adorable gamin she portrayed in *Rebecca of Sunnybrook Farm* (1917), *Pollyanna* (1920), *Sparrows* (1926), and others. Lacking also is the sheer exuberance of her playing opposite husband-to-be Charles "Buddy" Rogers in *My Best Girl* (1927), so appealing to modern audiences.

There is also exuberance in the performances of Douglas Fairbanks, the natural enthusiasm of a man who, like Pickford, is playing underage but knows he has the stamina for the task. He is the personification of Zorro in *The Mark of Zorro* (1920), of d'Artagnan in *The Three Musketeers* (1921), of Robin Hood in the 1922 film of that name, of *The Thief of Bagdad* (1924), and of the title character in *The Black Pirate* (1926). Here, Fairbanks gives us a fairy-tale world of which we want to be a part, but it is also a world with a far more adult complexion. Present is an undercurrent of sexual bravado in the Fairbanks swagger, much as can be found a decade later in the characterizations of Errol Flynn.

Both Pickford and Fairbanks have personality. The latter also possesses a balletic quality, similar in many ways to that of Chaplin. He was an accomplished boxer, gymnast, fencer, and horse rider in private life, and his onscreen stunts presented few problems. At the same time, he understood the need to pace himself, never to show any necessary exertion. If he had to jump a table, the table was lowered a few inches below the normal. Staircases had steps of lesser height. If he had to slide down a curtain or a ship's sail, he did it with poise. Always the actor sought to give the appearance of grace and ease. He had the natural movement of a dancer rather than the top-heavy appearance of a stuntman.

Mary Pickford and Douglas Fairbanks made only one film together, *The Taming of the Shrew* (1929). Despite their mutual background in the theatre, neither is able to rise to the occasion. Pickford lacks the fire to be the shrewish Katherine. Fairbanks has the style of Petruchio, but, like his wife, he displays little understanding of the Shakespearian dialogue and how it should be delivered.

Pickford ended her career in 1933 with *Secrets*, the only film in which she impersonated middle age, aging from eighteen to 75 and doing it remarkably well. Fairbanks was less successful in his last screen appearance, playing an aging roué in the British production of *The Private Life of Don Juan* (1934).

The couple split in 1933 and divorced three years later. Fairbanks married the British socialite Lady Sylvia Ashley that same year. Mary Pickford fooled around in film production but gradually sunk deeper and deeper into alcoholism. Lillian Gish always maintained that drinking was the family curse. It killed Mary's mother, Charlotte, who was influential early in her daughter's career, and it played a part in the demise of younger brother Jack Pickford (1896–1933), who somehow always managed to look debauched no matter how innocent the character he was portraying on screen.

Note: The papers of Mary Pickford are at the Margaret Herrick Library of the Academy of Motion Picture Arts and Sciences.

Bibliographies

Carey, Gary. *Doug & Mary: A Biography of Douglas Fairbanks & Mary Pickford.*
   New York: E.P. Dutton, 1977.
Herndon, Booton. *Mary Pickford and Douglas Fairbanks.* New York: W.W. Norton,
   1977. [contains a very lengthy bibliography of magazine articles, but page num-
   bers are not provided]
Talmey, Allene. *Doug and Mary, and Others.* New York: Macy-Masius, 1927.

Douglas Fairbanks

Bodeen, DeWitt. "Douglas Fairbanks." *Focus on Film,* no. 5, winter 1970, pp. 17–30.
Cooke, Alastair. *Douglas Fairbanks: The Making of a Screen Character.* New York:
   Museum of Modern Art, 1940.
Evans, Alice Belton. "He Knows What He Wants and He Does It." *National Board
   of Review Magazine,* January 1928, pp. 4–5, 10.
Fairbanks, Douglas. "Let Me Say This for the Films." *Ladies' Home Journal,* Sep-
   tember 1922, pp. 13, 117, 120.
———. "Why Big Pictures?" *Ladies' Home Journal,* March 1924, pp. 7, 103–104.
Hancock, Ralph and Letitia Fairbanks. *Douglas Fairbanks: The Fourth Musketeer.*
   New York: Henry Holt, 1953.
Herring, Robert. "Interview with Douglas Fairbanks, Sr." *Close Up,* no. 6, 1930, pp.
   504–508.
Lambert, Gavin. "The Last Heroes." *Sequence,* no. 8, summer 1949, pp. 77–80.
Lindsay, Vachel. "The Great Douglas Fairbanks." *Ladies' Home Journal,* August
   1926, pp. 12, 114.
Schickel, Richard. *His Picture in the Papers.* New York: Charterhouse, 1973.
Taylor, Charles K., Doug Gets Away with It." *Outlook,* April 14, 1926, pp. 560–562.
Thorp, Dunham. "How Fairbanks Took the Color out of Color." *Motion Picture Clas-
   sic,* May 1926, pp. 28–29, 87–90.
Tibbetts, John C. "The Choreography of Hope: The Films of Douglas Fairbanks,
   Sr." *Film Comment,* May-June 1996, pp.50–55.
Tibbetts, John C. and James M. Welsh. *His Majesty the American: The Cinema of
   Douglas Fairbanks, Sr.* South Brunswick, N.J.: A.S. Barnes, 1977.

Mary Pickford

Belasco, David. "Mary Pickford Came to Me." *Photoplay,* December 1915, pp. 27–34.
Brownlow, Kevin. *Mary Pickford Rediscovered: Rare Pictures of a Hollywood Leg-
   end.* New York: Harry N. Abrams, 1999.
Evans, Delight. "Mary Pickford, the Girl." *Photoplay,* July 1918, pp. 90–91.
Eyman, Scott. *Mary Pickford, America's Sweetheart.* New York: Donald I. Fine,
   1990.
Harriman, Mary Case. "Sweetheart." *The New Yorker,* April 7, 1934, pp. 29–33.
Johnson, Julian. "Mary Pickford, Herself and Her Career." *Photoplay,* November
   1915, pp. 53–62; December 1915, pp. 27–34; January 1916, pp. 37, 44; February 1916, p. 49.

Niver, Kemp. *Mary Pickford, Comedienne*. Los Angeles: Locare Research, 1969.

O'Higgins, Harvey. "To What Green Altar?" *New Republic*, February 15, 1919, pp. 80–81.

Pickford, Mary. "What It Means to Be a Movie Actress." *Ladies' Home Journal*, January 1915, p. 9.

———. *Sunshine and Shadow*. New York: Doubleday, 1955.

Spears, Jack. "Mary Pickford's Directors." *Films in Review*, February 1966, pp. 71–95.

Synon, Katherine. "The Unspoiled Mary Pickford." *Photoplay*, September 1914, pp. 35–40.

Whitfield, Eileen. *Pickford: The Woman Who Made Hollywood*. Lexington, Ky.: University Press of Kentucky, 1997.

Windeler, Robert. *Sweetheart: The Story of Mary Pickford*. New York: Praeger, 1973.

ARLINE PRETTY

Blanche Sweet is a real name, perfect for a silent film star, and so is Arline Pretty, which sounds too good to be true. (What was appropriate for silent films did not work later, and in the 1950s British film star Violet Pretty changed her name to Anne Heywood.)

Arline Pretty (Philadelphia, September 5, 1885–Los Angeles, April 14, 1978) was educated in Washington, D.C., where she was a member of the Columbia Players. She wanted to be a Broadway star but instead was lured to Tampa, Florida, to appear in local films aimed at promoting the city as a production center: "I don't think anyone ever saw those. I never heard of them, but I did get the experience which was good for me." The actress was briefly with Universal and then joined the Vitagraph Company in 1915. She was attractive enough that year to be elected Miss Brooklyn.

Vitagraph had produced its first serial, *The Goddess*, in 1915 as a starring vehicle for Earle Williams and Anita Stewart. The silly story involved a modern Joan of Arc raised on a desert island in the belief that she was a goddess. Arline Pretty was starred in Vitagraph's 1917 serial, *The Secret Kingdom*, the first episode of which was released on January 1st. While neither as pretty as Pearl White nor as adventuresome as Ruth Roland, Arline Pretty made an appealing serial heroine and followed *The Secret Kingdom* with *The Hidden Hand* (1917) and *A Woman in Grey* (1920), both released by Pathé. "They did make you tremendously popular," she recalled. "Because they were sixteen episodes, and you were in a theatre for sixteen whole weeks. I got thousands of letters and cards.

"You know I was always being kidnapped and Charles Richman was always rescuing me. In *The Secret Kingdom*, they took me to a place in Brooklyn, the top floor of one of those brownstones. Charles was to get a room in the next house, let a rope down to me, and I was to jump out and he'd take me across. Naturally I was a little nervous about it. I'd never jumped out of a four-storey place in my life—and never expected to. I had an evening dress on and they did make a belt to go under the dress with a hook on it. A man whose name was Eddie Wentworth had charge of the stunts and he said, 'Don't jump out until I call all right.' I thought I heard 'all right' and I jumped out. I went zooming down to the first floor and I was stuck. I'd be smashed to pieces if I'd gone all the way. Charles and Eddie came down and they were white as sheets. Because when I jumped out, nobody had a hold of the rope on the roof. They had put it around the chimney so it wouldn't fall off. They saw it start to go and ran as fast as they could and stopped it. Eddie said, 'Why did you jump before I said all right?' He nearly fainted because he realized he'd called 'hold tight' and it sounded like 'all right' to me."

Arline Pretty's feature films are not available for viewing, which is unfortunate as a few boast remarkable storylines. Her first, *The Man Who Found Himself*, released by World in 1915, has the hero, Robert Warwick, escape from Sing Sing by pretending to be a member of the World film crew shooting there. In Vitagraph's *The Dawn of Freedom* (1916), Revolutionary War hero Charles Richman is held in suspended animation and revived to lead the workers in a rebellion against the current owner of a coalmine on his property.

Arline Pretty was also a leading lady to Douglas Fairbanks in *In Again—Out Again*, released in April 1917, playing a pacifist fiancée to the war preparedness hero. In the Western *The Challenge of Chance*, released in July 1919, Arline Pretty plays opposite heavyweight champion of the world, Jess Willard.

In the 1920s, Arline Pretty's career was generally limited to second female leads in minor productions. She did appear in a couple of Metro films starring Viola Dana, for which her salary of $250 a week was not bad. Her last silent film was *Virgin Lips*, produced by Columbia in 1928.

I interviewed Pretty in connection with my book *The Big V: A History of the Vitagraph Company*. The actress was then living in a small apartment in a dingy building less than three blocks from Grauman's Chinese Theatre. After publication of *The Big V*, I invited her to a celebratory party. She refused, informing me she wished to have nothing to do with the book or its author. The reason? I had humiliated her by noting that with the coming of sound she had become an extra and so continued for the remainder of her career.

Bibliography

"Arline Pretty Leading Lady to Fairbanks." *Moving Picture World*, March 17, 1917, p. 1750.
"Arline Pretty Was Born That Way." *Photoplay*, June 1917, p. 74.
Montanye, Lillian. "The Pretty Miss Pretty." *Motion Picture Classic*, November 1919, pp. 60, 103.

ESTHER RALSTON

Paramount's 1924 release of the first and only live-action screen adaptation of *Peter Pan* confirmed the prominence of Betty Bronson as Peter Pan, and made stars of Mary Brian as Wendy, Virginia Brown Faire as Tinker Bell, and Esther Ralston as Mrs. Darling. It seems somehow appropriate that Tinker Bell's creator should enjoy old age in wealthy Leisure World, the California equivalent of Never Never Land for senior citizens, while Mrs. Darling ended her days in a trailer park in Ventura, California. Admittedly, it was an upscale trailer park, where one of Esther's brothers also lived, but it was still a trailer park. Mrs. Darling grew up and found life gets tougher as one gets old, particularly if one is an actress.

Esther Ralston (Bar Harbor, Maine, September 17, 1902–Ventura, California, January 14, 1994) began her film career as an extra in the late teens, after many years of touring with her family as part of "The Seven Ralstons," performing anywhere there was an audience. Her first screen role of any worth was as Mary Jane Wilks in William Desmond Taylor's 1920 production of *Huckleberry Finn*, with Lewis Sargent in the title role. She played an angel in Chaplin's *The Kid* (1921) but was cut from the film prior to its release and again worked with *The Kid*'s Jackie Coogan in *Oliver Twist* (1922). In all, Esther Ralston made more than twenty credited appearances in feature films before landing the role of Mrs. Darling in *Peter Pan*. It was as if, overnight, she had matured from teenage roles to motherhood.

Peter Pan also marked the beginning of a Famous Players–Lasky/Paramount contract, which continued through 1929 and saw Esther Ralston as a leading lady in 26 films. Along with Betty Bronson, she was the only cast member from *Peter Pan* to be featured in a second J.M. Barrie adaptation, *A Kiss for Cinderella* (1926). She was a competent, bright, and cheery leading lady to the likes of Richard Dix (*Lucky Devil* and *Womanhandled*, both 1925, *The Quarterback*, 1926, and *The Wheel of Life*, 1929), Edward Everett Horton (*Beggar on Horseback*, 1925), Warner Baxter (*The Best People*, 1925), Richard Arlen (*Figures Don't Lie*, 1927), and others.

The best of her silent work, and certainly the most accessible, is as Esther, the captain's daughter in *Old Ironsides*, directed by James Cruze, shot on location at Catalina, and first screened in December 1926. The film is a romance, with a young and surprisingly muscular Charles Farrell playing opposite Esther, an adventure epic, and, in part, the story of the U.S.S. Constitution, known as "Old Ironsides." "My favorite is *Old Ironsides*," said Esther. "My people came over on the Mayflower, and they fought in the Revolutionary War and the Civil War and the World War and Vietnam. I think because *Old*

Ironsides is history—American history—that meant more to me than any of the other pictures."

Old Ironsides, along with many other prominent Paramount releases, was edited by Dorothy Arzner, and Esther Ralston was the star of Arzner's first two directorial efforts, *Fashions for Women* and *Ten Modern Commandments*, both released in 1927. The films were not a happy experience for Esther, who objected to some of Arzner's directorial techniques which involved having the star sit in her lap and allowing her breasts to be fondled. It was obviously an example of sexual harassment, if not of the typical male-female variety, and outrageous as it might have been, one had to laugh at Esther's recounting of the episodes, complete with mock outrage and indignation.

Another amusing incident involved *Children of Divorce* (1927), in which Esther, as the product of a broken marriage, foolishly allows the man she loves, Gary Cooper, to be tricked into marriage by Clara Bow. The film is remarkable for the understated performance of Bow in the later scenes as she determines to kill herself. Director Frank Lloyd moves his camera in for a close-up of the unhappiness in Bow's eyes, and then, as she walks away through two sets of doors, having decided to take poison, the camera moves away from her, emphasizing the drama of the moment. Cooper is young and attractive but wears much too much makeup, and even a shower scene (quite unusual in a silent film) fails to capture his masculinity. Modern audiences tend to respond to the better-known leading players, but Esther Ralston not only dominates the film but also is uniform in her underplaying.

Clara Bow asked Esther if she liked Gary Cooper, to which the latter replied, "Yes, because he is such a good actor." Bow responded, "I like him too, because he allows me to take my dog in the tub with me when he gives me my morning bath."

Esther Ralson continued on screen through *San Francisco Docks* in 1941 and was a frequent television performer in later years, notably in NBC's *Our Five Daughters* (1961–1962). In the 1930s, she made a good second female lead to Joan Crawford in *Sadie McKee* (1934) and to Alice Faye in *Tin Pan Alley* (1940), and she is excellent as the American movie star in Walter Forde's superior British thriller *Rome Express* (1932).

Esther Ralston was, of course, the dominant figure at the trailer park, attending screenings of her films at the recreation center and frequently flying off to retrospectives and film buff tributes. She loved the attention of fans, except for one who always gave the impression of being very close to her but at the mention of whose name she would shudder. Esther, Mary Brian, and I were once walking across a San Francisco hotel lobby when Esther spotted this fan approaching. I have never seen an eighty-year-old lady move with such speed, urging us to follow in haste.

She very much felt the need to preserve her niche in film history. After reading a biography of Louise Brooks, that described Brook's performance in *The American Venus* (1926) as eclipsing that of Esther's, Ralston commented, "Hell, I didn't even know she was in the film!"

I had the opportunity to edit Esther's autobiography and became friendly in part because of that and also through out mutual friend, Mary Brian, who is the godmother to one of Esther's daughters. Mary and I frequently visited the trailer park, where Esther would serve us homemade lemon meringue pie. Despite the fact that Mary and Esther had been friends since *Peter Pan*, it seemed odd that they had so little to say to each other; always it was a matter of finding something to talk about. On our last visit, on August 16, 1992, Esther was only a few weeks shy of her 90th birthday, and yet she could still do a high kick to demonstrate her continued youthfulness. We had planned to drive up for her funeral on January 17, 1994, but that morning, a 6.0 earthquake hit Los Angeles. We never made it for a final farewell.

Bibliography

Drew, William M. "Esther Ralston" in *Speaking of Silents: First Ladies of the Screen.* Vestal, N.Y.: Vestal Press, 1989, pp. 186–211.

"The Girl on the Cover." *Photoplay*, October 1925, p. 76.

Hughes, Miriam. "Another Inegnue." *Photoplay*, January 1931, pp. 41, 108.

"I Wore Thousand-Dollar Dresses." *TV Guide*, August 18, 1962, pp. 26–28.

Prosser, Catherine S. "Just a Small Time Girl." *Photoplay*, April 1928, pp. 58, 111.

Ralston, Esther. *Some Day We'll Laugh: An Autobiography.* Metuchen, N.J.: Scarecrow Press, 1985.

Waterbury, Ruth. "Love and Esther Ralston." *Photoplay*, October 1926, pp. 63, 126–127.

Sincerely yours
Charles Ray

CHARLES RAY

Charles Ray has little to commend him to modern audiences. His round-faced boyish looks lack charm, and his characterizations of small-town or rural American youths whose naiveté and lack of sophistication never prevent their winning in the end do not ring true. In many respects, he is similar in style to Harry Langdon, playing under-age and under-intelligent types, except that for Ray the roles are dramatic and for Langdon they are supposedly comic. There is a further similarity between the two men. Both failed to realize their limitations as performers and overextended themselves by taking arrogant charge of their careers. Langdon's problem was that he did not understand that he was inferior to Chaplin, Keaton, and Lloyd and should not have attempted to emulate their self-controlled production activities. Charles Ray failed to comprehend that dramatic silent screen performance was dominated by women, and that male stars could never compete with Mary Pickford and others with their own production entities.

After a number of years as a minor stage actor, Charles Ray (Jacksonville, Illinois, March 15, 1891–Los Angeles, November 23, 1943) entered films as an extra for producer Thomas H. Ince in December 1912. He was to remain with Ince through 1920, playing supporting roles to William S. Hart in *The Grudge* and *The Conversion of Frosty Blake* (both released in 1915), eventually becoming a star in his own right, playing a Confederate soldier in the 1915 melodrama *The Coward*. By 1917, Ray had become firmly established in the characterization of the wholesome "hick." "I play these because I was born among such folks and know them," he explained to the *New York Dramatic Mirror* in 1920. The most entertaining of the Ray features, in large part because it is so silly, is *The Clodhopper*, released in June 1917, in which he plays a farm boy who comes to New York and becomes a cabaret star, performing the foot-stomping dance, the clodhop.

By 1920, Ince was releasing his films through Paramount. Ray spoke with Adolph Zukor about the possibility of continuing with Paramount at a bigger salary, but Zukor quickly realized the actor's ego was out of control. "I knew he was headed for trouble and did not care to be with him when he found it," wrote the producer in his autobiography, *The Public Is Never Wrong*. Ray formed his own production company, releasing through Associated First National. His first film, *45 Minutes from Broadway* (1920) was based on the George M. Cohan play; it was relatively successful, but Ray was no George M. Cohan. *The Old Swimmin' Hole*, released in February 1921, is a bucolic comedy and the only American silent feature containing no subtitles. It works not so much because of the pantomimic skills of the players but because the storyline is so negligible.

The film that brought Charles Ray down was *The Courtship of Myles Standish*, based on the Longfellow poem, released in December 1923. Wearing a long, blonde wig, Ray looked even more ridiculous than he had appeared in most of his earlier films. The film was financed by Ray, and its failure at the box-office forced the actor into bankruptcy. The actor's decline was not a solo effort. His wife, Clara Grant, whom he had married in November 1915 and whose visions of grandeur were more than the equal to those of her husband, ably assisted him. Jane Novak recalled, "I don't think Charlie was so ambitious as his wife was. They both had absolutely nothing when they were first married. Then he became such a big star, and she...If a tradesman dared ring the front door bell, she would really blow him out, and say, 'you're supposed to go round the back.' They spent so much money. They had this beautiful house in Beverly Hills. I was at Earle Williams's home for dinner, and Pat Powers from Universal was there, and Pat was telling us, 'Last night we were at a dinner party at Charlie Ray's, and he said, tomorrow they're going bankrupt.' They were having this enormous dinner party with a butler behind every chair. Pat said, 'I just looked at him and said, how can you do this if you're going bankrupt tomorrow? Who will pay the bills?' And he said, 'we thought it was the thing to do.' How could they? He was very naïve. He was much like the character he played on the screen. But he was a very sweet person, too."

Marian Trimble, the daughter of Vitagraph co-founder J. Stuart Blackton, also knew Ray at this time: "What a tragic figure he was...I had gotten to know him quite well, seeing him many Sundays at Patsy Ruth Miller's famous tennis parties, where my father and I distinguished ourselves as a doubles team. Charlie never played. He just sat there and had very little to say. I always wanted to take him on my lap and croon, 'There, there, it *isn't* so bad.'"

Following the bankruptcy, Clara Grant Ray opened a dress shop on Sunset Boulevard, and her husband began the downward spiral through lesser films and lesser producers. His last silent film, *The Garden of Eden* (1928), has him playing against type as a sophisticated resident of a Monte Carlo hotel. He is fifth billed in the credits. With the coming of sound, Charles Ray was reduced to bit parts and extra work. He and Clara divorced in 1935. A year earlier he had again filed for bankruptcy. "I'm not trying to stage a comeback," he said at the time, "I'm just looking for work." In 1935, Ray published, through California Graphic Press, a collection of short stories titled *Hollywood Shorts, compiled from incidents in the everyday life of men and women who entertain in pictures.* An undercurrent of anti-Semitism is evident in a number of the stories, suggesting that Ray blamed his downfall on the Jewish studio bosses such as Adolph Zukor, who came along replacing the earlier gentile producers such as Thomas H. Ince.

The independent studios of Charles Ray, located at 4401 Sunset Boulevard, later became the home of Monogram Pictures and, still later, public television station KCET. In 1979, the latter discovered that a portion of Ray's screening room at the studio was still extant hidden behind a fake wall. Once more, albeit briefly, Charles Ray came back into the spotlight.

Bibliography

"Before They Were Stars: Charles Ray." *New York Dramatic Mirror,* March 13, 1920, pp. 480, 505.

Bodeen, DeWitt. "Charles Ray." *Films in Review,* November 1968, pp. 548–568.

Brewster, Eleanor. "That Unclouded Ray." *Motion Picture,* April 1919, pp. 38–39, 107.

Hall, Gladys and Adele Whitely Fletcher. "We Interview Charles Ray." *Motion Picture,* March 1922, pp. 22–23, 100.

Martin, Minerva. "The Young and Debonair Charles Ray." *Photoplay,* October 1914, pp. 46–49.

Naylor, Hazel Simpson. "Keeping the Ray Focused." *Motion Picture,* January 1920, pp. 44–45, 111.

O'Hara, Kenneth. "Tom Ince's New Wonder Boy." *Photoplay,* January 1916, pp. 106–108.

Porter, Katherine Anne. "The Real Ray." *Motion Picture,* October 1920, pp. 36–37, 102.

Ray, Charles. "Something New in Dances—'Clodhopping,'" *New York Dramatic Mirror,* June 9, 1917, p. 32.

———. "It Pays to be Natural." *New York Dramatic Mirror,* July 31, 1920, p. 183.

———. "Confessions Made by a Star-Producer." *Photoplay,* November 1924, pp. 56–57, 110–111.

———. "I Spent a Million to Dress Up." *Photoplay,* September 1927, pp. 47, 131–132.

WALLACE REID

Long before Ramon Novarro and Rudolph Valentino, Wallace Reid was the screen's first matineé idol, and unlike his successors he was very much an American hero. Reid began a series of films dealing with fast cars with *The Roaring Road* (1919), in which he is an automobile salesman who wins the Santa Monica Road Race. In *The Firefly of France* (1918), Reid is an American aviator in France who captures German spies. In *Hawthorne of the USA* (1919), he is an American who brings democracy to a fictional European country. His roles may have required that he occasionally play non-Americans, but there was always a spirit of Americanism about the characters.

Because of his good looks and modest personality, Wallace Reid was very much in demand as a leading man to the top stars at Paramount, where he was under contract from 1915 until his death. He played opposite Geraldine Farrar in *Carmen* (1915), *Maria Rosa* (1916), *Joan the Woman* (1917), *The Woman God Forgot* (1917), and *The Devil Stone* (1917), and his presence undoubtedly helped audience accept someone from the upper echelon of the operatic stage in the more plebeian setting of the motion picture. Ann Little was a frequent leading lady in the teens, most notably in *Believe Me, Xantippe* (1918), in which John Barrymore had starred on Broadway. Little remembered Reid as "the most talented person you would know in the world" but also recalled that he was not pleased to discover on one of their films that the billing was "Ann Little and Wallace Reid" rather than the other way around.

Gloria Swanson starred opposite Reid in *The Affairs of Anatol* (1921) and *Don't Tell Everything* (1921). Bebe Daniels was also in the former and was Reid's leading lady in *The Dancin' Fool* (1920), *Sick Abed* (1920) and *Nice People* (1922). She recalled, "He and Valentino were two of the nicest men I've ever known."

Wallace Reid was born in St. Louis, Missouri, on April 15, 1891, the son of the popular stage actor, Hal Reid, who also worked in films as an actor and director. He was well educated and might have become a physician had he not decided to follow his father on stage. Reid entered films in 1910 with the Selig Polyscope Company and appeared in more than 100 short subjects for Vitagraph, Reliance, Universal, and others. He is easily recognizable in these films, often playing leading parts, but audiences do not appear to have noticed him until D.W. Griffith cast him as Jeff the blacksmith in *The Birth of a Nation* (1915). Reid appears in only one scene, a brutal fistfight, but there is almost a homoerotic quality to the sequence as Reid's shirt is literally torn from his body and he displays his muscular physique.

Cecil B. DeMille and Jesse L. Lasky were two executives who saw Reid's performance and were struck by his flawless features and body, his expressive eyes, slim good looks, and 180 pounds of muscle. They signed him to a Paramount contract. Wallace Reid starred in 32 Paramount features without incident. For the 33rd, *The Valley of the Giants*, released in August 1919 and based on the popular and much-filmed Peter B. Kyne novel, he went on location to the High Sierras. En route, the train in which the company was traveling was involved in an accident, and Reid was badly injured. Legend has it that he was prescribed morphine in order to ease his pain, and that the actor became addicted to the drug.

There are other stories. At least one contemporary told me that Reid was supplied morphine by his leading lady, Grace Darmond, who was well known around Hollywood as a drug dealer. Darmond was also notorious as a lesbian, being the woman for whom Jean Acker left Valentino on their wedding night. As far as the press and the public were concerned, Wallace Reid was a happily married family man. He and actress Dorothy Davenport, with whom he appeared in many films at Universal in 1913 and 1914, had married in October 1913. Reid was frequently photographed, pipe in mouth, book in hand and dog at his side, as an exemplary figure of American family values.

Some have disputed the image. Bebe Daniels was adamant that Reid was "unhappily married." Off the record, she expressed doubt that the actor should ever have married, being possibly bisexual. Claire DuBrey went further, insisting to me that Reid was "unsure of his sexuality." Did Wallace Reid embrace drugs as a means of escape from a family life to which he was doomed but which he did not want? Whatever the reality, Wallace Reid became a drug addict, and while he continued to act, he was beginning to show signs of drug abuse. He lost weight. His face became haggard. While filming his last feature, *Thirty Days*, in 1922, he collapsed on the set.

Dorothy Davenport, Mrs. Reid, gave a press conference announcing her husband's condition and blaming it entirely on the morphine he had been given after the train wreck. Reid entered a sanitarium, where he died on January 18, 1923. "He went off dope too fast," said Ann Little, "and that was what killed him. He tried but it didn't work." Wallace Reid's mother paid tribute to her son with a slim biographical volume, *Wallace Reid: His Life Story*. Mrs. Wallace Reid exploited her husband's death, producing the anti-drug feature *Human Wreckage*, released in June 1923. As friend Priscilla Bonner explained it, Mrs. Reid had to promote a career for herself in order to pay for the education and upbringing of her son and daughter, and the production of *Human Wreckage* and later films was a necessary exploitation of the family name. Those films have given Mrs. Wallace Reid a place in film history as a pioneering female producer and director.

Bibliography

Bodeen, DeWitt. "Wallace Reid." *Films in Review*, April 1966, pp. 205–230.

Cheatham, Maude S. "Wally, the Genial." *Motion Picture*, October 1920, pp. 32–33, 104.

Fletcher, Adele Whitely and Gladys Hall. "We Interview Wally." *Motion Picture*, September 1921, pp. 22–23, 100.

Gaddis, Pearl. "Wallace Reid of the Universal Company." *Motion Picture Story Magazine*, February 1914, pp. 102–103.

Gebhart, Myrtle. "Some Memories of Wallace Reid." *Picture-Play*, May 1923, pp. 26–29, 90.

Kingsley, Grace. "Romances of Famous Film Folk." *Picture-Play*, July 1921, pp. 51–53.

McGaffey, Kenneth. "Wandering with Wally." *Photoplay*, June 1918, pp. 59–60.

Reid, Bertha Westbrook. *Wallace Reid: His Life Story.* Los Angeles: Sorg, 1923.

Reid, Dorothy Davenport. "The Real Wally." *Photoplay*, March 1925, pp. 58, 100.

Reid, Wallace. "How I Got In." *Motion Picture*, January 1918, p. 59.

Scollard, York. "Wally the Wonderful." *Photoplay*, March 1916, pp. 76–77.

Shelley, Hazel. "Ideals of an Idol." *Motion Picture Classic*, March 1921, pp. 22–23, 68.

"Wallace Reid as We Knew Him." *Picture-Play*, April 1923, pp. 28–29, 90.

Sincerely,
Billie Rhodes

BILLIE RHODES

When I first came to Los Angeles in 1971, one of the first actresses I contacted was Billie Rhodes. I had seen a number of Christie comedy shorts in which she had appeared in the late teens, and was impressed by her charm and her light comedic style. In 1915, *Picture-Play* described her as "one of our best little laugh-provokers." I don't know that her characters ever generated much actual laughter, but she did make audiences smile as much if not more so than Mabel Normand, and had she had a mentor such as Mack Sennett rather than the distinctly second-rate comedy producer Al Christie, she might well have been a major feature-length comedienne.

Rhodes lived on Laurel Canyon in Studio City only a few blocks away from the house in which I was to spend much of my life. She was never to visit me, but I was a frequent guest at the four-unit apartment complex that she owned, eating the mini pizzas on which she seemed to thrive. She had been born Levita Axelrod in San Francisco on August 15, 1894, and by the time I knew her she had become a little old Jewish lady in her mid-70s.

After a brief stage career in stock and a tour on the Orpheum circuit, Billie Rhodes entered films with the Kalem Company at the suggestion of director George Melford; she made her screen debut in the two-reel drama *Perils of the Sea*, starring Carlyle Blackwell and released on September 20, 1913. At the close of her Kalem contract, Billie began to sing in nightclubs. As she recalled, "It wasn't long before Al Christie caught my hand one evening when I was about to sing and asked me to come over to the studio." Beginning in the summer of 1915, she was to appear in one comedy a week, usually playing opposite Neal Burns or Lee Moran, under the direction of Al Christie, who was releasing his films through the Universal-controlled Nestor Company. (Within a short space of time, Billie was being billed as "The Nestor Girl.") Billie was also seen in a minor role in Christie's first feature-length production, *Mrs. Plum's Pudding*, starring stage actress Marie Tempest, released in the summer of 1915.

When Christie entered independent production in the late summer of 1916, he took Billie Rhodes with him, and she was the star of his first independent production, *A Seminary Scandal*, released on September 18, 1916. Billie continued with Christie through 1918, and in April 1917, the producer began starring her opposite Jay Belasco in a series of Strand comedies. All were clean and wholesome and entirely devoid of the slapstick humor associated with Mack Sennett. At times, they might be considered somewhat dull, but they were never lifeless.

An overweight and under-talented comedian by the name of "Smiling

Billy" Parsons persuaded Billie Rhodes to leave Christie and embark on independent production. He starred her in a series of Capitol Comedies released through Goldwyn and a six-reel feature, *The Girl of My Dreams*, released by First National, all in 1918. The following year, Parsons starred Billie in three feature films, *Hoop-La*, *The Lamb and the Lion*, and *The Blue Bonnet*. He also married her, on February 12, 1919, but it was a short-lived relationship as he died on September 28 of the same year.

The death of Billy Parsons came at a bad time for Billie Rhodes. She was still cute and relatively young, but there was no one to guide her, and later feature films—*Miss Nobody* (1920), *His Pajama Girl* (1921), *The Star Reporter* (1921), *Fires of Youth* (1924), and *Leave It to Gerry* (1924)—did nothing for her career and were commercial and critical failures.

Billie Rhodes remarried in 1920 and in the mid-1920s, she went back to the stage and to night club entertaining. Despite having appeared in some 200 films, she was completely forgotten—even by the film buffs—but at the end of her life, she returned to the spotlight, teaming up with ragtime pianist Galen Wilkes and singing songs she had performed seventy years earlier. She died at her Studio City home on March 12, 1988.

Note: The papers of Billie Rhodes are at the Margaret Herrick Library of the Academy of Motion Picture Arts and Sciences.

Bibliography

Oderman, Stuart. "Billie Rhodes." *Films in Review*, December 1988, pp. 592–601.
Peltret, Elizabeth. "Billie Rhodes—Circus Girl." *Motion Picture Classic*, January 1919, pp. 26–27, 74.
Shannon, Betty. "The Devil's Little Daughter." *Photoplay*, July 1917, p. 97.

CHARLES "BUDDY" ROGERS

A leading man of some 38 feature films, including three in the United Kingdom, Buddy Rogers never overcame the "pretty boy" label, a label that was even more damning when coupled with the title "Mr. Mary Pickford." Buddy was the perennial college boy—even in old age with silver hair, he had the look of someone who might have been a regular at a fraternity reunion. At the start of his career, he had been considered for the roles subsequently played, respectively, by Charles Farrell and Ronald Colman in *Old Ironsides* (1926) and *Beau Geste* (1926), and rejected for both because he was simply too pretty. Paramount tried to promote him as the new Wallace Reid, but he lacked the masculinity and the muscles. As late as 1930, by which time his screen career was assured, there were still rumors behind his back that Buddy Rogers was the studio "pretty boy" and, perhaps worse, "a sissy."

As if to emphasize his masculinity and his bravado, Rogers starred, along with Richard Arlen and Clara Bow, in William Wellman's 1927 production of *Wings*, written by John Monk Saunders. As the young First World War flyer, Buddy Rogers demonstrates the capability to portray the spirit of youth and adventure, to mature on screen, and to perform stunts that so-called rugged leading men of later decades would be incapable of. Richard Arlen was already a qualified flyer, but Rogers had to spend 200 hours in the air, learning how to handle a plane at Kelly Field. He described Wellman as "tough, probably the ruggedest director I've worked with," a man who knew how to inject realism into his scenes: "Dick Arlen and I had a fight scene, so Wellman came to me the night before, and he said, 'You know Buddy, Arlen says he can smash your face up....He's going to beat the hell out of you.' He went to Arlen and said the same thing, and he got the best fight scene out of us you've ever seen. He was that type of director. And the drunk scenes, when I drank champagne, he made me get drunk. He wanted the real thing."

Buddy Rogers was a pilot with the Navy during World War Two, and when we first met back in May 1971, he recalled, "Thousands of young pilots would come over to me and say, Commander Rogers, you're responsible for me being a pilot. I saw your movie."

Charles Buddy Rogers was born in Olathe, Kansas, on August 13, 1904, the son of the publisher of the Olathe *Mirror*, and forever in Hollywood, he was always to be the small town boy from Kansas who made good and married its somewhat faded and past her prime queen. Spotted by a talent scout from Paramount, Buddy was brought to the company's Astoria Studios on Long Island, where for six months he was a member of the Paramount Acting School, appearing as the star in the graduating feature, *Fascinating Youth* (1926).

The actor remained the Paramount college boy, playing opposite Mary Brian, Nancy Carroll, and others in relatively unimportant features. He did have a small role in the W.C. Fields vehicle So's Your Old Man (1926), made an easy transition to sound with Abie's Irish Rose (1929), positively oozed charm singing "Peach of a Pair" to Nancy Carroll in the Technicolor musical Follow Thru (1930), and with Wellman tried unsuccessfully to repeat the popularity of Wings with Young Eagles (1930).

Bothered by the endless college boy roles offered by the studio, Buddy Rogers left Paramount on December 1, 1931, and signed up himself and his orchestra for a radio career with NBC. Leading an orchestra and performing his favorite party piece of playing the various instrument in the group perhaps gave Buddy Rogers his greatest satisfaction. He had formed his first band while still a student at the University of Kansas, and the idea for playing all the instruments in the orchestra had originated in the 1929 film Close Harmony.

Back in 1927, Buddy Rogers had been selected to play opposite Mary Pickford in My Best Girl, one of the most delightful of the later Pickford vehicles thanks in large part to the obvious chemistry between the two leading performers and the direction of the often unfairly maligned Sam Taylor. As Buddy recalled, "I was at a dance one Saturday night, and a woman who had adapted Wings said, 'What are you doing for lunch on Monday? I'll meet you in front of Paramount at twelve.' She drove up in her car, I got in, and we drove to another studio, and there was a big bungalow there. She said, 'Buddy, will you ring the doorbell? I'll park the car.' I rang the bell, and America's sweetheart with the curls opened the door. It was a plot to get me over there to see whether Miss Pickford might think I might be good for her leading man. I made a test, and a few days later, they called and said I had the part. When I was in college—and she later learned this—I preferred Norma Shearer to her. Didn't go over too well!"

Mary Pickford was further irritated when Buddy brought along a neighbor of his, Carole Lombard, and suggested that she play the sister in My Best Girl: "Mrs. Rogers said, 'Oh fine, but I don't think so at all.' She was so jealous."

The friendship between Pickford and Rogers grew in the 1930s, and on June 26, 1937, they married. It was Buddy's first marriage and Pickford's third. The actor remained devoted to his "star" and in later years, he was a popular silver-haired presence at screenings of My Best Girl, which he would always introduce with the words, "She was my best girl then, and she's still my best girl."

The impression, perhaps unfair, was that Mary Pickford throughout the marriage was the dominant partner in the relationship. Buddy had to move into Pickfair, living in permanent remembrance of his wife's second husband, and even had to endure her telling guests that Doug Fairbanks was "a real man." In 1945, Pickford did set up Comet Productions, almost as a play toy for Buddy, with her as president and him as vice president. He was allowed to continue his career, playing Lupe Velez's husband in three "Mexican Spitfire" movies (1941 and 1942), and producing his last in 1957, *The Parson and the Outlaw*, in which he also appeared as the preacher who befriends Billy the Kid. But there were unpleasant indications that Buddy's time away from Pickfair was barely tolerated.

Mary Brian, who had co-starred with Buddy in his second film, *More Pay—Less Work*, on loan-out to Fox in 1926, recalled being in summer stock with Buddy, and on opening night, Pickford telephoned him, drunkenly screaming that he should be at home, where she needed him, instead of out working for a salary that would not even take care of his phone bill. Just as Pickford took to the bottle, so did Buddy. Publicist Herb Sterne, a frequent guest at Pickfair, remembered nights when he, Buddy, and William Cameron Menzies would be so bored that they would raid the butler's pantry and get drunk on Scotch.

After Pickford's death in 1979, life changed for the better. Buddy had promised Mary that he would never remarry, but he must perhaps have remembered that his wedding vows included "love, honor, and cherish," but not "obey." In September 1980, he sold Pickfair and built a new home, the Pickfair Lodge, next door. On July 22, 1981, he married a fifty-year-old real estate agent, Beverly Ricone, with whom he had been friendly for a number of years. Mary Pickford had doubts as to how wisely Buddy might spend her money after she was gone, but, in reality, he distributed the funds to many worthwhile causes and in 1986 was honored with the Jean Hersholt Humanitarian Award from the Academy of Motion Picture Arts and Sciences. Buddy Rogers died in Rancho Mirage, California, on April 21, 1999.

Bibliography

Carter, Mary. "Buddy Has Arrived." *Cinema Art*, August 1927, pp. 21, 45–47.
Ingram, Alice. "Buddy Conquers Broadway!" *Photoplay*, June 1930, p. 88.
Rogers, B.H. "My Son Buddy." *Photoplay*, July 1929, pp. 34–35, 88, 94–96.
St. Johns, Ivan. "Necking with America's Sweetheart." *Photoplay*, October 1927, pp. 98, 106.
Slide, Anthony. "Charles 'Buddy' Rogers." *The Silent Picture*, no. 11/12, Summer-Autumn 1971, unpaged.
Watkins, Fred. "FFM Interviews Buddy Rogers." *Film Fan Monthly*, December 1970, pp. 8–22.

Clarine Seymour in *The Girl Who Stayed at Home* (1919).

CLARINE SEYMOUR

Nineteen-twenty was a bad year for both D.W. Griffith and for American filmgoers. That year saw the deaths of two of the director's brightest young stars, Robert Harron and Clarine Seymour, both of whom might have had brilliant careers ahead of them. Clarine Seymour had the makings of a flapper—before the flapper came into existence—and she had a natural, saucy quality that made her an appealing light comedienne. Her curly black hair was just ready for the bob of the new decade, and her eyes were two of the most bewitching on screen. Clarine Seymour was a blend of Dorothy Gish and Constance Talmadge, but she was also unique, very much her own personality, and a formidable acting talent. A month prior to her death, *Motion Picture Classic* featured Clarine Seymour on its March 1920 cover, noting "the screen has no prettier or more piquant comedienne."

Harron and Seymour were teamed in two features, *The Girl Who Stayed at Home* and *True Heart Susie*, both released in 1919. In the first, Seymour is cast as Cutie Beautiful (and she is!), a showgirl who makes a man of the spineless Harron character and sends him off to war. In one marvelous shot, she is seen busily knitting for the troops, thinking of the dangers that her husband is facing, while her feet respond to the music on the phonograph. As the title has it, "The upper part of her sad—but the feet still rag-time." In *True Heart Susie*, she is the other woman who steals Harron away from Lillian Gish. The film might belong to the latter, but Clarine Seymour works hard at stealing it away from Gish, ensnaring Harron and eventually dying as a result of her very minor unfaithfulness. Again, there is a brilliant subtitle as Harron sees his wife die, not knowing the cause of her death: "She died as she had lived—a little unfaithful."

Clarine Seymour (Brooklyn, New York, December 9, 1898–New York, April 25, 1920) was born into a relatively affluent family. She made her professional debut at a Methodist Church "entertainment" in 1916, and later that same year, Seymour entered films because of a reversal in her father's business activities. She worked for the Thanhouser Company and for Pathé and later appeared as a leading lady in comedy productions at Hal Roach's Rolin Company opposite Toto the Clown and not Harold Lloyd to whom she would have been better suited, and with Al Christie. In 1918, Victor Heerman directed a screen test of the actress for Griffith, and she asked him to persuade Robert Harron to play opposite her in the test. Heerman described her as "a very clever little thing," and Griffith obviously concurred.

After *The Girl Who Stayed at Home* and *True Heart Susie*, Griffith featured Seymour along with Richard Barthelmess in *Scarlet Days* (1919) and *The Idol Dancer* (1920). The latter is a Western and one of the worst films ever directed by Griffith. Seymour provides some comic relief to the posturing melodramatics of co-star Carol Dempster but not enough to save the film. Nowhere is the tragedy of Clarine Seymour's death more pointed than here; if only she might have lived and Dempster died, how much better would Griffith have fared in the coming decade. Ralph Graves also appeared in *Scarlet Days*, and after dismissing Dempster as "dopey looking," he described Clairine Seymour as "a beautiful girl, totally natural; she had this natural quality that was just beginning to come into vogue." As White Almond Flower in *The Idol Dancer*, Seymour holds an attraction, particularly with her dancing for both Barthelmess and Creighton Hale. In the end, the latter sacrifices himself in order that Barthelmess and Seymour can be saved from a horde of cannibals. Ultimately, the film is a waste of time for both its leads, but it did bring Seymour critical and popular praise. The films make it very obvious that Griffith was grooming both Seymour and Barthelmess for stardom in the 1920s.

Clarine Seymour signed a four-year contract with Griffith and began filming of the role subsequently played by Mary Hay in *Way Down East*, but she died suddenly and unexpectedly. Historian and literary critic Edward Wagenknecht paid tribute to her at his Methodist Church in Oak Park, Illinois. The text was subsequently published in 1920 by Seymour's father as *A Tribute to Clarine Seymour*, and, although only fifteen pages long, it is Wagenknecht's first published title, antedating his other books by some seven years.

Bibliography

Haskins, Harrison. "The Last Interview." *Motion Picture Classic*, July 1920, pp. 51–52, 83.

Peltret, Elizabeth. "Introducing Cutie Beautiful." *Motion Picture Classic*, July 1919, pp. 46–47, 76.

Shannon, Betty. "An Unfinished Story." *Photoplay*, July 1920, p. 81.

Lowell Sherman and Greta Garbo in *The Divine Woman* (1928).

LOWELL SHERMAN

D.W. Griffith is responsible for some of the greatest villains of the silent screen. There is the massive presence of George Siegmann, menacing Lillian Gish in *Hearts of the World* (1918). Donald Crisp plays against later type as the father, beating his daughter Lillian Gish senseless in *Broken Blossoms* (1919). Walter Long is a lumbering brute, in blackface, chasing and ulitimately causing the death of Mae Marsh in *The Birth of a Nation* (1915). Above all, there is Lowell Sherman, a suave and sinister villain, playing without melodramatic effect in a classic Griffith melodrama, *Way Down East* (1920). As Lennox Sanderson, Sherman lures Lillian Gish into a false marriage, impregnates and then abandons her and the unwanted child. He represents love to the young and friendless Anna Moore, and, later, he represents danger as he threatens to expose her to the Bartlett family, who has taken her in unaware of her past. Without Lowell Sherman as Lennox Sanderson, there would be no flight through the blizzard for the Gish heroine, no last minute rescue from the icefloe by hero Richard Barthelmess. In fact, there would be no story at all.

Lowell Sherman (San Francisco, October 11, 1888–Los Angeles, December 28, 1934) transformed villainy into an art form both on screen and on stage. He was no leering, moustache-tugging villain in the manner of Roy D'Arcy (who made an art of that artificial style of villainy), but rather Sherman underplayed, adding a touch of quiet nastiness to the evil doing. He was a purebred American villain with just the correct hint of European sophistication. Born to wear a tuxedo, Sherman was charming, but we, the audience, if not the heroine, knew that he was dangerous.

The actor, who had been on stage since the age of four, made his New York debut not as a villain but as the rider of the Pony Express in *The Girl of the Golden West*. For 224 performances at the Belasco Theatre, beginning November 14, 1905, Lowell Sherman impressed audiences as a true Western hero. With him in the cast were three other members-to-be of the film industry, T. Hayes Hunter, Frank Keenan, and James Kirkwood. Sherman confirmed his prominence as a screen villain by luring Norma Talmadge away from husband Frederick Burton in *Yes or No* (1920) and then abandoning her. That was always a popular move on Lowell Sherman's part. However, his screen career dates back to *Behind the Scenes* (1914), in which he is a friend of Mary Pickford and James Kirkwood. The following year, in *Always in the Way*, he plays Mary Miles Minter's father.

In the 1920s, Lowell Sherman was busy consolidating his reputation as the "Wickedest Villain on the Screen." He was a killer in *Bright Lights of*

Broadway (1923) and a Russian who lusts after both mother Belle Bennett and daughter Lois Moran in *The Reckless Lady* (1926). His actions as a German spy in *Convoy* (1927) force Dorothy Mackaill into prostitution, and in *The Divine Woman* (1928), he steals Garbo away from Lars Hanson.

Off screen, Lowell Sherman was as much a philanderer as he was on it. The actor was present with Roscoe "Fatty" Arbuckle at the rape/killing of Virginia Rappe in San Francisco in September 1921. If published reports are to be believed, the comedian told Sherman, "If you want to have an orgy, then get your own apartment." Like Arbuckle, he was ostracized by the film industry, albeit briefly, and Famous Players–Lasky canceled his contract. Lowell Sherman was married to actress Pauline Garon from 1926 to 1930, and, after his divorce, married Helene Costello. Despite all this blatant heterosexuality, some writers have actually suggested Lowell Sherman was gay. Nonsense!

In 1929, Lowell Sherman made an easy transition to sound as a villain in *Evidence*, but the following year, he turned to direction at RKO, initially directing himself opposite Bebe Daniels in *Lawful Larceny* and opposite Marion Nixon in *The Pay Off*. Two major productions from 1933 are *Morning Glory* with Katharine Hepburn and *She Done Him Wrong* with Mae West. A year earlier, Sherman found time to return to acting as the alcoholic film director Maximilian Carey in *What Price Hollywood?* If we didn't know that it takes discipline and talent to both act and direct, we might well be forgiven for assuming that Carey, with his wit, humor, and outrageous behavior, is a caricature of Lowell Sherman.

Some of Sherman's directorial methods were rather odd. While filming the outrageous screen version of Thorne Smith's far more outrageous novel *Night Life of the Gods* (1935), Lowell Sherman wore only his underwear, declaring it was too hot to wear more. He was assigned to direct the first three-color Technicolor feature, *Becky Sharp* (1935), but died 24 days into shooting. His footage was scrapped and reshot by Rouben Mamoulian. Ironically, Lowell Sherman died of pneumonia the same day as Universal previewed *Night Life of the Gods*. Could it be that his lack of clothing on the film set had anything to do with his death?

On a personal note, I have long been an admirer of Lowell Sherman's performance in *Way Down East*. He sets an example that all young men in this overly moralistic clime should follow. I have always assumed that the character of Lennox Sanderson would marry and have a son named Lennox Sanderson Jr., and in his honor, I used that pseudonym for a number of years while writing negative book reviews in *Films in Review* and essays in *Magill's Survey of Cinema*.

Bibliography

"The Charming Mansfield." *Photoplay*, July 1923, p. 52.

Kutner, Nanette. "The Wickedest Man on Screen." *Movie Magazine*, March 1926, pp. 47–48, 88–89.

"Wickedest Villain on the Screen." *Photoplay*, February 1921, p. 45.

PAULINE STARKE

Sitting with her husband, George Sherwood, in a small Santa Monica, California, apartment, Pauline Starke tries to answer my questions. She is no longer the freckle-faced kid who appealed to D.W. Griffith as a potential leading lady. She looks old. This is September 1975, and she *is* old. She looks not merely emaciated but positively desiccated. One feels almost uncomfortable trying to coax a response from a woman whose replies are monosyllabic at best. Most of the past she does not, or chooses not, to remember.

Silent cinema is a vague but happy memory: "It was like a big family, and everyone enjoyed it because there wasn't as much tension and all that. Everybody sort of chipped in, and it was easy work, very easy." As for her mentor and first director, D.W. Griffith, "He was very nice."

Born in Joplin, Missouri, on January 10, 1900, Pauline Starke came to Los Angeles with her mother, and when the latter began work as an extra, her daughter would accompany her: "I happened to be in the crowd when Griffith was selecting, and he said he admired my forehead so much. He used me then in quite a few pictures." The actress was initially an extra in *The Birth of a Nation* (1915)—"I was a white girl in the morning and a colored girl in the afternoon"—and then selected as one of the favorites of the harem in the Babylonian sequence of *Intolerance* (1916).

Pauline Starke had the look of a country girl, unspoiled, natural, and unfamiliar with makeup. As such, she was featured in a number of films produced by the Fine Arts Company, of which Griffith was the titular head and supervising producer, including *The Wharf Rat* (1916), *The Bad Boy* (1917), and *Cheerful Givers* (1917). As late as 1919, she was not a star; for example, she is the second female lead under Clara Kimball Young in that year's *Eyes of Youth*, which initially brought Valentino to national attention. By 1921, Pauline Starke does have star billing, along with Harry Myers, in the first version of *A Connecticut Yankee in King Arthur's Court*, but it is another actress, Rosemary Theby, who has the choicest role as Morgan Le Fay.

Metro-Goldwyn-Mayer signed Pauline to a contract in 1925 at a salary of $1,000 a week, rising the following year to $1,500, and her first starring role there was opposite Conrad Nagel in *Sun-Up*, based on the popular play by Lulu Vollmer. Co-starred with Starke is Lucille La Verne (as the widow Cagle) who had been the star of the play's original Broadway production, and who is, of course, quite magnificent as Mother Frochard, harassing Dorothy Gish in D.W. Griffith's *Orphans of the Storm* (1922). In *Sun-Up*, Starke is still the rugged, untiring, outdoor type, but quickly MGM changed her image to that of a glamorous Hollywood-style star. Nowhere is this change more apparent than in the two-color Technicolor extravaganza *The Viking*, co-produced with the Technicolor Corporation, and released in November 1929 with music and sound effects. From Missouri country girl, Pauline Starke was transformed to the blonde Viking beauty, Helga, displaying a goodly portion of bosom to greasy-looking and instantly forgettable leading man LeRoy Mason.

The Viking was the actress's last MGM release. She starred in a couple of talkies for Universal, *Man, Woman and Wife* (1929) and *What Men Want* (1930), and one for Columbia, *A Royal Romance* (1930), and then, as she put it, she was "involuntarily" retired from the screen. She was to have starred in the outrageously "camp" production of *The Great Gabbo* (1929) with Erich von Stroheim as the ventriloquist title character, but, after three or four days of shooting, director James Cruze replaced her with his wife Betty Compson. "That's one of the dirty tricks that are played on you in films," she remarked philosophically. There were a couple of very inconsequential B pictures in which Starke later starred, *Missing Daughters* (1933) and *$20 a Week* (1935), but there was no way these could help revive a career that was totally dead.

In 1927, Pauline Starke married comedy producer Jack White. They were divorced in 1931, and the following year, she married George Sherwood. He was not involved in film production, but, after playing bit parts at Essanay in the teens, he had formed his own stock company in Chicago and later went on to run the Music Box and the Vine Street Theatres in Hollywood. Sherwood starred Starke in his 1932 Broadway production of Kenneth Webb's *Zombie*, later filmed as *White Zombie*. The play ran a mere seventeen performances and was a disaster; the critic of the *New York Herald-World* called it "one of the worst" and the New York *Telegram* thought it had "the makings of a devasting comedy." The Sherwood-Starke marriage was a lasting and a happy one; the couple made trips to Europe and India. During her visits to India Starke actually made a return to the screen as an unbilled Western woman in *Nine Hours to Rama* (1962) and in the documentary feature *The Big Hunt* (1968). She died in Santa Monica on February 3, 1977.

Bibliography

Blake, Ivan. "Pauline Starke Destroys an illusion." *Cinema Art*, April 1926, pp. 22, 47.

Craig, Marion. "Snub-Nose, Freckle-Face!" *Photoplay*, November 1919, pp. 36–37.

French, Janet. "The Ugly Duckling Who Became a Great Beauty." *Photoplay*, June 1930, pp. 44–45, 143.

Hall, Gladys. "The Glad Sad Girl." *Motion Picture*, November 1921, pp. 56–57.

Herzog, Dorothy. "Yep—It's the Same Gal." *Photoplay*, July 1926, pp. 46, 117.

"Pity Poor Pauline." *Photoplay*, July 1918, p. 57.

Tildesley, Alice. "The Girl to Whom Nothing Ever Happened." *Motion Picture Classic*, February 1926, pp. 30–31, 77.

VALESKA SURATT. *See* **THE VAMPS**

GLORIA SWANSON

To the majority of Americans, Gloria Swanson as Norma Desmond in *Sunset Blvd.* (1950) is the archetypal silent film star, deranged, out-of-touch with reality, clinging desperately to the past, and wearing makeup that even Theda Bara might have rejected as over the top. If anything, for all its entertainment value, *Sunset Blvd.* does a disservice both to silent players and to Gloria Swanson. Just as Norma Desmond is not your typical silent star, so Gloria Swanson is not Norma Desmond.

Gloria Swanson (Chicago, March 27, 1897–New York, April 4, 1983) was not a one-dimensional player. Even in *Sunset Blvd.*, when she impersonates Chaplin, as she had done in *Manhandled* (1924), there is evidence of a comedic brilliance. As a waitress who dreams of becoming an actress in *Stage Struck* (1925), she engages in physical comedy, including a boxing match with Gertrude Astor, and parodies the type of star she was fast becoming in a dream sequence as Salome, closely modeled after Nazimova's performance.

Early in a career that began in 1914 with the Chicago-based Essanay Company, she had been considered as a leading lady to Chaplin, but just as she rejected the notion of being typecast opposite him, so, later, did she turn down Mack Sennett's suggestion that he turn her into a second Mabel Normand. "You aren't going to make a second anything out of me!" Cecil B. DeMille, who appears in *Sunset Blvd.*, made Swanson a star in a series of six films, beginning with *Don't Change Your Husband* (1919), sensibly casting her opposite some of the biggest leading men of the day, including Thomas Meighan and Wallace Reid. In the 1920s, Paramount continued the star-making process, allowing Swanson free reign in the production in France of *Madame Sans-Gêne* (1925), in which she portrays Napoleon's laundress. For an example of Swanson's dramatic power, one need look no further than *Zaza* (1923), directed by Allan Dwan, with whom Swanson formed the perfect combination. Her transformation from the flighty Zaza to the elegant Parisien Zaza is excellent; there is perfection in her walk as enters the theatre, stopping herself from kicking her maid on the backside, and as she fights with her theatrical rival Florianne. There is such a good French atmosphere to this production that one can well understand why Swanson was so warmly welcomed to Paris and the filming of *Madame Sans-Gêne*.

With *The Love of Sunya* (1927), Swanson formed her own production company, with financial assistance from Joseph P. Kennedy, who later became her lover, helped promote her second independent production, *Sadie Thompson* (1928), and, foolishly, allowed her to hire Erich von Stroheim to direct her in *Queen Kelly* (1928). Singing "Love, Your Magic Spell Is Everywhere," Swanson made a good transition to sound with *The Trespasser* (1929), but her career was basically over by the 1930s and, in large part, revived thanks to *Sunset Blvd.* Curiously, the actress failed to take advantage of the film and appeared in nothing more of worth on screen.

Swanson was an actress who understood what it was to be a star and what was expected of a star by her public. In September 1971, after lunch with Lois Wilson at Sardi's in New York, the two of us headed over to the Booth Theatre, where Swanson was starring in *Butterflies Are Free.* Lois had been very close to the actress since their time together at Paramount in the 1920s and wanted me to meet Gloria. A crowd was gathered at the stage door, as a limousine, complete with uniformed chauffeur drove up. The chauffeur opened the door, and a tiny figure, dressed more for the opera than a Wednesday afternoon in New York, descended from the automobile. Graciously, she stopped to wave to her fans and sign a couple of autographs, and then disappeared into the theatre, pursued by Lois and me. It was a memorable moment, despite Swanson's later angrily berating Wilson for bringing me into her presence. "I can't see him now. I can't talk to him now," she declared with a look in my direction that would surely have put both DeMille and von Stroheim in their place.

Note: Gloria Swanson's voluminous papers are at the University of Texas at Austin.

Bibliography

Albert, Katherine. "What Next for Gloria?" *Photoplay*, July 1929, pp. 64–65, 124–125.

Bodeen, DeWitt. "Gloria Swanson." *Films in Review*, April 1965, pp. 193–216.

Chierichetti, David. "Gloria Swanson Today." *Film Fan Monthly*, no. 164, February 1975, pp. 3–9.

Fletcher, Adele Whitely. "Instead of the Silken Gloria." *Motion Picture*, December 1921, pp. 28–29, 93.

"Gloria Glorified." *Photoplay*, August 1918, p. 28.

Lang, Harry. "So This Is Gloria!" *Photoplay*, September 1930, pp. 35–36, 84.

Kennedy, John Bright. "Drop That Pie!" *Collier's*, June 8, 1929, p. 28.

Martin, Mildred. "The Husbands in Gloria's Career." *Photoplay*, July 1934, pp. 40, 94.

Naylor, Hazel Simpson. "Piloting a Dream Craft." *Motion Picture*, April 1921, pp. 24–25, 87.

Nogueira, Rui. "I Am Not Going to Write My Memoirs." *Sight and Sound*, spring 1969, pp. 58–62, 109.

Quirk, Lawrence J. *The Films of Gloria Swanson.* Secaucus, N.J.: Citadel Press, 1984.

Remont, Fritzi. "The Delightful Contradictions of Gloria Swanson." *Motion Picture Classic*, July 1919, pp. 22–23, 72, 74.

St. Johns, Adela Rogers. "The Confessions of a Modern Woman." *Photoplay*, February 1922, pp. 20–22, 114.

————. "Gloria! An Impression." *Photoplay*, September 1923, pp. 28–29, 104–105.

Smith, Frederick James. "The Silken Gloria." *Motion Picture Classic*, February 1920, pp. 16–17, 83.

————. "Why I Am Going Back to the Screen." *Photoplay*, April 1937, pp. 14–16, 118.

Smith, Helena Huntington. "Ugly Duckling." *The New Yorker*, January 18, 1930, pp. 24–27.

Swanson, Gloria. "There Is No Formula for Success." *Photoplay*, April 1926, pp. 32–33, 117–119

————. *Swanson on Swanson*. New York: Random House, 1980.

Taylor, John Russell. "Swanson." *Sight and Sound*, autumn, 1968, pp. 201–202.

BLANCHE SWEET

Blanche Sweet was the first silent star whom I got to know well, someone with whom I remained close throughout her life. My correspondence file on her contains over seventy items, dating from 1969 until shortly before her death, in New York, on September 6, 1986. The first letter enclosed a hand-written essay on her and D.W. Griffith's first feature, *Judith of Bethulia*, which I published that same year in *The Silent Picture*. She angrily denounced my original title for my second book, *The Griffith Girls*—"It sounds like a trained line of high kickers...surely we deserve better than that"—and had me change the title to *The Griffith Actresses*. Aside from correspondence, Blanche proved quite devoted in her insistence that I escort her to various events. I was at her side when she opened the D.W. Griffith Theatre in New York on February 20, 1975, and on November 13, 1976, I was her escort to the 50th anniversary celebration of New York Local 644 of IATSE. We attended many screenings together at the Museum of Modern Art, as well as numerous dinner engagements.

A typical dinner with Blanche took place on May 29, 1978. The setting was a small, neighborhood Italian restaurant a couple of blocks from her Lexington Avenue, New York, apartment. Very loudly, she is arguing that Darwin's Theory of the Origin of the Species is wrong. She has also decided not to permit NBC to film her flying her kite in Central Park. You cannot just expect someone to go and fly a kite. Kite flying is serious business, demanding the correct climatical condition and the right temperament in the flyer. She is now quite drunk, indeed "as tight as a tick." "How tight does a tick get?" she asks. Two days later, we are seated in a conservative lunchroom, where Blanche informs me that revolutionaries are dear to her heart and hopes that the fire that has just occurred at the International Museum of Photography at George Eastman House has destroyed her film *The Warrens of Virginia* (1915).

Blanche generally prefers that we should lunch at the Museum of Modern Art, adding to the terror of the meal in that there will doubtless be someone who recognizes her and will strike up a conversation. At one memorable lunch, on March 22, the service was so bad that Blanche was literally screaming for butter and physically grabbing hold of a waitress, who threatened to have her evicted from the room. At the end of meal, Blanche informs me that, being a movie star, she will have to leave a tip, regardless of the service or the quality of the food.

I was determined to film a tribute to Blanche Sweet in the form of 30-minute, 16mm documentary, *Portrait of Blanche Sweet*. It takes a long time to save the necessary money to hire a film crew and an even longer time before I am eventually able to put the footage together. But on Wednesday, September 19, 1979, we are all set to shoot in Blanche's one-room apartment. She has discovered that construction work is going on in the property behind her apartment building, but the day before, she goes around and orders the men to cease work on the day of the shoot. They agree. While we are setting up the lights and the camera, Blanche takes the bus up to Bloomingdale's to have the department store staff help with her false eyelashes and makeup. Blanche is very fond of her false eyelashes. She will not be photographed without them. After the filming is over, she tells me she will keep them on until she goes to bed. Then, she will slowly peel them off and look at them with pleasure. *Portrait of Blanche Sweet,* which I describe as a one-sided conversation with the actress, is finally completed in 1982, and Blanche insists that it be the first film screened at the new Mary Pickford Theatre of the Library of Congress on May 11 of that year. Blanche, who has now strangely taken to referring to herself in correspondence as "me, myself only" is very pleased with the film, which she describes as "my biography."

Thanks to the efforts of Henry Hart, the first and longtime editor of *Films in Review,* Blanche was a member of the National Board of Review. As a result, she would often invite me to Board screenings when I was in New York. On one remarkable occasion, she harangued the conservative members of the organization on the need to support the communist regime in Cuba. When the Board made the mistake of naming Roman Polanski's *Macbeth* the Best Picture of the Year, she sent me a copy of an advertisement from the *New York Times* across which was written one word, "Ha!" Only Blanche could evoke such strong meaning from one simple word.

On April 1, 1975, Blanche and I celebrate the one-hundredth anniversary of D.W. Griffith's birth with a special program at the Library of Congress. I introduce the evening event, and Blanche makes some pungent comments in regard to the American Biograph films being screened—and also manages, quite rightly, to chastise the audience for its laughter during some of the shorts. Prior to the show, she and I are invited to appear live on Maury Povich's television program, *Panorama,* on WTTG-Washington, D.C. It is my first television appearance. I am very nervous. Blanche is highly amused and will for years to come insist to all and sundry that she was concerned I was about to faint. Miraculously, the show is a huge success, in large part because Blanche takes an instant dislike to Maury Povich, who has no idea who she is, and proceeds with quiet charm to skewer him.

In my capacity as resident film historian of the Academy of Motion Picture Arts and Sciences, I made the mistake of insisting that Blanche would be the perfect host for an October 1979 tribute to Mary Pickford. Everyone else wants Lillian Gish, but, foolishly, I argue for—and get—Blanche. It is to be first-class all the way, including accommodation at the Beverly Wilshire Hotel. Miss Sweet is bad-tempered and temperamental throughout. The hotel room is inadequate. The makeup man she has demanded is thirty minutes late. Her limousine from the hotel to the theatre fails to arrive. She walks into the reception, wagging her finger at me and threatening to take the next plane back to New York. Douglas Fairbanks Jr. offers his arm to escort her into the theatre, but she waves it away. She wants to check the house first and find out the size of the attendance.

She is the stereotypical temperamental silent star. After the program, she stalks out of the building, leaving her fans demanding autographs, telling me she wants to get away from "those people." On the car drive back to the hotel, she is furious that fellow participants Buddy Rogers and Douglas Fairbanks Jr. had spoken with sorrow at Pickford's passing, turning the evening into a somber affair. She insists that Buddy and Doug had no right to display their grief in public. "Buddy and Doug Jr. were having fun autographing everything but the walls in the Academy lobby," Blanche wrote later. "Too bad they couldn't have controlled their crying a little better before an audience."

In the back seat of the car is Dido (Madame Jean) Renoir, whom Robert Gitt had given a lift to the event. Dido is vastly amused by Blanche, who has no interest in even saying hello to her, and for years after, Dido will ask sarcastically at each meeting, "And how is Miss Blanche Sweet?" The next day, prior to Blanche's departure for New York, Jetta Goudal hosts a luncheon in her honor at the Beverly Wilshire Hotel. Even Goudal is worn down by Blanche's temperamental behavior.

Throughout her life and her career, Blanche Sweet was to remain a semi-revolutionary, an old-fashioned liberal within an industry that was increasingly conservative in outlook and philosophy. Blanche was an iconoclast who cared little for what others thought of her and who, ultimately, ruined her own career through bad judgment and careless behavior. "I'd been called temperamental at one time. I really wasn't," she explained to me. "All I wanted was to do things a certain way. If they weren't done that way, I put up a fight."

Born Sarah Blanche Sweet in Chicago on June 18, 1896, her father had deserted her mother, who died shortly after Blanche's birth, and so she was raised by her grandmother, a woman for whom she always had overwhelming praise and who must, presumably, take the credit or blame for Blanche's singular personality. Like most actors and actresses who began their careers on stage as infants, Blanche and her grandmother needed money. At eighteen months old, Blanche was carried on stage in the classic melodrama, *Blue Jeans*. In 1909, while Blanche and her grandmother were in New York, it was suggested that Blanche try for film work at American Biograph:"My grand-mother and I went down. We made inquiries at a window, they gave us a form and we filled that out, and heard nothing. Then we made our way up to the Edison Company, and we had better luck there. They put me into a film the next day as an extra. All I remember about it was that it was raining, and I was under an umbrella. Then they gave me a picture, *A Man with Three Wives* [1909].

"Then the same person who said go down to the Biograph, said, did you see Griffith? We said, 'We just saw a window and a form.' 'Well go down and see Griffith.' So we did. I made my first appearance at Biograph, which was as an extra in *A Corner in Wheat* [1909]. It seems to me that we, the extras, only got three dollars a day. I've never been very good at remembering what I was paid. The only thing that ever registered was when I got my first ten thousand dollars a week. I remember that!"

Blanche Sweet was to remain with Griffith and American Biograph for five years, replacing Mary Pickford as its leading player and, in turn, being replaced by Lillian Gish. The style and appearance of the three actresses is so diverse that it is impossible to compare one to the other. Blanche is still a teenager with "puppy fat," unlike the ethereal Gish, and lacks the obvious personality of Pickford. She is a more natural actress than either of the two. *The Lonedale Operator*, released on March 23, 1911, is undoubtedly Blanche's best known one-reel short for the company, with its typical Griffith cross-editing and last minute rescue, but it is not a film that shows off the actress to advantage.

Far superior is *The Painted Lady*, released on October 24, 1912, in which Blanche actually creates a complex character, that of a young and repressed girl without suitors who is coerced into believing that only through the use of makeup will she attract a lover. That lover is subsequently and inadvertently killed by her when she finds him breaking into the family home. "Something of a tour de force for both the director and his star," wrote Vincent Canby in the *New York Times* (January 23, 1975). A British film collector, John Cunningham, discovered a 35mm nitrate print of the film and very generously made a 16mm print of it for me. I screened it for Blanche at the Museum of Modern Art on October 1, 1971, and from that moment on it became her favorite Biograph appearance. In later years, she would even provide detailed accounts of its making, despite recalling nothing of the film when first she saw it. Blanche was very good at "remembering" when necessary; if she didn't know the answer to an earnest film scholar's question, she would visit the Museum of Modern Art and research the subject.

Blanche did have vivid memories of Griffith's production methods: "He had nothing down on paper. He would have an idea, maybe it was his own idea, maybe something he bought. Then you'd start elaborating on the individual scenes. You do this, you do that. You started improvising, and doing it as you thought it should be done or could be done. If it was all right, good. But if it wasn't, he'd say, 'No, let's do something else.' If you didn't start opening it up, he'd get up and show you. And that's what really pulverized you. He wasn't a good actor on the stage, he wasn't a good actor in the few films that he made. He was a magnificent actor as a director. I've never seen better acting on anybody's part. He could do a woman just as perfectly as he could do a man's part. He would do it so well that you were simply crushed.

"I wasn't particularly impressed with Griffith in the beginning. He was just somebody who was directing a film. I guess it took me a good year or more to realize I was working with a very unusual man, a very understanding person, a person who knew a great deal about people and things and acting. It might also be that his personality was growing and, maybe, he was developing along with the films that he was developing."

Griffith's and Blanche's last film for American Biograph was the feature-length *Judith of Bethulia*, with Blanche in the title role of the Jewish widow who falls in love with and kills Holofernes, the enemy of her people. Aside from its spectacular battle scenes, the four-reel drama is poor melodrama and in some respects inferior to many of Griffith's short subjects. Blanche and I looked at the film in 1975, and after the screening, Blanche turned to me and whispered, "It seems like twelve reels."

When Griffith left American Biograph, Blanche went with him, as leading lady, to Mutual, where she starred in *The Escape, Home Sweet Home,* and *The Avenging Conscience,* all released in 1914. (As a result of wearing thrift shop clothes for *The Escape,* Blanche contracted scarlet fever.) She had every reason to believe that Griffith was to remain her director and would select her to play Elsie Stoneman in *The Birth of a Nation* (1915). Instead, he selected Lillian Gish, and Blanche accepted a lucrative offer from Cecil B. DeMille.

"I was supposed to be in *The Clansman—The Birth of a Nation.* But then the DeMille faction came after me and offered me a lot of money. I went to Griffith and expected him to say, 'No, I need you.' He didn't. He told me to go, go, go. I was disappointed and very hurt. I was scared. Mary Pickford said somewhere that when she said she was going, he just blessed her and said I'll miss you. He certainly didn't bless me. He never got in touch with me afterwards, which I felt he should. He never said a word to me. I felt guilty because I hadn't seen him in the last years of his life. I still feel guilty about that. I should have overcome that bias, but it took me years to realize how much the man had done for me. I couldn't go to the [memorial] ceremonies in Kentucky. I did go to his funeral, although I don't believe in funerals. There were quite a lot of people there, but, on the other hand, all of Hollywood should have been there, standing. There have been a lot of men and women who have done a great deal for films, contributed a lot, but nobody did quite as much as he did. I really felt that everybody who ever worked in the films should have been there. Well, that's one reason why I don't believe in funerals."

At the same time, Blanche was willing—at least in private—to acknowledge the director's faults. While making a short with an Indian theme, Blanche recalled how she had expressed her admiration of the physique of one of the Indian extras, dressed only in a loincloth. In anger, Griffith turned to her and said, "Nigger lover."

Blanche's remembrance of the studios on East 14th Street were vivid. The studios proper were on the first floor, entered through double doors, with a section railed off for Griffith's office, with the "front offices" situated in the front of the building. Costumes and props were stored in the basement, and on the second floor was a small projection room. Blanche was instrumental in placing a plaque on the wall of the building currently at 11 East 14th Street. I was honored to be asked by her to come up with the wording of the plaque, which was officially unveiled on November 30, 1975, and stolen shortly thereafter. "The junkies got it during the 17 day strike of doormen, where there was no protection by pickets after midnight," Blanche wrote me.

Blanche made two features for DeMille—*The Warrens of Virginia* and *The Captive*, both released in 1915—followed by another seventeen for Famous Players-Lasky between 1915 and 1917. "I had a terrible time," remembered Blanche of working with DeMille. "I was terrified of him. Here I was, going out on my own, whatever I did had to be me and nobody else. I was with a strange director that I didn't know anything about. His version of the story was that he was terrified of me! He was working with a Griffith player who was supposed to have quite a reputation, and he didn't know much about films."

Blanche was dismissive of both *The Warrens of Virginia* and *The Captive*, much preferring *The Ragamuffin*, *Blacklist*, and *The Sowers*, all released in 1916 and directed by Cecil's brother, William C. de Mille, who "had a more subtle way of doing things."

Marshall Neilan directed three of the Famous Player-Lasky productions from 1917, *Those without Sin*, *The Tides of Barnegat*, and *The Silent Partner*, and the couple planned to marry in 1922. (Neilan had earlier been married to another American Biograph actress, Gertrude Bambrick.) Blanche remembered first meeting Neilan when he was an actor at American Biograph:

"I don't think Marshall amounted to very much as an actor. He was passable, good-looking, as good as a lot of them. But he had ideas, always a little ahead of their time and a little advanced."

When Blanche left Famous Players-Lasky in 1917, she was absent from the screen for two years. She always refused to discuss this period, which was possibly connected with a drug addiction problem. When she did return in 1919, it was under Neilan's direction in *The Unpardonable Sin*, an independent production with a World War One theme. It was followed by a series of feature films, dismissed by Blanche as "what I knew I shouldn't do." She had "a lovely feeling" doing *Fighting Cressy* (1919) because of its Bret Harte source. *Help Wanted—Male* (1920), directed by Henry King, was "a bore." In large part because of her friendship with Clarence Badger and his wife Betty, she enjoyed *Quincy Adams Sawyer (1922).*

The most important production from this period is *Anna Christie*, the first screen adaptation of the Eugene O'Neill play, produced by Thomas H. Ince in 1923, with John Griffith Wray directing, and William Russell, George Marion, and Eugenie Besserer providing strong support. Ince paid $35,000 for the screen rights and spent $165,000 on the production. There were problems. John Griffith Wray insisted on using a megaphone even for the close-ups. A disturbed Blanche Sweet asked that Thomas Ince retake some of the scenes, only to discover that he was as excitable as his director. In the summer of 1977, Blanche went to see Liv Ullman on stage in *Anna Christie* and announced, "She was better than I was. When you're a vain actress, that's going a long way." Blanche did not express the same feelings in regard to Garbo's appearance in the 1930 sound adaptation and bitterly regretted that she was not asked to repeat her performance in the title role.

Blanche's version of *Anna Christie*—although it is equally the vision of Ince and Wray—is far more expansive than the later Garbo feature, taking time to show the Swedish fishing village were Anna was born, her life in Minnesota, what has forced her into prostitution, and even brief scenes of her father Chris (George Marion) in Shanghai. Unfortunately, the outdoor scenes have such a splendid documentary quality that they clash awkwardly with the obvious studio sets. Blanche displays strong emotion as she talks to Marthy (Eugenie Besserer) and berates Chris for not having been "a regular father." The change in Anna when you next see her on Chris's barge, sitting in the rain, is quite amazing—as if she has been reborn. Equally exhilarating are other scenes on the barge as Anna hangs out the washing and talks to Matt (William Russell).

Anna Christie was followed by a second film for Ince, *Those Who Dance* (1924): "We said, 'We'll do *Those Who Dance*, which will be a popular boxoffice

film, and if *Anna Christie* doesn't make too much money, we can salvage it.'"
While she might appear in two or more films for the same producer, Blanche
was unwilling to sign multi-picture contracts. She once told me, she had been
offered the role of Diane in *7th Heaven* (1927) but rejected it because the
producer, Fox, had insisted she sign a longterm contract.

Marshall Neilan and Blanche joined forces creatively and commercially
in 1924, through a contractual arrangement with MGM to direct and star,
respectively, in a series of independent feature films, to be released through
the studio, for which the couple was to accept entire responsibility. There
were problems in that Neilan and MGM chief Louis B. Mayer were, as Blanche
put it, "pre-natal enemies," but the arrangement did result in two major films,
Tess of the D'Urbevilles (1924) and *The Sporting Venus* (1925), both shot on
location in Britain. The couple also planned to film Rebecca West's *The Return of the Soldier*. "We did make a few exteriors," recalled Blanche, "And we
talked many times with Rebecca West, who I admired greatly as a writer, as a
person, but we never finished the film. Later Warner Bros. bought it from me
for Bette Davis. They never made it."

MGM and Marshall Neilan became embroiled in vitriolic litigation, which,
curiously, did not hurt Blanche, who later worked again for MGM in *The
Woman Racket* (1930). As a result of the success of her romantic partnership
opposite Ronald Colman in *The Sporting Venus*, she was again paired with
him in *His Supreme Moment* (1925). Both Lillian Gish and Blanche Sweet
expressed disappointment to me at Colman's lackluster lovemaking on screen,
although Blanche did point out that he had great legs. When I mentioned this
to Mary Brian, she assured me that Colman was a great lover, but she admon-
ished me not to ask her how she knew.

After five more indifferent features, Blanche and Neilan were reunited
for one last time in *Diplomacy* (1926), which Blanche had seen and admired
on stage as a vehicle for Gladys Cooper. Blanche had wanted to appear as the
adventuress, Countess Zicka, but producer Paramount objected, concerned
at the character's negative quality. This, despite Blanche's having portrayed a
prostitute in *Anna Christie*. As a result, Arlette Marchal was signed for Zicka,
and Blanche was forced to play the much-maligned wife. "You should never,
never do that," she told me. "Either play what you want or, if you don't like it,
don't play it."

With her marriage to Marshall Neilan in ruins—he had been having an
affair with Gloria Swanson among others—Blanche returned to England to
star in *The Woman in White* (1929) for Herbert Wilcox. Upon her return, she
and Neilan were divorced. Seven years later, Blanche married actor Raymond
Hackett, to whom she was devoted. She always spoke of him with affection,

telling me that when he died in 1958, she arranged for his corneas to be donated to someone in need, knowing they would then see the world through her husband's eyes.

With the coming of sound, Blanche's film career was approaching its close. No matter that she had been a stage performer as a child and had a good speaking voice, she had been on screen for almost twenty years, and that was too long in an industry fixated with youth. There was a vaudeville tour and a starring role in a one-reel Vitaphone short, *Always Faithful* (1929), in which she is an about-to-be unfaithful wife whose husband pretends not to know of her plans. In *Always Faithful*, Blanche's presence is commanding and her voice faultlessly pleasing. Of her three sound features, all released in 1930, *The Woman Racket*, *Show Girl in Hollywood*, and *The Silver Horde*, it is the second that still entertains and finds new admirers for Blanche Sweet. Here, she is former silent star Donna Harris, playing a crucial supporting role in the rise to stardom of Dixie Dugan (portrayed by the inexorably dreadful Alice White). Before an attempted suicide, Donna Harris tells Dixie that she is 32 years old, and "When you are over thirty, you are older than those hills out there."

Did she mind playing a faded silent star? "No, I was young enough not to have that bother me. Had I been a fading star, I probably would have been troubled by it." Was she happy with the film? "Not particularly. I don't know why I did it. I'd known director Mervyn LeRoy for a long time, and I let him influence me. He talked me into it. I didn't like the picture."

When she made *Show Girl in Hollywood*, Blanche told me she had no reason to believe that she did not have a full life and career awaiting her: "I had a whole big future ahead of me." She never recorded "There's a Tear for Every Smile in Hollywood," which she sings so well and so movingly in the film, but it remains indelibly linked to her. Whenever Richard Griffith, the former curator of film at the Museum of Modern Art, saw her, he would always sing a line or two.

At the end of her Hollywood career, in reality there was not too much professionally ahead for Blanche Sweet. In 1935, she played the second female lead on Broadway in the Robert E. Sherwood play *The Petrified Forest*. The two leading men, Humphrey Bogart and Leslie Howard, were in the process of becoming major Hollywood stars, but Blanche was not invited to join them for the Warner Bros. screen adaptation. She occasionally found work in radio and early television in the 1950s, but for a while, Blanche was reduced to working in a Los Angeles department store as a sales clerk. After Raymond Hackett's death, she moved to New York, where she became a fixture at events at the Museum of Modern Art. She was a devoted supporter of its staff in times of trouble and would always be on the picket lines during strikes. She delighted at spotting a Rockefeller entering the building, being able to hurl abuse at him or her.

We continued corresponding almost until the end; my last meeting with her took place at the Bellevue Hospital, New York, on October 12, 1984. She was remarkably cheerful and mentally alert. We talked of inconsequential things, and she told me, "You were always goodlooking, but now you are positively handsome." How can one not like an actress with such sensibility?

After her death, Blanche had made arrangements for her body to be used for research at the College of Physicians at Columbia Presbyterian Medical Center. In her last years, she had relied on social security and minimal dividends from Con Edison stock to take care of her needs and had also been provided with assistance from the Actors' Fund of America. In a codicil to her will, she left various items to friends, including her 16mm print of *Anna Christie* to me and her large collection of photographs to the Museum of Modern Art. "I'll be glad when this is all over, so I can catch up with Raymond, or at least have oblivion," she wrote. "But it's been a lovely world despite its troubles." As one might expect with Blanche, the troubles were not over. With incredible arrogance, the Actors' Fund chose to ignore Blanche's wishes, and her personal effects were basically trashed. On a positive note, Martin Sopocy, who had taken care of Blanche in her final years, arranged the naming of a lilac in her memory. White with faint hints of blue (for Blanche's eyes) and pink, "syringa x hyacinthiflora 'Blanche Sweet'" came into being thanks to donations from Blanche's various friends, whom Martin and I approached. Even Lillian Gish, who would refer to Blanche as "Miss Sweet and Sour" generously contributed. The lilac was officially unveiled at the Brooklyn Botanic Garden on April 28, 1990. On September 18, 1990, Blanche's ashes were scattered under her lilac at the Garden. I would have been there, but earlier that day, en route to New York, I was detained and accused of being a terrorist (a story that belongs elsewhere). If there is a heaven, I know Blanche must have been looking down and laughing her head off at my predicament.

Bibliography

Ames, Courtney. "The Real Blanche Sweet." *Picture-Play*, August 1916, pp. 98–101.

Bodeen, DeWitt. "Blanche Sweet." *Films in Review*, November 1965, pp. 549–570.

Carr, Harry C. "Waiting for Tomorrow." *Photoplay*, May 1918, pp. 69–70.

Courtlandt, Roberta. "The Girl Who Reads Tennyson between Scenes." *Motion Picture*, April 1916, pp. 143–145.

Drew, William M. "Blanche Sweet" in *Speaking of Silents: First Ladies of the Screen*. Vestal, N.Y.: Vestal Press, 1989, pp. 212–245.

Ettinger, Margaret. "An Impression of Blanche Sweet." *Cinema Art*, September 1926, pp. 42–43.

Hall, Gladys. "Confessions of a Star: Blanche Sweet." *Motion Picture Classic*, October 1928, pp. 16–17, 70, 87.

Higgins, Steven,"Blanche Sweet: gli anni alla Biograph." *Griffithiana*, no. 5–6, March-July 1980, pp. 73–90.

———. "Introduzione a Blanche Sweet." *Griffithiana*, January 1982, pp. 73–76.

Lewis, Kevin. "Blanche Sweet and Marshall Neilan." *Films in Review*, June/July 1981, pp. 351–356.

———. "Happy Birthday, Blanche Sweet." *Films in Review*, March 1986, pp. 130–140.

Pratt, George C. "The Blonde Telegrapher: Blanche Sweet." *Image*, vol. 17, no. 1, March 1975, pp. 21–25.

St. Johns, Adela Rogers. "An Impression of Blanche Sweet." *Photoplay*, September 1924, pp. 58–59, 107.

Sherwood, C. Blythe. "Big Little Blanche." *Motion Picture*, December 1920, pp. 30–31, 100.

Slide, Anthony. "Blanche Sweet and Anna Christie." *The Silent Picture*, no. 14, spring 1972, pp. 12–13.

Smith, Frederick James. "The New Blanche Sweet." *Motion Picture Classic*, November 1918, pp. 16–17, 71.

Sweet, Blanche. "Keep Your Public Guessing." *Motion Picture Director*, August 1926, pp. 21–23.

———. "Griffith, a Big Step Forward, and Judith." *The Silent Picture*, no. 5, winter 1969/70, pp. 9–10.

CONSTANCE TALMAGE

Of the three Talmadge sisters, Norma was the great dramatic star and Constance (Brooklyn, New York, April 19, 1900–Los Angeles, November 23, 1973) the great light comedienne. The third sister, Natalie (1899–1969) was married to Buster Keaton at the height of his career and that was probably sufficient in and of itself. Constance Talmadge was barely sixteen years old and had been on screen in inconsequential films for only a couple of years when D.W. Griffith cast her as The Mountain Girl in the Babylonian story in *Intolerance* (1916). The visual humor and, above all, the pacing is remarkable, as she chews green onions to ward off suitors in the marriage auction, fends off the advances of her lover, Elmer Clifton as the Rhapsode, and moons over her hero, Belshazzar (Alfred Paget). Talmadge provides an everchanging variety of mood swings, from pout to serenic smile. One of the funniest and most outrageous moments in the film has Talmadge, who must have understood the phallic symbolism, milk a goat as her face records her desire for Belshazzar.

Constance Talmadge never gave quiet as extraordinary a performance again. With maturity came sophistication, and this is suggested by the brief footage of her shot in 1919 when the Babylonian sequence was reissued under the title of *The Fall of Babylon*. As The Mountain Girl who no longer dies but is united with the Rhapsode, she looks older, which of course she is, and somehow less energetic. In regard to *Intolerance*, what is even more remarkable is that one is inclined to forget that The Mountain Girl does not constitute the actress's only contribution to the film. She also appears in the French story, playing a serious role, Marguerite de Valois, and billed as Georgia Pearce. The modern viewer sees only her wedding procession, but there was apparently much more to the characterization. The only scenes in *Intolerance* where an audience does not see Constance Talmadge are those involving the chariot, where she is doubled by Annette Defoe.

Aside from *Intolerance*, Talmadge also worked under Griffith's supervision in a handful of 1915 and 1916 Fine Arts features, including *The Missing Link* (1915) and *The Matrimaniac* (1916), in which she is Douglas Fairbanks's leading lady. When sister Norma married Joseph Schenck, he was persuaded to take control of both his wife's and his sister-in-law's careers. The first film Constance Talmadge made for her own company was *The Lesson*, released in May 1918, in which she plays a small-town girl who visits New York and eventually realizes that she was happier back home. The film was somewhat lackluster, and in order to improve the Talmadge films, Schenck hired Anita Loos and her husband, John Emerson, as writers. Emerson died in 1956, but

Loos lived on until 1981, and thus had the opportunity to present without argument her interpretation of the writing partnership. Just as Loos is singularly creative in the non-fiction she wrote on Hollywood history, she is probably equally dishonest in taking credit for the Loos-Emerson films away from her husband. She has taken credit for the writing of *Intolerance*, when it is obvious that her contribution was limited to the comic titles dealing with The Mountain Girl. John Emerson may have been an alcoholic, but he was a major writer long before Anita Loos teamed up with him, and there is no reason to doubt that Emerson did more than his share in writing the Constance Talmadge and other silent films.

In the teens, Constance Talmadge and Dorothy Gish double-dated with Robert Harron and writer-director Victor Heerman. Talmadge at this time had much the same hoyden quality as Dorothy Gish. Of Talmadge, who was nicknamed "Dutch," Heerman told me, "Everybody loved her and everybody had a great time when they were with her." Eventually, Dorothy married actor James Rennie and Talmadge married a Greek importer named John Pialoglou. Both marriages ended in divorce. Talmadge married three more times; the final one in 1939 to stockbroker Walter Michael Giblin was a lasting one.

Joseph Schenck continued to supervise Constance Talmadge's career into the 1920s, when there were fewer films but with higher production values than ever before. Both she and Billie Dove were showgirls in *Polly of the Follies* (1922). The following year, she played the title role in *Dulcy*, based on a dumb female character created on stage by Lynn Fontanne. For a while Dulcy became a slang term for a stupid but well-meaning woman, and there was even a comic strip in 1923, "Dulcy, the Beautiful Dumbbell," supposedly authored by Constance Talmadge. The best of the later Talmadge films available for viewing is *Her Sister from Paris* (1925), which provides the actress with a double role, that of a dutiful wife and her vamp/dancer twin sister. The pair switch identities and confuse and confound the former's husband, played by Ronald Colman.

Joseph Schenck had worked out a lucrative production deal with First National, whereby Talmadge received a little over $93,000 for each film, plus another $37,500 for her mother, identified as "the manager of the artist." It is safe to assume that least 50 percent of the amount paid by First National constituted profit for the actress. With the coming of sound, the First National agreement was terminated in 1927. Talmadge made one last silent film, *Venus*, for United Artists release, and happily retired.

Bibliography

Bodeen, DeWitt. "Constance Talmadge." *Films in Review*, December 1967, pp. 613–630.

Goldbeck, Willis. "Tonsils and Terpsichore." *Motion Picture*, May 1922, pp. 24–25, 98.

Hall, Gladys. "Confessions of the Stars: Constance Talmadge." *Motion Picture Classic*, November 1928, pp. 18–19, 70, 83.

Kingsley, Grace. "The Wild Woman of Babylon." *Photoplay*, May 1917, pp. 80–82, 148.

Loos, Anita. *The Talmadge Girls*. New York: Viking Press, 1978.

McGaffey, Kenneth. "Convalescing with Constance." *Motion Picture*, April 1 919, pp. 50–51, 105.

O'Reilly, Edward S. "A Date with Connie." *Photoplay*, September 1920, pp. 54–55, 102–103.

Smith, Frederick James. "Tomboy Constance." *Motion Picture Classic*, July 1919, pp. 16–17, 76.

Talmadge, Constance. "Rire et faire rire." *Cinema Art*, November 1926, pp. 44–45.

———. "The Tragedy of Being Funny." *Motion Picture*, August 1927, pp. 54–55, 102.

Talmadge, Margaret L. *The Talmadge Sisters, Norma, Constance, Natalie*. Philadephia: J.B. Lippincott, 1924.

NORMA TALMAGE

While there are dramatic performances in individual silent films that stand out—most notably Mae Marsh and Miriam Cooper in *Intolerance*—there is only actress whose entire silent career is exemplary of the best in dramatic performance. That performer is Norma Talmadge, each one of whose characterizations is unique and created with a dramatic force unlike that found in any other actress. "With Norma Talmadge every part is a separate and distinct creation," wrote Adela Rogers St. Johns in 1926. "And when you see her upon the screen, you never see Norma Talmadge. You, as an audience, know absolutely nothing of the woman, Norma Talmadge."

Norma Talmadge (Jersey City, New Jersey, May 26, 1897–Las Vegas, December 24, 1957) could play both modern and period roles, and whoever the director might be, she was able to control and modulate her performance to the part. She was a natural dramatic actress, with an emotional intensity where necessary and a quiet presence at other times. The double tragedy is that while many of her films have survived they do not get screened, and because they are not lightweight affairs, easy to watch and understand, they require more from their audiences than do lesser silent productions with lesser silent stars.

Panthea (1917) was the first film for her own production company. Based on a popular play by Monckton Hoffe, it was a dramatic tour de force for Olga Petrova on stage and similarly on screen for Talmadge. The actress made many films with Sidney Franklin, quite a few of which are little more than program pictures, but also *Smilin' Through* (1922), one of the greatest screen romances of all time. In *Within the Law* (1923), again based on a popular play (this time by Bayard Veiller), Talmadge is a New York shopgirl wrongly accused of theft who becomes a blackmailer. *Graustark* (1925) has her as the princess of a mythical kingdom who wins approval from her people for marriage to an American commoner. New York or Ruritania, the setting mattered little when the performance was uniformly good. In 1926, Talmadge played the title role of *Kiki* in the French romantic comedy, and was as good, if not better, than Mary Pickford in the 1931 sound remake.

Alexandre Dumas fils's tragic heroine, Marguerite Gautier, was an obvious role for the actress, and, again, her 1927 version of *Camille* is the equal of, and certainly less studied, than the later Garbo production. In *Camille*, Talmadge plays opposite her offscreen lover, Gilbert Roland, and sparks fly just as they do in the couple's other silent films, *The Dove* (1927) and *The Woman Disputed* (1928). The last was a not entirely successful farewell to an era, and it was followed by two sound productions, *New York Nights* (1929) and *DuBarry: Woman of Passion* (1930), which are not without interest from a technical standpoint but are hampered by an actress whose voice sadly sounds inappropriate to her appearance and bearing.

The oldest of the Talmadge sisters, Norma Talmadge began her professional career as a youngster posing for song slides, and, in late 1910, she joined the Vitagraph Company. She first came to public attention as the young woman accompanying Sidney Carton (played by Maurice Costello) in the tumbril on his way to the guillotine in the company's three-reel 1911 production of *A Tale of Two Cities*. The part is insignificant yet highly relevant from a dramatic standpoint, and just as it made a star of Norma Talmadge, so did the same role in the 1917 version help draw attention to Florence Vidor. Talmadge left Vitagraph in the summer of 1915 after starring in its major anti-German propagandistic drama, *The Battle Cry of Peace*. She worked under D.W. Griffith's supervision, if not direction, at Fine Arts during 1916. Curiously, if modern audiences know Talmadge at all, it is because she is the star of the much-screened, drug-related Fine Arts production, *The Devil's Needle*. The film does little for the actress or for the drug issue.

On October 20, 1916, Norma Talmadge married producer Joseph M. Schenck, and he supervised, nurtured and sustained her career, much as Irving Thalberg later did at MGM for Norma Shearer. Schenck and Talmadge divorced in April 1934. That same year, she married entertainer George Jessel, divorcing him in 1939, and in 1946, the actress made a final marriage, to Las Vegas physician Dr. Carvel James.

Coming out a luncheon engagement at the Vendome Restaurant in West Hollywood in October 1935, Talmadge was besieged by a group of fans asking for autographs. "Run along kiddies. I don't need you now," she told them. And with those words, a proud star of the silent screen walked away into history.

Bibliography

"Before They Were Stars: Norma Talmadge." *New York Dramatic Mirror*, April 17, 1920, pp. 744, 765.

Carr, Harry. "Slumbering Fires." *Motion Picture Classic*, December 1922, pp. 32–33, 77.

———. "The Millionaire Actress." *Motion Picture Classic*, July 1925, pp. 42, 71.

"A Day with Norma Talmadge of the Vitagraph Company." *Motion Picture Story Magazine*, November 1914, pp. 107–110.

Fletcher, Adele Whitely. "Floating Island on Olympus." *Motion Picture*, March 1921, pp. 22–23, 109.

Hornblow, Arthur, Jr. "Norma Talmadge." *Photoplay*, August 1915, pp. 99–102.

Lachmund, Marjorie Gleyre. "Our Norma." *Motion Picture*, January 1917, pp. 110–112.

Loos, Anita. *The Talmadge Girls*. New York: Viking Press, 1978.

MacDonald, Margaret I. "Norma Talmadge, a Modern Female." *Moving Picture World*, July 21, 1917, p. 390.

Naylor, Hazel Simpson. "That Tantalizing Talmadge." *Motion Picture*, October 1918, pp. 100-103.

Oettinger, Malcolm H. "Beauty and the Bean." *Picture-Play*, April 1922, pp. 42-44, 88.

St. Johns, Adela Rogers. "The Lady of the Vase." *Photoplay*, August 1923, pp. 38-39, 104.

———. "Our ONE and ONLY Great Actress." *Photoplay*, February 1926, pp. 58, 136-137.

Schallert, Edwin. "The Challenge to Fame." *Picture-Play*, June 1924, pp. 33-34, 110.

Service, Faith. "The Amazing Interview." *Motion Picture Classic*, January 1920, pp. 22-23, 87.

Spears, Jack. "Norma Talmadge." *Films in Review*, January 1967, pp. 16-40.

Talmadge, Margaret L. *The Talmadge Sisters, Norma, Constance, Natalie*. Philadelphia: J.B. Lippincott, 1924.

Talmadge, Norma. "How I Got In." *Motion Picture*, October 1917, pp. 109-110.

Vance, Elsie. "Norma Talmadge—the Adorable." *Photoplay*, February 1915, pp. 68-70.

Alice Terry and Rex Ingram.

ALICE TERRY

Two leading ladies of the silent screen who were married to their directors were Enid Bennett (Mrs. Fred Niblo) and Alice Terry (Mrs. Rex Ingram). Both, it was suggested were nothing blondes with influential meal tickets, and while the comment might be partially true of End Bennett, whose biggest role was as Maid Marian in the 1922 Douglas Fairbanks vehicle, *Robin Hood*, which was not directed by her husband, it is far from an accurate description of Alice Terry.

The problem Alice had at the height of her career was that she was the wife of Rex Ingram, and she was doomed to be his leading lady in films that were dominated by their male stars. She holds her own opposite Rudolph Valentino in *The Four Horsemen of the Apocalypse* (1921), but not in their second film together, *The Conquering Power* (1921). Lewis Stone's dual role in *The Prisoner of Zenda* (1922) assures his prominence there, and even he is overshadowed by Ramon Novarro in *Scaramouche* (1923). Novarro was, of course, Rex Ingram's successor-discovery to Rudolph Valentino, and he starred opposite Alice Terry in *Where the Pavement Ends* (1923) and *The Arab* (1924), as well as the non-Ingram directed *Lovers?* (1927). They make a beautiful couple, but which is the most beautiful is sometimes difficult to determine. Alice Terry is a passive film star, subjugated to the will of her husband-director (at least on screen); "pliant clay" is how one fan magazine writer described Alice.

When Alice is separated from Rex, as she was in late 1924 and 1925, at a time when the marriage was in jeopardy, MGM cast her in *The Great Divide*, with Conway Tearle, and *Confessions of a Queen*, again with Lewis Stone, and loaned her out to Paramount for *Any Woman* and *Sackcloth and Scarlet*. Away from Rex Ingram, Alice Terry was the legitimate star, and, particularly in the two Paramount releases, minus a recognizable leading man, she affirms her boxoffice popularity.

Born Helen Taafe in Vincennes, Indiana, on July 24, 1900, Alice was, as her name suggests, of Welsh ancestry. She entered films as an extra in the mid-teens along with a friend, Claire DuBrey. For two years, she also worked in the cutting rooms at Famous Players–Lasky. As early as 1916, she receives screen credit as Alice Taafe, with *Photoplay*'s commenting of her work in *Not My Sister*, "She is an added starter and looks very promising." For Rex Ingram, Alice appeared in uncredited bit parts in *The Day She Paid* (1919), starring Francelia Billington, and *Shore Acres*, starring Alice Lake. She was co-leading lady, with Francelia Billington, in the English melodrama *Hearts Are Trumps*, released in December 1920. She should not be confused with a

Vitagraph actress of the teens who also used the name of Alice Terry. Alice is actually a brunette. She first wore a blonde wig in *Hearts Are Trumps*, to differentiate her character from that of Francelia Billington. In *The Four Horsemen of the Apocalypse*, Alice again wore the wig, because her character, Marguerite Laurier, is described as a blonde, and retained the hairpiece thereafter.

Bette Davis once commented that she had never been a film fan, but as a kid, she had seen *The Four Horsemen of the Apocalypse* about five times: "I went to watch the scene where he [Valentino] kneels and takes off Alice Terry's shoes. I was made for that one scene. I hoped one day some man would do the same for me." Rex Ingram did not share Bette Davis's enthusiasm for his film; according to Alice he didn't like it because he had never been to South America, where much of the production is set, and thought the film was "all wrong."

Ingram had insisted that Alice learn to speak French for her role in *The Four Horsemen of the Apocalypse*. Despite being a silent film, some directors did consider it appropriate that performers speak the language of the characters they were portraying. For example, in *7th Heaven*, it is very obvious that Janet Gaynor and Charles Farrell are actually speaking French—at least in the close-ups. A knowledge of French was convenient when, in 1924, Rex and Alice took up residence on the French Riviera, and the director adopted the Victorine Studios in Nice as his new production headquarters. The move to Europe was coincident with Metro, for whom Ingram was the highest paid director, becoming Metro-Goldwyn-Mayer. So antagonistic was Ingram toward new studio head Louis B. Mayer that an agreement was worked out whereby his films would be billed as Metro-Goldwyn productions. Mayer's name was not to appear anywhere on screen or in publicity. Alice seized on this arrangement as a means to relaxation from work. As she recalled, whenever she felt the urge to get away from Rex and the studio, she would scour publicity and find an inadvertent reference to one of her husband's films being a Metro-Goldwyn-Mayer production. The offending publicity would be shown to Ingram, he would have a temper tantrum and close down production, and Alice would go off to the beach.

According to Alice, *Mare Nostrum* was the only one of his films that Rex liked, and as far as she was concerned, it was the only one of her appearances of which she was proud. Here, she is Freya Talberg, a German spy modeled after Mata Hari. Far from being the patrician beauty who simply seems to stand around in so many of her films, Alice gives a performance and is at her most emotional best, quiet and yet with her body tense, as she goes off to her execution.

The Magician (1926) is Ingram at his visual best, but like so many of the director's films it lacks excitement. It is fascinating to look at, but basically dull, despite its grand guignol storyline, the grotesque characters so beloved of Ingram, and an ending that would be later become clichéd for the horror film, with hero and heroine looking back as the mad scientist's tower is engulfed in flames. Alice and leading man Ivan Petrovich have little to do, with Paul Wegener as the crazed scientist dominating the action. *The Garden of Allah* (1927) must have appealed to Ingram with its religious overtones, and Alice Terry is beautifully photographed and particularly moving here. I saw the film with cinematographer Lee Garmes and Mrs. Harry Lachman, whose husband was production manager. Mrs. Lachman recalled that Ingram would sit around for hours, doing nothing except read from the Koran; "he was just going through a phase," explained Garmes.

Weight problems had always plagued Alice. She would joke that "Ince always wanted me to diet. And every time I came down those stairs from the dressing rooms at Inceville, he would ask, 'Alice, what do you have behind your back?'—and it was always a chocolate éclair." Once Rex insisted that she walk from Nice to Marseilles in an effort to lose weight, but the moment Rex disappeared, Alice would have her sister Edna pick her up in a car and drive her to the next destination where she would eat all she wanted. Eventually, Louis B. Mayer issued a dictate. Alice must either give up candy or give up movies. Without hesitation, she chose the latter option.

Alice Terry and Rex Ingram were married in Pasadena on November 5, 1921, during the making of *The Prisoner of Zenda*. It was a curious marriage, lasting until Ingram's death in 1950, but one that may not even have been consummated. Film critic and founder of the film department at the Museum of Modern Art, Iris Barry, described the relationship as "a gallant and loyal companionship," which it very obviously was. The couple did adopt a young Arab boy, Kada Ab Del Kadir, but what happened to him in unknown. Director Robert Florey told me that he was asked at one time by the French authorities to check on the welfare of the teenager, and he had become a delinquent with a bad reputation around Hollywood.

Alice made no effort to hide the fact that she and Rex did not share accommodation—in Nice, she and Edna lived on the second floor and Rex occupied ground floor rooms—and that her longtime lover was actor Gerald Fielding. Born in Darjeeling, India, on July 6, 1910, Gerald Fielding was ten years younger than Alice. The couple must first have met when he played the small role of Bonnie in Ingram's last silent production, *The Three Passions*, in 1929. Fielding looks rather effeminate as Dmitri in *The Scarlet Empress* (1933), but as early as July 1, 1929, the British fan magazine, *Film Weekly*, noted a remarkable similarity in appearance between him and Ingram, without, apparently, realizing how deep the similarity was. When Alice and Fielding became lovers is unclear. Herb Sterne always claimed that Fielding was bisexual, and that Alice had stolen him away from fellow actor Michael Whalen which suggests that the relationship did not develop until the mid- to late 1930s. When Gerald Fielding died in Encino, California, On June 3, 1956, he was married, and presumably had ended his affair with Alice.

Rex Ingram also sought companionship of the opposite sex, and a close friend noted the presence of four of his mistresses at his funeral. When Alice was asked how she could invite Ingram's mistresses to the post-funeral party, she responded who cared because she was the only one could call herself Mrs. Rex Ingram. Neither Ingram nor Alice was gay, but Alice was very broadminded. She remained a close friend of Ramon Novarro and was fully aware of his personal situation. In the 1930s, she allowed him, Barry Norton and other gay actors to escort her to gay Hollywood nightspots, thus serving as a "beard" for their gay lifestyles. Her partnering of gay actors led a gossip columnist in *The Hollywood Reporter* to question who she and they were trying to fool. It was all very obvious to those in the know, and all very civilized.

As noted, Alice Terry was a competent film editor and she had obviously learned direction from a master. Thus, when Ingram became incapacitated and too moody to work, she would take over direction of his features. In 1931, when Ingram began production of what was to be his last film and his only talkie, *Baroud,* Alice was named co-director. Ingram starred in the film, as a French legionnaire, and Alice directed all the scenes in which he appeared. "Rex could play any part in a film, a cripple or an old lady, but when it came to playing himself, it was a different story," commented Alice.

Baroud was released in the U.S. in 1933 as *Love in the Morocco,* received only minimal bookings and was a critical failure. The problem is that the production is painfully amateurish, badly acted, and only a semi-documentary quality saves it from being a total disaster. After the film was released, Selznick wired Ingram and offered him a contract as an actor. Rex was horrified. What is obvious from *Baroud* is that Alice was an all-round filmmaker, an actress who could handle many aspects of the creative process, but was too modest to acknowledge her worth.

Baroud might not have marked the end of Alice's film career. Obviously, she still enjoyed the studio atmosphere, and on November 10, 1933, she filmed a screen test at Warner Bros. for German director G.W. Pabst's only American film, *A Modern Hero.* The part for which Alice was tested is presumably that played by Jean Muir opposite an aging and somewhat pudgy Richard Barthelmess.

When Rex Ingram decided to return to Los Angeles, he instructed Alice to find a home by a river, with trees and mountains in the background. While out drinking with some of her women friends, Alice was about to throw up and asked that the car be stopped. She got out, fell down on the ground and vomited. Looking up, she saw a property in Studio City on the banks of the Los Angeles River, which is generally little more than a trickle. It was tree-shaded and a short distance away was the Santa Monica Mountains. Alice had found a new home for her and Rex. The property, on Kelsey Street and now demolished, consisted of the main house at the east end, where Alice lived, Ingram's studio and residence to the west, and stables, later converted into an apartment, on an incline by the river. When Ingram died, Alice and her sister Edna moved into the Ingram's studio, which was smaller and easier to maintain.

After Ingram's death, Gerald Fielding wanted to move in with Alice but sister Edna forbade it. Edna was always in control. She had been an extra in films, like Alice, but then married a financial advisor. Edna knew how to bear a grudge. When working in films, she had given her money to her mother who, in turn, passed it on to brother Robert. Because of her brother's abuse of her income, Edna refused to allow his son, Robert, to enter the house, and would not permit Alice to have anything to do with her nephew. Of course, after Alice's death, the nephew, who is now deceased, took to appearing at screenings of films by Alice and Rex, speaking authoritatively of his aunt and uncle.

Rex Ingram was a good painter and sculptor, and, in retirement, Alice also took up painting. (On the walls of my dining room, I have oil paintings by Alice of Rex, their villa in niece and the Victorine Studios). The couple were affluent, and Alice added considerably to her wealth when she filed suit in July 1951, asking for $750,000 in damages from Edward Small and Columbia Pictures, claiming she was libeled in the film biography *Valentino* (in which she is not mentioned by name). According to Alice, the film depicted misconduct between herself and Valentino. The suit was settled out of court in January 1953 for an undisclosed sum believed to be half-a-million dollars.

It has been asserted that Alice Terry in old age became a recluse. Such a suggestion is far from the truth. She had put on weight, but was not obese, and, in all truth, as she would explain, having to visit the beauty parlor to take care of her hair, and to replace her comfortable slippers with shoes was a chore. Although on one memorable occasion, she did take everyone over to the home of cinematographer William Clothier, Alice basically preferred to entertain at home with Sunday afternoon parties in the mid- through late 1970s. The bill of fare was usually cold ham and Mumm's champagne. There were many funny stories, sometimes at Ingram's expense but often at her own. Never did Alice get sentimental over Ingram's death, as has been suggested. Jack Hewson, who lived on the property from the 1950s through the 1980s, recalled that Alice would often ask him to accompany her to restaurants for dinner, insisting they go on to an after-hours club for drinks. Alice was known to insist on wearing a full-length white mink coat, with matching hat, for such dinner engagements. She was always so proud of her appearance in mink and so sure that all the other women were envious.

I first wrote of Alice Terry in *The Idols of Silence* back in 1976, and she was so pleased with my comments that she gave the book as a Christmas present to all her friends: "I believe that's the first time I have ever been treated so nicely. Your reviews were so good I am glad you exist today. It makes me feel good for the first time that I was ever in the movies. You must have had a hard time finding the nice things to say. Usually they said I was adequate—I used to hate that word."

I would stop by Alice Terry's home from time to time, dropping off reading matter. She particularly enjoyed the monthly film buff publication *Films in Review* and show business autobiographies: "I read all these books about Valentino, and I always think that Valentino was never like that. He was always agreeable, tried hard to please everybody." She was convulsed with laughter upon reading Pola Negri's autobiography, in which the actress wrote of dropping rose petals on the bed in which she and Valentino would make love. As far as Alice was concerned, neither was capable of the sexual act—at least as far as a member of the opposite sex was concerned.

Our last meeting took place on June 18, 1981. I was surprised when Alice's nurse stopped me and said she wanted to say hello. She looked much the same, but was quickly confused. I would try and agree with her when she said something that was patently wrong, and then I would be embarrassed at being caught out in a lie.

In the end, alzheimer's put a stop to the parties and to the fun. The nurses who had responsibility for Alice's care abused her. She had always refused to be photographed and, in particular, she rejected Roddy McDowall's persistent requests both to meet and photograph her. Only when she could no longer fend for herself did McDowall force his way in, with the cooperation of the nurses. His photographs of Alice are an insult to this fine lady. To look at them is to look at a face where anger at her own impotence is present in the eyes, but which is also dead to the outside world. Alice Terry died in a Burbank hospital on December 22, 1987.

Note: The scrapbooks of Alice Terry are at the Margaret Herrick Library of the Academy of Motion Picture Arts and Sciences.

Bibliography

Barton, Ralph. "You Never Know Your Luck." *Photoplay*, October 1921, pp. 21, 97.

Beach, Barbara. "Rex and His Queen." *Motion Picture*, January 1922, pp. 22–23, 102.

Bodeen, DeWitt. "Rex Ingram and Alice Terry, Part One." *Films in Review*, February 1975, pp. 73–89.

———. "Rex Ingram and Alice Terry, Part II." *Films in Review*, March 1975, pp. 129–142.

Cheatham, Maude. "The Waking Beauty." *Motion Picture Classic*, July 1921, pp. 32–33, 74.

Evans, Delight. "She Wants to Be Wicked." *Photoplay*, December 1922, pp. 45, 108–109.

Howe, Herbert. "When Alice Played a German Soldier with a Beard." *Photoplay*, February 1925, pp. 59, 98–99.

———. "Presenting Rex Ingram in Baroud." *New Movie Magazine*, March 1932, pp. 37–39.

Johaneson, Bland. "Alice & Miss Terry." *Photoplay*, January 1924, pp. 41, 104.

Manners, Dorothy. "Old Friends Talk of Alice Terry." *Picture-Play*, September 1925, pp. 89, 100.

Oettinger, Malcolm. "Should a Wife Tell?" *Picture-Play*, March 1924, pp. 84–85, 104.

Thayer, Mamie. "Alice of Old Vincennes." *Picture-Play*, May 1921, pp. 45–46, 95.

FLORENCE TURNER

It is odd that the first two pioneering actresses of the silent screen should both have been named Florence. Florence or Flo—what an old-fashioned name, inappropriate for Florence Lawrence (1890–1938), who had a youthful charm when she entered films at the American Biograph Company in 1908, but most apt for her rival, Florence Turner, who always had an aura of age and maturity. She is not a great beauty, although there is a hint of Latin loveliness there. The face is too easily molded, too easily misshapen for comic effect. It is Turner's adaptability and talent for impersonation that stands her out above other early actresses, but it is that same quality that dooms her to second-class status today. She is not attractive enough to warrant our attention.

Born in New York on January 6, 1887, Turner spent a number of years on stage and in vaudeville before joining the Brooklyn-based Vitagraph Company in 1907. At that time, she was hired not merely as an actress, but also as a bookkeeper, pay clerk, accountant, and wardrobe woman. One had to be talented in many fields to impress an early film producer! Turner starred in a vast number of one-reel short subjects, including Shakespeare adaptations and Southern melodramas. She was the sole performer in a 1911 short titled *Jealousy*, "a study in the art of dramatic expression." A year earlier, she had consolidated her popularity by making the first personal appearance by a screen star at a movie theatre (in Brooklyn). She was a little old for the title, but she was recognized as "The Vitagraph Girl," and there was even a popular song written in her honor.

Leading man James Morrison knew her well: "Close friends always called her Flo T. [She had] a very nervous temperament, but easy to work with. She was a worker. She never put on airs. You'd never really know she was a star, but, of course, she was."

When Turner left Vitagraph in 1913, it was not to join another American producer, but to travel to England, where she set up her own production company with Vitagraph director Larry Trimble. In all, she starred in more than 25 British films, prominent among which is a five-reel adaptation of *Far from the Madding Crowd* (1915) and *My Old Dutch* (1915), opposite international music hall star, Albert Chevalier. As evidenced by another 1915 feature, *East Is East*, in which surprisingly can be found Edith Evans, Turner's films are superior to all British productions of the period. Not that that is a great compliment.

In 1916, she and Trimble returned to the United States. Trimble's widow Marian denied to me that there was anything romantic in the relationship between the two, and further insisted that physical problems prevented Turner's enjoying any sort of sex life and kept her a spinster. In the three years she had been away, the American film industry had changed drastically, with many of the old producers fading away and the feature film replacing the short subject. There was really no room for Turner as a leading lady, and in 1922 she decided to return to England. Unfortunately, there were also changes, very different ones, in the British film industry. Production was hampered by lack of funds and lack of public interest in native films, and by 1924 the slump was such that all production ceased. A chastened Florence Turner came back again to the United States. The passage for her and her mother was paid by Marion Davies, who found Turner a small role in her production of the historical drama, *Janice Meredith*.

James Morrison recalled, "The whole business had leapt ahead of her. Larry Trimble came to me and he said, 'Jim, Flo T. wants to get back into pictures, and I think she can.' We got a little company together; the people who were in it worked for nothing because we loved Flo T. We did scenes from *My Old Dutch*, but nothing ever came of it." In reality, Trimble was hired by Universal to direct a new screen version of *My Old Dutch*, but the starring role went to May McAvoy.

Small roles were all that were left for the pioneering actress, usually those of the mother, as in the 1927 Buster Keaton vehicle, *College*. By the 1930s, Turner was playing extra, and early in the next decade, she entered the Motion Picture Country House, where she died on August 28, 1946. Just as Florence Lawrence had died, a forgotten suicide victim, so was Florence Turner assigned to obscurity, yet thirty years earlier, Norma Talmadge had said of Turner, "I would rather have touched the hem of her skirt than to have shaken hands with St. Peter."

Note: Florence Turner's scrapbooks and papers are at the Los Angeles County Museum of Natural History.

Bibliography

Crocombe, Leslie. "The Girl of the Film: Florence Turner." *Pictures and the Picturegoer*, June 6, 1914, pp. 358–360.

Denig, Lynde. "Larry Trimble Brings Turner Films." *Moving Picture World*, August 19, 1916, p. 1223.

Gates, Harvey. "Florence Turner Talks about Acting." *New York Dramatic Mirror*, October 30, 1912, p. 28.

Hoffman, Hugh. "Florence Turner Comes Back." *Moving Picture World*, May 18, 1912, p. 622.

Moen, L.C. "Florence Turner Returns to America." *Motion Picture News*, May 24, 1924, pp. 2430–2431, 2433.

Peltret, Elizabeth. "The Return of Florence Turner." *Motion Picture Classic*, February 1919, pp. 28–29, 72–73.

Slide, Anthony. "Florence Turner" in *The Big V: A History of the Vitagraph Company*. Metuchen, N.J.: Scarecrow Press, 1987, pp. 37–43.

Turner, Florence. "Putting 'Move' into 'Movie,'" *Motion Picture Studio*, April 15, 1922, p. 13.

RUDOLPH VALENTINO. *See* **THE LEGENDS**

THE VAMPS

Theda Bara, Louise Glaum, Kitty Gordon, Olga Grey,
Alice Hollister, and Valeska Suratt

The vamp was a character unique to silent films, neither heroine nor villain-ess. She was a predatory female, whose behavior was so distinctly lacking in eroticism that she was positively asexual. Many actresses might spend time vamping the leading man, but only a handful gained distinction at the art and craft. Their popularity was sustained not through any acting talent, but rather because of the manner of their performance. The vamp, or more accurately vampire, owes her existence to a painting, "The Vampire," by the Victorian artist, Sir Edward Burne-Jones, and to an 1897 verse of the same title by Rudyard Kipling that begins with the words, "A fool there was and he made his prayer...."

The best-known exponent of the vamp is **THEDA BARA** (Cincinnati, Ohio, July 22, 1890–Los Angeles, April 7, 1955). Born Theodosia Goodman and

given the name Theda Bara, an anagram of "Arab Death," by a publicist, she came to the screen in January 1915 in a lurid William Fox production, *A Fool There Was*, based on the Kipling verse and a 1909 play by Porter Emerson Browne. When Bara uttered the immortal words, "Kiss me, my fool," contemporary audiences gasped and modern audiences laughed, as well they might. She is not a good actress, and a rediscovery of her films, the majority of which are lost, will not alter her reputation. Her 1919 retirement made sense, and when she returned briefly to the screen for two films in 1925 and 1926 it was to parody herself. In real life, she was apparently both charming and intelligent, a sophisticated wife to director Charles Brabin. George Walsh was her leading man in *The Serpent* (1916), directed by brother Raoul, and he described her as "a grand person, very, very fine." Fan magazine writer Adele Whitely Fletcher knew her socially:

"She was one of the best informed women that I have ever known. She knew who she was. I think she started my interest in food. She would pick me up in her chauffeur-driven car, and we would go to a place in Jersey, where they served beautiful Italian food, then we went out to a place on Long Island, where they did beautiful seafood. Always we'd stop along the road, and the chauffer would take out a silver cocktail shaker and we'd have a martini or maybe one-and-a-half martinis, just enough to whet the appetite."

Theda Bara was not the first screen vamp. As early as 1910, the Selig Polyscope had released a one-reel short, *The Vampire*, the star of which is unknown. **ALICE HOLLISTER** (Worcester, Massachusetts, September 28, 1886–Costa Mesa, California, February 24, 1973) became the first recognized vamp, playing the adventuress Sybill in Kalem's three-reel short, *The Vampire*, released on October 15, 1913. The highlight of the production is the "Vampire Dance," performed by Bert French and Alice Eis. Hollister also starred in a second film, *The Vampire's Trail*, a two-reel short, released on August 3, 1914.

The greatest of vamps is the least known, and she is **OLGA GREY** (Budapest, Hungary, 1897–Los Angeles, April 25, 1973), the only major D.W. Griffith-trained vamp, plying her craft in a handful of Fine Arts productions in 1915 and 1916. Despite being born Anushka Zacsek in Hungary, she was always referred to by Dorothy Gish as "That Russian femme fatale." An extra in *The Birth of a Nation* (1915), Olga Grey was cast as the Bible's best-known reformed vamp, Mary Magdalene, in *Intolerance* (1916), following in the footsteps of Alice Hollister who played the same Biblical character in Kalem's 1912 *From the Manger to the Cross*. Grey entered films without explanation in 1914, and disappeared, equally without reason, in 1919. She was not the only vamp who learned her craft with D.W. Griffith. Equally impressive is Viola Barry (1894–1964), stealing Lillian Gish's husband, Walter Miller, away from her in the 1913 American Biograph two-reel short, *The Mothering Heart.*

KITTY GORDON (Folkestone, England, April 22, 1878–Brentwood, N.Y., May 26, 1974) starred in some 22 features between 1916 and 1919, and she was expert at the art of vamping without turning her face to the camera. "Miss Gordon's opulent back is alone an example of perfect dramatic technique," wrote the *New York Dramatic Mirror* (October 21, 1914). Kitty Gordon came from the stage, making her London debut in 1901 and her New York debut in 1905; Victor Herbert had written the 1911 operetta, *The Enchantress* for her, and she remained active through 1952, when she appeared on television in *Life Begins at 80.*

Also from the theatre, with far lesser a pedigree, came **VALESKA SURATT** (Terre Haute, Indiana, June 28, 1882–Washington, D.C., July 2, 1962). An exotic dancer and star of playlets on the vaudeville stage, Suratt starred, as a vamp, in eleven feature films between 1915 and 1917, and then returned to vaudeville. Contemporary critics described her as "ornate." She was also very obviously crazy. "Am I not Satan's ward, in the eyes of my audience?" she asked a 1916 fan magazine. By the time she came to write her unpublished autobiography, she had changed sides and become the Virgin Mary incarnate. It is easy to laugh at a creature such as Valeska Suratt, but her later life was far from easy and bordered on tragedy. By the 1930s, she was living in one room at a shabby New York hotel, and when novelist Fannie Hurst arranged a benefit performance on her behalf, Suratt lost the $2,000 raised through gambling, retaining only enough to purchase six eggs and a bouquet of roses.

Another vamp making the world safe for sin during the First World War, as fan magazine writer Herbert Howe put it, was **LOUISE GLAUM** (Baltimore, Maryland, September 4, 1900–Los Angeles, November 25, 1970), who entered films in 1911 with Pathé and by 1912 was a leading lady with the Nestor Company. She rose from slapstick comedy, playing opposite Alkali Ike, to ingénue to vamp, and confirmed her reputation with her vamping of the new minister in William S. Hart's *Hell's Hinges* (1916). Her best surviving film is *Sex* (1920), in which she makes her first appearance, suspended in the center of a giant spider's web, performing "The Spider Dance," espousing the philosophy, "Grab everything you want and never feel sorry for anyone but yourself." A lighted cigarette in a woman's hand here personifies sin. "Time the inscrutable—who patiently creates that he may as patiently destroy" reaps a revenge on the vamping Miss Glaum in a manner that might well have won approval later from the Production Code Administration, whose morality if not physical presence was as powerful in 1920 as it would be a decade-and-a-half later. Glaum marries William Conklin only to have her protégée, Peggy

Pearce, come along and steal the apparently desirable Mr. Conklin away from her.

Louise Glaum retired in the mid-1920s and taught acting in Los Angeles. As Louise Harris, she was a prim, businesslike and unremarkable elderly lady, who neither in physical form nor manner resembled one of the screen's great vamps.

Despite the melodramatics and mediocrity of the vamps, they remained relatively well known to later audiences, their performances exemplary of how modern audiences perceived of the leading ladies of the silent screen. On November 10, 1955, a musical titled *The Vamp* opened at the Winter Garden Theatre on Broadway, starring Carol Channing as Flora Weems, a composite of Theda Bara and Pola Negri, and featuring Steve Reeves as "Muscle Man." The show ran for sixty performances, proving that the vamp was still a viable commercial proposition.

Bibliographies

Theda Bara

Bara, Pauline. "My Theda Bara." *Motion Picture Classic*, January 1921, pp. 19–20, 79.

Bara, Theda. "How I Became a Vampire." *Forum*, July 1919, pp. 88–93.

Bodeen, DeWitt. "Theda Bara." *Films in Review*, May 1968, pp. 266–287.

Courtlandt, Roberta. "The Divine Theda." *Motion Picture*, April 1917, pp. 59–62.

Evans, Delight. "Does Theda Bara Believe Her Own Press Agent?" *Photoplay*, May 1918, pp. 62–63, 107.

Franklyn, Wallace. "Purgatory's Ivory Angel." *Photoplay*, September 1915, pp. 69–72.

Gebhart, Myrtle. "The New Theda Bara." *Picture-Play*, September 1925, pp. 16–17, 114.

Genini, Ronald. *Theda Bara: A Biography of the Silent Screen Vamp, with a Filmography*. Jefferson, N.C.: McFarland, 1996.

Golden, Eve. *Vamp: The Rise and Fall of Theda Bara*. Vestal, N.Y.: Emprise Publishing, 1996. [No contemporary bibliographic citations are listed in this book]

Hall, Gladys and Adele Whitely Fletcher. "We Interview Theda Bara." *Motion Picture*, November 1922, pp. 20–22, 116.

McKelvie, Martha Groves. "O-o-o-h Theda!" *Motion Picture Classic*, September 1918, pp. 24–25, 68.

Mullett, Mary B. "Theda Bara, Queen of the Vampire." *American Magazine*, September 1920, pp. 34–35.

Petrova, Olga. "Mme. Petrova Interviews Theda Bara." *Shadowland*, March–April 1920, pp. 43–44, 74.

Smith, Agnes. "The Confessions of Theda Bara." *Photoplay*, June 1920, pp. 57–58, 110–111.

Smith, Frederick James. "Keeping That Appointment with Theda Bara." *Motion Picture Classic*, February 1919, pp. 16–17, 78.
"What It Means to Live under the Same Roof with the So-Called Vampire." *Theatre*, October 1918, p. 258.

Louise Glaum

Bruce, Betsy. "T'was Ever Thus." *Motion Picture*, January 1919, pp. 62–63, 97.
Drew, Robert. "Siren Stuff." *Motion Picture*, March 1922, pp. 72–73, 96.
Lee, Carol. "A Vampire Who's Proud of It." *Motion Picture Classic*, March 1917, pp. 44–46.
Milton, Martha. "I've Vamped Enough." *Motion Picture Classic*, August 1918, pp. 29–30, 73–74.
Smith, Frederick James. "Living Down Her Past." *Motion Picture Classic*, December 1917, pp. 52–53.
Taylor, Mary Keane. "The Luxurious Louise." *Motion Picture Classic*, June 1919, pp. 48–49, 62, 72.

Kitty Gordon

"Mother-Not-Ashamed-of-Daughter." *Photoplay*, January 1919, p. 61.

Olga Grey

Grey, Olga. "How I Learned to Act." *Motion Picture*, December 1916, p. 69.
"A Vamp with a Goulash Name." *Photoplay*, February 1917, p. 73.

Alice Hollister

"Alice Hollister." *Motion Picture Classic*, April 1917, p. 38.
Courtlandt, Roberta. "Alice Hollister of the Kalem Company." *Motion Picture*, February 1915, pp. 94–96.
Shelley, Hazel. "The Original Vampire." *Motion Picture Classic*, July 1921, pp. 62–63, 89.

Valeska Suratt

Bacon, George Vaux. "Valeska Suratt of Terre Haute." *Photoplay*, March 1916, p. 89.
May, Lillian. "A Siren at Home." *Motion Picture*, December 1916, pp. 113–116.
Suratt, Valeska. "Sneering at Satan." *Picture-Play*, August 1916, pp. 32–37.

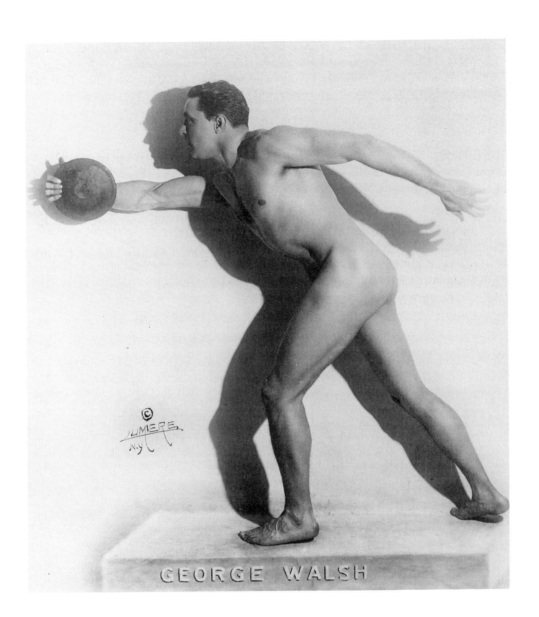

GEORGE WALSH

George Walsh

Pomona is a small, dusty community east of Los Angeles. It is not exactly a glamorous spot for a movie star, but here I am in June 1972 at the ranchstyle home of leading man George Walsh. Perhaps "ranch" is too grand a description for the one-story home and single field that appear to comprise the Walsh homestead. In the house is a large, slobbering dog. In the field is an equally large, slobbering horse. George Walsh looks as aged as his animals, but he is friendly and happy to talk of the past. He is as proud of his former athletic prowess as his film career, boasting of his exploits on the baseball and football fields, his swimming and his rowing expertise. There is still a hint of a footballer's build here, and I can well understand why Walsh is so pleased with the nude photographs of his muscular rear, shot in the late teens, that he insists on sharing them with me. Somehow his rugged features do not match that devastatingly handsome body.

Born in New York on March 16, 1889, Walsh boasts of his Irish immigrant background, although his father was actually born in the English industrial city of Sheffield. Neither George nor his older brother Raoul (1887–1980) entered the family's thriving tailoring business. Raoul entered films with D.W. Griffith at American Biograph and became a prominent director of action dramas. After college, George joined the Brooklyn Dodgers as an outfielder in 1914, but after being laid up in mid-season with typhoid, he decided to join his brother in Hollywood. The two took up residence at the Hollywood Hotel on the corner on Highland Avenue and Hollywood Boulevard, and almost immediately, George found work as an extra in Westerns.

Walsh has the small and unimportant role of the bridegroom of Cana in the Judean story of *Intolerance* (1916), and while working on the film, he met Seena Owen, who plays the Princess Beloved. The couple married in February 1916, but it was a stormy relationship, ending in divorce, and Walsh claimed that she had tried to kill him. Brother Raoul also married an actress, Miriam Cooper (with whom George co-starred in a number of films), and that was an equally unhappy marriage.

In 1916, George Walsh was signed to a long-term contract by William Fox, with one of his first films being *Blue Blood and Red*, directed by Raoul: "We wrote the story on the train, coming out to California, my brother and I, and when it came to naming the main characters, why I knew they were supposed to be high class people, and I immediately thought of DuPont. I was playing the young son, and I put his name in as Reginald, without dreaming or knowing there was such as person, belonging to the DuPont family in Delaware. He was an honor student at Harvard, and in the picture he's shown up as not knowing anything.

"When the picture was released, Mr. Fox got a letter from DuPont's lawyer, expressing indignation about maligning his family and his son, and he wanted the picture immediately destroyed. The picture was going big, so Fox had his lawyer write back that they would change all the names and eliminate any reference to DuPont. Well that wasn't enough. They wanted the picture destroyed. Fox said, all right, I'll destroy it, but I'll make another one showing that you have made millions of dollars furnishing shot and shell for the armies fighting over there [in Europe], killing thousands of men. That was the last he heard of a DuPont!"

Walsh made his last film for Fox in September 1920. He had been making $1,500 a week, and Fox offered him $2,000, but knowing that Pearl White had been signed to a contract at $4,000, Walsh demanded the same figure. Fox refused, and Walsh quit the studio. The most important of Walsh's Fox features is probably *The Honor System* (1917), directed by brother Raoul and co-starring Miriam Cooper, but the titles mean nothing. They were "star" vehicles intended to promote Walsh's athleticism and his ability to perform stunts of which other leading men would be physically incapable. Walsh enjoyed making the films, and that much was apparent, even if the performances might be considered somewhat wooden or heavy-handed.

Walsh made fewer films in the 1920s through no fault of his own. He did portray Rawdon Crawley in Hugo Ballin's 1923 production of *Vanity Fair*, and that same year, he was cast as Don Diego opposite Mary Pickford in Ernst Lubitsch's *Rosita* set in the early 1800s:

"I had a very unique costume of that period, flesh tights, very tight around here [the crotch]. Lubitsch and Mary and her mother had gone into the projection room to see the previous day's rushes, and I was waiting for them to come back. I see Lubitsch coming, and the closer he gets, the more he looks and looks, and finally he's looking at me down here. 'Now don't feel badly about this. Mrs. Pickford, she don't like it. In Europe, this would be wonderful, but Mrs. Pickford, she don't like it.' That, of course, would have drawn attention from Mary I guess. We had to take the whole thing over again, and I had to strap my privates down."

George Walsh had a healthy sense of humor about sexual matters. He recalled a visit to Montreal, where a madam offered him fifty dollars to go with her; Walsh was particularly pleased that the previous week, the same madam had approached Jack Dempsey and offered him only $25. He was equally proud of his performance as a female impersonator in an unidentified film: "I went to the dressing room at lunchtime and naturally unfastened my corset to eat. The call came to return, my dresser came in to help me, and he's kneeling down in front of me, working on the corset. It was a hot day and I left my door open. The night watchman was walking down the hall and he stood there looking. Here I was with this long hair hanging down and this guy kneeling in front of me. 'What's the matter, can't you find it?' he said, and away he went."

As a result of his performance in *Vanity Fair*, Walsh was signed to a long term Goldwyn contract in February 1923. It might have appeared advantageous, but it was anything but in that Goldwyn planned to star the actor in the title role of its upcoming production of *Ben-Hur*. Walsh spent, in his words, not one minute working on the film. Screenwriter and erstwhile producer June Mathis, who had selected the actor—"she just felt that I was the ideal one"—was removed from the production, Goldwyn became part of Metro-Goldwyn-Mayer, and the new company chose Ramon Novarro for the part: "It was a terrible blow and a terrible thing. It was too bad it had to happen like that. I was the last one to find out. I was handled very, very cruel. I'll never forget Frank [Francis X.] Bushman, a grand, grand individual. He stayed on and played Messala. When I was leaving, I went to his bungalow and we had a farewell. He said, 'George, this is the worst thing that I have ever seen happen to a performer in all my experience. Why'd you'd even be better in my part.' You can't get anything higher than that. Loews [the MGM parent company] deliberately tried to give the impression to the public that I had fallen down and they had to replace me with this other fellow. They never tried to set things right for me in the eyes of the public. As they say in the prize ring, struck me a low blow."

From Goldwyn and MGM, it was a long way down as Walsh discovered. In December 1924, he signed a contract with the obscure Chadwick Pictures Corporation (best remembered today for its 1925 production of *The Wizard of Oz*, starring Larry Semon and Oliver Hardy). Walsh starred in five Chadwick features in 1925 and 1926, followed by seven in 1926, 1927 and 1928 for Samuel Zierler's Excellent Pictures, still a further step down. Walsh identified I.E. Chadwick as "a nice fellow," who "would have done some big things." But he didn't.

It was Raoul who came to his younger brother's aid, appointing him an assistant director on the 1930 epic sound Western, *The Big Trail*. There were small roles in the 1930s, often in his brother's films, and George Walsh gave his farewell performance on screen as a quartermaster in the 1936 Mae West vehicle, *Klondike Annie*, directed by Raoul. It was also Raoul who provided his brother with a new career, importing a couple of Irish thoroughbred race horses in 1930, which George trained, and, four years later, helping George obtain a trainer's license. With obvious pleasure, George Walsh told me, "I got started on the horses and I've been with the horses ever since. Never went back." As he explained, "I train these horses they way that I trained myself—and I did pretty good."

George Walsh died in Pomona on June 13, 1981. In retrospect he was a genuinely nice guy whom fate, in the form of MGM, furnished a raw deal.

Bibliography

Beach, Barbara. "The Gladiator of the Screen." *Motion Picture Classic*, August 1919, pp. 18–19, 85.

Blythe, Tony. "That Walsh Family." *Motion Picture*, November 1921, pp. 66, 93.

Conley, Walter. "George Walsh." *The Silent Picture*, no. 10, spring 1971, unpaged.

Holland, Larry Lee. "George Walsh." *Films in Review*, April 1982, pp. 220–225.

Naylor, Hazel Simpson. "Catching up with George." *Motion Picture*, October 1918, pp. 32–34, 122.

Schallert, Elza. "Is He the Screen's Worst Actor?" *Picture-Play*, March 1924, pp. 20–21, 115.

Slide, Anthony. "George Walsh." *The Silent Picture*, no. 16, autumn 1972, pp. 12–16.

HENRY B. WALTHALL

There is no other player from the silent era so closely associated with one screen role than Henry B. Walthall. For better or worse, he will always be the "little colonel" of *The Birth of a Nation*, the epitome of the Southern gentleman and to some, the symbol of Southern racism. Everything that Walthall accomplished prior to *The Birth of a Nation* might be considered training for that film, and nothing he did later could possibly compare to that one single performance. Even his personality would seem to mirror that of the character he portrayed. In her autobiography, Lillian Gish wrote that "'Wally,' as he was affectionately called, was everything in life that his 'little colonel' was on the screen, dear, patient, lovable."

Like his mentor D.W. Griffith, Henry Brazeale Walthall was a Southerner, with perhaps a little more affluent family background than the director, but certainly influenced by the same Southern history and culture. He was born, one of eleven sons, on a farm near Columbiana, Shelby County, Alabama, on March 16, 1878. He studied law, but quit to fight in the Spanish-American War, and then took up acting, making his New York debut in 1901. He was cast in popular Southern melodramas of the day, including Edward McWade's *Winchester* and Lottie Blair Parker's *Under Southern Skies*. In 1909, a chance encounter with a friend and fellow actor, James Kirkwood, resulted in a meeting with D.W. Griffith at the American Biograph Company. Griffith was already familiar with Walthall's stage work, and immediately cast him in *A Convict's Sacrifice*, released on July 26, 1909.

Walthall appeared in more than 100 American Biograph shorts from 1909 through 1913, and, with a short break at Pathé, was to remain with Griffith until 1915. "He loved Wally," recalled Blanche Sweet. "He thought he was a fine actor, and he never really had much to say about Wally's acting. He showed him very little. He just said, 'Well, here's the situation,' this, that and the other, or 'a little less Wally,' or 'a little more Wally.' He respected and depended upon Wally as an actor." Blanche played Judith to Walthall's Holofernes in Griffith's first and American Biograph's only feature-length production, *Judith of Bethulia*, released on March 8, 1914. At only five feet, six inches, Walthall lacked the stature of Holofernes, but, as Blanche remembered, Griffith's attitude was, "Wally will play it big."

The actor did not immediately go with Griffith when the director moved from American Biograph to the Reliance-Majestic organization, but he was starred in two 1914 features there, *Home, Sweet Home* and *The Avenging Conscience*. In the latter, a psychological drama, Walthall is an anti-hero, the nephew who dreams vividly of murdering his uncle, demonstrative of the actor's ability to handle unsympathetic and even villainous roles with which he is not generally associated.

Walthall had played Southerners in many American Biograph shorts, and he was the obvious choice for Ben Cameron, the "little colonel," who fights valiantly for the Southern cause in the Civil War, returns to a community devastated by war and Northern carpetbaggers and conceives of the Ku Klux Klan in *The Birth of a Nation*. This being a silent film, the audience, of course, never hears Walthall, but one knows instinctively that here is a proud and noble Southerner, a perception that is a tribute to both actor and director. As one critic dubbed him, Walthall was now "The Edwin Booth of the Screen," but rather than capitalize on the success of *The Birth of a Nation*, he left Griffith, first joining the Balboa Amusement Company in Long Beach, California, and then the declining Chicago-based Essanay Company in the late spring of 1915.

Both Walthall and his actress wife, Mary Charleson, remained with Essanay through May 1917. Walthall's only production for Essanay that has the remotest interest is *The Raven* (1915), in which he plays Edgar Allan Poe, and which has obvious links to *The Avenging Conscience*, suggested by Poe's "The Tell-Tale Heart." After leaving Essanay, Walthall was promoted as available at $2,500 a week, a ridiculously high figure when one considers that at Balboa, two years earlier, he was earning only $250 a week.

There were, of course, no takers, and Walthall formed his own independent production company, releasing through Paralta, the first two films from which, *His Robe of Honor* and *Humdrum Brown* (both 1918), were both directed by Rex Ingram. In 1918, Walthall returned to Griffith's direction. It was announced that he was to appear in *Hearts of the World*, but instead, he was cast as Sir Roger Brighton in Griffith's minor, and "lost" production of *The Great Love*. Walthall was directed again by Griffith a dozen years later in *Abraham Lincoln* (1930), in which he has the minor role of Colonel Marshall. Perhaps Griffith resented Walthall's leaving him after *The Birth of a Nation*, although one would be hard pressed to find a suitable role for him in the director's next film, *Intolerance*, and it may well have been that the actor was encouraged to leave. Whatever the reason, Griffith was very ambivalent in his attitude toward Walthall. In 1926, fan magazine writer, Frederick James Smith, asked the director to name the greatest actor with whom he had worked: "He thought for a while. 'Arthur Johnson, I guess,' he said. 'Yes, Arthur Johnson. Henry B. Walthall was excellent in romantic roles. Perhaps a little too florid . . . But Johnson was matchless in everything—modern, romantic, comedy.'" For Griffith to select the relatively obscure Arthur Johnson (1876–1916), who worked for him at American Biograph from 1908 to 1910, is incomprehensible.

By the late teens, Henry B. Walthall's career was in rapid decline. With neither the beauty of a Valentino or the insouciance of a Jack Mulhall, Walthall was out of style as a leading man in the 1920s. He made many films, but only a handful in the late 1920s are famous titles and not because of his appearance in them: *Three Faces East* (1926), *The Road to Mandalay* (1926), *The Scarlet Letter* (1927), *London after Midnight* (1927), and *Wings* (1929).

With the coming of sound, the situation improved. Walthall had a solid stage background, and his voice was quiet yet authoritative. He was particularly good at portrayals of dotty professors or scientists. In 1932, in *Chandu the Magician*, he is that extraordinary contradiction in terms, a humanitarian who invents a death ray. In 1935, in *Dante's Inferno*, he is the sideshow operator, offering his patrons a glimpse of hell. In 1936, in *The Devil-Doll*, he is the ultimate mad scientist—"You think I'm mad; the world would too, if it knew what I was going to do"—experimenting with the shrinking of humans.

It was John Ford who provided Walthall with one last opportunity to match his performance as the "little colonel." In the Will Rogers vehicle, *Judge Priest* (1934), Walthall dominates the last reel, as, in the role of the Reverend Ashby Brand, he recalls the final struggles of the Confederacy during the Civil War, proudly holding the confederate flag. The image and the language may be unacceptable in our revisionist society, which has denigrated and diminished D.W. Griffith and his contribution to the art and craft of filmmaking, but it is still powerful and still evocative of an age, society and culture that is largely gone. Just as Griffith brought to the screen a history that was to him both personal and unquestionable, so does Henry B. Walthall breathe life into the characters from that history.

Henry B. Walthall was to have played the High Lama in Frank Capra's production of *Lost Horizon*, but died on June 17, 1936, before shooting commenced. The following day, when he returned to Los Angeles, D.W. Griffith was told of the actor's death, and made the following comments to a reporter from the *Los Angeles Times*, noting that with Walthall's passing, there could be no suggestion that *The Birth of a Nation* be remade. The words are a fitting tribute to the one actor who came closest to the director's persona:

"I don't know whether you could call him a great actor, but of this I am certain—he had a great soul.

"It is given perhaps to many to have great souls; it is given to only a few to be able to express that soul to the entire world by means of an expressive face and body, as Henry Walthall did in *The Birth of a Nation*.

"Of course, the world doesn't know and doesn't bother much about that sort of thing, but he had a poet's imagination and a beautiful face that could express the soul and imagination he possessed.

"He was a gentleman, and, as Hollywood puts it, 'a sweet guy.'"

Bibliography

Cohn, Alfred A. "The Reformation of 'Wally.'" *Photoplay*, December 1917, pp. 31–33.

Donnell, Dorothy. "I Remember When." *Motion Picture Classic*, November 1925, pp. 40–41, 71.

Gaddis, Pearl. "He Isn't the Little Colonel Any More." *Motion Picture*, September 1921, pp. 38–39, 88.

Griggs, John. "Here Was an Actor!" *Films in Review*, March 1952, pp. 118–124, 131.

Hall, Gladys. "The Little Colonel Carries On." *Motion Picture*, January 1929, pp. 42, 93, 95.

McGaffey, Kenneth. "The New Walthall." *Motion Picture*, May 1919, pp. 32–34, 101.

Owen, Kenneth. "The Little Colonel." *Photoplay*, August 1915, pp. 27–30.

Peltret, Elizabeth. "Walthall and the Little Colonel." *Motion Picture Classic*, November 1918, pp. 49–50, 80.

Smith, Russell E. "Henry Walthall of the Mutual Company." *Motion Picture Story Magazine*, April 1914, pp. 114–115.

Williamson, Edwin. "The Early Days of Henry B. Walthall." *Picture-Play*, August 1916, pp. 83–89.

KATHLYN WILLIAMS

The leading lady with the Chicago-based pioneering film producer, the Selig Polyscope Company, Kathlyn Williams progressed with ease to the portrayal of mature women of the 1920s, and always impresses with her low-key performances. She was not a great beauty, but she had strong, attractive and enquiring features. Colonel William N. Selig, founder of the company that bore his name, also maintained a menagerie of wild animals available for his productions and for rental to other producers, and even when surrounded by an elephant, a lion, a chimpanzee or other animals from the Selig Zoo, Kathlyn Williams never lost her quiet, ladylike dignity.

Born in Butte, Montana, on May 31, 1888, Williams studied drama at Wesleyan University before making her film debut with the American Biograph Company in 1910. She made only three films for the company before joining Selig, with which she was to remain for the next six years. She played Henriette, one of the two orphans—Winnifred Greenwood was the other—in *The Two Orphans* (1911), which Selig had filmed earlier in 1907 and which was remade by D.W. Griffith as *Orphans of the Storm*. She played the title role in the first motion picture serial, *The Adventures of Kathlyn*, the first episode of which was released in December 1913. She wrote, directed and starred in a 1914 one-reel short, *The Leopard's Foundling*. And she was Cherry Malotte in the first film adaptation of Rex Beach's novel, *The Spoilers*, a nine-reel feature, released in March 1914. Along with William Farnum (as Roy Glennister), Williams turns in a superior performance, overcoming antiquated and unimaginative direction by Colin Campbell.

From Selig, Kathlyn Williams moved on to producer Oliver Morosco and Paramount. Something of the later, more mature roles she was to portray is evidenced in George Melford's *The Cost of Hatred* (1917), in which Williams plays both the mother and the daughter of an abusive judge. Williams is at her best under William C. de Mille's direction in *Conrad in Quest of His Youth* (1920), in which Thomas Meighan as Conrad searches for his youth, after World War One, and discovers the bitter truth that life changes and the past cannot be restored. Providing a dose of reality is Kathlyn Williams as Mrs. Adaile, whom Conrad remembers as once being the most beautiful woman in the world.

When the Paramount contract ended in 1921, Kathlyn Williams became a freelance player, no longer the ingénue but now the reliable older woman, the featured character player in productions such as *The Dancer Spanish* (1923), *The Wanderer* (1926) and *Our Dancing Daughters* (1928). She made an easy transition to sound, and continued to appear on screen through 1935.

Both of her husbands were associated with Selig as actors: Robert Allen, whom she married in 1913 and divorced in 1916, and Charles Eyton, whom she married in 1916 and divorced in 1931. In January 1950, Williams was involved in a serious automobile accident that resulted in the amputation of her right leg. It left her bitter and dispirited. She died in Los Angeles on September 23, 1960.

Bibliography

Bodeen, DeWitt. "Kathlyn Williams." *Films in Review*, February 1984, pp. 66–79.
Burgess, Beth. "The lady of Lions Reconsiders." *Photoplay*, January 1917, p. 138.
Carter, Aline. "Untouched by Ennui." *Motion Picture*, August 1921, pp. 53–54, 99.
Denton, Frances. "Kathlyn's Memory Box." *Photoplay*, November 1917, pp. 76–78.
Howe, Herbert. "The Diplomat of Hollywood." *Photoplay*, September 1924, p. 63.
"Popular Players." *Moving Picture World*, August 23, 1913, p. 832.
Schmid, Peter Gridley. "An Animal Chat with Kathlyn Williams." *Motion Picture Classic*, January 1917, pp. 32–36.
Smith, Bertha H. "A Nervy Movie Lady." *Sunset*, June 1914, pp. 1323–1325.

For Tony —
Fondly —
Lois Wilson

LOIS WILSON

Hollywood basically wasted Lois Wilson's talents. She was a pretty, not a beautiful star, and producers tended to cast her to type, completely ignoring the fact that she could act—very well—in a number of characterizations. As she would so often complain to me, any actress could have played many of her most prominent roles. Of James Cruze's production of *The Covered Wagon* (1923), in which she plays Molly Wingate, "I'm very happy to have appeared in that. It was a great picture, but I think anyone that photographed well and knew anything about silent pictures, I think a great many actresses could have played that part just as well, maybe better." Of *The Vanishing American* (1925), in which she is the white schoolteacher, loved by the Native American played by Richard Dix, "I think it was a great picture for him. I think almost any leading woman could have played my part and I'm not proud of my work in it. I don't think I was very good in that picture. I realized what a great performance Richard gave, and I was a little bit ashamed of mine."

Born in Pittsburgh on June 28, 1894, Lois Wilson was the most famous of four sisters who entered films. The others were Connie Lewis, Diana Kane and Janice Wilson. She made her debut in Lois Weber's *The Dumb Girl of Portici* (1916) after winning a beauty contest organized by Universal. As she told it, the night before she was scheduled to be filmed, dragged across the set by her hair, her grandfather died. This tragic event helped her to play the scene more emotionally. Under contract to Universal, Lois moved to Los Angeles, initially living with character actress Laura Oakley, and established herself as J. Warren Kerrigan's leading lady. "He was a darling, kinda like a big brother to me," said Wilson of the homosexual Kerrigan who was often identified as her fiancé. She was not too impressed with Kerrigan's performance opposite her in *The Covered Wagon* and felt that Jack Holt would have been better suited to the role. The other actor with whom Wilson, who never married, was romantically linked was Richard Dix: "We were engaged at one time. I didn't marry him. I'm sorry."

In 1919, Wilson signed a long-term contract with Famous Players–Lasky, with whom she remained until 1926 and for whom she contributed her finest screen performances. She had the second female lead, after Leatrice Joy, in Cecil B. DeMille's *Manslaughter* (1922), the second female lead to Pola Negri in *Bella Donna* (1923), was the love interest in Edward Everett Horton's *Ruggles of Red Gap* (1923), went to Ireland to play opposite Thomas Meighan in *Irish Luck* (1925), appeared with sister Diana Kane opposite Ben Lyon in *Bluebeard's Seven Wives* (1925), and was again Richard Dix's girl friend in *Let's Get Marriage* (1926). In the Rudolph Valentino vehicle, *Monsieur*

Beaucaire (1924), Lois plays Queen Marie of France and Lowell Sherman is King Louis XV:

"The thing that I was surprised about Valentino was his gaiety and his sense of humor. All I ever heard about was the great lover, and, of course, as the Queen of France and quite a bit older I didn't experience any of that. Lowell Sherman would say things under his breath. The King would do needlepoint, and he said, 'Don't worry Queenie, I'm knitting a little bra for you.' I nearly died laughing, and I had to be so severe and proper."

In all, Wilson appeared in more than thirty Paramount features. She found particular enjoyment in seven produced at the company's Astoria, New York, studios. She loved the city, and lived there until sister Diana's ill health persuaded her to return to Los Angeles in the 1970s. The director whom she most disliked at Paramount and refused to discuss was Irvin Willat, responsible for *Rugged Water* (1925). The director whom she most liked working with was William C. de Mille. Of his brother, Cecil, she commented, "Sarcastic but a fine director," and was delighted to boast to him, "You got me in a picture but I didn't play a glamour girl." Of William, he was "one of the luckiest things that happened to me."

Of the half-a-dozen films that the pair made, the best is, without question, *Miss Lulu Bett*, based on the Zona Gale play, released in November 1921. Here, as the title character, looking as plain as a film actress could possibly be without sinking into melodrama, she is the title character, "the family beast of burden, whose timid soul has failed to break the bonds of family servitude."

It was five years later and toward the end of her relationship with Famous Players–Lasky and Paramount that Wilson again had the opportunity really to act, this time as Daisy Buchanan to Warner Baxter's Jay Gatsby in the first screen adaptation of F. Scott Fitzgerald's *The Great Gatsby*:

"Adolph Zukor started to call me the Sunshine Girl, and I got a little tired of, you know, the end of the picture, always fading into the sunlight. I wanted to play a wicked woman. Daisy wasn't exactly wicked, but she was certainly more sophisticated than the parts I had been playing. Herbert Brenon decided I was to do the picture. Mr. Zukor was in Europe at the time, and when he came back and discovered that I had made the picture, he was furious. He said, 'You play a bitch. We don't like you play bitches.' I was rather prudish earlier in my career, and I had said, when seeing all the pictures that Cecil B. DeMille used to make, I will never take a bath on the screen, I will never take a drink on the screen, and I will never cut my hair. Well, I did all three for *The Great Gatsby*! I loved playing a bitch!"

Lois Wilson continued to appear on screen with the coming of sound, making over forty additional films. She is memorable as Shirley Temple's mother who dies early in *Bright Eyes* (1934), and ended her screen career as Virginia Mayo's mother in *The Girl from Jones Beach* (1949). In the 1930s, she turned to the stage for a living, recalling the words of William C. de Mille that "If you are a good character actress, you'll never die in the theatre." When de Mille saw her on stage, he told her, "I'm very proud of my pupil. All the things I've said about you have come true." In 1968, Lois understudied Lillian Gish in *I Never Sang for My Father* on Broadway, and two years later, she appeared in a production of *The Mad Woman of Chaillot.*

On visits to New York, Lois Wilson was always a gracious hostess at her elegant Sutton Place apartment. She was equally charming, her eyes always sparkling with good humor, on visits to her sister's Studio City home. In time, Lois suffered severe memory loss. She had no idea as to one's identity, although was quite happy to talk anyway. Eventually, she relocated to a niece's home in Reno, where she died on March 3, 1988.

Note: The papers of Lois Wilson are at Kent State University.

Bibliography

Brynn, Celia. "The Nice Girl." *Picture-Play*, November 1921, pp. 29, 100–102.

Cheatham, Maude. "Even as You and I." *Motion Picture*, December 1921, pp. 22–23, 87.

Chic, Mlle. "What I Had to Learn in Pictures." *Moving Picture Weekly*, April 15, 1916, p. 18.

Collins, William A. "Lois Wilson." *Films in Review*, January 1973, pp. 18–35.

Delvigne, Doris. "What's in a Name?" *Motion Picture*, August 1919, pp. 58–59, 106.

Drew, William M. "Lois Wilson" in *Speaking of Silents: First Ladies of the Screen.* Vestal, N.Y.: Vestal Press, 1989, pp. 246–272.

Gaddis, Pearl. "The Girl Who Couldn't Be Discovered." *Motion Picture*, May 1917, pp. 96–98.

Gassoway, Gordon. "Lois the Lovable." *Motion Picture Classic*, September 1922, pp. 38–39, 75.

Hall, Gladys. "Confessions of the Stars: Lois Wilson." *Motion Picture Classic*, April 1929, pp. 20–21, 74–75.

Johaneson, Bland. "Must She Commit Murder?" *Photoplay*, March 1924, pp. 37, 129.

Service, Faith. "You Can't Keep a Good Trouper Down." *Motion Picture*, September 1931, pp. 80, 104.

Shelley, Hazel. "A Puritan in Pictures." *Motion Picture Classic*, September 1921, pp. 32–33, 85.

Summers, Murray. "An Interview with Lois Wilson." *Filmograph*, vol. 1, no. 4, 1970, pp. 2–10.

MARGERY WILSON

Margery Wilson was a multi-talented individual. To label her a silent star is a gross misnomer. She was also a film director, a writer, a radio broadcaster, and a personal counselor on self-improvement and on charm. A D.W. Grififth discovery, she had some of the ethereal presence of Lillian Gish, mixed with a healthy dose of earthy reality. In old age, the resemblance between her and Lillian was quite startling. I was with her at Los Angeles International Airport, returning from a program at Pacific Film Archive in Berkeley, and a stranger came up and asked Margery if she was Lillian Gish. Despite the element of charm, a field with which she was closely associated in the 1930s, there was a hardness to Margery Wilson's character. Pride of place in her home was an oil painting of her and daughter Elizabeth. When asked what had happened to her only child, she replied that she had died young of cancer, adding it was her own fault in that she was a heavy smoker. She displayed no sympathy for her daughter, and asked for no sympathy at her loss.

Here was a determined and ambitious woman, who had a great sense of her own correctness and an avid belief in her own Protestant approach to religion. In later years, the latter predominated, and at one incredibly boring dinner party, Margery entertained her guests with a reading from her latest work, *God Here and Now*, published at the age of 81. Her belief in herself was strengthened by her publisher, Prentice-Hall deciding to reprint her 1961 text, *Double Your Energy and Live without Fatigue*, in 1983, with no prodding from the author.

She was very kind and generous. The West Hollywood home where she lived when we first met had been left to her by a client as a residence for the remainder of her life. When that client's son married and needed a house, she willingly handed the place over to him, and moved to an apartment in the Park LaBrea complex. She was very much the actress. When I filmed her for the documentary, *The Silent Feminists: America's First Women Directors*, she was virtually bed-ridden. She sat slumped in a chair, refusing to replace the bed shawl around her shoulders with something more glamorous. I despaired that anything could come of the situation, but the moment the lights were lit and the camera began rolling, she perked up, the years seemed to fall away, and she was again the well-spoken, self-assured Margery Wilson.

Sarah Barker Strayer was born on October 31, 1897 in Gracey, Kentucky, where her mother was "taking the waters": "I was born in such a hurry that the doctor barely had time to get to our house. And he lived just across the street. I was born in a hurry, and I've been in a hurry ever since." Mother was the head of the English and music departments at Kentucky's Sandy

Valley Seminary, and so her daughter was given a thorough training in the arts of elocution, recitation, singing and acting. At the age of fourteen, Sarah became a professional actress, and rather than bring shame on the family name, she adopted the name of Woodrow Wilson's daughter, Margery.

Margery Wilson came to Los Angeles and the Reliance-Majestic Studios (later Fine Arts) in order to get her sister into films:

"I looked in the equivalent of the yellow pages of the telephone book and discovered the name of Reliance and Majestic Films. I'd seen some of them and I thought they were pretty bad, so I thought I'd try my approach out on a lesser studio and see what was wrong with it before I ruined my chances with a big one. The gateman was a strange, disagreeable-looking creature. I handed him my engraved card and looked the place over, as though I was considering buying it."

She met with Griffith's colleague, Frank Woods. and talked at length about her sister: "Mr Woods kept sinking in his chair, and going down and down and down. Finally he roused himself and said, 'Well, Miss Wilson, if your personality photographs, we'll be able to make a star of you.' He asked me if I would make some tests. I said No. 'Give me something to do that's real, give me a little part in a picture. I don't mind being an extra if I can just get close to the camera with a real idea.' So he did.

"Griffith came a few days later. I was always a bookish person, and so I had stacks of books wherever I went. I was moving from one dressing room to another. The place was filthy and the dust was about an inch thick. I had been cleaning up, and I had my head tied up in an old dust rag, a dirty old apron on and filthy gloves. I was carrying a pile of books. I couldn't see around them. I went around a corner and smack into a man, and the books went in all directions. I thought, 'Oh, my dear books on this dirty ground.' I was on all fours, picking up these books, and I saw these well-shod feet and these soft hands helping me. I sat back on my heels and looked up, and it was Griffith. The tears just flowed. Mr. Griffith helped me up, put his arms around me, and said, 'Stop crying child. Pull yourself together and come into my office at four o'clock.' He called after me, 'you'll make it. Whatever it takes, you've got it.'"

Initially, it was Griffith's intention to have Margery portray St. Veronica, the young woman whose dead child Christ brings back to life on his way to the crucifixion in *Intolerance*. She was further to play a slave in the auction sequence of the Babylonian story. Neither part eventually made it into the released film, although Griffith did shoot the St. Veronica sequence with another actress. Ultimately, Wilson was cast as Brown Eyes, the young girl betrothed to Eugene Pallette in the French Story, who, on the eve of her marriage, is massacred along with her fellow Huguenots:

"The very dramatic scene was when my lover, having fought his way across Paris to get me, arrives too late. I've already been killed. He picks me up, defies the soldiery, and, of course, they shoot him. I'm limp in his arms and he falls with me. We took that scene about five times. In one of those falls, I injured my spine. A big lump came on it, and it's still there. But it's never caused me any great trouble, so I never told Mr. Griffith."

As he did with other members of his company, Griffith asked the actress to help research her section of *Intolerance*: "Mr. Griffith had a way of giving the oddest people great responsibilities when he wanted to, when it struck him. I was a teenager, and he gave me the responsibility of getting all those costumes together. I had to go to a library, make tracings and drawings, and then get to the costume department. The wardrobe mistress was just out of her mind because I wanted everything just like those old drawings. That was a wonderful way he had of getting people just totally involved in what he was doing. Everybody who had any contact whatever with Griffith always came off with a tremendous growth somewhere, somehow he put a stamp on them."

Griffith cast Margery Wilson in two 1915 Fine Arts productions that he supervised but did not direct: *Double Trouble*, the second Douglas Fairbanks film, and *Bred in the Bone*, with Dorothy Gish. He also loaned her to Thomas H. Ince, and Margery was William S. Hart's leading lady in five productions: *The Primal Lure* (1916), *The Return of Draw Egan* (1916), *The Desert Man* (1917), *The Gun Fighter* (1917), and *Wolf Lowry* (1917). In the fall of 1916, she was no longer a Griffith actress but a member of Ince's stock company, appearing in his Triangle-Kay Bee productions.

Margery Wilson was both intelligent and ambitious, and in 1920, she embarked on a new career as a director with her own production company. She directed a two-reel comedy, *Two of a Kind*, in the summer of 1920. She both directed and starred in her first feature-length effort, *That Something*, shot in 1920 and released in 1921, which is concerned with "that unnameable thing that makes of a man a success or a failure." On location in Vermont in the early 1920s, Wilson directed two features, *Insinuation* and *The Offenders*. "I was a critic's actress," she explained to me, "and, unfortunately or maybe fortunately, I began to believe what the critics said about me. That's why I thought I could branch out and make my own films." None of the films directed by Wilson have survived and reviews of them are scanty. She was proud of the two Vermont productions, claiming somewhat erroneously, "I was the first person who ever made a film—not the Italians, not *The Bicycle Thief*—but Margery Wilson was the first person to make a film without a studio, without a single set. I was the first person in the wide world to do it! I wrote it, directed it, produced it, acted in it, and sold it!"

Those directorial efforts marked the end of Margery Wilson's film career. How odd it is that once a woman moves away from the obvious occupation of acting to the more creative endeavor of directing and producing, her career evaporates. Margery also wed Grover P. Williamson, and as she put it, "I married a man who didn't want me to do anything." In fact, she did continue as a creative individual, and as early as 1928, she wrote a monograph on actress Dolores Del Rio. In the 1930s and 1940, Margery produced a series of books on self-improvement, including *Charm* (1930), *The New Etiquette: The Modern Code of Social Behavior* (1937) and *How to Make the Most of Your Wife* (1947).

With her early experience in elocution, Margery Wilson was in demand with the coming of sound to teach film actors how to speak: "My speech and diction was considered tops. I trained practically all the people in Hollywood except Garbo for the talkies. Jack Gilbert had a high, squeaky voice, and when he first appeared as the great lover with sound, people actually laughed. It was too bad, because he was a darling person and a very close friend of mine. I met him at the Ince studios. He was nineteen years old, skinny as a rail and he had an enormous nose and a huge Adam's apple. He grew to his nose as a puppy does to his feet. He was very much in love with Enid Bennett, who afterwards married Fred Niblo. We made a little foursome and we all had to go riding in Jack's first automobile. Well, I was able to lower Jack's voice two tones, but it was too little, too late. He'd already made a mess of it. Poor Jack was just born for tragedy—nothing quite worked for him."

By the 1930s, Margery Wilson had an international reputation as an authority on charm, heading a New York charm school for debutantes. Her name appeared frequently in the press as a "charm expert," and in 1934, she was asked to name "The Ten Most Charming People in America": Anne Lindbergh, Will Rogers, Lady Mendl, Mary Pickford, Alexander Woolcott, Madame Schumann-Heinck, the Reverend Harry Emerson Fosdick, sculptor Gutzon Borglum, Ambassador Robert W. Bingham, and Jane Addams. Margery died in an Arcadia, California, convalescent home on January 21, 1986.

When I first met Margery Wilson in 1972 at a reception at the Alexandria Hotel in downtown Los Angeles I displayed a remarkable lack of charm when I asked, being entirely ignorant of anything she had done since *Intolerance*, where she had been for the past fifty years. My naivete notwithstanding, she did invite me to her home, and she gave me my first taste of a root beer float. In subsequent years, she would always refer to that first root beer float and even told other interviewers about it. Some five years later, she remarked, with customary honesty, on the weight that I had put on, and noted that on our first meeting I had looked "rather beautiful." What greater compliment could one ask from the first lady of charm?

Note: Margery Wilson's career as a director is discussed in my *The Silent Feminists: America's First Women Directors*, Lanham, Md.: Scarecrow Press, 1996, pp. 71–81.

Bibliography

Jordan, Orma. "Kentucky Babe." *Photoplay*, October 1916, p. 41.
Norton, Helen. "Brains, Brown Eyes and Buttons." *Motion Picture*, March 1919, pp. 30–31, 105.
Slide, Anthony. "Margery Wilson." *The Silent Picture*, no. 17, 1973, pp. 17–24.
Wilson, Margery. *I Found My Way*. Philadelphia: J. B. Lippincott, 1956.
Woodside, J.B. "She Was Padded to Fame." *Photoplay*, December 1917, pp. 83, 127.

Claire Winsor, with Lowell Sherman, in *Grand Larceny* (1922).

CLAIRE WINDSOR

There is an enigmatic quality to her features, the suggestion of a passion raging just under the surface. Claire Windsor was beautiful, but never strikingly so until she got older. Then, she became an acknowledged aging beauty—rather like Fannie Ward had been in an earlier age. Lois Weber discovered her, and Windsor's best work is in the five feature films produced and directed by Lois Weber between 1920 and 1921: *To Please One Woman* (1920), *What's Worth While?* (1921), *Too Wise Wives* (1921), *The Blot* (1921), and *What Do Men Want?* (1921).

Each of the films deals with the male-female relationship, and Windsor (and Weber) are helped tremendously in that the male in three of the films is Louis Calhern who was to go on to a distinguished stage career. There is little drama in the stories, and whatever emotional intensity exists is created by Claire Windsor's character. Always, Windsor is the gentle, trusting female to whom life happens rather than someone who creates her own life. The beauty is in the spirit, and somehow, thanks to a meeting of minds between director and star, Claire Windsor is able to suggest that inner quality in her performance.

Claire Windsor was born with the unlikely name of Ola Kronk in Cawker City, Kansas, on April 14, 1897. She was already a professional dancer, a single parent with a three-year-old son, when she arrived in Los Angeles in 1920. After working as an extra in a couple of features directed by Allan Dwan, Windsor was spotted by Lois Weber while carrying a luncheon tray in the Robert Brunton Studios cafeteria. She was signed to a one-year contract at a salary of $150 a week, and renamed Claire Windsor. The name was selected by Weber because she felt it captured what she perceived as the English, patrician beauty of the actress.

Weber and Windsor might have continued to work together had their films been successful at the boxoffice. They were not, and the actress signed a contract with Samuel Goldwyn. She was later under contract to MGM from 1924 to 1926, earning an initial $500 a week, rising to $800. At the same time, Carmel Myers and Aileen Pringle were earning $750 a week at the studio, and May McAvoy was taking home $2,750 a week. From 1925 to 1927, Claire Windsor was married to Bert Lytell, who had once been the highest paid male star at Metro, but whose career was rapidly declining. Windsor was a very busy actress in the 1920s, but none of her post-Weber films are worthy of consideration, and neither are any of her occasional appearances in sound films through the mid-1940s.

The actress was involved in two highly publicized escapades. In July

1921, while horseback riding in the Hollywood Hills, she disappeared for two days. Chaplin offered a $1,000 reward for her safe return, and there were rumors that he was planning to marry her. It was all a publicity stunt. Less a stunt and more an embarrassment was a suit for alienation of her husband's affection brought against the actress by the wife of Oakland, California, banker Alfred C. Read Jr. in September 1933. After a lengthy, vitriolic and highly publicized court battle, Mrs. Read was awarded $75,000, and her poor husband was found guilty of stealing eleven dollars from the vindictive Windsor.

I met Claire Windsor only once, when she was honored at a reception at the Alexandria Hotel in downtown Los Angeles in April 1972. She was a stunningly beautiful grandmother. In a desperate attempt to revive its image, the hotel had named a room on the 12th floor in her honor. We were all taken up and allowed to tour the room, which seemed as much as an anticlimax to the cocktail party as the unveiling of the Claire Windsor bedroom was an anticlimax to a substantial film career. Claire Windsor died in Los Angeles on October 23, 1972. The Alexandria became a welfare hotel, closed to the public. The fate of the Claire Windsor bedroom is not known.

Note: The scrapbooks and other papers of Claire Windsor are at the Cinema Library of the University of Southern California.

Bibliography

Albert, Katherine. "Claire Windsor Talks of Herself." *Cinema Art*, December 1926, pp. 28–29.

Cheatham, Maude. "The Heroine." *Motion Picture Classic*, April 1922, pp. 20–21, 79.

Gassaway, Gordon. "Ola Kronk, Really." *Motion Picture*, September 1921, pp. 24–25, 93.

"Give Credit to Kansas." *Photoplay*, June 1922, p. 69.

Goldbeck, Willis. "A Year and a Tear." *Motion Picture Classic*, April 1921, pp. 22–23, 72.

Smith, Agnes, A Chat with Claire Windsor." *Picture-Play*, January 1923, pp. 43, 102.

FAY WRAY

Fay Wray has the good fortune or, more accurately, the misfortune to be associated with only one film. Thanks to her role as leading lady to an ape in *King Kong* (1933), she is assured of a permanent place in film history. At the same time, the role and the film do a disservice to a performer who may not have been a great actress, but who had many prominent parts to her career. She screamed as well as she does in *King Kong* in Michael Curtiz's *The Mystery of the Wax Museum* (1933). The makers of *King Kong*, Meriam C. Cooper and Ernest Schoedsack, are equally well served by their leading lady in *The Four Feathers* (1929), and Fay Wray can boast work for many other major directors, including Josef von Sternberg (*Thunderbolt*, 1929), Frank Capra (*Dirigible*, 1931), Raoul Walsh (*The Bowery*, 1933) and, most importantly, Erich von Stroheim (*The Wedding March*, 1928).

Filmmakers selected Fay Wray because she was competent, compliant and, above all, intelligent. She understood the prominence of *King Kong* in her career but was happier talking of other films:

"I don't think I did anything as enduring. For the rest, I did a few interesting things and a lot of not so interesting things. *King Kong* has a kind of mythical character, which I respect, and its endurance has been remarkable. I guess it's because I really love the people that made it that I have a feeling for it."

Fay Wray was married to two prominent screenwriters, John Monk Saunders and Robert Riskin. In 1930 Saunders wrote a series of *Liberty* magazine short stories that, the following year, became the novel *Single Lady*, introducing the character of Nikki, an American girl living in Paris shortly after World War One, whose insouciance hides an intelligent and emotional psyche. Saunders put a lot of Fay Wray into the character, and his wife starred in the 1931 musical comedy, *Nikki*, which had a brief run on Broadway, and in which her leading man was a pre-Hollywood Cary Grant. Helen Chandler does well as Nikki in the 1931 screen adaptation of the novel, *The Last Flight*. I first contacted Fay Wray after writing an essay on Saunders for the *Dictionary of Literary Biography*. Pieces in that compendium are not exactly noted for their emotional appeal, but after reading my comments on her first husband, Fay Wray burst into tears, announcing, "You have expressed a sensitivity and an understanding about his work that is outstanding."

I had admired Fay Wray's work in silent films and also her later, more mature roles, including such innocuous pieces as *Tammy and the Bachelor* (1957) and *Summer Love* (1958), as well as the made-for-television drama, *Gideon's Trumpet* (1980), in which she is Henry Fonda's dowdy landlady. "The thing that was different about the role was I tried to make myself look as awful and plain as I could. Unfortunately I succeeded. Some of my friends thought I was an idiot to do that. In fact, I got a good deal of pleasure out of wearing no makeup and looking dreadful."

The actress lived in a sterile, but expensive, apartment block in the Century City development. She was sensibly dressed, with a sensible hairstyle, and a very sensible attitude toward her career. The ingénue image of the Fay Wray of silent films was gone, replaced with a maturity that was strong and forceful when necessary. She explained that she almost never did any interviews, but "I have this very good feeling about you." The feeling apparently continued, because we met at social events many other times through the years, and she was always enthusiasticly charming.

Fay Wray (her real name) was born in Alberta, Canada, on September 15, 1907. After the separation of her parents, Fay's mother, determined to escape the cold, moved to Los Angeles and enrolled her daughter at Hollywood High School:

"It was very simple to know people who were involved in the industry. Through friends I got an extra role one day and the very next time a 'bit' to do at the Century Comedies. As a result of these two times I got a leading lady role in *Gasoline Love* [1923]. I was walking in front of the studio and the owners were coming out. I guess they remembered having seen me on those other two occasions. They asked if I would like to do this leading lady thing, and the appropriate answer was yes. I'd always been in love with films. I'd been in love with acting. That was the one thing I seemed to have great pleasure from, aside from being in school, which I loved.

"I had known of a man who was the head of the Hal Roach Studio, F. Richard Jones, and it seemed to be no problem to go to the studio and ask for an appointment with him. I told him I would like to work, and he said, 'I think we can give you a six-month contract.' Today it would seem that would be an impossibility, but it just so happened that way. I was at Hal Roach about six months, and then moved on to Universal.

"I didn't look down on comedies. I would rather have been a comedienne than a leading lady. To be a foil to a male comedian, that was a little dismaying to me. I thought that if I was going to be in comedies I could be comic, but I learned soon that leading ladies are not supposed to be funny, just decorative."

After Western shorts at Universal with Art Acord, Hoot Gibson and Al Hoxie, Fay Wray made her feature film debut in *The Coast Patrol*, released in March 1925. The film was produced by the Poverty Row filmmaker Bud Barsky who had the good fortune in 1931 to acquire a group of chimpanzees that he starred in a series of short subjects and rented out to MGM for the

"Tarzan" productions. "It was a B-minus production," said Fay of *The Coast Patrol*. "Bud Barsky was a round little fellow, who smoked cigars a lot and wanted me to change my name to June Darling."

Fay Wray's big break came with her casting in Erich von Stroheim's *The Wedding March*. Initially, she had been rejected by one of the director's colleagues because she was not a blonde and she was too tall. The latter was resolved by Fay's losing a few inches from the pile of hair on her head, and she was taken in to see von Stroheim:

"He paced up and down and told me the story of *The Wedding March*, and asked me if I could play Mitzi. I told him I could. He held out his hand and said, 'Goodbye Mitzi.' I was so thrilled, I just began to cry, and from that moment on he seemed very secure about me.

"There was something quite different about him than I would have expected. He was very real. He had great energy. He was personable. He was dressed very casually, and there was none of that austere raiment that you might expect. He had written the story and, as you know, he played it. He did all things. He was all things. There was a total creative quality about him. I don't remember much about his auditory direction, but he certainly talked me through the scenes. There was music on the set, his music, the music of Vienna. It was very stimulating."

Stroheim might have cast Fay Wray in later films, but when Paramount took over the film from producer Pat Powers, the director was, as so often happened, removed from the scene. Fay became a Paramount contract star, making an easy transition to sound, but unhappy with the studio's casting decisions: "I had no choice as to the films, and that was an uncomfortable feeling. I felt that had I done two more films with von Stroheim or at least a director who had a strong artistic integrity (which I think he did), who knows?"

She was unhappy with both the role of a gangster's moll and her director, Josef von Sternberg, on *Thunderbolt*: "It just didn't feel right, and he was not the great communicator that von Stroheim was. He was a cold person, and his wife at that time, Riza Royce, was much more articulate."

Fay Wray remained busy in the 1930s, and also made four films in England in 1935. Her 1928 marriage to John Monk Saunders ended in 1939, and he committed suicide the following year. With her 1942 marriage to Robert Riskin, she retired from the screen. "To stop working was a pleasure." However, when Riskin became seriously ill and unable to work in 1950, Fay Wray was forced to resume her career: "It just became essential for me to start working again." She retired officially in the early 1980s:

"I don't seem to need to act. I think about it in a fantasy way. But I do love motion pictures, and I've always been very glad to have been associated with them. I don't know of any other medium that's more vital or influential."

Note: The scrapbooks and other papers of Fay Wray are at the Cinema Library of the University of Southern California.

Bibliography

Albert, Katherine. "The New Fay Wray?" *Photoplay*, January 1930, pp. 6, 102.
Craig, Carol. "Pert Pioneer." *Movie Classic*, August 1935, pp. 36, 77.
Kinnard, Roy. "Fay Wray." *Films in Review*, February 1987, pp. 84–93.
Spensley, Dorothy. "Snatched from Slapstick." *Photoplay*, January 1927, pp. 58, 119.
Wray, Fay. *On the Other Hand: A Life Story.* New York: St. Martin's Press, 1989.

Index